Life Writing

Life Writing

Essays on Autobiography, Biography and Literature

Edited by

Richard Bradford

First published 2010 by
PALGRAVE MACMILLAN

Palgrave Macmillan in the UK is an imprint of Macmillan Publishers Limited,
registered in England, company number 785998, of Houndmills, Basingstoke,
Hampshire RG21 6XS.

Palgrave Macmillan in the US is a division of St Martin's Press LLC,
175 Fifth Avenue, New York, NY 10010.

Palgrave Macmillan is the global academic imprint of the above companies
and has companies and representatives throughout the world.

Palgrave® and Macmillan® are registered trademarks in the United States,
the United Kingdom, Europe and other countries.

ISBN 978–0–230–20252–8   hardback

This book is printed on paper suitable for recycling and made from fully
managed and sustained forest sources. Logging, pulping and manufacturing
processes are expected to conform to the environmental regulations of the
country of origin.

A catalogue record for this book is available from the British Library.

A catalog record for this book is available from the Library of Congress.

10 9 8 7 6 5 4 3 2 1
19 18 17 16 15 14 13 12 11 10

Printed and bound in Great Britain by
CPI Antony Rowe, Chippenham and Eastbourne

Contents

Notes on Contributors

Martin Amis is regarded as one of the most influential and innovative voices in contemporary British fiction. He has published twelve novels, six volumes of non-fiction and a memoir *Experience* (2000). His most recent novel *The Pregnant Widow* is unashamedly autobiographical.

Timothy C. Baker is a lecturer in Scottish literature at the University of Aberdeen. He is the author of *George Mackay Brown and the Philosophy of Community* (2009), as well as articles on contemporary Scottish and American writing.

Stanley Black is Senior Lecturer in Hispanic Studies at the University of Ulster, Coleraine, where he teaches Spanish history, politics and culture. He is the author of *Juan Goytisolo and the Poetics of Contagion* (2001) and editor of *Juan Goytisolo: Territories of Life and Writing* (2007). His book, *Spain since 1939* is due to be published by Palgrave Macmillan in 2009.

Richard Bradford is Research Professor in English at the University of Ulster. He has published eighteen books on a variety of topics, from Milton through theories of metre and prosody to Russian Formalism. His biographies of Kingsley Amis (*Lucky Him*, 2001), Philip Larkin (*First Boredom, Then Fear*, 2005) and Alan Sillitoe (*The Life of a Long Distance Writer*, 2008) received excellent reviews in British, Irish and US newspapers. He is currently working on the authorised biography of Martin Amis and his book *Poetry. The Ultimate Guide* will be published by Palgrave Macmillan in 2010.

Kevin De Ornellas lectures on English Renaissance Literature at the University of Ulster. He has published widely on representations of animals in early modern texts.

Ruth Fainlight was born in New York City, but has lived in England since the age of fifteen. She has published thirteen collections of poems in England and the USA, as well as two volumes of short stories, translations from Portuguese and Spanish, and has written libretti for the Royal Opera House and Channel 4 TV. Books of her poems have appeared in French, Italian, Portuguese, Romanian and Spanish translation. She received the Hawthornden and Cholmondeley Awards in 1994, and is a Fellow of the Royal Society of Literature. Her 1997 collection, *Sugar-Paper Blue*, was short-listed for the 1998 Whitbread Award. Her latest collection of poems is *Moon Wheels*, 2006, and a

Collected Poems is scheduled for 2010. Her new translation of Sophocles' *The-ban Plays*, in collaboration with Robert Littman, will be published in Spring 2009.

Graham Gargett is Professor of French Culture and Ideas at the University of Ulster, a Member of the Royal Irish Academy, and past President of the Eighteenth-Century Ireland Society (2000–2006). His publications include *Voltaire and Protestantism* (1980), *Jacob Vernet, Geneva and the 'Philosophes'* (1994), and a monograph on the abbé Trublet published in the *Studies on Voltaire and the Eighteenth Century* (1996). He also co-edited, with Geraldine Sheridan, *Ireland and the French Enlightenment, 1700–1800* (1999), and in recent years has published several articles on Goldsmith. A study on *Oliver Goldsmith and Voltaire* is in the advanced stages of preparation.

Alexis Grohmann is Senior Lecturer in Hispanic Studies at University of Edinburgh. His main research interests include Spanish literature post 1970, especially the work of Javier Marías and Arturo Pérez-Reverte; the novel of adventure; the genre of the newspaper column by writers; and, more generally, the art of digression in literature.

Tim Hancock is interested in exploring disparities between the interests, values and priorities of poets and literary critics, and has published research related to this field on the work of Lowell, Mina Loy, Paul Muldoon, Ciaran Carson, as well as on the academically disdained subject of modern love poetry. He teaches modern literature at the University of Ulster.

Andrew James is a lecturer in English at Chikushi Women's University in Dazaifu, Japan and a doctoral student in English literature at the University of Ulster. He is examining the development of the narrative voice in Kingsley Amis's fiction. He holds Master's degrees in English literature from Mississippi State University and in TESL/TEFL from the University of Birmingham, England. His most recent publication is an essay on Amis's *One Fat Englishman* in *Englishness Revisited* (2009)

E. H. Jones is a Lecturer in French at the University of Leicester. Her research interests focus on twentieth-century French and Francophone life writing, particularly the works of Serge Doubrovsky and Hervé Guibert. She also has a strong interest in Cultural Geography and *Spaces of Belonging* (2007), her recent monograph, seeks to forge a new conceptual framework for the interdisciplinary space between Geography and Literary Studies.

Andrew Keanie is a lecturer at the University of Ulster, Northern Ireland. He is the author of *Wordsworth and Coleridge: Views From the Meticulous to the Sublime* (2007). He is also the author of the first full-length book on Hartley

Coleridge since 1931, *Hartley Coleridge: A Reassessment of his Life and Work* (2008). He is a poet and musician, and lives in Derry with his wife and daughter.

Nicola King is Visiting Research Fellow (and formerly Senior Lecturer) in English at the University of the West of England, Bristol. She is the author of *Memory, Narrative, Identity Remembering the Self* (2000) and numerous articles on contemporary fiction and autobiography, most recently on Terry Eagleton and Gillian Rose in the issue of *Rethinking History* on Academic Autobiography. She is currently working on memoirs in which writers develop and represent their relationship with nature and the environment.

Claire Lynch holds a doctorate from the University of Oxford. Her first book *Irish Autobiography: Stories of Selves in the Narrative of the Nation* will be published in 2009. She is currently working on the Burnett Archive of Working Class Autobiography held at Brunel University in London.

Richard Maguire studied at University of Ulster before taking a long break. He is currently finishing his PhD in Mourning and Melancholia in Gay Men's Autobiography at King's College London. He is organising his own conference on Queer Autobiography in the summer of 2009. He teaches Queer Theory, Poetry and London literature at King's and Arcadia University's overseas programme.

Deirdre O'Byrne lectures at Loughborough University. She has published articles on twentieth-century Irish fiction, and is working on a book on Irish women's rural writings for Palgrave Macmillan. She is involved in community events related to literature and Irish Studies, and is Chair of Nottingham Irish Studies Group.

Dale Salwak is Professor of English at southern California's Citrus College and a recipient of Purdue University's Distinguished Alumni Award along with a National Defense Education Act fellowship from the University of Southern California. He is the author of numerous books, including *Teaching Life: Letters from a Life in Literature.*

Alan Sillitoe was born in Nottingham, England on 4 March 1928. He left school at fourteen, for factory work, until at seventeen becoming an air traffic control assistant. After four years in the Royal Air Force as a wireless operator he returned from Malaya for demobilisation but was found to have tuberculosis. During his recovery he decided to become a writer. Much of the 1950s he lived in France and Spain, where he wrote many poems, and his first novel, *Saturday Night and Sunday Morning*, published in 1958. The following year came his second book, *The Loneliness of the Long Distance Runner* – both made into films. Since then he has written novels, stories, poems, plays, travel books, and stories for children. His *Collected Poems* was published in 1993. *Gadfly in Russia* (2007) is about his travels in that country.

D. J. Taylor is the author of two acclaimed biographies, *Thackeray*, and *Orwell: The Life*, which won the Whitbread Biography Prize in 2003. He has written seven novels, the most recent being *Ask Alice* (2009). He is also well known as a critic and reviewer, and his other books include *A Vain Conceit: British Fiction in the 1980s* and *After the War: the Novel an England since 1945*. His *Bright Young People. The Rise and Fall of a Generation: 1918–1940* was published in 2008.

David Thorley is a journalist and freelance writer with research interests in seventeenth and eighteenth century literature, and in particular the rhetorical approaches taken by writers of that period to personal illness. His contribution to this volume is drawn from his research on the topic for a thesis at Oxford University.

Introduction and Acknowledgements

Richard Bradford

This volume was inspired by the Conference on Life Writing held at the University of Ulster, Coleraine, in June 2007, convened to reflect the diversity and dynamism of this new and as yet ill-defined field of study.

The delegates and contributors to the volume come from various branches of Literary Studies, and around half the chapters are concerned with questions attendant upon the biographical and autobiographical aspects of literature. However, one immediately feels obliged to follow such a statement with a qualification; that while these chapters share a number of similarities there is an equal amount of heterogeneity in approach, perspective and methodology.

Andrew James (Chapter 1), for example, fixes upon the compulsive yet guilt-ridden propensity of Kingsley Amis to incorporate within his work perverse and sometimes embarrassing aspects of his life. Deirdre O'Byrne (Chapter 2) shifts the perspective from the singular to the tribal and examines how the life and work of Elizabeth Bowen and Annabel Goff reflect the collective sense of loss and displacement felt by many twentieth century writers of Anglo-Irish descent. Tim Hancock (Chapter 3) returns us to the particular and offers a nuanced insightful account of the interplay between the minutiae of Robert Lowell's verse and the fabric of the poet's experience. In his reflections on the relationship between the lives and work of Anthony Powell and George Orwell, D.J. Taylor (Chapter 4) shows how both writers create channels between the figures they invent and the ones they variously imagine or fear themselves to be; an uncomplicated yet aesthetically enthralling game of auto-psychoanalysis. Graham Gargett (Chapter 5) pursues the conundrum of Oliver Goldsmith's 'life' as a narrative and an assembly of details notoriously resistant to accurate depiction. Gargett, concentrating on *History of the Earth and Animated Nature*, raises the question of whether Goldsmith deliberately set out to mislead biographers. A similar theme is taken up by Dale Salwak's engaging and disarmingly honest account of his personal dealings with Kingsley Amis, a figure who can, according to his mood, be magnetically real and unfathomably evasive (Chapter 6). Hartley Coleridge has inevitably always existed in the shadow of his esteemed father, Samuel Taylor, but in his chapter Andrew Keanie, author of the most recent biography of Hartley, provides us with an insight into a literary life beset by tragedy (Chapter 7). My own contribution (Chapter 9) is a brief and I confess somewhat speculative history of modern literary biography from its gestation in the Renaissance to its more recent, unsettled relationship with academia. Kevin De Ornellas (Chapter 8) causes us to think again about the relationship between the real and the invented in his fascinating discussion of literary horses, including the most famous anthropomorphosised equine in English, Black Beauty.

It is already apparent that even among those chapters with a closely related agenda of concerns – principally the relationship between the author's life and the text – the subject matter effectively eschews anything resembling a theoretical paradigm. The individualism of literary writers both in their approach to their vocation and through their personality and predisposition, supplemented by a limitlessly varied fabric of contexts and circumstances, ensures that the raw material of research determines the manner of analysis rather than the other way around. This might well be the unacknowledged explanation for the curious and uncomfortable relationship between literary biography and academia. The former began to flourish in Europe in the 17th and 18th centuries and has more recently been tolerated, frequently with suspicion, as a houseguest of academic criticism and scholarship.

This subject is touched upon in my own chapter (9) and in Tim Hancock's (Chapter 3), but I shall here offer a brief summary. In literary studies the so-called New Critics ordained that the text rather than the writer should be the primary, some argued the exclusive, subject of scrutiny. Undue attention to the foibles and experiences of the latter was seen as amateurish, a dilution of aesthetic and intellectual rigour with speculative imaginings on what a writer might have meant or thought. The theoretical successors to this generation, the Structuralists and Poststructuralists, were even less tolerant of the presence of the author, with Barthes famously announcing his extinction by the united forces of the arbitrary sign system and the text.

As a consequence one might expect that those disposed toward literary biography would feel somewhat alienated from the prevailing academic environment: the Theory Wars are over but the Theorists prevail over the ongoing armistice. But what the Conference demonstrated, and this volume records, is that there is no clear line of demarcation between those who would, say twenty years ago, have been dismissed as recusants or eccentrics – that is conventional literary biographers – and those whose approach to the concepts of identity and the recording of existence involve questions customarily associated with Theory or philosophy. The emergence of biography in recent decades as one of the most profitable branches of publishing carries with it a slipstream of vexatious issues, all of which have been present if somewhat dormant within the fabric of European writing and culture since the Renaissance. For example, when we record a 'Life' do we reassemble fragments whose only claim to authenticity is their existence as coherent units of language? Can something which is comprised of, on average, 4–500 pages of seamless narrative and which occupies the attention of the reader, often at intervals, for no more than 12 hours in total seriously make claims to be an accurate account of perhaps 80 years of experiences, some calculated, some random, others internalised or confidential, many forgotten or subject to irreconcilable dispute? Does the Life of a writer tell us more about the importance or gestation of their writing than impersonal evaluative scrutiny? What is and what is not biography or autobiography? Obviously when the appellation 'fiction' is attached to a story it involves the claim, or admission, that the piece is made up exclusively of inventions and untruths. But novels, plays or poems which owe their existence to very real events have long been acknowledged, often by their authors, as concomitant features of the creative process. At the other end of this spectrum units of language that were not primarily intended for public dissemination – diaries, notebooks, correspondence, jottings – can be seen as in themselves both illuminating and candid examples of autobiography, with the writer addressing only themselves and as a consequence exempt from the confining responsibilities either to a readership or to significant others.

All of these issues, and more, are dealt with in chapters by Stanley Black, Claire Lynch, Alexis Grohmann, E.H. Jones, David Thorley, Timothy C. Baker, Nicola King and Richard Maguire.

Stanley Black's contribution on Juan Guytisolo (Chapter 10) sets the agenda. Guytisolo, in his words, experimented with fiction and autobiography 'to confirm…the unsalvageable distance between ungraspable reality and the text which in vain attempts to capture it'(Chapter 10). Grohmann's contribution (Chapter 11) is a concise and illuminating survey of how autobiography blends with other generic types and modes in the contemporary European novel, causing us again to question our routine perceptions of what distinguishes fiction from truth-based discourses. On a related theme Jones (Chapter 12) obliges us to re-examine the boundaries between the sub-genre of 'autofiction' and its purely fictional and non-fictional counterparts. While David Thorley (Chapter 13) does not engage specifically with these issues, his fascinating scholarly piece provides a pertinent supplement to the questions raised by them. His subjects, 17th-century diarists, were writing in a period when the differences between fiction and fact, reflection and truth, were ill-defined; writing was a largely private, intimate activity rarely sanctioned and made public by the press and as such the work of his subjects prefigures many of the 20th and 21st century debates on the relationship between reality, text and subjectivity. Lynch (Chapter 14) tackles the epistemological and generic ambiguities that surround the notion of 'autobiography', averring that it is in truth a hybrid genre comprising elements of fiction, history and documentary with no presiding conventions regarding their relative significance.

Autobiography is also the subject of chapters by Baker and King. King (Chapter 15) examines the ways in which writers attempt to recover, in mature adulthood, events and emotions experienced in childhood and adolescence, and Baker (Chapter 16) concerns himself specifically with the remembrance and recording of the death of someone close to the autobiographer. Significantly, both involve in their discussions literary and non-literary writers, raising the issue of the function of reason and creativity in the verbalisation of memory and emotion; Andrew Motion features in both chapters. Richard Maguire's study (Chapter 17) of the letters, diaries and monologues of the gay artist David Wojnorowicz presents us with two states of fragmentation and displacement, one felt and internalised by Wojnorowicz and the other apparent to him in the social landscape of the US during the 1980s and 90s.

By presenting this collection as comprised of two spheres of interest, literary biography and the less definable field of what might be termed writerly engagements with selfhood, it is not my intention to imply that Life Writing is a house divided by dogma and affiliation. It is certainly the case that among the second group one encounters regular engagements with the major presences of Poststructuralism and contemporary cultural theory – de Man and Derrida feature in four of these chapters, for example – but one should not make the mistake of assuming that the theses developed and espoused by these thinkers are incompatible with current work in the ostensibly more traditional zone of literary biography. As stated above critical biography has for some time been treated as the poor and disorganised relation of serious literary studies, a consensus reinforced by an abundance of post-Saussurean credos which present the self, the individual, more as the product of language than its source or subject. Now, however, a more mature third generation of theorists is involved in qualifying and revising such postulations – a process exemplified in the above chapters - and literary biographers have become far more sceptical with regard to ever being able to obtain a precise unambiguous model of the relationships between an author, their circumstances and the text. In short, Life Writing is providing the location for a mutually enlightening dialogue between two sets of writers and thinkers who, even a decade ago, would have held irreconcilable points of view. The Ulster Conference and as a consequence this volume will we hope provide an important early record of what shows all the signs of maturing into a most exciting and innovative branch of literary studies and the humanities.

I have left until last three individuals who, both at the Conference and in the volume, contribute greatly to cementing this new alliance: living writers themselves. Alan Sillitoe is a novelist, poet, dramatist and travel writer who in *Raw Material* (1972) offered one of the most enthralling accounts of how he perceived the intersections and divergences between his life and his writing. In his chapter here he returns to this subject, and addresses it with modesty and candour (Chapter 18). Ruth Fainlight's poetry involves the otherwise unlikely combination of rich stylistic elegance and an appetite for unalloyed emotion. In her piece she tells of how aspects of her life and temperament have fed the latter and enabled her to accomplish the former (Chapter 19). Martin Amis is no stranger to controversy, to the extent that opinions on him are frequently so vociferous and divided that we lose sight of their subject; are we concerned with the man or his work? Chapter 20 is a transcription of his interview from the Conference in which he provides us with some rare insights into the biographical groundings of his fiction, into his life in general, his relationships with his father and his own opinions on literary biography.

The Conference was organised and coordinated by Dr Tim Hancock and Dr Stanley Black, without whom this volume would not have been possible. Maria Campbell provided invaluable assistance with the editing and preparation of the typescript. Thanks are due also to Professor Pól Ó Dochartaigh, then head of the Humanities Research Institute, now Dean of Arts and Humanities, for his assistance with funding for the event.

Paula Kennedy and Steven Hall of Palgrave Macmillan have provided tireless assistance, and Ann Marangos has done a fine and heroic job as editor.

Part I
Literary Biography

1

In Search of Peter Quennell: Redefining the Self in *The Biographer's Moustache*

Andrew James

The Biographer's Moustache (1995) is a novel about a mediocre journalist of Scottish descent who attempts to write a biography of a pompous, wordy writer who has been out of print for years. Its convoluted questioning of life through art seems to have doomed it to both critical and commercial failure. David Sexton wrote of Amis's comedic sentences that "their fatigue is infectious" (6) while Jenny Turner concluded that "*The Biographer's Moustache* finds itself a good half century out of date in the very week of its publication" (2). While writing the novel, Amis was assisting his own biographer, Glaswegian and former Fleet Street journalist, Eric Jacobs. The relationship between Jacobs and Amis as a backdrop to *The Biographer's Moustache* is well-documented, but the role of literary biographer Peter Quennell as the model for the writer Jimmie Fane has not been thoroughly examined. Jacobs himself revealed the connection:

> If there is a model for [Jimmie Fane] it is Peter Quennell, a much-married literary gent of Graham Greene-Anthony Powell vintage. Quennell would pop into the Queen's pub where Kingsley would consign him to the fringes of the conversation on the grounds that he was a bore, apt to mumble. Poor Quennell was suffering the disabilities of old age but that did not spare him from Kingsley's harsh enforcement of his rules of congeniality.
>
> (Jacobs 2000, 5)

For Amis, writing against acquaintances was a pattern he established in his first novel, *Lucky Jim* (1953), with the deployment of his father-in-law, Leonard Bardwell, as Professor Welch and Philip Larkin's girlfriend, Monica Jones, as Margaret Peel. Other prominent examples include the manipulative Lady Baldock in *I Want It Now* (1968), based upon Elizabeth Jane Howard's friend Dolly Burns (Jacobs 1995, 298–9) and Colin Howard, Amis's former brother-in-law, as Geoffrey Mabbott in the 1978 novel *Jake's Thing* (Leader 2006 674). In each of the above cases, Amis does not seem to have been exacting literary revenge even though the depictions are all decidedly negative.

3

He just found the mannerisms and behaviour of the models irritating. There is also precedent for Amis using other writers as the basis for fictional characters, as the Yorkshire-born Pope of *The Alteration* (1976) was based upon John Braine (Jacobs 1995, 168). But Peter and Marilyn Quennell occupy a unique place in Amis's fiction as the only people to play prominent roles in three of his books. They became an awful elderly couple in the 1990 novel *The Folks that Live on the Hill*, a work that Amis dedicated to Peter Quennell even though he was depicted as a doddering fool. Anthony Powell, who suspected the dedication was intended to ease Amis's guilty conscience (24), had discovered the fictional possibilities of Peter Quennell long before Amis, having used him as the model for Mark Members in *A Dance to the Music of Time* (Allason and Marshall, Screen 12).

In a marked departure from habit, five years after the publication of *The Folks that Live on the Hill*, Amis recycled the Quennells in *The Biographer's Moustache*. Amis rarely reused either real-life models or fictional characters. The most prominent examples, Jenny Bunn and Patrick Standish, the principal characters in *Take a Girl Like You* (1960), were, more precisely, revisited at a distance of twenty-eight years in *Difficulties with Girls* (1988). The only other character who recurred in Amis's novels was the ephemeral L(azy) S(od) Caton, modelled on R.A. Caton, the publisher of Amis's first poetry collection. Caton had cameos in several early novels, though his character is never developed in any detail. He was finally killed off in *The Anti-Death League* (1966), having served primarily as a joke between the author, attentive readers, and fellow-writers such as Philip Larkin, who had also experienced the evasive R.A. Caton. But even if Quennell in his declining years was poor company, it is hard to believe that Amis used him in *The Biographer's Moustache* simply to poke fun at him. Quennell died in 1993, a year before the composition of the novel, and Amis had already mercilessly satirized both husband and wife for the second time in his *Memoirs* (1991). Rather, Amis used Quennell as the model for Jimmie Fane because, as he stated in an essay on the use of autobiography in fiction, a novelist's heroes are always "vehicles of his self-criticism" ("Real", 25). Contrary to the view of reviewer David Nokes that Amis and Fane "are pretty much indistinguishable" (7), Amis used Quennell to ensure that they could be distinguished. Jimmie Fane tells the reader emphatically what and who Kingsley Amis is not. Perhaps distracted by the presence of obvious autobiography in *The Biographer's Moustache*, most critics have failed to see Fane as anything other than a distortion of the author himself. However, Amis would have agreed with Terry Eagleton's assertion that "Even if a novel states actual facts, it does not somehow become truer" (90) for by deliberately distorting the relationship between himself and Eric Jacobs through the blending of Quennell into Fane, he offers an intriguing analysis of his own character one final time. Through Quennell-Fane, Amis presents his views on language, art, and life.

The first point of contrast between Quennell and Amis is linguistic. Matters of language were always of great importance to Amis, as evidenced by his collected writings on grammar and usage, the posthumously published *The King's English* (1996). Though Amis often whimsically states his preferences and relishes deliberating on minor stylistic matters, he claims to be more interested in preserving common sense than in settling scores. Through an appropriately alcoholic metaphor, he explains: "A rational being prefers being understood, and served, to being right" (3). When speaking, the natural approach is best: "My tolerance wears thin when I hear an accentuation that seems to me wilfully or absurdly eccentric" (3). For Jimmie Fane, too, any issue of language or pronunciation is "a prime concern" (59) and he refers to Fowler's guide to English usage, which Amis himself revered and, for the most part, followed. But Fane differs from Amis in his use of language to denigrate others and prove his own social superiority. Fane asks his biographer to pronounce "curriculum vitae" (15) and "tissue" (57) in order to sneer at him and, in his fawning on the rich, is revealed as a snob even though he insists that he is not. He cites the *Oxford English Dictionary* in his defence, arguing that snobbery entails an exaggerated respect for wealth and social position while his respect is "by any reasonable standards perfectly proper" (83). Fane, in fact, belongs to the group that Amis called "wankers", defined in *The King's English* as

> prissy, fussy, priggish, prim and of what they would probably misrepresent as a higher social class than one's own. They speak in an over-precise way with much pedantic insistence on letters not generally sounded, especially Hs. Left to them the language would die of purity, like medieval Latin. (23)

Amis would probably have agreed with Jimmie Fane's logic when he argues that the second word in "curriculum vitae" must be pronounced "like vie-tee" and not "vee-tye", "Since we're supposedly talking English rather than Latin or Italian" (15). However, the inconsequentiality of the discussion and Fane's motivation – to embarrass his biographer – make him a wanker rather than a language purist. Fane also has an inflated opinion of his own class status, believing himself to be out of "*a* top drawer but not of *the* top drawer, the one with dukes and marquises in it" (180).

In *The King's English*, Amis is critical of the use of foreign languages – particularly French – for affectation. He devotes three pages to the proper pronunciation of French loan words, and declares that French should be avoided if an equivalent English expression exists. The snobbish tendency to insist on the overly correct French pronunciation is lamented, as Amis notes that, when spoken, "hors d'oeuvres" is almost an "infallible wanker-detector" (80). In the portrait of the Quennells in Amis's *Memoirs*, matters of language usage and French are both significant and the same points reappear in *The Biographer's Moustache*. After becoming reacquainted with Peter Quennell in a wine bar in the 1960s, Amis reports that he was invited to his Chelsea home for "luncheon" (242). *The Biographer's Moustache* opens with Jimmie Fane and his fourth wife Joanna quibbling over the difference between "lunch" and "luncheon". Joanna promises "not to arrange anything frightfully stuffy [like luncheon] ever if [Jimmie'll] help by calling things by their right names" (1). Gordon Scott-Thompson has been invited to discuss his proposal to write Fane's biography, and he brings his girlfriend, Louise, whose presence allows Amis to return to the theme of properly naming things and people. When introduced to Louise, Fane repeats her name and says, "Does that mean you're French? If I may say so you don't look it." She replies that she is "English all the way back as far as I know" (8). In his *Memoirs*, Amis describes a confrontation with Marilyn Quennell at one luncheon. He and his first wife, Hilly, arrived to discover that Marilyn had forgotten anyone was coming and Peter had failed to invite other guests. Amis made "some mildly derogatory comment" about the menu of "squashed quiche lorraine, a salad of lumps of tomato and onion, and ice cream with mangoes" (244) which prompted Marilyn, darkly drawn as "a bit manic-depressive with a fondness for vodka" (243), to erupt: "You're a great fat bum [...]. What you write is a load of rubbish and you can't even speak French. You are extremely boring and very rude and who the hell do you think you are anyway, I'd like to know" (244). Displaying uncharacteristic forbearance, Amis "managed a laugh at this, and stayed on. Hilly walked out. Either that evening or the next they were round at [his] place for drinks" (244–5). Embedded in Marilyn Quennell's insults are some delicate personal issues for Amis. While he would not have disputed his weight problem, to be dismissed as a boring writer or companion would have been insulting for someone who considered the entertainment of others of great personal and professional importance. As for French- the place for it was clearly in France. Amis craftily links French with irrationalism and affectation. There is no reason why Amis should speak French, just as Louise's name does not serve as proof of French lineage. The names "Amis" and "Louise" may have some distant connection to France, but the curiosity of the Quennell-Fanes betrays a pompous insistence upon origins and class.

In the second volume of Peter Quennell's memoirs, *The Wanton Chase*, French conversation often appears without translation, perhaps implying that anyone sufficiently cultured to read Quennell must be fluent in French. This implication would not have pleased Amis, whose general principle in the discussion of French loanwords in *The King's English* is that foreign languages must not be used to exclude monolingual anglophones. Quennell frequently mentions Proust and his enormous influence on his own life: "During middle age I studied the London background, and categorised my friends and acquaintances from a distinctly Proustian point of view" (105). Amis did not believe contact with, let alone detailed knowledge of, foreign cultures and languages to be a mark of urbanity and the discussion of language and culture conducted via Jimmie Fane throughout *The Biographer's Moustache* highlights the difference between acquisitive and inquisitive behaviour. The Fanes' acquisitiveness is apparent at the opening luncheon which is attended by an Italian count who does not speak English and "from first to last ha[s] nothing to say" (10). He has been invited not for his conversation but because the Fanes sometimes visit his *palazzo* and he is a member of the nobility. Jimmie Fane makes no attempt to speak with him even though, according to Joanna, he speaks Italian fluently (51). The count has no importance as anything other than an exotic nobleman.

In his *Memoirs*, Amis expresses general disinterest in the trappings of culture and particular distaste for the homes of the rich. After confessing to not liking the Quennells' "irritatingly pretty house", he explains:

> It is a defect of mine that I hate having to notice and perhaps admire others' possessions on display, or just prefer to have as little to do with houses as possible, though I can see the point of living in one. I once most rewardingly disconcerted some elevated and well-off fellow who asked me, in a tone that expected an affirmative answer, if I would like to "see round" his rather grand house by replying with a tolerant smile, "No thank you." But I digress. (243)

The luncheon at the Quennells' is preceded by a description of their home's interior: "Spectacular artificial flowers were arranged with great style all over the place, not least on the dining-room table, on which lay also two cats and a lot of valuable or valuable-looking plates and silver" (244). Amis draws attention to projected appearances to suggest the cultural acquisitiveness of the Quennells: the flowers are spectacular and stylized, but artificial; the plates are probably valuable, and there are a lot of them. In *The Biographer's Moustache*, then, the narrator's vague description of the furnishings in the Fane house superficially indicates Gordon Scott-Thompson's lack of cultural refinement when it is actually an affirmation of Amis's distaste for the Quennells' prettified house: "The ceilings had the look of having been the work of somebody in particular and over the sideboard there hung an oil painting of foreign parts that had a distinctly pricey appearance" (11). While Amis the novelist and autobiographer is unimpressed by price tags and high art, much of *The Wanton Chase*, Peter Quennell's memoirs, represents a catalogue of the homes of the rich and Bohemian he has visited (95). Amis's bias against perceived cultural acquisitiveness might have coloured his judgement for, in celebrating Quennell's life, Michael Grant offered a different view of his home and companionship: "Many is the enjoyable hour I spent in [Peter's] and Marilyn's house in Cheyne Row, and I confess that when we once exchanged houses I took the opportunity to look through his collection of personal photographs, some of which would have lent considerable added zest, if it was needed (as it is not), to his autobiographies" (50). Amis certainly does not seem to have considered that self-restraint was a part of Quennell's personality, or that he came by his interest in houses quite naturally, since his father was an architect with a "love of quality" (Quennell 1976, 21).

In *The Biographer's Moustache*, Amis satirizes the hypocritical snobbery of the Fanes. Though they are not members of the aristocracy and they are scathingly critical of both snobbery and privilege, they are also eager to rub shoulders with their social superiors. Fane tells Scott-Thompson, "I like people of wealth and rank as a group, they're the people I want to mix with" (85) and later confesses to being a "frightful old arse-creeper of the nobility" (180). The depiction fits the persona of Quennell in *The Wanton Chase*, though Amis in his own memoirs actually attributes the use of the term "arse-creeping" to Marilyn Quennell. She says of Evelyn Waugh: "Horrible little man. What I couldn't bear about him was the way he arse-crept rich and important people." After deriding Waugh for praising an acquaintance's house and belongings, she concludes: "Little fart. You know I used to be Lady something. Nobody could have made more fuss of me while I was. And nobody could have started ignoring me quicker when I stopped being it" (245). Similar ground is covered in *The Biographer's Moustache* through the second Mrs. Fane, whose status has been upgraded from Rosie to Lady Rowena due to a fortuitous marriage. It is rumoured that Jimmie Fane will leave Joanna for Rosie's wealth and new-found title (242). Like Marilyn Quennell, Joanna accuses others of snobbery and pretension, but commits both crimes in her affair with Scott-Thompson. She rarely lets him finish a sentence and addresses him as though he were her social inferior. When he tries to calm her, she says: "For Christ's sake don't tell me I'm being hysterical, there's a good boy" (206). In bed, Scott-Thompson confesses his love but she makes no reply for "She was either asleep or, what was in effect the same thing, closed for maintenance" (216). Thus, Joanna herself has become an object, like wealth or status, to be maintained. Earlier in the novel she is similarly depicted, post-coition, entering maintenance mode but satisfied with her acquisition: "She made a noise like someone sampling a more than usually delicious chocolate and turned on her side" (153). The extent to which art begins to imitate life and characters intertwine and overlap is reflected in Paul Fussell's remark that "To some, [Amis's] *Memoirs* […] seemed to document those unattractive, Evelyn Waugh-like prejudices" (7). When Amis heard Marilyn Quennell criticize Waugh, he saw only the irony and hypocrisy in someone who longed for the respect accorded the nobility laughing at a sycophant. Though he was not a snob and would never have admitted to sharing anything more than the English comedic instinct with Waugh, Amis too ended up causing offence to many people who considered themselves his friends.

Another of the important functions served by Jimmie Fane in *The Biographer's Moustache* is that of pernicious romantic. Most Amis heroes are, at best, realists and, at worst, cynical opportunists. The employment of Quennell as model afforded Amis the opportunity of portraying a view of life fundamentally antipathetic to his own. Gordon Scott-Thompson is the last in the line of cynical realists which began with the protagonist of *Lucky Jim*. Scott-Thompson has inherited Dixon's intellectual boredom and limited sense of morality and he occasionally makes pronouncements that could have come from Dixon's mouth. Dixon's oft-quoted line summarizing his opportunistic approach to life – "nice things are nicer than nasty ones" (1953, 140) – is reinterpreted by Scott-Thompson to read, "human beings were good at avoiding unpleasant things if they could and making the best of them if not" (138). In sum, both would prefer to coast through life rather than to struggle at self-improvement. The lack of a satisfactory moral explanation for character motivation in Amis's novels has led to negative commentary – most famously, perhaps, by F.R. Leavis, who called him a "pornographer" (Amis 1991, 217) – but even critics such as Humphrey Carpenter who are sympathetic to Amis's artistic aims have seen an "amoral moral" at the centre of the Amisian world. According to Carpenter, this states "that you should take care of your own feelings before you consider other people's" (72). However, an examination of both Quennell and Fane shows that Amis's position is not so much amoral as it is anti-romantic. They have a weakness for epiphanic glimpses of beauty while Amis is intrigued by the volatile unpredictability of human nature. Quennell the romantic often pontificates on artistic beauty in his two-volume autobiography. He provides "three incidents, selected at random, that [he] shall never forget" (180) as examples of beauty: a valley in south-western France; a woman's neck on a London bus; and the movements of his pet cat, Suki. He explains the inclusion of the third example in the following way: "Dogs often parody human emotions; a cat's occasional display of feeling is all the more effective because it is so obviously histrionic, and seldom followed, when it has achieved its end, by the smallest show of gratitude" (1980, 183–4). Thus, Quennell's conception of beauty is irrational, epiphanic, and Bohemian and Amis's familiarity with Quennell's character surely led him to have Fane tell Scott-Thompson that he wrote "predominantly to create beauty" (176). In contrast, Amis always avoided serious discussions of art and literature with his friends because he feared that too much talk would lead to creative paralysis. Eric Jacobs reported that "Literary matters as a subject of social intercourse always made Amis uneasy" (1995, 77). This approach to art and literature was, in part, responsible for the cooling of relations between Amis and Philip Larkin:

> Writer though he was to his fingertips, the literary world was not his. He preferred the heterogeneous company of pub and club. For one thing, fiction and poetry were to him a kind of private transaction between writer and reader, best not discussed in public, particularly by writers themselves who were apt to be put off their stride by too much chatter about what they were up to. On this view, theory was the enemy of practice. (Jacobs 2001, 30)

Through Peter Quennell, the romantic novelist who has run out of things to say, Amis suggests that romantic visions of aesthetic beauty are anathema to literary creation. Although Fane claims that he had "no gift" for novels, Amis would have the reader believe that he failed because of his inability to accurately capture reality. After reading some of Fane's novels, Scott-Thompson notes a "preference for the unexpected when the obvious would have served perfectly well or even, perhaps, stronger in the context" (144). The awkward presentation of reality which results from an obsession with aesthetics is precisely the fault Amis thought he had identified in American novelists who, in *The King's English*, he wished would "come off it" and "be natural" (11). Thus, Amis-as-realist confronts the romantic Quennell. To Amis, Quennell is overly concerned with the package at the expense of its contents, as this brief explanation of the difference between their personalities indicates:

> As his work on Byron, Boswell and many others will show, Peter's interest in literature and in writers is mainly biographical and personal. This bias is reflected in his conversation. Time and time again I will try to keep the focus on, say, *The Village* and Peter will shift it languidly but inexorably to Crabbe's opium addiction. (1991, 245)

In order to distinguish himself from Quennell, who suggests that essential truths are revealed in epiphanic moments, Amis, in *The Biographer's Moustache*, teases readers. After Scott-Thompson and Fane arrive at Hungerstream, the country seat of the drunken Duke of Dunwich, for a weekend party two insoluble puzzles are presented. First, duke greets biographer by asking something that sounds like, but is not, "Have you had much experience of puttock-sleighs?" When Scott-Thompson answers that he has not, the duke replies, "You'll soon get the hang of it" (163). Fane imaginatively suggests that the duke might have meant "buttock slaves" but for the intellectually vapid Scott-Thompson the phrase remains meaningless (181). When he asks for a clarification, the duke claims not to understand the question. Finally, as the visitors assemble in front of the estate to say their goodbyes, the duke suddenly remembers: "That phrase you wanted me to explain. I knew what it must have been almost as soon as you asked me. Actually you hadn't got it quite right. It was – ." And the explanation of puttock-sleighs is "lost in a mechanical roar", as the car engine starts and Scott-Thompson is driven away from Hungerstream (211). In a similar episode, Scott-Thompson and Fane watch the duke attempt to mount a horse. He fails and is towed, half in the saddle with one foot in a stirrup, for about a hundred yards. The horse disappears at a gallop around the corner of the house then reappears seconds later riderless (182). The observers wonder if the comedy has not, perhaps, been staged for their benefit, but decide that it could not have been timed so perfectly to coincide with their own return from a walk in the countryside. Later, at cocktail hour, the duke surfaces uninjured and smartly dressed (184). The reader cannot help but wonder about the significance of both events. Though Amis might have used the puzzles to suggest that contemporary English aristocrats lack purpose and that beneath their posh exterior is an interior too mundane to merit analysis, he is also leading the reader down blind alleys. Where Peter Quennell offers epiphanies, Amis teases with riddles.

While it would be impossible to determine whether Mark Members or Jimmie Fane more closely resembled Peter Quennell, the differences in the two novelists' approaches is revealing of Amis's purpose. In comparing his writing to Anthony Powell's, Amis concluded: "I make things up, whereas Powell writes down what has happened" (Amis 2001, 1018). Though the distinction may be fine, if Amis's fiction is not autobiographical it is always self-reflexive. Amis considered his third novel, *I Like It Here* (1958), his worst because it followed Powell's creative method: "I really cobbled it together out of straightforwardly autobiographical experiences in Portugal, with a kind of mystery story rather perfunctorily imposed on that. The critics didn't like it, and I don't blame them really" (1975, 10). *The Biographer's Moustache* also drew upon straightforward autobiography, with the imposition of Peter and Marilyn Quennell onto the story, and it too offers an extended commentary on art. Robert H. Bell was one of the few critics to praise *The Biographer's Moustache*, calling it "a thoroughly enjoyable and intelligent novel, treated shamefully by British reviewers, some of whom seemed impatient for Amis to hush and die like a good chap" (15). It may be intelligent but for many readers it fails to satisfy because it is full of nasty people. The biographer is a dullard; the writer, a shit; and the women, grasping, predatory, and hard. As John McDermott once noted, Amis is "too interesting a novelist, too cunning a tactician, to allow one side to have all the best tunes" (121) and it is refreshing to find that in his final novel Amis reserves most of the best repartees for the women. And yet he seems to have forgotten Jim Dixon's maxim that nice things are nicer than nasty ones and begun to revel in nastiness. Perhaps it is fair to say, as Zachary Leader has of his later novels, that Amis really did come to "enjoy causing offence, as he did in real life" (306).

Like the fictional biographer, Gordon Scott-Thompson, Amis was not one to heed advice. Immediately after he is warned to stay away from Fane's wife, Scott-Thompson begins an affair with her. And although he temporarily bows to the consensus opinion that he looks better without facial hair and shaves off his moustache, he has grown it back by novel's end. The moustache is another of Amis's blind alleys which leads to nothing beyond the author's determination to irritate and provoke. Still, the blind alleys serve a similar purpose to that of Fane-Quennell in the novel. They warn the reader not to become overly enamoured with appearances. Even if Scott-Thompson is more attractive without the moustache, he remains an uninteresting person. To Amis, Peter Quennell was a literary hanger-on, following the greats to their homes, notebook in hand. Amis, however, aspired to be one of the greats. By envisioning himself, an aging writer cooperating with an inexperienced biographer, as Quennell, Amis gives himself a backhanded compliment. Thus, when critic Peter Bien lamented of Jacobs's work that it is too bad this "authorized biography leaves us with such a bad opinion of this talented man" (414), one wonders what he would have thought of *The Biographer's Moustache* for Jimmie Fane is worse than Amis and less talented. *The Biographer's Moustache* suggests, then, that things and people can always be worse. If the reader considers Kingsley Amis a disagreeable fellow, he becomes even less agreeable with the addition of some of Peter Quennell's character traits.

Bibliography

Allason, Julian and Keith Marshall (2007). "Models for Characters in Anthony Powell's *A Dance to the Music of Time*". 24 May. 16 screens. <http://www.anthonypowell.org.uk/dance/dancewho.html>

Amis, Kingsley (1953). *Lucky Jim*. London: Penguin.

—— (1958). *I Like It Here*. London: Victor Gollancz.

—— (1960). *Take a Girl Like You*. London: Victor Gollancz.

—— (1966). *Anti-Death League*. London: Victor Gollancz.

—— "Real and Made-Up People" (1973). Repr., 1998. *Critical Essays on Kingsley Amis*. Ed. Robert Bell. New York: G. K. Hall: 23–7.

—— (1975). "Interview with Michael Barber.". *The Paris Review* 59:64 (Winter): 1–33.

—— (1988). *Difficulties with Girls*. London: Hutchinson.

—— (1990). *The Folks that Live on the Hill*. Bath: Chivers Press.

—— (1991). *Memoirs*. London: Hutchinson.

—— (1995). *The Biographer's Moustache*. London: Flamingo.

—— (1996). *The King's English*. London: Harper Collins.

—— (2001). *The Letters of Kingsley Amis*. Ed. Zachary Leader. London: Harper Collins.

Bell, Robert H. (1998). "Kingsley Amis in the Great Tradition and in Our Time". *Critical Essays on Kingsley Amis*. Ed. Robert H. Bell. New York: G.K. Hall, 2–16.

Bien, Peter (1996). "Kingsley Amis: A Biography by Eric Jacobs". *World Literature Today* 70.2 (Spring): 413–14.

Bradford, Richard (1998). *Kingsley Amis*. Plymouth: Northcote House.

Carpenter, Humphrey (2002). *The Angry Young Men: A Literary Comedy of the 1950's*. London: Allen Lane.

Eagleton, Terry (2003). *After Theory*. London: Penguin.

Fussell, Paul (1994). *The Anti-Egotist: Kingsley Amis, Man of Letters*. New York: Oxford University Press.

Grant, Michael (1993). "Sir Peter Quennell, 1905–1993: An Appreciation". *History Today* 43 (Dec.): 50.

Jacobs, Eric (1995). *Kingsley Amis: A Biography*. New York: St. Martin's Press.

—— (2000). "Dear Martin, Yours Eric". *The Times*. 11 May: 3–5.

—— (2001). "The Day I Became a Ghost". *British Journalism Review* 12.26: 26–32.

Jones, Richard (1996). "Is That All There Is?" *The American Scholar* 65.4 (Autumn): 4 pp. 23 Aug. 2006 <http://lion.chadwyck.com/search>

Leader, Zachary (2006). *The Life of Kingsley Amis*. London: Jonathan Cape.

McDermott, John (1989). *Kingsley Amis, an English Moralist*. New York: St. Martin's.

Nokes, David (1995). "Boring for Britain". *The Sunday Times*. 20 Aug.: 7.

Powell, Anthony (1997). *Journals 1990–1992*. London: Heinemann.

Pritchard, William H. (1995). "Appreciating Kingsley Amis". *The Hudson Review* 48.1 (Spring): 137–44.

Quennell, Peter (1976). *The Marble Foot*. London: Collins.

—— (1980). *The Wanton Chase*. London: Collins.

Sexton, David (1995). "The life and the wife". *Times Literary Supplement*. 8 Sept.: 6.

Turner, Jenny (1995). "Amis among oiks". *Guardian*. 31 Aug. 25 May 2007: 2.

2
Pictures and Places: Enclaves of Illusion in the Life-writings of Elizabeth Bowen and Annabel Goff

Deirdre O'Byrne

Elizabeth Bowen, writing in *Seven Winters* of the Dublin home where she spent half the year as a girl, tells us that 'A house where a child no longer is is virtually rolled up and put away' (7), in explanation of her innocent belief that the building exists meaningfully only while she occupies it. This statement has multiple ironies for Bowen's readers today. If we take the sense of 'house' as in dynasty, that too is 'rolled up and put away' when it no longer has a child in it. Bowen, an only child, and childless heir to her ancestral home, records its demolition in the 1963 Afterword to her family history, *Bowen's Court*. This was first published in 1943 (459), the same year as *Seven Winters*. The book is both chronicle and catalogue of Bowen's Court – she describes the rooms and their contents in some detail, and pays particular attention to ancestral portraits, assessing the character of their subjects by their appearance. Bowen presents herself as movie director and camerawoman in her resolution to concentrate on a unity of setting: 'When Bowens leave Bowen's Court they go off the screen' (282). She tells us that she has some male cousins, but there is an air of finality about the Afterword, suggesting that the house of Bowen is being wrapped up and put into storage in Elizabeth's memory and memoir. This article unfurls selected life-writings of Bowen and another Anglo-Irish writer, Annabel Goff, and unpacks some of the metaphors of enclosure and encapsulation that abound in their stories.

Goff, born in 1940s Ireland, calls her 1990 autobiography *Walled Gardens: Scenes from an Anglo-Irish Childhood* (1994). Just as Bowen enfolds her family history in a narrative named for their ancestral house, so Goff chooses symbols of shelter and conservation for her title. The subtitle notifies us that her life-story has, like Bowen's autobiographical writings, a strongly visual and spatial element. When she died, Bowen was working on an autobiography to be called *Pictures and Conversations*, and one chapter in the published fragment is called 'Places' (1975). Goff recalls two memorable enclosed gardens, one at her first childhood home, Glenville, and the other at her maternal grandparents' house, Ballinacourty. In her text, these two enclosures function as more than mere spaces – they are a crucial part of how she reconstructs her childhood.

The memoir opens with her father's funeral – which may be a homage to *Bowen's Court*, whose first edition closes with the burial of the author's father (447). After the funeral service, Goff and her sister revisit the site of Glenville. The house itself is gone, but some stables and outbuildings remain, and she writes: 'We should have been able to work out where the house used to stand, since the weeping ash which had once *dominated* the lawn, still remained, but we were unable to' (9; my italics). That weeping ash is one of the many examples of the uncanny ability of the Anglo-Irish to surround themselves with symbols of their own decline, something I will discuss in more detail later. The tree, no longer having a lawn to dominate, has concomitantly lost its power to aid the sisters in the location of their former home. However, it's the absence of significant built structures that Goff finds spatially confusing: 'It was some time afterward that I understood why I couldn't work out where the house used to be. There was not a trace of the greenhouses or the walled garden' (10).[1] The walled garden in her mind acts as an indispensable *aide-mémoire*, enclosing and protecting her childhood memories. Without it, she is unable to situate her younger self.

In both *Bowen's Court* and *Walled Gardens*, the writer chooses past over present, recollected edifices over current empty spaces or replacements. Even though each woman has seen for herself that her childhood home no longer stands, she continues to go there in her mind, validating primary memories and repudiating the over-laying of secondary ones. Goff says she has 'no visual memory of what any of the [site] looked like that afternoon' of her father's funeral:

> If I could remember that I would have to stop believing that Glenville still exists. I would have to admit that it is no longer possible to run up those steps, enter the hall ... and go into the library, where the whole family would be waiting for me. (9)

Bowen's Afterward is similarly resistant to accepting the obliteration of her home. Her consciousness, like that of Goff, is a preservative, and, furthermore, functions as a conjuror-saviour who can resurrect the dead: 'When I think of Bowen's Court, there it is' (459). Goff overcomes the mere fact of her father's demise by comforting herself with the 'idea that I can still make my father laugh'. She writes about this in terms of re/collecting: 'In some ways, my father's death did not interrupt every aspect of my relationship with him .... The tiny incidents and ironies which I used to collect for my letters to him are no longer committed to paper, but they are still collected' (7).

Goff's resourceful mother turns the Anglo-Irish propensities for collecting and capturing their ancestors in portraiture into a successful career. Although her daughter doesn't say so, it's clear that the auctions where she acquires her artefacts are part of the dissolution of the Ascendancy. Pictures, often of military subjects, join the hordes of Catholic Irish being shipped to the United States. Goff notes dryly that 'their ultimate purchasers, we were told, often claimed them as ancestors' (175–6). If we adopt Elizabeth Bowen's habit of ascribing feelings to painted subjects, we can imagine the uniformed gentry's emotions on this replanting of the Planters.

As we have seen, Goff attributes considerable cartographical power to the walled garden in her parents' home, Glenville. Her account of her maternal grandparents' home, Ballinacourty, attaches even more significance to a similar structure. She describes the garden as consisting of two parts. Next to the main enclosure is a smaller space, the remains of a building:

> The opening to this ruin remained, as did the outer walls .... I still dream of this smaller garden, regularly and undramatically, but vividly enough not to be sure whether what I remember is an accurate picture of a past reality or a gradually developed illusion. The memories of the small garden ... are warm and golden with a sense of well-being and sunshine .... [T]he walls were high enough to keep out the wind and the sound of the wind. (99)

So the walled garden is not just part of her memory, it is a recurring visitor in her current life, albeit to her dreamworld, and she is aware that it is an active agent in the shaping of her memory-bank. Goff the autobiographer is writing in a period when the Anglo-Irish world she inhabited as a girl is already gone, but her dreaming self returns to a womb-like structure in which no winds of change intrude – even their sounds are excluded. As the title of Ken Loach's film *The Wind That Shakes the Barley* attests, 'wind' was a code word for the Irish independence movement, which heralded the end of the Anglo-Irish world inhabited by Bowen and Goff.[2] Goff's foregrounding of this encompassing space and its sheltering qualities suggests that her memory and subconscious are nostalgic for a former, privileged existence. Her sleeping self follows in her paternal grandmother's footsteps; in Grannie [sic] Goff's world, 'Changing times and standards were ignored' (156).

Goff's childhood home Glenville has been replaced by a dairy plant, and the site of Ballinacourty is now occupied by a cement factory, tangible manifestation of progress and re/construction. Goff grew up in post-Independence Ireland, but in her dreams she returns to a prelapsarian space which is, significantly, the remnant of a ruin. Thomas Hyde, a friend of Elizabeth Bowen, visited the site of Bowen's Court with her, and his assessment of the atmosphere of the walled garden, which outlived the house, is equally open to metaphorical interpretation. In a letter he writes that 'Inside the walled garden was like a fantasy world' (Glendinning, 1993, 232). The proposed title of Bowen's unfinished autobiography, *Pictures and Conversations*, is from the opening of Lewis Carroll's absurdist fantasy *Alice in Wonderland* (Glendinning, 1993, 229; Carroll, 1997). Goff differentiates between the Anglo-Irish and their compatriots in their imaginary lives: 'I think that the native Irish could not afford to entertain illusions and that it is very likely that the Anglo-Irish could not afford not to do so' (35).

The concepts of fantasy and a parallel existence are marked in Anglo-Irish fiction, for instance, in Oscar Wilde's *The Picture of Dorian Gray* (1974), Bram Stoker's *Dracula* (1983)[3] and Sheridan le Fanu's 'Carmilla' (1987). These texts, like Goff and Bowen's life-writings, challenge the accepted boundaries of life and death. Much of Elizabeth Bowen's fiction is similarly imbued with Gothic tendencies. For instance, her short story 'Hand in Glove' suggests that a character is strangled in the attic by the glove of a deceased aunt (775). So, in virtually haunting and being haunted by their Un-Dead houses, Goff and Bowen could be said to be fulfilling an Anglo-Irish stereotype.

A prominent motif of Gothic literature is the ruined castle. When Annabel Goff's father moves to Kinsale, the seventeen-year-old feels a strong emotional attachment to one local feature, the ruined Charles Fort: 'It was where I experienced most clearly the call of the past, the sense that I was being told something important which would prove of value to me'. This Anglo-Irish relic, like her grandparents' walled garden, induces in her a 'feeling of well-being' (204). The emotional attachment to ruins is a marked trait of the Anglo-Irish. In Bowen's *The House in Paris*, Uncle Bill displays photographs of the ruined remains of his former home (1941). Grubgeld confirms that this class 'frequently understand their [autobiographical] stories as testimonies to the ruin of one way of life' (xx). Joan de Vere's calls her autobiography *In Ruin Reconciled* (1990), a phrase taken from a poem by her relative Aubrey de Vere (v).[4]

Elizabeth Bowen writes in *Bowen's Court* that 'this is a country of ruins' and 'ruins feature the landscape' (15), implying that, in her estimation, a countryside without ruins is somewhat lacking (15). 'Yes, ruins stand for error or failure [she writes] – but in Ireland we take these as part of life' (17). Nevertheless, she professes to be glad that Bowen's Court is demolished completely and 'never lived to be a ruin' (459), which may be interpreted as a declaration that though 'error and failure' may be a part of others' lives, she, Elizabeth Bowen, has no wish to associate herself with them, despite that all-inclusive 'we'.

Bowen (1899–1973) was born into a world she describes as 'late-Victorian' (*Seven*, 31). The Victorians are well known for their morbid sensibility, and their influence permeates Bowen's writing. In *Seven Winters* (1943), it is clear that her imagination was actively gothic even in her early years. This is what she tells us about her perceptions on walking around Dublin:

> often I felt a malign temperament at work. *Stories* of gloom would add themselves to the houses, till these shut out the sky. The streets tautened

and the distances frowned. Walking down Upper Mount Street or Lower Baggot Street I at once had the feeling of being in the wrong, and Leeson Street became a definite threat. (30, my italics)

She attributes her anxiety to a fear of the unknown: 'No swamp or jungle could hold more threats than the tacitly ruled-out parts of one's own city' (17). Coming from the descendent of Cromwellian planters (*Court*, 62), this description echoes the fear of the native population that pervades so much colonial writing. But significantly, Bowen presents herself a child who is already making up stories which anthropomorphise architecture. Several of her books contain buildings in the title: *Bowen's Court* (1998), *The Hotel* (1927), *The House in Paris* (1941), or as a central feature, as in *The Last September* (1929).

As adult autobiographer, Bowen rationalises her fears about Dublin's streetscape: 'Perhaps a child smells history without knowing it – I did not *know* I was looking at the tomb of fashion' (*Seven*, 30, italics Bowen's). Note the noun of fatal incarceration. She goes on to qualify her fears: 'In fact, the climatic moodiness of South Dublin ... must have existed only in my eye' (31). This supposition, that her eye/I is the originator of gothic fantasies, claims subjective responsibility for her perceptions. However, her description of the interior décor of her nursery suggest that these fantasies may have their origins precisely in her seeing eye. '[M]y nursery was planned to induce peace', she writes, but two pictures hanging there belie that intention. Bowen remembers these two pictures 'sharply' as 'they were openings into a second, more threatening reality' – she is sensing the existence of a parallel universe. Her descriptions of the pictures conjure up macabre subjects hilariously inappropriate for a nursery, especially that of an imaginative child:

> The first ... [depicted] Casabianca standing against the flames. The boy stood in ecstasy on the burning deck. In the other, a baby in a wooden cradle floated smilingly on an immense flood .... All round, from the lonely expanse of water rose only the tips of gables, chimneys and trees. (13)[5]

Unsurprisingly, these gothic scenes 'induced in [Elizabeth] a secret suspended fear of disasters – fires and floods'. The child Bowen is too young to be conscious of the impending catastrophe facing her Anglo-Irish community, but given how many Big Houses were lost to fire, the Casabianca picture is portentous. With her characteristic dry humour, Bowen posits that the picture of the boy in the fire 'must ... have been chosen for its heroic subject' and was 'there to stimulate courage – for [her] father and mother, like all Anglo-Irish people, saw courage ... as an end in itself' (13). The picture of the child adrift in a flood, and the 'dread of a tidal wave' it induces in the girl Elizabeth, eerily presages not only the loss of her uncle, decades later, on the Titanic (*Pictures*, 48), but, metaphorically, the flood of debt which finally engulfs her class and caste.

Co-incidentally, *The Rising Tide* is the title of a 1937 novel by Molly Keane (1984), another Anglo-Irish writer, and a friend of the adult Bowen.[6] In fact, the 'rising tide' which the child Elizabeth dreads comes close to swamping some Anglo-Irish, inhabiting homes 'with roofs like sieves' (Bence-Jones, 1987, 287) unable to cope with Irish precipitation. In *Twilight of the Ascendancy*, Bence-Jones tells us that 'at Tervoe in County Limerick, ... Lord Emly, smoking innumerable cigars, moved from room to room as the rain came in'(261), displaying Casabiancian aplomb. Bence-Jones goes on to report that 'The rain came no less abundantly through the leaky roof of Lismehane in County Clare, clattering into enamel jugs and basins put out to catch the drips', so the owner Colonel George O'Callaghan-Westropp surrounded by his 'mangy terriers' (261) could no doubt have sympathised with the cradled infant afloat with its cat.[7]

Bowen names her chief fear in contemplating the Moses-like child: 'What would become of the cradle in a world in which everyone else was drowned?' (*Seven*, 13). This question suggests a child who already imagines her world as beset with threatening forces, and who identifies herself as a lone survivor. She lives to experience the reality of being a child of the house of Bowen, trying to keep afloat in Bowen's Court, effectively the cradle of her dynasty. Her world, Anglo-Ireland, by then contained so few survivors that they might as well all have been drowned.

Critics often see Bowen as the very embodiment of the disappearing Anglo-Irish world, an opinion which may be influenced by her life-writing. For instance, in the autobiographical 'Origins', she refers to 'my more or less synonymous race and family: the Anglo-Irish' (*Pictures*, 14). Gearóid Cronin dubs her the 'last heir and chronicler' of her culture (Cronin, 1991, 160). Victoria Glendinning writes that 'When [Bowen] died the Anglo-Irish literary tradition died with her' (Glendinning, 1993, 2). If it did, it rapidly resurrected itself in exemplary texts such as John Banville's *Birchwood* (1998), Jennifer Johnston's *Fool's Sanctuary* (1987), Aidan Higgins's *Langrishe, Go Down* (1993) and Molly Keane's *Good Behaviour* (1983), but Glendinning's allegation nevertheless proves that Bowen is not alone in identifying herself as a child inhabiting apocalyptic times. Her editor says 'Courage was something she never lacked' (*Pictures*, xxxvii), so perhaps the nursery pictures did have the desired effect on her psyche.

She retains an interest in art, and studies it as a young woman (Glendinning, 1993, 41), but when she tries to acquire a painting of Bowen's Court to hang in her new home in England, she is informed by the intended artist that the roof has been removed. Soon afterwards, the house is demolished (4). Thus an interest in art prognosticates catastrophe for Bowen in her later years as it did in her early childhood.

Courage and its accompanying attributes are highly commended in Annabel Goff's *Walled Gardens*:

> Self-sufficiency and inner resources were what I most admired in my grandmother. Recently I've come to realise that most members of my family who survived ... had these qualities to quite an advanced degree. In a society based on such depths of reserve, if you don't have one or the other, you tend to perish. (158)

She goes on to give her definition of courage 'as understanding that behaving well in adversity is its own reward, and that there is no viable alternative' (159). Bravery is needed in this beleaguered world. Like young Bowen, the child Annabel has an active imagination which is preyed on by what she terms 'morbid fantasies. I was a fearful child and the things I feared came in order. Death, ... poverty [and] ghosts' (42–3). Goff does not mention if the décor of her nursery set off these 'fantasies', but she is specifically 'afraid that [her] parents would die' and remembers experiencing 'rage, confusion and insecurity' when her father makes a 'casual reference ... to his old age' (43). This is somewhat understandable in light of the fact that her father is fifteen years older than her mother (178), which may make him seem elderly and vulnerable to his young daughter. She later discloses that her parents' marriage is not a happy one, which could explain some of her feelings of insecurity. Marital incompatibility can of course happen in any society, but as Goff and Molly Keane report, suitable suitors are hard to come by in Anglo-Ireland (Goff, 1994, 195; Quinn, 1990, 74–5), and Goff gives a prime example of a 'trapped' wife in her portrait of family friends Scottie and Creed. Annabel eavesdrops on the 'courageous' Scottie, intuiting that she can learn lessons from her fortitude within a wreck of a relationship (30), as she feels she can glean messages from 'ruined Georgian house[s]' (7).

Young Annabel finds her 'fear, rage, confusion, insecurity ... all impossible to communicate'. This reticence has endured: 'Even now I hesitate to say what it is that frightens me' (42). Naming one's fears, the adult Goff tells us, is tempting fate. And yet she names them here in her autobiography, suggesting that her childhood fears no longer have relevance (or that writing is not the same as verbal utterance). Her narrative reveals that her parents eventually divorced, her father is dead at the time of writing, and the important houses of her girlhood are gone, so the worst has already happened in that world of her youth. Those early fears did manifest themselves and she lived through them. Her book functions as a repository of her fear-filled childhood, a means of laying her ghosts to rest by encasing them within covers.

In *Bowen's Court*, Elizabeth Bowen writes: 'It has taken the decline of the Anglo-Irish to open to them the poetry of regret: only dispossessed people know their land in the dark' (132). Anglo-Irish 'poetry of regret' comes in many forms, including autobiography, though it is a kind of poetic justice that the sometime-dispossessors are experiencing loss for themselves. Bowen, however, does not believe in 'repining', which she regretfully notes as having become a habit among her race: 'in my own day, I hear a good deal too much of it' (*Court*, 187). She copes, like that other famous author-in-exile, James Joyce, by turning her loss into literature. Joyce boasts that Dublin could be rebuilt from his writings (Budgen, 1972, 67–8), and his *opus* functions for us as a literary reconstruction of that now-vanished city scene of the early twentieth century. The exiled Bowen likewise reconstructs her former home in her life-writing, especially in *Bowen's Court*. The house lives within the writer as a source of courage: 'I suppose that everyone, fighting or just enduring, carried within him one private image, one peaceful scene.' (Note that male pronoun, which I'll come back to later.) 'Mine was Bowen's Court. War made me that image out of a house built of anxious history' (457).

Bowen tells us in the 1963 edition of *Bowen's Court* that the original book was written during the second world war. She begins it in the summer of 1939 and finishes it in December 1941 (453, 456–7). Reading of Bowen's early life, it is difficult to escape the notion that the writer as a girl undergoes her own personal wars and 'anxious history'. In the winter of 1905–1906 when she is six years old, doctors advise that her brilliant but nervous father Henry Bowen should be separated from his wife Florence and their only daughter – a child to whom he is much attached: 'he constantly wished to be with me, and to take me for walks' (416), Elizabeth's poignantly relates. His wife and child move to England, while Henry stays in Ireland. Echoing that nursery picture mentioned earlier, Grubgeld describes Bowen and her mother Florence in England as 'unmoored ships, tied together and drifting' (92). The family is reunited after five years, but by that time, Florence has cancer, and she dies when Elizabeth is thirteen. So, by the time she leaves girlhood, Bowen has suffered her own evacuation experience: parted from a parent, home – and country – she loves, disorientated, and with no clear idea of the reasons behind the separations. Small wonder that her family home becomes such an anchor for her.

If Bowen's Court, the house, is a psychic presence to its chronicler (Cronin, 1991, 143–4), it also functions as her doppelgänger. In the early days of her parents' marriage, the couple live in Dublin because of her father's career, and their daughter speculates on the attitude of the house to this move: 'It may be said that Bowen's Court met and conquered the challenge of emptiness – but on the house the conquest has left its mark: it is to these first phases of emptiness that I trace the start of the house's strong *own* life' (*Court*, 403, italics Bowen's). Thus the 'family storyteller', as she dubs herself (69), anthropomorphises the family home, attributing to it the qualities she subsequently had to develop in herself as that challenging couple's daughter: ability to, not just cope with, but conquer, feelings of loss and abandonment, and subsequent self-reliance.

Women who display courage and initiative come forcefully to life in *Bowen's Court*. Mary Crofts, a cousin of the Bowens, is described admiringly as 'a figure to watch' (86), being 'intrepid [and] fearless', an assessment the biographer makes on observing the 'bold bad eyes' captured in Mary's portrait (100). The author provides an amusing example of bold female self-enclosure which gives access to male power. Given alternative versions of an eavesdropping episode which lead to a Miss St Leger becoming 'the only lady Freemason', Bowen prefers the popular story that reports her hiding in a grandfather clock over the family account which depicts her passively falling asleep on a sofa. Bowen, assessing the 'dogged, impassive look' of Miss St Leger's portrait, 'support[s] the clock version' (6). Incidentally, Bowen's short story 'The Inherited Clock' attaches uncanny powers to an old clock (Bowen, 1983, 623–40), and as Lis Christensen explores, timepieces recur as motifs in her fiction (150–1). Bowen's chosen fable of the female Freemason is interesting in that it depicts a woman being admitted to an exclusively male society through her own agency. The literary world of Bowen's era, and especially, the Anglo-Irish literary canon, is male-dominated, but Bowen is widely recognised as a writer of considerable merit.

As Bowen judges her ancestors and their peers through portraits, so we can draw our conclusions from the photographs included in the book. The author strides purposefully across the lawn towards us in the first, with the house in the background. This is Elizabeth Bowen's 'court', her domain. In other photographs, we see some of the courtiers – like herself, remarkable women of letters: Carson McCullers and Iris Murdoch. As Johannes Wally writes, 'Bowen's Court became an important literary salon' (104), and this can be read as an attribute of the hostess as much as of her homeplace.

In recording the many Roberts and Henrys in her antecedents, the writer turns kingmaker: 'I have, for clearness, numbered my ancestors as though they were kings – and, in a sense, every man's life *is* a reign, a reign over his own powers' (*Court*, 145; italics Bowen's). By that logic, that crowns her, as their heir, Queen Elizabeth. Like the most famous holder of that title, this Elizabeth arrived where a son was anticipated, in Bowen's case so strongly that the foetus was already christened Robert (404). The later Elizabeth is also attracted to androgyny. In *Bowen's Court*, she records that 'On weekdays I wore a Robert-like, buttoned-up coat, and was gratified by strangers calling me "Sonny"' (406). This incident is more specific in *Seven Winters*; she recalls: 'I had the *triumph* of being called 'Sonny' by a conductor who lifted me off a tram' (16; my italics). Both women, when referring to their professional role, use a male pronoun – Elizabeth Bowen characterises the fighting, enduring (*Court*, 457), and writing self as male (*Pictures*, 36). Neither bears a child, thus precipitating a problematic succession. Apart from the first chapter, which is named for the house, each chapter of *Bowens' Court* is named for the reigning heir. This practice suggest that the house itself is the primary ruler. Elizabeth does not name the final chapter after herself, which might suggest some reticence in crowning herself queen, but she tells us in 'Origins' that '"History" inebriated me' as a teenager (Pictures, 26; quotation marks Bowen's), so she cannot fail to see the parallels between herself and the Virgin Queen. Bowen writes: 'I am not a "regional writer" in the accredited sense' (*Pictures*, 35), but in writing of her family and its heritage, she and other Anglo-Irish writers create a fictional region of their own: that nebulous imaginary territory called 'Anglo-Ireland', which she names as her place of origin in her plans for her autobiography (62). Catholics 'were simply "the others", whose world lay alongside ours and never touched' (*Seven*, 44). She tells us that her parents created, in their marriage, 'a world of their own', and that she too 'began to set up her own' (11), and in this they are a microcosm of the behaviour of the Anglo-Irish as a community. Peter Somerville-Large quotes Lady Fingall's description of her Anglo-Irish compatriots as inhabiting 'a world of their own, with Ireland outside the gates' (355). This has an echo in the walled gardens that Goff describes – enclaves which exist in the surrounding countryside, but remain sheltered from it and its prevailing winds.

Notes

1. I have written elsewhere about the irony that the Anglo-Irish were skilled gardeners but failed to propagate their own species (O'Byrne, 2008)
2. A poem by Katharine Tynan (Tynan, 1891, 57) and a song by Robert Dwyer Joyce (Laverty, 2006, 33) share the title and Irish-Independence-related theme of Loach's film. Dwyer Joyce's version is sung by a woman in a scene from the film depicting the wake of a young rebel. Tynan was a friend of Yeats, whose championing of the Anglo-Irish way of life is well documented. His book *The Wind Among the Reeds* (1891) endeavours to conserve an even earlier world than theirs, that of ancient Celtic mythology.
3. One of Goff's childhood homes, Ballinaparka, has a gothic quality in common with Dracula's castle – it is frequently visited by bats. She recalls her mother 'valiantly swiping at them with a tennis racket' (166–7), an interesting use of transferable skills; as Bowen depicts in *The Last September*, the Anglo-Irish were very keen on tennis.
4. The title is ironic on several counts. Joan de Vere is clearly not reconciled to the fact that as a female she is excluded from inheriting Curragh Chase, the family home (de Vere, 1990, 46). The title is from Milton's *Paradise Regained* (iv, 413) and as the house burned down, it never can be regained. Also, despite the 'Anglo-Ireland' of the title, much of the book depicts the author abroad, suggesting that she, like Elizabeth Bowen, inhabits a psychic space called 'Anglo-Ireland', wherever they happen to be physically living.
5. Felicia Hemans, who wrote the poem 'Casabianca', which begins 'The boy stood on the burning deck' (Hemans, c.1890), lived in Dublin from 1831. The figure of Casabianca also appears in Stoker's *Dracula*; the captain who lashed his hands to a mast in order to direct his ship to shore, when he foresees his own death, is compared to him (1983, 80).

6. The title of Keane's novel *Good Behaviour* (1983) also occurs in Bowen's writing: 'In the interest of good manners and good behaviour people learned to subdue their own feelings' (Bowen, 1950, 199). Given the theme of repression in Keane's novel, this is unlikely to be a coincidence.

7. The fact that a cat shares the cradle with the child is hardly reassuring to the girl Elizabeth, who 'was not very fond of animals' and would choose a stuffed dog over a real one *(Seven*, 47) – another instance of fantasy being preferred to reality.

Bibliography

Primary sources

J. Banville (1998) *Birchwood* (London: Picador).

E. Bowen (1927) *The Hotel* (London: Constable).

—— (1929). *The Last September* (London: Constable).

—— (1941). *The House in Paris* (London: Victor Gollancz).

—— (1943). *Seven Winters* (London: Longman).

—— (1950). *Collected Impressions* (London: Longman).

—— (1975). *Pictures and Conversations* (London: Allen Lane).

—— (1983). *The Collected Stories of Elizabeth Bowen* (London: Penguin).

—— (1998). *Bowen's Court* (Cork: Collins).

L. Carroll (1997*) Alice's Adventures in Wonderland and Through the Looking Glass* (London: Puffin).

A. Goff (1994) *Walled Gardens: Scenes from an Anglo-Irish Childhood*, (London: Eland).

F. D. Hemans (c.1890) *The Poetical Works of Mrs Hemans* (London: Warne).

A. Higgins (1993) *Langrishe, Go Down* (London: Minerva).

J. Johnston (1987) *Fool's Sanctuary* (London: Hamish Hamilton).

M. Keane (1983) *Good Behaviour* (London: Deutsch).

—— (1984). *The Rising Tide* (London: Virago).

P. Laverty (2006) *The Wind That Shakes the Barley*, screenplay (Cork: Galley Head).

S. le Fanu (1987) 'Carmilla' in A. Ryan (ed.), *The Penguin Book of Vampire Stories* (Harmondsworth: Penguin) 71–137.

K. Loach (2006) (dir.) *The Wind That Shakes the Barley* (Sixteen Films).

J. Milton (1968) *Paradise Regained: Samson Agonistes, 1671* (Menston: Scolar Press).

B. Stoker (1983) *Dracula* (Oxford: Oxford University Press).

K. Tynan (1891) *Ballads and Lyrics by Katharine Tynan* (London:Kegan Paul).

O. Wilde (1974) *The Picture of Dorian Gray* (Oxford: Oxford University Press).

W. B. Yeats (1899)*The Wind Among the Reeds* (New York: J. Lane).

Secondary Sources

M. Bence-Jones (1987) *Twilight of the Ascendancy* (London: Constable).

F. Budgen (1972) *James Joyce and the Making of Ulysses and other writings* (Oxford: Oxford University Press).

L. Christensen (2001) *Elizabeth Bowen: The Later Fiction*, (Copenhagen: Museum Tusculanum Press).

G. Cronin (1991) 'The Big House and the Irish Landscape in the Work of Elizabeth Bowen', in J. Genet (ed.) *The Big House in Ireland: Reality and Representation* (Dingle: Brandon) 143–61.

J. de Vere (1990) *In Ruin Reconciled: A Memoir of Anglo-Ireland 1913–1959* (Dublin: Lilliput).

V. Glendinning (1993) *Elizabeth Bowen: Portrait of A Writer* (London: Phoenix).

E. Grubgeld (2004) *Anglo-Irish Autobiography: Class, Gender, and the Forms of the Narrative* (Syracuse, NY: Syracuse University Press).

D. O'Byrne (2008) 'Last of their line: the disappearing Anglo-Irish in 20th-century fictions and autobiographies' in M. Busteed and J. Tonge (eds) *Irish Protestant Identities* (Manchester: Manchester University Press) 51–68.

J. Quinn (1990) (ed.) *A Portrait of the Artist as a Young Girl* (London: Mandarin).

P. Somerville-Large (1995) *The Irish Country House: A Social History* (London: Sinclair-Stevenson).

J. Wally (2004) *Selected Twentieth-Century Anglo-Irish Autobiographies: Theory and Patterns of Self-Representation* (Frankfurt: Peter Lang).

3

Of Skunks and Doorknobs: Robert Lowell and 'The Business of Direct Experience'

Tim Hancock

The American writer Richard Tillinghast, once a student and friend of Robert Lowell, opens his memoir on the poet with an attack on critical approaches that assume an unbridgeable gap between a writer's life and his work:

> "My thinking is talking to you," Lowell wrote in a late poem to his friend Peter Taylor, emphasizing the personal quality of his poetic discourse. This emphasis contradicts a tendency, dating from the early days of Modernism, and particularly popular with the New Critics, to evoke "the speaker" of a poem, to avoid at all costs the idea that the speaker may be the same person as the author.[1]

In contrast, Tillinghast argues that, 'to Lowell [...] life and art were one' (ibid., p. 54), and seeks to shed light on his poetry by giving 'a fully rounded sense of what he was like as a person' (p. 3). By adopting this approach, Tillinghast takes advantage of the privilege of some insider's knowledge, but (as he is well aware) also transgresses against laws laid down and observed by the men who shaped Lowell's own early views on what poetry criticism should be. Once a student of John Crowe Ransom, the man often credited with giving the New Critics their name,[2] Lowell was to acknowledge in 1963 that the rigours and strictures of this school were still in his blood,[3] and that his admiration for Ransom had not palled since he wrote an enthusiastic review of his teacher's own poetry twenty-five years earlier: 'Proudly we declare that common and quotidian experience is beneath the grace of art' wrote Lowell in this article, a phrase that rings with the precocious (not to say pompous) self-assurance of a New Critical acolyte, a chosen-one.[4] For the aspiring New Critic, knowledge of the author's own 'common and quotidian experience' was little more than a distraction from the quest for an objective, 'correct' interpretation of the poem itself – the 'professional' reader's sole and proper focus of attention. For the fledgeling poet, life and art seemed less indivisable than hierarchically separated, with the latter clearly trumping the former.

Just *how* distracting a writer's life and reputation could be had been revealed, in 1929, by I.A. Richards in his notorious study of mis-reading habits, *Practical Criticism*; a year later model student William Empson showed everyone how it should be done in *Seven Types of Ambiguity*, the book which established a standard of impersonal 'close-reading' that many academics who followed would aspire towards. Lowell was clearly deeply influenced by the ideas of such men: there is a photograph of him standing amongst the teaching staff of the Kenyon College 1950 Summer School, an illustrious group that included Ransom, L.C. Knights, Delmore Schwartz and Empson himself. Yet if Lowell and Empson look at ease in this company, both were instinctive rebels against the strictures and practices of their New Critical contemporaries, and both were to become – in their different ways, but for similar reasons – iconoclastic figures in the world of mid-century poetry and academic poetry criticism. In 1957 an irascible Empson described the 'new rigour' as a 'campaign to make poetry as dull as possible';[5] he was to indicate the grounds of his attack most succinctly in the transgressive title of his last collection of essays, *Using Biography* (published posthumously in 1985). Similarly, reviewing Stanley Kunitz's *Father and Son* in 1962, Lowell first attacked the dullness of much contemporary close reading, before going on to adopt his own decidedly idiosyncratic critical approach:

> My first questions are cheating personal ones that mean much to me, but which are no doubt uncritical and unanswerable by careful reading. I want to know if Kunitz and his own father are the father and son. Is the countryside the country around Worcester, Massachusetts, where Kunitz grew up and I went to boarding school? What happened to his sister?[6]

Lowell's 'cheating' questions contravene a basic law of the New Criticism, the law that states – as Eliot famously put it – that the 'man which suffers' is separate from the 'mind that creates', and that understanding of the latter, if this is to be an ambition at all, can only be achieved through a close reading of the poem, the right and proper subject of the critic's attention. Lowell's tone may be playful in this review, but his sin goes beyond merely posing one or two prohibited questions: it is hard to imagine a more serious violation of established practice than his suggestion that the poetry itself might *not* be one's overriding concern, rather that it might be used as a vehicle by which to get to know another writer, or just another man, a friend. The experience of Lowell's students during the 1960s indicates that this alternative set of priorities was also displayed in his classroom. Judith Baumel has noted how he 'enjoyed bringing the lives of poets to bear on their work'; Helen Vendler concludes that

> this, in the end, seems to me the best thing Lowell did for his students; he gave them the sense, so absent from textbook headnotes, of a life, a spirit,

a mind, and a set of occasions from which writing issues – a real life, a real mind, fixed in historical circumstance and quotidian abrasions.

(Meyers, p. 289)

Looking back at another photo, this time one of the poet alone taken during his period as New Critial acolyte, an older and somewhat battle-weary Lowell portrays his younger self as a sort of expendable junior hit-man of some impersonal academic mafia:

> I lean against the tree, and sharpen bromides
> to serve our great taskmaster, the New Critic,
> who loved the writing better than we ourselves ...[7]

This is not entirely dismissive: the young poet has contributed towards the great task of linguistic clarity by assiduously paring the clichés from his work; however, rather than his achievement, it is his youthful servility that now strikes the older Lowell: the natural order of things has been inverted as author obediently writes to serve a critical praxis, a praxis that – it is implied – may not have that author's best interests at heart. Lowell notes the 'tension' in his pose, suggesting that the health of writing is here being secured with little regard to the health of the writer. Although physically strong, Robert Lowell was not a healthy man. The repeated experiences of mania, depression and relationship turmoil that punctuated his life led him to sympathise with the vulnerable individual behind the words, that individual who had – in his youth – absorbed a critical ethos that declared his own 'life', his day-to-day experience, to be of no great matter, essentially beside the critical point. Lowell implies here and elsewhere that his generation had internalised a set of values that, while bolstering their self-belief as guardians of the language, effectively undermined their self-esteem as human beings; in Lowell's mind, the New Critical cult of impersonality had become indelibly associated with inhumanity. This situation is neatly encapsulated in his late elegy 'For John Berryman', wherein Lowell describes the 'generic' life offered to his cohort of '*Maudits*', and baldly states:

> 'We asked to be obsessed with writing,
> and we were.'[8]

On the one hand, this recalls the intensity of shared convictions regarding the importance of art; on the other, such convictions are now undermined by a self-conviction, as – given the context of Berryman's alcoholism, mental health problems and suicide – the dominant message is that such obsession should be regarded as an illness, one that, the poem hints, was wilfully contracted.

Lowell's own mental breakdown in 1954 clearly contributed towards his loss of faith in the adequacy of an aesthetic that sought to leave quotidian experience behind, and can been seen as marking a turning point in his career. Five difficult years later, the acolyte was to announce himself apostate by publishing the appropriately entitled *Life Studies*, the book in which the 'business of direct experience', as he was later to call it (see Meyers, p. 71), finally took centre stage in his work. In a transition that has been widely acknowleged (not least by the poet), Lowell foresook the 'complicated, difficult, laboured poems' (ibid., p. 82) he had written in the 1940s to experiment with looser, autobiographical pieces, a product of contact with the more liberal aesthetic legislation observed by the emerging 'Beat poets' in California, and of pschyotherapy that involved the recording of childhood reminiscences and research into recent ancestry. *Life Studies* may, for its author, have reflected a new inward focus on family relations and personal psychology, but the book immediately struck a chord with a wider audience, being celebrated as a traumatic but necessary wake-up call from what Lowell coined the 'tranquillized *Fifties*',[9] a much-needed break with conformity that heralded the sixties cult of self-expression.[10] For Lowell's New Critical coterie, however, *Life Studies* seemed little short of a betrayal. Allen Tate's response, in a private letter to his friend, says much about his own values and expectations, and about the poet's straying from the right and true path in this landmark volume: '*All* the poems about your family, including the one about you and Elizabeth, are definitely *bad*', he wrote, 'composed of unassimilated details, terribly intimate, and coldly noted, which might well have been transferred from the notes from your autobiography without change'.[11] Tate may have flinched from the intimate 'details', but this was not the main source of his ire; after all, the New Critic, an admirer of John Donne and indebted to F.R. Leavis, invariably desired poetic metaphor to be grounded in 'concrete' emotional reality. More problematic was the 'unassimilated' nature of these details: autobiography was apparently being offered in the raw rather than transformed by art into something symbolically resonant and generally available to readers who had no knowledge of the author's personal circumstances. Lowell appeared to be offering his old friends (to borrow Yeats's celebrated formula) the 'bundle of accidents and incoherence that sits down to breakfast' rather than the man 'reborn as an idea, something intended, complete'.[12] Tate went on to remind the writer that his 'fine poems in the past' had demonstrated 'an imaginative thrust towards a symbolic order', but that he was now presenting 'in causerie and at random' scattered items of experience that, according to this critic at least, would only be of interest to himself (quoted in Hamilton, p. 237). The 'items of experience' scattered through *Life Studies*, conveyed as they are in loose forms that verge on – indeed in one part move into – prose, offended the sensibilities of critics for whom, as Terry Eagleton has put it, poetry offered 'a cloistered alternative to material history'.[13] Readers such as Tate tended to view the fully achieved poem as 'a spatial figure rather than a temporal process', a timeless artefact that had been 'plucked free of the wreckage of history and hoisted into a sublime space above it' (ibid., p. 48). The 'wreckage of history' – in this case Lowell's personal and ancestral history – is all too evident in *Life Studies*, and more to the point, all too ongoing. As we reach the last pages of this book we increasingly sense unfinished business, with final lines generating an impression less of 'fully achieved' symbolic order than of further wreckage about to fall down around the poet's ears: 'We are all old timers, / each of us holds a locked razor' ('Waking in the Blue', p. 96); 'Gored by the climacteric of his want, / he stalls above me like an elephant' ('To Speak of the Woe that is in Marriage', p. 102). At the very end, we are left facing the unnerving presence of a mother skunk who 'will not scare' ('Skunk Hour', pp. 103–4). More on the significance of this skunk later.

Allen Tate baulked at the 'unassimilated details' in *Life Studies*, but for Lowell such details seem to have become vitally important, and it was the very fact that they *were* unassimilated, unworked-up, that seems to have mattered to him. As he was to put it in a much later poem, 'mere' description and transcription consoled him in a way that the symbolic transformation of life could not:

> I see
> horse and meadow, duck and pond,
> universal consolatory
> description without significance,
> transcribed verbatim by my eye.
>
> ('Shifting Colors', *Day by Day*, pp. 119–20)

Here was an allegiance that Lowell was to declare repeatedly in interviews conducted during the 1960s and 70s: 'The needle that prods into what really happened may be the same needle that writes a good line'; 'the poet needs to keep turning to something immediate and alive'; 'the problem with poetry is that it doesn't necessarily have the connection with life'; 'I wished to describe the immediate instant' (Meyers, pp. 75, 90, 97, 158). Perhaps most revealing of all is Lowell's conversation with Frederick Seidel, published in the *Paris Review* in 1962. Arguing that 'almost the whole problem of writing poetry is to bring it back to what you really feel', Lowell complained that contemporary verse had 'become too much something specialized that can't handle much experience' and demanded 'some breakthrough back into life' (Meyers, pp. 72, 55). Having stated his (somewhat revisionary) belief that what made his own 'earlier poems valuable' seemed 'to be some recording of experience' (p. 60), Lowell offers in passing a small example of the sort of 'unassimilated detail' that might open up a new channel between art and life:

> You may feel the doorknob more strongly than some big personal event, and the doorknob will open into something that you can use as your own.

A lot of poetry seems to me very good in the tradition but just doesn't move me very much because it doesn't have personal vibrance to it. I probably exaggerate the value of it, but it's precious to me. Some little image, some detail you've noticed – you're writing about a little country shop, just describing it, and your poem ends up with an existentialist account of your experience. But it's the shop that started it off.' (p. 72)

While this doorknob failed to make it into *Life Studies*, a comment by Lowell in a symposium on 'Skunk Hour' reveals that it was nevertheless a source of inspiration for that poem:

'I was haunted by the image of a blue china doorknob. I never used the doorknob, or knew what it meant, yet somehow it started the current of images in my opening stanza'[14]

It may also be that the 'little country shop' that Lowell mentions as another unassimilated detail is the same as that found in the poem's fourth stanza:

And now our fairy
decorator brightens his shop for fall,
his fishnet's filled with orange cork,
orange, his cobbler's bench and awl.

I want to return to such details, and to the mystery of the missing door-knob later, but at this point it is worth noting that 'Skunk Hour' was the one poem in *Life Studies* that generally escaped New Critical censure; more than that, it was widely celebrated. On 11 October 1957, two years before the book's publication, Lowell sent a letter containing the poem to his close friend and literary critical conscience, Randall Jarrell. It prompted an enthu-siastic response, one with which Allan Tate concurred in his own letter to Lowell later that year (see Hamilton, pp. 234, 237). Subsequently, it has been this, 'his greatest poem' (according to Stephen Gould Axelrod)[15] that has, more than any other piece in the book (and probably in Lowell's entire oeu-vre), been singled out for attention and almost unqualified praise from within academia. The mere fact that so many close readers have had so much to say about 'Skunk Hour' testifies to its palatable nature for the critical commu-nity, but this does not necessarily indicate a new willingness, on the part of the critical establishment, to accommodate Lowell's autobiographical urges. In fact, examining the grounds for praise suggests quite the opposite to be the case. The poem also, as I want to go on to show, reveals something of Lowell's own mixed feelings where the relationship between 'life and art' was concerned.

One of the most detailed responses to 'Skunk Hour' was given by John Fred-erick Nims, whose methods and conclusions trace the classic New Critical route of interpretation: having discerned an initial tension, transcended by symbolic resolution in the poem's final stanzas ('a strange sort of reconciliation [...] but a restoration of balance none-the-less'), Nims hoists 'Skunk Hour' into the sublime space already occupied by other representatives from the great tradition by concluding that it is 'a sort of "Hamlet" or "Lear" in miniature'.[16] Here, then, in the transgressive volume's final poem, was the 'imaginative thrust towards a symbolic order' that the likes of Tate found to be conspicuously lacking elsewhere in *Life Studies*, such order being implicit in the form of 'Skunk Hour' (with its regular stanzaic structure and relatively stable rhyme scheme) as well as its content, which moves from general observation ('the season's ill') through specific, 'concrete' memory ('I watched for love cars'), to what Lowell has himself described as 'ambiguous affirmation' in the shape of the apparently totemic skunk. Not only did 'Skunk Hour' offer a route that the New Critics found easy to follow, it also offered them some reassuringly familiar scenery along the way by gesturing towards issues that preoccupied writers whose first allegiance had been to the Agrarian Movement and the southern states, issues such as the decline of a traditional social hierarchy (represented by the 'hermit heiress'), the rise of vulgar materialism (represented by the 'summer millionaire'), and the lasting value of religious belief in a time of spiritual decline (represented by the 'Trinitarian Church'). Lowell knew exactly what his friends and (perhaps just as significantly) his most influential critics wanted to read. Coming right at the end of *Life Studies* – a book full of gristly material that the poet knew many would find hard to stomach – you could see 'Skunk Hour', then, as the sweet symbolic dessert, served up as compensation to allow these readers to go home happy. It offered a reassuring hint that the apostate poet might, after a troubled time, be coming back into the fold.

There has been no shortage of formalist interpretation of 'Skunk Hour', and the general impression left by such commentary is of an arcane and transcendent work that, though rooted in a recognisable world, has its true significance in its symbolic structure, somewhere outside of history. As Sandra Gilbert writes, 'It is in 'Skunk Hour' that I have long felt and continue to feel with particular keenness the resonance of something beyond 'mere' factuality'.[17] Gilbert interrogates the poem's characters in search for meaning and significance that transcends 'mere factuality', the accidental details of life, time and location: she would, for example, have us believe that Nautilus Island's hermit heiress is really 'Circe, Hecate, Ishtar, Venus, the goddess of love turned goddess of death in an All Soul's Night world where the graveyard shelves upon the town' (ibid., p. 75). Lawrence Kramer is more open to the possibility of autobiographical intent, but his psychoanalytical approach ultimately eschews the unassimilated details of day-to-day experience for a cast of Freudian archetypes: the first four stanzas, according to Kramer, constitute 'a symbolic geography of Lowell's distorted Oedipal triangle', with the 'hermit heiress' being a version of Lowell's mother, the 'summer

millionaire' his father, the 'fairy decorator' (in a somewhat unlikely transformation) Lowell himself. Such readings leave the impression that everyone in
'Skunk Hour' is *really* somebody else, or several others, with the determined
skunk being the most overdetermined of all: to Kramer she is a 'nurturing
mother' who is yet 'invested with a phalllic aspect', a 'totem, mascot, fugitive
from a beast fable';[18] others have seen her as symbol of fecundity, survival,
repressed desire, spiritual crisis, mania, domesticity, anti-domesticity, and so
on. Whatever, to the critics she is rarely just a skunk; the merely factual may
be a necessary starting point for the poem, but it seems unacceptable as a
interpretive destination. For academic readers of 'Skunk Hour', the details of
the poem are primarily valued in so far as they resonate symbolically.

In this context, we might turn for illumination to Lowell's own response
to the various interpretations offered in the symposium on his poem:

> Very little of what I had in mind is untouched on; much that never
> occurred to me has been granted me. What I didn't intend often seems now
> at least as valid as what I did. My complaint is not that I am misunderstood;
> but that I am overunderstood.

(Ostroff, p. 107)

An academic context invariably brought out this poet's fidelity to life over
text, to recollection over interpretation, and this is partly his way of displaying his poetic credentials and license: *he* is the true artist who does
some teaching on the side, rather than the teacher / critic who produces
the occasional slim volume of poems. Having said that, when Lowell spoke
of *Life Studies* and 'Skunk Hour' he consistently returned to 'the immediate
instant',[19] perhaps in reaction to formalist criticism that dwelled so exclusively on matters that transcended that instant. Other poets have noted this
focus of attention in Lowell: Elizabeth Bishop – to whom 'Skunk Hour' was
dedicated – wrote in her dust-jacket appraisal of *Life Studies* that whenever
she read one of her friend's poems, she felt 'a chilling sensation of here-
and-now'; Seamus Heaney has since perceptively noted how Lowell's poems
seem to be 'sustained by the updraft of energy from "acute personal reminiscence". Yet the reminiscence itself is unmysterious, coming from a recent
past or a just-sped present'.[20] Fellow poets steeped in and sympathetic to
Lowell's writing have been, it would appear, more struck by the sensation of
'here-and-now' in his work than by the symbolic 'beyond-and-always' that
has preoccupied many critics. Stephen Gould Axelrod's comment that Lowell's late poem 'George III' 'moves from a historicist retrieval of particulars
to a poetic sense of something more universal than historical data' may be
taken as axiomatic of this general direction of criticism here;[21] yet evidence
that, in writing 'Skunk Hour' at least, the poet was moving in exactly the
opposite direction to this makes, I would suggest, a temporary reversal of
the usual critical trajectory from source to symbol a worthwhile exercise. As

Lowell himself told V.S. Naipaul, *Life Studies* is 'about direct experience, and not symbols' (Meyers, p. 146).

Lowell's second wife Elizabeth Hardwick noted that the characters in 'Skunk Hour' 'were living, more or less as he sees them, in Castine that summer', and that 'the details, not the feeling' of the poem 'were rather alarmingly precise' (Hamilton *Biography*, p. 267). This precision was alarming because 'Skunk Hour' kicked up a bit of a stink in the small Maine community: Philip Booth, another Castine resident and friend of Lowell's, recalled that ' "our fairy decorator" (mentioned in stanza 4) left town soon after the book's publication'. Booth also mentions, in passing, that he had advised Lowell to change what was once a 'twelve knot yawl' (as it appears in an early draft of stanza 3) to a 'nine knot yawl' (as it appears in the final text).[22] Faithfulness to such minutiaea as the plausible cruising speed of a boat seems, then, to have been important to Lowell, and a similar motivation can be detected behind other revisions that he made to this poem, with one unpublished draft entitled 'Inspiration'[23] proving particularly revealing. Perhaps the most obvious difference between this draft and the *Life Studies* version is in the cast of characters that appear in the first half of the poem. Neither the decorator nor the millionaire exist in the earlier text; lines connected with the former were originally associated with Lowell himself:

> Writing verses like a turk
> I lie in bed from sun to sun
> There is no money in this work,
> You have to love it.

Hence a rather self-pitying general complaint about the thankless task of lying around writing poetry is replaced by the vividly recalled orange details of a 'little shop', based on that run by one who we know to have been living in Castine that summer. The movement from generalities to historical specifics during the compositional process is also reflected in small, but telling changes: the insertion of a personal pronoun in 'our summer millionaire', 'our fairy decorator', and 'our back steps', for example. By such means, the narrator integrates himself and his poem into the local community; the people and things to which he refers are made to seem a little less symbolic, a little more mundane and familiar to us. The dedication of 'Skunk Hour' to Bishop, Lowell's guest in Castine during the summer of 1957, serves its own function, shifting the tone of the first four stanzas from that of detached social commentary towards something more closely resembling a personal letter: Lowell might be updating local gossip about mutual acquaintances in this part of the poem, with the repetition of 'still' in the first stanza contributing to this impression as it generates a sense that these people remain alive and well, living not only in the eternal present of the text but also in the village at time of writing.

If Lowell uses the present tense in order to generate an impression of 'now' in 'Skunk Hour', other techniques are deployed to reinforce the sense of 'here'. Stanza five of the published poem is little changed from the fourth stanza of 'Inspiration', but the little change is a revealing one: by turning 'my old Ford' into 'my Tudor Ford', the poet identifies the two door model he is thinking of – another revision towards historical particulars along the lines of the 'nine knot yawl'. Further modifications seem to have be made with a similar aim in mind: the substitution of a definite for an indefinite article before 'Trinitarian Church', for example, which assures us that Lowell has a specific and familiar building in mind: this is not just any church, it's the one whose narrow white spire still rises over the village's Main Street. The third line of the final stanza has been altered more dramatically: what now reads 'a mother skunk with her column of kittens swills the garbage pail' was once simply 'a skunk glares in a garbage pail'. Lowell, whose early poetry had rarely strayed far from regular stress patterns or syllabic count, now veers dramatically from tetrameter as the anonymous skunk acquires the particulars of gender and offspring. Here we see form momentarily opening itself up and distending in response to pressure exerted by the details of experience.

Just *how* faithful to life are the details in this poem only becomes clear when one has some visual knowledge of the Castine area – knowledge which, thanks to the internet, no longer requires an air fare.[24] Nautilus Island, which is in fact connected by a narrow isthmus to the mainland, lies only a few hundred metres from the Castine seafront and directly faces the converted boathouse in which Lowell spent his summers writing poetry; the 'eyesores' facing the Nautilus Island shore are, then, buildings on the same strip as the poet's own residence. By opening his poem with a gesture to this island and its hardy inhabitant, the poet is implicitly locating his own place of writing and defining his field of vision. Also visible to him would have been Blue Hill, which rises on the skyline about ten miles directly east of Castine. When he describes this hill as covered in a 'fox stain', Lowell finds a particularly apt metaphor to capture its distinctive colour in the fall: both tree foliage and the local blueberry barrens turn a dramatic rust red at this time of year.[25] Castine's cemetery – setting for the narrator's voyeuristic noctural journey – 'shelves on the town' in so far as it is located on the plateau of a low rise north-east of the village centre; the fact that this space, unlike most of the Castine promontory, is devoid of trees, reminds us that Lowell's description of 'the hill's skull' functions not only as a symbolic memento mori, but also a pictorial description of a space that has been shorn of its natural vegetation.

Such details contribute towards the sense of urgency and immediacy that many have sensed, but few have adequately accounted for, in 'Skunk Hour'. The darkened 'love-cars', the song on the bleating radio, the enriched atmosphere ... all are indicators of the compelling draw of the 'here-and-now'.

In some respects, with her dominant presence and apparently endless interpretability, the skunk herself could be regarded as something of a distraction from the general tenor of the poem; but if this fecund survivor is to be seen as symbolic of anything, you could argue that it should be 'life' itself: she is the walking present tense that rudely confronts the poet with its compelling and unassimilatable immediacy. Lowell, who had once pictured himself lying 'in bed from sun to sun', has been raised and drawn to the top of his back steps by such quickening influences; he now sees himself, at the end of the poem, as not so much hoisted above and beyond the wreckage of history, but as located in a very precise location between house and Castine common. Having ridden the sustaining updraft of energy provided by these specific images and reminiscences, he has finally reached a thrilling yet precarious perch from which – we sense – there will be no easy return to the marital home.

Robert Lowell's desire to transport the compelling and ineffable present tense into his poetry was to find its most extreme manifestation in his *Notebook* poems, which he described as focused on 'day to day' details ('the lamp by a tree out this window on Redcliffe Square ... or maybe the rain'), and 'always the instant, sometimes changing to the lost. A flash of haiku to lighten the distant' (Meyers, p. 157). Having said that, the tortuous textual history of these fourteen-liners reminds us that, if it is important to take Lowell's oft-repeated commitment to writing 'life' fully on board, we should in doing so not lose sight of his artistry – as Alex Calder has noted, 'although all process poems make concessions towards artifice, few make so many as *Notebook 1967–68*.'[26] Lowell was a notorious reviser – 'you didn't write, you *re*wrote', as, in an elegy to his lost friend, he has Jarrell tell him (*History*, p. 135) – and much of this rewriting was done *after* publication: the *Notebook* poems, which first saw the light of day in May 1969, were revised for a second edition in July and revised again for a third in January 1970, before 'all the poems' were 'changed, some heavily' when the original volume was split into three separate books in 1973.[27] No doubt some of these revisions, as we have seen with 'Skunk Hour', were intended to take the art closer to the actuality of experience, but even so Lowell was clearly moving away from the ostensible ambition of his 'process poem', which was essentially to catch day-to-day thought and experience on the wing. All of which generated an impression of bad faith and arbitrariness that exhasperated the likes of Calvin Bedient, who concluded that 'Lowell was ready to say almost anything, then take it back and replace it with its opposite.'[28] Helen Vendler has provided us with a nice example of Lowell's casual infidelity to life in his last book, *Day by Day*:

> For all their air of verbatim description, these poems, like all poems, are invented things. They are invented even in little. Lowell once handed me a draft of a new poem, called "Bright Day in Boston." It begins, "Joy

of standing up my dentist, / my X-ray plates like a broken Acropolis ... / Joy to idle through Boston." I was struck by the *panache* of standing up one's dentist, and said so; "Well, as a matter of fact," said Lowell sheepishly, "I actually *did* go to the dentist first, and *then* went for the walk" [...] The life of desire is as evident in these poems as the life of fact.[29]

Lowell's sheepishness here is telling evidence – there is a sense that he felt himself 'found out' not living up to the standards of verisimilitude that he had elsewhere so vocally championed. Whatever, such information exposes the inadequacy of Tillinghast's assertion that 'life and art were one' for this poet; neither Robert Lowell's art, nor his life, could exactly be described as harmonious, and more often than not what we sense when we read his poetry is a tension between these things: life and art were two essentially incompatable authorities that were vying for control of his pen.

As it turns out, the writing history of 'Skunk Hour' not only illustrates this poet's stated desire to get back to the details of experience, it also usefully illustrates the limits of this allegiance. In the symposium on his poem, Lowell attributes the voyeuristic vignette of its fifth stanza to an anecdote he had heard about Walt Whitman, thus undermining the autobiographical basis of what appears on the surface to be a vivid personal memory. Yet he may have been laying a false trail here, because another unpublished draft of what was to become 'Skunk Hour' traces the experience back to a journey he had shared with Elizabeth Bishop:

> And we, we drove a car into the night
> And climbed the tar's bald skull above the bay
> To watch the moon whose mind is not quite right[30]

At this point one is tempted to ask a no doubt uncritical cheating personal question: do the roots of this poem lie in an attempted seduction which Lowell, given his own marital status and Bishop's homosexuality, subsequently wanted to cover up? Whatever, we can see that this poet's compulsion for veracity only goes so far: he may have entered the confessional with *Life Studies*, but he was evidently putting a spin on his sins. The poet was, of course, fully aware of his own 'artistry' and, sheepish moments aside, was generally happy to confess it – as he told an interviewer in 1965, 'My "autobiographical" poems are not always factually true. I've tinkered a lot with fact. You leave out a lot, and emphasize this and not that. Your actual experience is a complex flux. I've invented facts and changed things, and the whole balance of the poem was something invented'.[31] So, our strong impression that Lowell felt art had to get back to the unassimilated world of experience has to be counterbalanced by an appreciation that, for this poet, all experience – good, bad and ugly – was just raw material with the potential to be re-fashioned by the metamorphic processes of art.

Whatever happened to that mysterious doorknob? Putatively a source of inspiration for the first half of 'Skunk Hour', it was not to appear in Lowell's poetry until a few years later, fulfilling slightly different functions in two versions of the poem 'Waking Early Sunday Morning'. In the first of these, published during 1965 in the *New York Review of Books*, the doorknob offers a mundane alternative to 'the great / subjects' that the poet cannot find it in his heart to write about, reflecting therefore a diminution of his ambitions: the imaginatively compelling blue china doorknob is here transformed into colourless 'old china doorknobs', which are then further reduced to the status of 'slight, useless things to calm the mad.' When the poem finally appeared in *Near the Ocean* two years later, Lowell's once 'unassimilated' detail from Castine life had been – like Castine itself – fully assimilated into the universally available, infinitely meaningful world of poetic metaphor:

> In this small town where everything
> is known, I see His vanishing
> emblems, His white spire and flag-
> pole sticking out above the fog,
> like old white china doorknobs, sad,
> slight, useless things to calm the mad.[32]

Once offered as an ineffable source of inspiration, something that Lowell failed to incorporate into his poetry ('I never used the doorknob') and refused to interpret ('or knew what it meant'), the doorknob is now freighted with symbolic weight: it has become an unlikely emblem of the retreating deity. On the one hand, it seems that Lowell retained a great enough allegiance to the unassimilated details of life to feel the need to include this unassuming doorknob *somewhere* in his poetry, and indeed not in any old poem: 'Waking Early Sunday Morning', with its memorable description of an 'unbuttoned' President 'swimming nude', was from the start intended as an attention-grabbing showpiece. Yet the image is not comfortable here, and Lowell's inability to determine its rightful place and, more importantly, to allow it to stand only for itself – 'description without significance' – reflects the limits of his allegiance to life. We are left with a detail that, rather than opening a door on reality, is displayed on a mantelpiece to invite admiration; what had originally spurred the poetic imagination is here reduced to the status of used goods.

Just as guilt and infidelity were recurring themes in Lowell's life, so the theme of his guilt at artistic infidelity *to* life recurs throughout his art; the centrality of the unresolved tension between art and life within a number of significantly placed poems – such as the title poem of *The Dolphin* – indicates its lasting importance for this poet:

> I have sat and listened to too many
> words of the collaborating muse,
> and plotted perhaps too freely with my life[33]

Yet Lowell's continuing need to confess only betrays the extent to which his early-learnt contempt for the merely quotidian remained ingrained within him. The tension posed an aesthetic problem – and provided a poetic seam – that he never really worked out. The issue remains unresolved in his last volume, indeed in the last poem of his last volume, a vacillating Yeatsian argument with the self wherein the debate is between the desire to 'make something imagined / not recalled' and the desire to 'say what happened' ('Epilogue', *Day by Day*, p. 127). Initially dismissive of the 'threadbare' art of his eye, which has produced a poetry 'paralyzed by fact', Lowell softens, characteristically moving towards an embrace of experience in this poem, and concluding with a resolution to dedicate his art to the fragile and precious fact of existence:

> We are poor passing facts,
> warned by that to give
> each figure in the photograph
> his living name.

This devotion to life is associated with 'the grace of accuracy' that Lowell discerns in the luminous realism of Vermeer; and yet the poet's recourse to an image from high art in this poem, to Vermeer's 'girl solid with yearning' rather than to some passing fact from his own 'lurid' past, seems indicative of loyalties that remained divided to the end. For this was to be Lowell's last word on the subject: he died of a heart-attack within a month of the poem's publication.

Notes

1. Tillinghast, *Robert Lowell's Life and Work: Damaged Grandeur* (Ann Arbor: University of Michigan Press, 1995), p. 2.
2. Ransom, *The New Criticism* (Norfolk, Connecticut: New Directions, 1941). J.E. Spingarn used the phrase as the title of a lecture which predated Ransom's book by thirty years, reprinted in Burgum, Edwin Berry, ed. *The New Criticism: An Anthology of Modern Æsthetics and Literary Criticism*. (New York: Prentice-Hall, 1930), pp. 3–25.
3. 'Robert Lowell in Conversation', with Al Alvarez, *The Review* 8 (August 1963), in Meyers, Jeffrey, ed., *Robert Lowell, Interviews and Memoirs* (Ann Arbor: University of Michigan Press, 1988), p. 82.
4. Quoted in Hamilton, Ian, *Robert Lowell: A Biography* (London: Faber and Faber, 1983), p. 59.

5. 'Donne the Space Man', *Essays on Renaissance Literature: Volume 1, Donne and the New Philosophy*, ed. John Haffenden (Cambridge: Cambridge University Press, 1993), p. 122.

6. 'Stanley Kunitz's "Father and Son"', in Robert Lowell, *Collected Prose*, ed. Robert Giroux (London: Faber and Faber, 1987), p. 83.

7. 'Picture in *The Literary Life, a Scrapbook*', *History* (London: Faber and Faber, 1973), p. 127.

8. *Day by Day* (London: Faber and Faber, 1978), p. 27.

9. 'Memories of West Street and Lepke', *Life Studies* (London: Faber and Faber, 1959), p. 99.

10. See especially Rosenthal, M.L., 'Poetry as Confession', *Nation* 189 (Sept 19 1959), pp. 154–5.

11. Quoted in Hamilton, p. 237.

12. Yeats, 'A General Introduction for my Work', *Essays and Introductions* (London: Macmillan, 1961), p. 509.

13. *Literary Theory: An Introduction* (Oxford: Basil Blackwell, 1983), p. 146.

14. Anthony Ostroff, ed, *The Contemporary Poet as Artist and Critic: Eight Symposia* (Boston: Little Brown, 1964), p. 109.

15. Axelrod, ed. and introd., *The Critical Response to Robert Lowell* (Westport, CT: Greenwood, 1999), p. 19.

16. 'On Robert Lowell's "Skunk Hour"', in Ostroff, ed, pp. 98, 97.

17. Gilbert, 'Mephistophilis in Maine: Rereading "Skunk Hour"', in Axelrod, Stephen Gould and Helen Deese, eds, *Robert Lowell: Essays on the Poetry* (Cambridge: Cambridge University Press, 1986), p. 74.

18. Kramer, 'Freud and the Skunks: Genre and Language in *Life Studies*', in Axelrod & Deese, pp. 89, 91.

19. Hamilton, Ian, 'A Conversation with Robert Lowell', in Meyers, p. 158.

20. Heaney, 'Lowell's Command', *The Government of the Tongue* (London: Faber & Faber, 1988), p. 145.

21. Axelrod, 'Lowell's Living Name: An Introduction', in *Robert Lowell: Essays on the Poetry* (Cambridge: Cambridge University Press, 1986), p. 21.

22. Booth, 'Summers in Castine: Contact Prints, 1955-1965', in Meyers, p. 203.

23. Reprinted in Axelrod, *Robert Lowell: Life and Art* (Princeton: Princeton University Press, 1978), p. 250.

24. Google Earth reference: Castine: http://maps.google.co.uk/maps?ie=UTF8&q=castine+maine&ll=44.399448,−68.798447&spn=0.249222,0.462799&z=11&iwloc=addr&om=1

25. A photo of this phenomenon can be viewed at http://www.bluehillbaygallery.com/na/06bluehillharbor-sm.jpg

26. Calder, '*Notebook 1967–68*: Writing the Process Poem', in Axelrod and Deese, eds, p. 136.

27. See Lowell, 'Note to the New Edition', *Notebook* (London: Faber and Faber, 1970), p. 264; 'Note', *History* (London: Faber and Faber, 1973), p. 9.

28. Bedient, 'Illegible Lowell (The Late Volumes)', in Axelrod and Deese, eds, p. 144.

29. Vendler, 'Robert Lowell's Last Days and Last Poems', in Meyers, p. 303.

30. Quoted in Wittek, Terri, *Robert Lowell and Life Studies: Revising the Self* (Columbia: University of Missouri Press, 1993), p. 112.

31. Howard, Jane, 'Applause for a Prize Poet', in Meyers, p. 94.

32. *Near the Ocean* (London: Faber and Faber, 1967), pp. 13–16.

33. 'Dolphin', *The Dolphin* (London: Faber and Faber, 1973), p. 78.

4

Projections of the Inner 'I': Anthony Powell, George Orwell and the Personal Myth

D. J. Taylor

In Anthony Powell's novel *Books Do Furnish A Room*, the tenth volume of the *Dance To The Music of Time* sequence, there is a bravura description of the novelist 'X. Trapnel', an exotic, protean, terminally elusive character whom Powell later admitted was based on that rackety denizen of war-time Soho pub-land, Julian Maclaren-Ross. Powell's account is worth quoting in full, for it offers not only an panoramic survey of Maclaren-Ross's mental landscape but perhaps the best example of Powell's technique, whether in real life or on the printed page, of dealing with the individual personality. Trapnel, according to Powell's narrator Nicholas Jenkins, 'aimed at many roles'.

> Trapnel wanted, among other things, to be a writer, a dandy, a lover, a comrade, an eccentric, a sage, a virtuoso, a good chap, a man of honour, a hard case, a spendthrift, an opportunist, a *raissoneur*; to be very rich, to be very poor, to possess a thousand mistresses, to win the heart of one love to whom he was ever faithful, to be on the best of terms with all men, to avenge savagely the lightest affront, to live to a hundred years and honour, to die young and unknown but recognised the following day as the most neglected genius of the age. Each of these ambitions had something to recommend it from one angle or another, with the possible exception of being poor – the only aim Trapnel achieved with unqualified mastery ...

This passage represents perhaps the fullest exposition of a concept that looms very large in all of Powell's novels – the personal myth. It goes all the way back to Arthur Zouch, the protagonist of his third novel, *From A View to a Death*, a socially ambitious painter on the prowl in hunting country, who considers himself an *ubermensch* and is eventually killed by a bolting horse. Elsewhere in his work, Powell makes the point that what happens to the average human being during the course of his or her life isn't really important. The decisive influence – and the decisive stimulus – is what he thinks happens to him, and what he imagines that other people make of these

41

circumstances. Life, according to Powell, is a process of self-mythologising, an endless projection of oneself and those around one into roles and guises that enable the mythologist to cope with the set-backs and changes of plan that the average life throws up in the path of the person living it.

The concept of the personal myth is all the more eye-opening when one applies it to Powell himself. There is a deeply revealing moment in a volume of the journals that he compiled in his Somersetshire-bound old age when he considers an academic study of his life and work called *Time and Anthony Powell*. This 'pleased him', he records, because it represented him as 'a poor boy made good.' At which point this particular reader's jaw dropped a notch or two, for Powell, as he made no bones of conceding, was the son of a Lieutenant-Colonel who went to Eton and Balliol College, Oxford, married an earl's daughter and lived for half-a-century in the distinctly up-market surroundings of the Chantry, Near Frome, Somerset.

And yet if a study of Powell's novels teaches us anything, it is that what may on the surface be a hulking social distinction is often, when closely examined, subject to an infinite number of gradations and qualifications. Powell belonged, investigation reveals, to a part of the Edwardian upper-middle-class that preferred to spend what money it had on education for its sons. At Eton and Oxford, consequently, he spent most of his time with 'smart' and well-connected people whose wealth and prestige he could never hope to emulate. When in the late 1920s he wanted to marry a woman named The Hon. Adelaide Biddulph and was cut out by his friend Henry Yorke, the novelist Henry Green, not an army officer's son but a wealthy, aristocratically descended businessman, he ascribed the defeat to his relative poverty. All this has enormous implications both for the way in which Powell lived the next seventy years of his life and for his books, with their relish both of smart life and of bohemia, their pointed observation of the social barriers that are breaking down around their characters and the oblique, sometimes abnormally detached register of their narrative voice.

In his four volumes of memoirs, perhaps even more so in his three volumes of journals, Powell writes with great shrewdness about the personal myths peddled or aspired to by his literary contemporaries. When he remarks, for example, that Evelyn Waugh, once he had achieved literary fame and social success, always behaved as if he were a duke one very significant part of Waugh's public personality looms unerringly into view. Discussing George Orwell, whom he knew intimately for nearly a decade, he offers an extraordinary account of an incident that took place in the nursery of Powell's younger son, John, in the winter of 1947. Powell had gone to fetch a book. Coming back he found the child's bed things slightly disturbed and Orwell looking with a rather suspect interest at a painting on the wall. Re-arranging the covers, Powell discovered, to his great surprise, a nine-inch Bowie knife. 'Oh yes' Orwell remarked, when this came to light, 'I'd forgotten I gave him that to play with.' All this, Powell decided, was 'much too big to be ignored'. What was Orwell doing with the knife? Why did he not want to be seen playing with the child? Powell's conclusion was that Orwell had created a kind of tableau, the equivalent of a mid-Victorian moral painting, the strong man moved by the child's weakness, whose central requirement was that he had to be discovered creating it.[1]

Using Powell's template, my aim here is to examine Orwell's novels from the point of view of his personal myth, to speculate on the way in which he regarded himself as a human being and the manner in which he projected these visions of himself into his art.

As a proportion of the whole, and given the twenty years he spent 'smothered under journalism', as he once put it, Orwell's six published novels represent only a tiny fraction of his output: the half-million word tip of a cascade of paper which, I once surreally calculated, would be enough to carpet Norwich city centre. The most obvious question to begin with is: how did he go about writing it? And the answer is in the curious, occasionally random, at all times obliquely personal way in which most novelists go about writing books. It tends to be forgotten that the majority of novels praised for the coherence of their structure and the singularity of their vision are written in a very prosaic way and, should you not happen to be Marcel Proust or James Joyce, for very prosaic reasons. Samuel Johnson, for example, wrote *Rasselas* in a week to defray the expenses of his mother's funeral; the pithy, interrogative dialogue of Alexandre Dumas's fiction is the result of his being paid at so many centimes a line. Orwell's novels are full of odd, individual fragments which the biographer, following in his wake, can sometimes pick up on the edge of the trail: the discovery, for example, that 'Dorothy' the heroine of his second novel, *A Clergyman's Daughter*, is the name of a girl over whose affections he actually fought with her fiancé, George Summers, on Southwold common in 1934; or that 'Manor Farm', in *Animal Farm*, is part of the name of a tiny culvert in Southwold High Street, twenty yards away from the home of Orwell's parents.

The most decisive twitch on the biographical thread came when I went to interview an old gentleman with the euphonious Suffolk name of Bumstead, who as a Southwold grocer in the 1930s supplying the Blair seniors remembered being given a wedding present by them when he married and cut dead by them if they came across each other in the street on a Sunday. At the end of our chat, just as I was getting up from my chair, Mr Bumstead fired a parting shot. "That George Orwell" he said, with the air of one who makes some absolutely startling revelation, "he put my brother in his book!" This was a bombshell. Which book? Where? "You go home and look in that *Nineteen Eighty-Four*" Mr Bumstead advised, "and you'll see, *he put my brother in his book*." I went home and subjected my ancient Penguin paperback to a thorough-going overhaul. And there it was. There in the scene in which Winston Smith, having been seized by the Thought Police in the love-nest he shares with Julia above Mr Charrington's shop, is dragged off to the Ministry of Love, where he watches a man attempt to palm a starving prisoner a piece of bread. "Bumstead" yells a voice from the telescreen, "2713 Bumstead J! Let fall that piece of bread." Jack Bumstead, in other words, the grocer's son from Southwold who, fifteen years before, had lived in a house on the other side of the High Street from Orwell's parents and had lain awake on summer nights listening to the sound of their son's typewriter clacking across the street.

Faced with a work of the imagination written by a flesh and blood subject, biographers tend to turn horribly reductive, however understandable their motivation or emphatic the warnings trailed in front of them by the novelist himself. 'I am not I' Evelyn Waugh noted at the beginning of *Brideshead Revisited*, 'thou art not he or she: they are not they.' The ways in which novelists 'put themselves into their books'– to render this transformation down to its crudest level – are as varied as the human experience they set out to represent. In *A Dance to the Music of Time* Anthony Powell uses the trick of self-effacement, consigning himself to the margins of the sequence, in the guise of his alter-ego Nicholas Jenkins, because he realises that a position centre-stage would compromise the objectivity about human affairs that is his aim as a writer. Writing something about William Cooper, the other day, I realised, alternatively, that the older he got the more liable Cooper was to write disguised autobiography. His retirement from the Civil Service, removal to his mansion flat at Putney Bridge, his hip replacement – all this was transferred, more or less unmediated, to the world of his novels. Orwell differs from Powell and Cooper in that his fiction consists almost exclusively of *projections* of himself, devious imaginary structures erected on the foundations of his own psychology and the particular environments in which he found himself when he wrote them. Nowhere, perhaps, is this grounding in the kind of person that Orwell imagined himself to be more evident than in what Orwell thought of his novels after, and in some cases even before, he had finished writing them. As a human being, and to a lesser extent as a writer, Orwell was obsessed with the idea of failure. His attitude to his fiction, consequently, is usually one of bitter disparagement. In 1946, for instance, shortly after the publication of *Animal Farm*, the book which made his name, he wrote the famous essay 'Why I Write' for a little magazine named *Gangrel*. He hoped in the future to write another work of fiction, he told *Gangrel*'s handful of readers. 'It is bound to be a failure, every book is a failure ...' Every book? *Ulysses* and *Vanity Fair* and *A La Recherche du Temps Perdus*? All of them?

There is no getting away from this blanket disavowal of his own and everybody else's talent, for it had been there since the very start of his career. The idea of using a pseudonym and transforming himself from 'Eric Blair' to 'George Orwell' was first proposed to his agent in 1932 on the grounds that he was 'not proud' of his first book, *Down and Out in Paris and London*. *A Clergyman's Daughter*, his second novel, was written off as 'bollix' – a word I have not actually found in any dictionary. *Keep The Aspidistra Flying*, his fourth, over which he claimed to have sweated blood in his efforts to create a work of art in the months devoted to its composition, was later marked down as a pot-boiler, written simply to get his hands on Victor Gollancz's £100 advance. Neither novel would he even allow to be reprinted during his lifetime: a new edition of *A Clergyman's Daughter* had to wait until 1960, ten years after his death and twenty-six after its first publication. There is a pattern to all this. Generally speaking, Orwell seems to have decided shortly after, or in some cases before, publication that what he had written was a mess in which a promising idea or good material had somehow defied his ability to render it down. Even *Nineteen Eighty-Four*, he told Malcolm Muggeridge, was a good idea that had crumbled in his hands.

And if the books are failure, so are the people who wander around in them. Each of Orwell's protagonists, when it comes down to it, is a study in failure, a matter of life not sustaining its early promise, dreams cast down into dust. Flory in *Burmese Days* is a lonely fantasist, whose best years have been squandered in drink and whoring; Dorothy in *A Clergyman's Daughter* is an old maid at twenty-eight; Comstock in *Keep The Aspidistra Flying* a moth-eaten minor poet turned sour by his blighted hopes. Even George Bowling in *Coming Up For Air*, perhaps the most resourceful and worldly – the least like Orwell, in fact – of this desperate crew, is irrevocably caught up in the ooze and stagnation of a life lived out with the mirthless Hilda in the shadow of approaching war. Each of Orwell's novels, by extension, is the story of a rebellion that fails, of an individual – in the case of *Animal Farm*, a mini society – who, however feebly or obliquely, attempts to throw over the traces. Each ends in more or less the same way, with the protagonist humbled, defeated, sent back to square one. Flory shoots himself. Dorothy returns to the sedative thraldom of her father's rectory. Gordon succumbs to the insidious embrace of the money god. George Bowling creeps home to the West London suburbs in shame. Winston Smith, brain-washed and re-educated, knows that he loves Big Brother. There is no way out. The best one can hope for is a kind of coming to terms with the weight of this environmental quicksand, the 'he is dead but won't lie down' idea peddled by the epigraph to *Coming Up For Air*, or Julia's 'We're not dead yet' in *Nineteen Eighty-Four*. The truly startling thing about this atmosphere of failure, inanition and spiritual servitude is that it is Orwell talking about himself.

Meanwhile, there is another question that needs answering. Even failures can be categorised. What kind of writer – and this in an era where literary affiliations were highly important – did Orwell think he was? Here a fascinating dualism applies. 'Why I Write' contains a statement of what Orwell thought his ambitions were as a very young man:

> So it is clear what kind of books I wanted to write, in so far as I could be said to want to write books at that time. I wanted to write enormous naturalistic novels with unhappy endings, full of detailed descriptions and

arresting similes, and also full of purple passages in which words were used partly for the sake of their sound. And in fact *Burmese Days*, which I wrote when I was thirty but projected much earlier, is rather that kind of book.

Many of these ambitions survived the lure of political commitment to which Orwell succumbed in the mid-1930s. Above all, they are detectible in his influences. *A Clergyman's Daughter* borrows extensively from the 'Night Town' scene in *Ulysses*, but in general the salutes registered in Orwell's novels are to a rather elderly collection of bygone English writers, firmly detached from the modernist tide then sweeping over the literature of the inter-war period. *Burmese Days* is drenched in essence of Maugham. Anthony Powell, having read *Keep The Aspidistra Flying*, commented that 'the Gissing had to stop'. Appropriately enough, for a novel whose hero's father is a put-upon small shopkeeper in a flyblown market town, *Coming Up For Air's* most conspicuous debt is to the H.G. Wells of *The History of Mr Polly*. In fact, one of the absconding Mr Polly's key encounters – when he returns to his old home, now a tea shop, and is served by his wife – is mirrored by George Bowling's half-minute in the tobacconist's shop behind whose counter lounges Elsie, his first love, now a slack-jawed hag.

So half of Orwell – a half that was never extinguished, always popping up behind the ideological barricades – was a pure aesthete. The other half, forged in the crucible of the Spanish Civil War, knew exactly what kind of age he was born into. Again, to borrow from 'Why I Write':

> The Spanish war and other events in 1936–7 turned the scale and thereafter I knew where I stood. Every line of serious work that I have written since 1936 has been written, directly or indirectly, against totalitarianism and for democratic Socialism, as I understand.

The 1930s are littered with the bones of novelists who had difficulty in harmonising the two sides of Orwell's literary nature. In *Burmese Days* half of him is anti-Imperialism's avenging angel, and the other half a newcomer to a distant land with a rapt, painter's vision who is periodically overwhelmed by sheer over-excitement with scene. In *Keep the Aspidistra Flying*, half of him is a near-hysterical critic of the capitalist racket and the other half the projection of an almost 'ninetyish' sensibility itching to write nature notes about mist-dimmed hedges and dew that glitters on the hedges with a diamond flash.

And behind these two contending impulses, it can't be too often stressed, lies the figure of Orwell himself: a man who despite all evidence to the contrary, considered himself a failure, and believed that wherever he was set down in the world, whether in the Burma of the 1920s or on a remote Scottish island in the 1940s, that he was being watched. Each of his five realist novels plays what is essentially the same trick – the setting up of a solitary anti-hero in opposition to a hostile world. That world is at heart Orwell's own – the world of a Burmese village, a Suffolk market town or a Hampstead bookshop – in each case twisted subtly out of kilter, decorated with all the subliminal horrors that oppressed Orwell as much as his characters. The terrible immediacy of *Nineteen Eighty-Four* to its original readers derived from the fact that its landscape was not some Huxleyite world of plastic and chrome but the vistas of bomb-cratered central London that Orwell glimpsed from the windows of the 53 bus as he made his way home from *Tribune*'s offices in the Strand each evening.

Burmese Days, to begin at the beginning, is an odd book altogether: an 'Eastern' novel built on a conventional foundation, but decked about with the most fantastic figurative garnishes. Flory is a disillusioned teak merchant in his thirties, unmarried (though he has a Burmese mistress, Ma Hla May), bored with the handful of local Europeans with whom he is forced to associate, and finding civilised conversation – and an audience for his harangues about the Raj – only in the company of an Indian hospital doctor. To make matters worse, Flory is disfigured by a hideous birthmark. The arrival in Kyauktada of Elizabeth, the twenty-year-old, marriage-minded niece of hard-drinking Mr Lackersteen gives Flory unexpected hope, only for him to be cut out by an aristocratic army officer, Lieutenant Verrall. Meanwhile, Kyauktada generally is subject to the machinations of an unscrupulous native magnate, U Po Kyin, who is cheerfully blackmailing and bullying himself to prominence. Having seen off Verrall and covered himself in glory by performing heroically in a failed native uprising, Flory is thrown over by Elizabeth when U Po Kyin bribes the now discarded Ma Hla May to make a public scene in the Kyauktada church. Flory takes the gentleman's way out.

All this is accompanied by some wounding dissections of the evils of British rule in the East and some devastating portraits of the whisky-sodden wrecks and amateur humorists who infest the Kyauktada club. All the same, the most striking thing about the novel is not its anti-Imperial sentiment, but the extravagance of its language: a riot of rococo imagery that is allowed to get dangerously out of hand. The face of U Po Kyin's servant in one of the early scenes recalls 'a coffee blancmange'. A bit later, in the gardens of the club, a native servant moves through the jungle of flowers 'like some large, nectar-sucking bird.' Then, in the space of two pages, a lizard clings to the wall of Flory's house 'like a heraldic dragon', light rains down 'like glistening white oil' and the noise of doves produces 'a sleepy sound, but with the sleepiness of chloroform rather than a lullaby'. Towards the end of the novel, the figurative touches look as if they were filched from out of the *Yellow Book*. Camp-fire flames dance 'like red holly'; Flory and Elizabeth's canoes move through the water 'like long curved needles threading through embroidery.' Finally, the language loses all relation to the things it is trying to describe. The moon rises out of a cloud-bank 'like a sick woman creeping out of bed', while storms chase each other across the sky like squads of cavalry. This is a testimony to the hold that Burma exerted on Orwell's imagination, but it is also the mark of a faintly old-fashioned aesthetic sensibility – like something out of a poem by Richard Le Gallienne – which never entirely disappeared from his work.

Flory, with his birth-mark, his sexual pessimism and his fatal deracination, is not Orwell, who as far as we know spent a blameless five years in Burma and, whatever his private misgivings about the regime he served, came home from it in 1927 not to make an anti-Imperialist gesture but on a medical certificate. But, in a formula patented over the next fifteen years, he is a *version* of Orwell sent to dramatise and exemplify some of Orwell's most deeply held beliefs about human behaviour. So, too, is Dorothy Hare, the heroine of *A Clergyman's Daughter*, Orwell's second novel, written in a little over six months in 1934, while its author was in Southwold recuperating from illness, and published by Victor Gollancz in 1935. Given that Dorothy is a twenty-eight year-old spinster with a neurotic habit of correcting minor personal failings by jabbing the end of a pin into her arm, this might seem an odd claim to make, although Orwell's great friend Richard Rees insisted that in describing Dorothy's features – 'a thin … unremarkable kind of face, with pale eyes and a nose just a shade too long' – he was describing a feminised version of himself. And yet, awash with personal preoccupations and experiences, *A Clergyman's Daughter* turns out to be one of those curious novels in which a writer's private demons contend with a mass of reportage masquerading as background.

Living a life of semi-genteel bondage slaving for her clerical father in his musty Suffolk rectory, terrified of sex but pursued by a seedy middle-aged rake named Mr Warburton, Dorothy suffers a breakdown. Discovered sitting in an amnesiac state by the roadside in a London backstreet by a tramp and his mates, she spends a fortnight picking hops in Kent before finding out who she is. The prompt is a newspaper report of a 'rector's daughter' vanished from the family hearth having last been observed in a close embrace with Mr Warburton. Migrating to London, letters to her father unanswered, Dorothy ends up in a prostitute's boarding house in Lambeth Cut, is rescued by her father's baronet cousin and put to work in a dreadful private school before being rescued by Mr Warburton who arrives providentially in a taxi. Her chief accuser turns out to have been sued for libel. Her reputation in Knype Hill unexpectedly restored, Dorothy goes home, refusing Mr Warburton's offer of marriage, to a slightly modified version of her former circumstances.

For all the occasional red herrings cast into the reader's path, *A Clergyman's Daughter* is essentially a matter of Orwell making use of material drawn from his own life. Part one is a sharply drawn, naturalistic account of a Suffolk market town of the kind he had lived in on and off for the past five years. Part two offers an opportunity to re-heat some of his tramping and hopping exploits. The night in Trafalgar Square, though pastiching Joyce, uses his own experiences from the summer of 1931. Part four is framed by the memories of his teaching days in west London. Understandably, juxtaposing all this disparate material – Suffolk, hop-picking, down-and-out London, private school teaching – presented Orwell with huge technical problems. On one level the novel is simply an exercise in bridge-building in which the central character frequently tumbles into the water below. Reading it one is constantly struck by the way in which Dorothy falls in and out of the book, pushed aside by the torrents of reportage, and the ultimate effect is faintly incongruous – a feeling of personal experience, peculiar to the author, grafted onto an imagined psychology that is much less able to deal with it. In the end, Dorothy is a vehicle for Orwell, rather than the other way around.

The same kind of projection characterises *Keep The Aspidistra Flying* (1936), although the final version of the author that emerges from these 250 or so pages of ground-down dissatisfaction is a much more cunning and deviously manipulated alter-ego. Of all the novels that Orwell produced in the 1930s, this – being a book about a literary man – is the one most closely associated with him as a writer. Yet it exists at a decidedly odd angle to the kind of person he was and was becoming – on the one hand supplying yet another fiction-alised view of a world that can very easily be identified with his own, on the other moving several stages beyond it to magnify his own obsessions in a slightly absurd and occasionally rather self-pitying way. Gordon Comstock is a failed poet whose distaste for respectable life – symbolised by the dismal plant of the title - has led to his giving up his job as an advertising copywriter and taking a job in Mr Mckechnie's book. He is supported in this by his chief professional patron, Ravelston, and his girlfriend Rosemary, the one because he respects Gordon's principles, the other because she, albeit chastely, loves him. Eventually, Gordon's affairs lurch towards crisis. Going out on the raz-zle after receiving an unexpected cheque from an American magazine he loses his job and ends up working in a two-penny lending library, a come down even by the standards of second-hand bookselling. Visiting him in the squalor of his shabby lodgings, Rosemary finally consents to sleep with him. Confronted with the inescapable fact of her pregnancy, Gordon faces a stark choice: either he abandons her or takes a decent job. The decent job wins out, and the novel ends with them, newly married, taking possession of a tiny flat off the Edgware Road.

There are substantial distinctions to be made between author and hero. Gordon is an isolated figure, railing at the Bloomsbury editors who won't publish his poems in their snooty magazines. Essentially Rosemary and Rav-elston are his only friends and the novel, again, illustrates Orwell's trick – a trick carried all the way through to *Nineteen Eighty-Four* – of setting up the solitary victim in opposition to a hostile world. By contrast, Orwell's own life in Hampstead, to which he had removed at the end of 1934, was comparatively lively, filled with interesting relationships, plenty of time to write and plenty of opportunities to see his work in print. But *Keep the Aspidistra Flying* is still crammed with autobiographical fragments – the description of the police cell in which Gordon fetches up after his night on the tiles is lifted from an unpublished essay from 1932. [2] His early aestheticism, too, was much in evidence. Occasionally this would twist itself into a more grotesque, 'modernist' image – the tram which slides across the square in which Mckechnie's bookshop is situated 'like a raucous swan of steel', but most of the touches are painterly, as when Gordon, hungrily eyeing up the female talent at a street market, sees three teenage girls whose faces 'cluster side by side like a truss of blossom on a Sweet William or Phlox.' When he stares at the most arresting of the trio, ' a delicate flush like a wave of aquarelle flooded her face.'

To set against this is a small but insistent prophetic note. The aeroplanes are coming, Gordon reflects early on in the novel; the whole world will soon be going up in a roar of high explosive. "My poems are dead because I'm dead. You're dead. We're all dead people in a dead world" Gordon lectures Rosemary. Even the advertising campaign that Gordon works on after his return to the agency – a preventative against sweaty feet canvassed by way of the slogan 'P.P. (pedic perspiration) – WHAT ABOUT YOU', which is reckoned to have a 'sinister simplicity', seems only a step or two away from the looming world of Big Brother and the Thought Police.

But we have heard this note before. Ask what the wider landscapes of Orwell's '30s novels are about, and the answer, or one of the answers is 'them', the malign exterior forces which Orwell thought were at work interfering in other people's lives. If the people in his novels – Flory, Dorothy, Gordon, George Bowling in *Coming Up For Air* – share a single characteristic it is their author's tendency to victimise them, to place them at the centre of a hostile world from which they cannot escape and where their every movement is subject to constant surveillance. The provincial backwater of Knype Hill in *A Clergyman's Daughter* is represented as a cauldron of spite and back-biting, scores being settled behind the lace curtains and the privet hedges, gross libels and calumnies crackling down the phone wires. 'It was one of those sleepy, old-fashioned streets, that look so ideally peaceful on a casual visit and so very different when you live in them and have an enemy or a creditor behind every window.' *Every* window? Surely some of the town's 5,000 or so inhabitants practise Christian charity? But this is what Orwell does with his characters. He cuts them off, places them – isolated, friendless, vulnerable – at the mercy of huge, unappeasable forces. There is a dreadful scene, also in *A Clergyman's Daughter*, in which Dorothy is harangued and humiliated by a gang of puritanically minded parents, having explained to their children a sexual reference in *Macbeth*. Her employer, Mrs Creevy's role, both before and after, is that of head conspirator – ceaselessly keeping an eye on Dorothy, her whereabouts and her attitude to her job. Gordon Comstock is less intimidated by his gorgon of a landlady, but even so his life is a series of furtive concealments: brewing illicit cups of tea in his room while listening for the sound of feet on the stair. Bowling in *Coming Up For Air* has a terror of being found out. His journey in search of the Thames Valley haunts of his boyhood – Orwell's own juvenile stamping ground – is coloured, and eventually undermined, by the thought that his wife's spies will be on his tail. When he half hears the emergency radio broadcast featuring a woman of the same name his first thought is that it must be one of Hilda's dodges, a cruel and elaborate ruse dreamed up with the aim of making him suffer. All this adds up. The telescreen, *Nineteen Eighty-Four's* great symbolic invention, is not an adventitious fictional device, but something central to the ideas he held about the world.

Meanwhile there is another crucial aspect of Orwell's self-projection that no account of *Nineteen Eighty-Four* can quite ignore. This is not a work of fiction – although most critics doubt that all the events described in actually happened – but 'Such, such were the joys', the 15,000 word account of Orwell's time at the Eastbourne preparatory school, St Cyprian's, unpublished for many years after his death on the grounds of the serious offence it would give to the school's still living proprietors. Dripping with animosity, accusing the headmaster and his wife, Mr and Mrs Wilkes of physical and mental cruelty and a snobbishness that would not have disgraced Lady Catherine de Burgh, the essay carries the two essential signature marks of Orwell's novels, which is to say that it contains, in the figure of the pre-teenage Eric Blair, a haunting picture of a lost, excluded outsider, whose individuality and happiness is being constrained by what is effectively a police state with 'Sambo' – the boy's name for the headmaster – as its all-seeing, ever-vigilant eye. At one point Orwell is sent on an errand to Eastbourne. Straying off the prescribed path to buy chocolate in a sweet shop, he emerges to find a man staring intently at his school cap. Naturally, Orwell represents his younger self as realising, the man is a spy placed there by Sambo. This seemed a perfectly logical explanation. 'Sambo was all-powerful: it was natural that his agents should be everywhere.'

When was 'Such, such were the Joys' written? The woman who acted as Orwell's secretary in the mid-1940s remembered making a fair copy from a bleary and apparently much-travelled typescript. But who typed the original, and when? Orwell had announced his intention of 'writing a book about St Cyprians's' to his fellow-pupil Cyril Connolly as far back as 1938. But a much more likely completion date is 1945–6. At any rate, it is at least probable that a considerable part of the work on 'Such, such were the Joys' was done when Orwell was incubating, or indeed writing, what became *Nineteen Eighty-Four*. Over the years many a critic has speculated that this expose of the totalitarian mind is on one level a projection of his infant misery, an autocratic world that has its roots in a boys' boarding school. But it could be argued, equally plausibly, that the trick is being played the other way around – that Orwell's mature views on authoritarianism and its psychological consequences encouraged him to recast his memories of St Cyprian's in a more sinister shape. The idea of the school as a police state, Mrs Wilkes with her arbitrary favouritism, the calamitous consequences of loss of favour – all

this, it could be said, is the mental baggage of *Nineteen Eighty-Four* shifted back in time. Whatever the answer to this riddle, there is some kind of relationship between the essay on boyhood and the dystopian novel, certainly sufficient to suggest that both took root in Orwell's mental landscape at the same time.

The point that *Nineteen-Eighty-Four* labours is the one that had animated Orwell's journalism since at least 1940, if not before. Any regime at war with its neighbour will commit acts of cruelty and tell lies. This Orwell matter-of-factly accepted. One of his chief complaints about the BBC Eastern Service, where he worked as an increasingly disillusioned talks producers between 1941 and 1943, was not that it broadcast propaganda, but that the propaganda it did broadcast was fatally ineffective. But a totalitarian regime does these things to sustain something integral to itself, to wield power for its own sake. Perhaps the most revealing moment in *Nineteen Eighty-Four* comes when O'Brien demands of Winston if he begins to understand what kind of world 'we' are creating. It is 'the exact opposite of the stupid, hedonistic utopias that the old reformers imagined' – a world of fear, treachery and torment. The ancient tyrants invoked by Porteous, the retired schoolmaster in *Coming Up For Air*, as Hitler's forebears, were simple hooligans. The totalitarians of the twentieth century are engaged on something much more insidious – not to tell a man that 2+2=5, but to convince him that it was so.

There is something sacerdotal about O'Brien as he pronounces this analysis – and a few pages before he has remarked that 'We are the priests of power. God is power' – but there is also something schoolmasterly, the sense of a patient, occasionally exasperated pedagogue urging on a backward student who may still 'make good' if he is sufficiently goaded. Orwell even notes that O'Brien 'assumed again the air of a schoolmaster questioning a promising pupil.' But the faint gestures towards his own early life – Mr Wilkes, perhaps, catechising contenders for the Harrow History Prize – make perfect sense in the novel's wider context. *Nineteen Eighty-Four* is, in fact, a kind of palimpsest, constantly refined and brought up to date, in which the early entries re-emerge to assume an unexpected resonance. The early sections, in particular, can be read as a conscious re-framing of the landscape of *Keep The Aspidistra Flying*. As Winston looks out of the window of Victory Mansions in the opening chapter, 'Down in the street little eddies of wind were whirling dust and torn paper into spirals' (Compare this with the ribbon of paper that 'fluttered fitfully like a tiny pennant' outside Mr McKechnie's bookshop. And every so often comes a twitch – subtle, but unmistakeable to anyone who knows Orwell's work – on the thread of his own memory. 'Want to see the hangings! Want to see the hangings!' chants the daughter of Winston's neighbour Parsons, referring to the execution in the park of Eurasian prisoners with round Mongol faces. Orwell had attended a very similar occasion in Burma a quarter of a century before. Finally there is an extraordinary moment, like a bullet winging its way back across time, when

Winston summons up the vision of Mrs Parsons in her slatternly kitchen, 'a woman with a lined face and wispy hair, fiddling helplessly with a blocked waste-pipe.' Orwell had seen such a face years before as he walked up the back-alley in the north of England and converted it into *The Road to Wigan Pier's* most enduring image.

Having completed *Nineteen-Eighty Four* on Jura at the end of 1948, Orwell collapsed, was taken away to a sanatorium in the Cotswolds and subsequently to University College Hospital London, where he died in January 1950. There were two fictional projects in his mind in the months before he died – one a long novel set in 1945, of which no trace survives, but assumed to be the third component in a trilogy of which *Animal Farm* and *Nineteen Eighty-Four* were the opening salvos, the other revealed in a conversation with his publisher, Fred Warburg, in June 1949. 'I asked him about a new novel, and this is formulated in his mind – a nouvelle of 30,000 to 40,000 words – a novel of character rather than ideas, with Burma as background.' Some notes and an unfinished draft survive, probably written in the spring of 1949.[3] Set in 1927 – the year of Orwell's own return from Burma, neatly enough – 'A Smoking Room Story' features a young man named Geoffrey 'Curly' Johnson, sent home by his firm for drunkenness, who combines a dislike of the American and English businessmen on the ship with social insecurity: he is wary of the bright young people who swarm aboard at Colombo. There is also mention of a Burmese woman, Ma Yi, his mistress, and the 'dust and squalor of his house, the worn gramophone records, the piled up whiskey bottles ...'.[4] Predictions of what Orwell might have thought and wrote, in which newspapers delight, are rarely worth the paper they are written on, but in terms of his fiction Orwell looks as if, at 46, he was returning – as his heroes Thackeray, Dickens had done before him – to the world of his own early life.

And where, finally, does this leave Orwell and his achievement? The location of a writer's primal literary impulse down among the lumber of his own experience is often thought to diminish him, to be regarded, for some reason as a form of sleight of hand. As Kingsley Amis once complained to Philip Larkin about Anthony Powell, a writer incidentally, whom Amis profoundly admired: 'it did suddenly strike me how fed up I was about all those real people and real incidents he's put in his books. I thought you were meant to *make them up*, you know, like a novelist ...'.[5] Observers of the fictional scene, from New Critics to Continental theorists – hardly any of them, it should be pointed out, novelists themselves – periodically rise up to assure their audiences that it is possible to separate a novel from the creative intelligence that fashioned it, when all that has really been proved is that in the last resort, in highly artificial circumstances, *they are ultimately separable*, which is not quite the same thing. A novel-reader and a biographer will perhaps look for different things in Orwell's fiction. The novel reader will look for plot, pace and character and that distinctive individual take on the passing human traffic. The biographer will look for Orwell. This biographer found both, inextricably bound up in the personal mythologizing that is such a central part of Orwell's elusive personality.

The history of the English novel in the 1930s has been subject to a great deal of retrospective teleology, and we tend to regard Orwell as a much more significant operator in it than critics who had not had the benefit of studying *Nineteen Eighty-Four* did so at the time. But we read, and will continue to read, his fiction for the reason that we continue to read the work of any great writer, both for what it tells us about the person who wrote it and what it tells us about ourselves, the people we are, have been, and shall become.

Notes

1. *To Keep the Ball Rolling: The Memoirs of Anthony Powell: Volume I: Infants of the Spring* (1976), pp.140–1.
2. 'Clink', in Peter Davison, ed. *George Orwell: The Complete Works: Volume X: A Kind of Compulsion, 1903–1936 (1998)*, pp. 254–60.
3. Davison, ed. *The Complete Works: Volume XX: Our Job is to Make Life Worth Living* (1998), pp.131–3.
4. *Ibid*, 188–99
5. Zachary Leader, ed. *The Letters of Kingsley Amis* (2000), p.950.

5
Goldsmith and the Art of Indirect Autobiography[1]

Graham Gargett

It is an obvious paradox that, although Oliver Goldsmith arguably played a significant role in the development of biographical writing in English,[2] he was notoriously cagey about his own life, and his biographers have had a dreadful time producing an adequate Goldsmith biography. The last real attempt was in 1977, John Ginger's *The Notable Man*, which, though admirable in several ways and certainly very readable, has many important gaps.[3] In a way this dearth of information apparently willed by the author is strange. If we take, for example, Goldsmith's own biography of Beau Nash, which dates from 1762, what strikes one immediately is the amount of documentary material that Goldsmith has assembled, particularly letters.[4] Yet he made not the slightest attempt to help his own future biographers. The volume of his letters published in the 1920s by Katherine Balderston is slight in the extreme.[5] One hesitates to say that he actually suppressed his letters, but he certainly made no attempt whatsoever to preserve them. Towards the end of his fairly short life, he did dictate the briefest of autobiographical accounts, a couple of pages, to his friend Thomas Percy, later Bishop of Dromore in Co. Down. Percy was supposed to be Goldsmith's biographer, but he was either too lazy or too occupied elsewhere ever to do anything much with this material, except to produce what is called 'The Percy memoir', in other words a few comments based on the text that Goldsmith had provided.[6] It is as if Goldsmith almost foresaw what would happen. As if he wanted to leave behind a tantalisingly sketchy though controlled account of his life. As if the obvious gaps and lacunae were not his personal responsibility or as if he wanted to play with posterity. That this is not mere speculation is surely illustrated by one of his early letters. On 14 August 1758 he wrote, from the Temple Exchange Coffee House, Temple Bar, in London, to his friend Robert Bryanton, in Ballymahon, as follows:

> There will come a day, no doubt it will – I beg you may live a couple of hundred years longer only to see the day – when the Scaligers and Daciers will vindicate my character, give learned editions of my labours, and bless

the times with copious comments on the text [...] How will they bewail the times that suffered so much genius to lie neglected. If ever my works find their way to Tartary or China, I know the consequence. Suppose one of your Chinese Owanowitzers instructing one of your Tartarian Chianobac-chi – you see I use Chinese names to show my own erudition, as I shall soon make our Chinese talk like an Englishman to show his. This may be the subject of the lecture: -

" 'Oliver Goldsmith flourished in the eighteenth and nineteenth cen-turies. He lived to be an hundred and three years old, [and in that] age may justly be styled the sun of [literature] and the Confucius of Europe. [Many of his earlier writings, to the regret of the] learned world, were anonymous, and have probably been lost, because united with those of others. The first avowed piece the world has of his is entitled an 'Essay on the Present state of Taste and Literature in Europe,' – a work well worth its weight in diamonds. In this he profoundly explains what learning is, and what learning is not. In this he proves that blockheads are not men of wit, and yet that men of wit are actually blockheads.[7]

I think one can certainly detect a ludic element in the almost contrived dearth of information about Goldsmith's life.

But there is arguably another side to it. It suited Goldsmith very well *dur-ing* his life in London to be vague and offhand about his background. He was always known in Johnson's circle as 'Dr. Goldsmith', often as 'Dr. min-imus' in contrast to 'Dr. major' – obviously Johnson himself. Yet it seems fairly certain that Goldsmith never got a doctorate of any description. Cer-tainly none of his biographers has ever found the slightest piece of evidence. Perhaps no one could reasonably blame Goldsmith for having pretended that he was a 'doctor' during his difficult early years in London. But a man who could contrive to fail the very simple examination to become a ship's surgeon, the only one out of some twenty candidates in December 1758 to achieve this feat,[8] is unlikely to have had any sort of real medi-cal qualification, whether from the University of Padua, as he claimed, or anywhere else.

I want to argue that Goldsmith continues this type of ludic mystification in his writings. He plays with his readers, by very obviously drawing on his own experiences in portraying his characters. This may seem a fairly banal thing to do, common to many or even most authors, but Goldsmith takes it to such an extreme that his biographers have often quite simply attributed to him actions and events that happen to certain of his characters. Yet Goldsmith refuses to do anything as simple as merely transferring actions and events wholesale. There are no doubt some points where the double identification is valid, but he is not trying to compose a second-hand autobiography, and we should be very careful not to go too far down the road that some Goldsmith biographers have taken.

Some examples will illustrate this point. Goldsmith's most famous comedy, *She Stoops to Conquer*, is arguably based on a case of mistaken identity which some claim happened to Goldsmith in his youth.[9] His first book, referred to in the letter quoted earlier, was *An Enquiry into the Present State of Polite Learning* (1758). Basically this describes the cultural development of modern Europe, but it also contains passages recalling events in Goldsmith's life. For example, he attacks the system of 'sizars' in Trinity College, Dublin. A sizar was the beneficiary of a type of student scholarship, but one that compelled him to wait at table for other, richer, students. Goldsmith himself had been a 'sizar', and had hated the humiliation involved.[10] Goldsmith's first great success, *The Chinese Letters*, usually known under its revised title of *The Citizen of the World*, was also clearly already in Goldsmith's mind when he wrote the letter to Bryanton quoted earlier. One of the main characters, 'The Man in Black', describes his youth in letter 27, and his father sounds very much like Goldsmith's – a poverty-striken clergyman who nonetheless spends his money freely on helping the poor and who fails to give his own children a due sense of the importance of money. Like the Man in Black, Goldsmith himself was a notorious spendthrift and was credited with giving away his money hand over fist to those who were actually in need or who were able to convince him that they were.[11] Above all, the passage in Goldsmith's works which has most appealed to critics is chapter 20 of *The Vicar of Wakefield*, which describes the travels of George Primrose, the Vicar's son.

To put this in context, a very brief summary of Goldsmith's life is required. Born in the Irish midlands around 1728, he was a less than brilliant student at Trinity College, Dublin, then spent a couple of years back home in Ballymahon, finally being sent by his family to study medicine in Edinburgh. After a year and a half he tired of this and took himself off to Leyden, where he claimed that the teaching would be much superior. Once again, however, a year or so later, he absconded, spending a period wandering around Europe that we know virtually nothing about. After the death of his uncle, Thomas Contarine, who had provided some financial support, Goldsmith left the continent and went, not back to Ireland, but to London, which he had never previously visited. His literary career began in 1757, when he was taken on as a reviewer for the *Monthly Review*.[12] After a few difficult years as a reviewer and essayist, he came to widespread notice with the *Chinese Letters* and achieved real fame with his didactic poem, *The Traveller*, in 1764. There followed *The Vicar of Wakefield*, *The Deserted Village*, and *She Stoops to Conquer*, as well as a considerable number of 'compilations' and *œuvres de circonstance*.[13] Goldsmith died after a short illness in 1774, probably at the age of 45.[14]

The mysterious time on the continent has understandably intrigued biographers and critics. Goldsmith told Thomas Percy laconically:

He [...] went (about 1753) to Padua in Italy, where he staid 6 months & saw Venice, Florence, Virona, & all the North Part of Italy. His Uncle dying while he was at Padua, he was obliged to return back thro France &c. on Foot, lodging at Convents chiefly of the Irish Nation. After spending in this perigrination once [*sic*] a year he came to settle in London this was about the breaking out of the War in 1756.[15]

Self evidently, however, there must have been so much more. And the missing detail is often supplied by Goldsmith's biographers from the apparently similar experiences of the fictional George Primrose. Like Goldsmith Primrose begins his continental travels in Holland, but rather than going there to study medicine, he aims to teach the Dutch English. Thereafter he travels to Louvain, and to Paris, where he becomes governor, or 'travelling tutor', to a young man of fortune, who journeys with him to Leghorn, from whence the pupil decides to sail back to England, leaving his tutor there in the lurch. Goldsmith claims none of this in his own case, but this has not stopped biographers from applying some – or nearly all – of what he writes about George Primrose to the author himself. Thus Goldsmith has been portrayed as travelling to Geneva as the tutor of a young English 'lord', like George Primrose begging board and lodging from French peasants by playing his flute – and so on. Earlier in chapter 20 of *The Vicar of Wakefield*, there are other reminiscences of Goldsmith's own life. Like him, George Primrose is a not very effective usher, or assistant teacher, at a boy's school: 'I had rather be a turnkey in Newgate', he declares:

> I was brow-beat by the master, hated for my ugly face by the mistress, worried by the boys within, and never permitted to stir out to meet civility abroad. But are you sure you are fit for a school? Let me examine you a little. Have you been bred apprentice to the business? No. Then you won't do for a school. Can you dress the boys hair? No. Then you won't do for a school. Have you had the small-pox? No. Then you won't do for a school. Can you lie three in a bed? No. Then you will never do for a school. Have you got a good stomach? Yes. Then you will by no means do for a school.[16]

Probably written about six years after Goldsmith himself had been a teacher in Dr. Milner's Classical School in Peckham, this passage arguably still reeks of his irritation.[17] Yet, if it is a pseudo-autobiographical text, the mixture of fact and fiction is evident. Goldsmith *had* himself had smallpox, so here he differs from George Primrose. But it had disfigured him, and he was generally considered ugly, not helped by his premature balding, so the mistress's hatred for his ugly face certainly rings a bell. In the Percy memoir, there is only the briefest of mentions of this part of his life:

> The Revd Dr Milner, a dissenting Minister of note, who kept a Classical School, at Peckham in Surrey, having a long fit of illness of which he

soon after died, becoming acquainted with him thro' his son, who was
also a young Physician, invited him to take the care of School During his
illness [...][18]

Clearly, the Percy memoir is a sanitised account of Goldsmith's life, dictated
when he had become famous and wished the more difficult moments of his
career to be glossed over as far as possible. Yet it is as if the carefully-suppressed
details cannot help bursting out in his writings: there we see the irritation,
the indignation, the annoyance, the sheer drudgery that must have characterised his time as a schoolmaster. So here fiction probably does trump
a would-be factual account by the author. But are passages like this in *The
Vicar of Wakefield* autofiction?[19] The whole question seems to me very complex and almost impossible to resolve. Just as every person's character has
different layers, and just as we respond perhaps differently to certain situations throughout our lives as we strive to construct more successfully a social
or professional persona, in just the same way an author like Goldsmith functions on several levels. He purposely uses incidents from his life or feelings
and reactions to flesh out and give inner life to his fictional creations; at the
same time he may sometimes or even often involuntarily reveal his beliefs
and feelings more effectively through his characters; and clearly, in the case
of Goldsmith he also plays with his readers, especially in his works of fiction.

When we turn to his so-called 'compilations', the situation is quite different. One of Goldsmith's most underrated achievements is arguably his *History
of the Earth and Animated Nature*, for which he was paid the vast sum of 800
guineas. This was a sort of compendium, published in 1774, an encyclopedia
not only of natural phenomena, but of animals, birds, plants, in short the
entire natural world as far as it was then known.[20] The work was hugely successful, and its pedagogical impact must have been enormous, since it went
into umpteen editions, and was reprinted well into the nineteenth century.[21]
John Ginger goes some way to acknowledging this, though even his praise
has a somewhat patronising ring about it:

It would [...] be wrong to exaggerate the shortcomings of *The History of the
Earth and Animated Nature*. This was a lucid and immensely readable work
which kept its popularity: only by the 1840s had its built-in obsolescence
begun to show itself.[22]

Ginger's main criticism is that Goldsmith was 'no more than an enthusiastic
amateur', and that he 'had spent the better part of five years re-arranging
other people's findings'. Basically, Ginger regards the work as a 'waste of
Goldsmith's talent, an undertaking he had 'brought [...] on himself through
his improvidence'.[23] Yet it is difficult to think of any scientific work that will
not have become somewhat 'obsolescent' some seventy years after its composition, even if the author is a 'real' scientist.[24] The task of popularising

or 'vulgarising' scientific knowledge and discoveries was, and remains, a vital one, and those writers who pioneered this *genre* in the seventeenth and eighteenth centuries were far from necessarily prostituting their talent, as the distinguished examples of Fontenelle and Voltaire show very clearly.[25] Apart from anything else, the dedication of the first Irish edition (1777) to the Speaker of the Irish House of Commons, Edmund Sexton Pery, and the impressive subscription list, including a whole raft of printers and booksellers ordering multiple copies, is eloquent testament to the interest in Goldsmith's native country.[26] More serious than this, though, is Ginger's complete failure to appreciate the sheer interest, fascination and enthusiasm which permeates the *History of the Earth and Animated Nature*. Goldsmith has frequently been accused of plagiarism – often justifiably, especially at the beginning of his writing career. As an apprentice journalist and essay writer, he drew freely on the work of others, especially French authors like Marivaux and Voltaire.[27] But in the *Animated Nature*, Goldsmith is scrupulous about revealing his sources, and these are many and varied, from recognised scientific treatises to recent newspaper articles. John Ginger once again seems vastly to underrate Goldsmith's work when he refers to him 'emerging from the long hours he had spent grappling with Buffon or Lucretius' (as if most of the *Animated Nature* had been merely compiled from the writings of these two authorities), and to the 'nuggets of science or pseudo-science' that Goldsmith scattered into conversations with his friends.[28] Not only is the implication that Goldsmith had little idea of what he was writing about unfair and inaccurate, based as it is largely on the mockery to which Goldsmith was subjected by Johnson and his cronies, it totally fails to recognise that Goldsmith's fascination in this huge panorama of all aspects of nature, from the formation of the earth to the minutest of microscopic species, reveals an aspect of his character which biographers have often missed, or merely ridiculed. As well as this, the *Animated Nature* provides many direct anecdotal glimpses of the author's life which are unique in his *œuvre* and which seem to have been noticed by hardly any Goldsmith critics or biographers.[29]

The pseudo-biographical material is evident in many places, as witness a passage in the article devoted to the otter. Goldsmith suddenly disagrees with Buffon, whose account he has been following, with a recollection of his own childhood, beside the River Inny, near Ballymahon:

> We learn from Mr. Buffon that this animal, in France, couples in winter and brings forth in the beginning of spring. But it is certainly different with us, for its young are never found till the latter end of summer; and I have frequently, when a boy, discovered their retreats, and pursued them at that season.[30]

Like this extract, several other passages provide us with information which appears to refer to Goldsmith's youth in Ireland. Admittedly, some passages may be based merely on his reading, as – for example – when he observes that 'in several parts of Ireland and the highlands of Scotland, the goat makes the chief possession of the inhabitants'.[31] Similarly, the comment that 'The few [stags] that still remain wild are to be found on the moors that border on Cornwall and Devonshire; and in Ireland, on most of the large mountains of that country'[32] might not necessarily indicate personal knowledge. But, when Goldsmith, a propos of May bugs, relates that 'In Ireland they suffered so much by these insects, that they came to a resolution of setting fire to a wood of some miles in extent, to prevent their mischievous propagation',[33] one is already less certain, since this comment comes immediately after another anecdote regarding the year 1751, while Goldsmith was a young man in Ireland. Remarks about polecats ('I have seen them burrow near a village, so as scarcely to be extirpated'[34]) and foxes ('I have seen these animals, when taken earlier in the woods, become very tame'[35]) also seem more likely to refer to Goldsmith's youth in Ireland than to his relatively urban existence in England, all the more so since the polecat was largely confined to Scotland and Ireland. And little doubt seems possible when Goldsmith devotes several paragraphs to 'the great Irish wolf-dog', an animal, he observes, 'which is very rare, even in the only country in the world where it is to be found', particularly since he adds later:

> The largest of those I have seen, and I have seen above a dozen, was about four feet high, or as tall as a calf of a year old [...] the gentleman who bred them assuring me, that a mastiff would be nothing when opposed to one of them, who generally seized their antagonist by the back: he added, that they would worry the strongest bull-dogs in a few minutes, to death.[36]

One even wonders if this comment about the superiority of the Irish wolf hound over the (British) bull dog is not a covert or subliminal example of Goldsmith emphasising his Irish origins.

Other passages give still clearer information about Goldsmith's activities as a young man in Ireland. As regards the wolf, he remarks: 'They are said to have infested Ireland long after they were extirpated in England; however, the oldest men in that country remember nothing of these animals',[37] a claim hardly likely to have been based on reading. And no doubt whatsoever remains in the section entitled 'The elk'. Here Goldsmith talks about the giant elks which we now know to have inhabited Ireland after the last great Ice Age, whose remains have been found in places like the outskirts of Belfast:

> If we were to judge of its size by the horns, which are sometimes fortuitously dug up in many parts of Ireland, we should not be much amiss in ascribing them to an animal at least ten feet high. Of these I have seen, which was ten feet nine inches from one tip to the other.[38]

Goldsmith's early interest, as well as his characteristic method of reasoning by analogy, is apparent:

> I remember, some years ago, to have seen a small moose-deer, which was brought from America by a gentleman of Ireland; it was about the size of an horse, and the horns were very little larger than those of a common stag: this, therefore, serves to prove that the horns bear an exact proportion to the animal's size; the small elk has but small horns; whereas those enormous ones, which we have described above, must have belonged to a proportionable creature.[39]

Already anticipating the accusation of guesswork, Goldsmith adds: 'In all the more noble animals, nature observes a perfect symmetry; and it is not to be supposed she fails in this single instance.'[40] No doubt Johnson and others might have mocked, but on this occasion Goldsmith's hunch turns out to have been quite correct. Another, amusing, example of Goldsmith's Irish observations concerns the seal. 'How long this animal lives is […] unknown', he comments, before adding:

> […] a gentleman whom I knew in Ireland, kept two of them, which he had taken very young, in his house for ten years; and they appeared to have the marks of age at the time I saw them, for they were grown grey about the muzzle; and it is very probable they did not live many years longer.[41]

As well as suggesting information about Goldsmith's formative years in Ireland, the *Animated Nature* also shows that he was a frequent and interested visitor to the Tower of London, forerunner of the London Zoo, and to 'the Queen's menagerie at Buckingham-Gate', where he found a zebra to be 'even more vicious' than one described by Buffon:

> Upon my attempting to approach, it seemed quite terrified, and was preparing to kick, appearing as wild as if just caught, although taken extremely young, and used with the utmost indulgence.[42]

Goldsmith also observed 'some years ago in London' an animal 'of the cow kind', which he feels that neither Buffon nor 'any other naturalist' that he knows of 'has hitherto described', possibly a yak.[43] In addition, he saw lions,[44] a 'catamountain' or ocelot,[45] a 'siagush' or serval,[46] and an 'ounce', whose keeper, to Goldsmith's concern, could put his hand through the bars and receive obvious affection from the animal.[47] It was probably too at the Tower that Goldsmith was astonished by his first view of an elephant, although he 'had taken care to prepare [his] imagination':

> I found my ideas fall as short of its real size as they did of its real figure; neither the pictures I had seen, nor the descriptions I had read, giving me adequate conceptions of either.[48]

In addition we find clear hints about Goldsmith's largely mysterious sojourn on the Continent. His section on sheep prompts him to comment on 'their following of the shepherd's pipe', which he had always thought an 'invention' of 'the old pastoral poets', 'before [he] had seen them trained in this manner'. However, 'in many parts of the Alps', he observes, 'and even in some provinces of France, the shepherd and his pipe are still continued, with true antique simplicity'.[49] Goldsmith also mentions game in the environs of Paris in terms that make it sound as if he spent a reasonable amount of time there:

> I never walked out about the environs of Paris, that I did not consider the immense quantity of game that was running almost tame on every side of me, as a badge of the slavery of the people; and what they wished me to observe as an object of triumph, I always regarded with a kind of secret compassion; yet this people have no game-laws for the remoter parts of the kingdom [...][50]

In addition, Goldsmith describes having seen scorpions,[51] and he remarks that, in some countries, frogs 'are distinguished by the ludicrous title of Dutch Nightingales'. 'Indeed', he adds, 'the aquatic frogs of Holland are loud beyond what one would imagine'.[52] Here we surely find an echo of the less than enthusiastic opinion the young Goldsmith had expressed about the Dutch in letters sent home to Ireland. Other glimpses of his personal life emerge, whether – presumably – from his early years living a garret in London ('I have often seen' a spider constructing its web),[53] or from a later stage of his career; musing about the tortoise and its habits, he comments: 'I have seen several of them about gentlemen's houses, that, in general, appear torpid, harmless, and even fond of employment'.[54] And yet other remarks reveal aspects of Goldsmith's character: his dislike of the cruelty of cats ('Of all the marks by which the cat discovers its natural malignity, that of playing and sporting with its little captive [a mouse] before killing it outright, is the most flagrant');[55] his delight in birds ('These splendid inhabitants of the air possess all those qualities that can soothe the heart and cheer the fancy');[56] his pleasure, 'while I was writing this history', at reading about a 'she-fox', who had carried a cub in her mouth 'for some miles' – ' I was not displeased', is the conclusion, 'to hear that this faithful creature escaped the pursuit, and at last got off in safety'.[57] Unsurprisingly, Goldsmith did not like the flea, remarking, with obvious knowledge, that it 'bites with greater severity' in some countries than in others: 'Its numbers in Italy and France are much greater than in England; and yet its bite is much more troublesome here, than I have found it in any other place'.[58] Even worse is the bug, 'another of those nauseous insects that intrude upon the retreats of mankind; and that often banish that sleep, which even sorrow and anxiety permitted to approach'. Lack of space unfortunately prevents me from quoting much of this long, and deeply-felt passage, though the end again gives a hint of Goldsmith's travels abroad:

> [...] happily for Great Britain, they multiply less in these islands, than in any part of the continent. In France and Italy the beds, particularly in their inns, swarm with them; and every piece of furniture seems to afford them a retreat. They grow larger also with them than with us, and bite with more cruel appetite.[59]

It seems to me that no future biographer of Goldsmith can afford to pass over the rich pickings to be found in *An History of the Earth and Animated Nature*, which even provides fascinating information about Goldsmith's theistic beliefs,[60] about Descartes,[61] and about materialism and the *philosophes*.[62] His personal comments, as we have seen, are direct, revealing, and tantalising.

But there is another type of intervention which brings us back – not perhaps to the ludic – but to Goldsmith's early career and to the idea of the writer wearing a mask. In his perceptive study, Richard C. Taylor observes that Goldsmith needed to establish common ground with his readers and that his predecessors, for example in *The Spectator*, had done so by assuming the role of, say, the Gentleman reader.[63] It was difficult for a penniless young Irishman to do this, although on occasion he attempted to do so. A little later he would successfully assume the mask of the foreigner in London, ostensibly a Chinaman, a mask which enabled him to expose the eccentricities of the English as seen by an outsider. But even earlier than this he exploited the persona of the much-travelled man, a persona for which – clearly – he was just as well qualified. A bizarre example is his *Memoirs of M. de Voltaire*, probably composed at the very time he was failing the ship surgeon's exam mentioned earlier – in other words the last weeks of 1758. This extraordinary piece teems with the most flagrant errors yet is so convincingly written that modern biographers of Voltaire have quoted parts of it. Goldsmith specifically claims to have witnessed an impassioned discussion between Voltaire, Diderot and Fontenelle in Paris and to have heard anecdotes of him while in Berlin, both impossible claims.[64] Yet Goldsmith clearly empathised so much with Voltaire that some passages in the *Memoirs* sound as if they might apply as well to Goldsmith himself. The most striking one is this:

> There is perhaps no situation more uneasy than that of being foremost in the Republic of letters. If a man, who writes to please the public, cannot, at the same time, stoop to flattery, he is certainly made unhappy for life. There are an hundred writers of inferior merit continually expecting his approbation, these must be all applauded, or made enemies, the public must be deceived by ill-placed praise, or dunces provoked into unremitting persecution. This undertribe in the literary commonwealth perfectly understand the force of combinations, are liberal in their mutual

commendations, and actually enjoy all the pleasures of fame without being so much as known to the public. While the man of eminence is regarded, as an outcast of their society, a fit object at which to level all their invective, and every advance he makes towards reputation, only lifts his head nearer to the storm; till at last he finds, that, instead of fame, he has been only all his life earning reproach, till he finds himself possessed of professing friends and sincere enemies.[65]

This is arguably a very fair description of Goldsmith's own situation as his career developed,

If we try to put Goldsmith's ambiguous engagement with biography and autobiography into some sort of critical context, one feels that he could very well have said, just like Doubrovsky: 'L'autobiographie, ce panthéon des pompes funèbres, l'accès m'en est interdit. D'accord. Mais je puis m'y introduire en fraude. Resquiller, à la faveur de la fiction, sous le couvert du roman'.[66] True, Goldsmith wrote only one novel, and even that was in some ways a satirical pastiche of the *genre*, but we may supplement this with his other works of fiction. When a young Irishman in London, Goldsmith for several years had no desire whatsoever to reveal too much about himself. Even after he became famous, Goldsmith remained coy in the extreme. He played with his readers, consciously it seems to me, and unconsciously, mystifying them, and later his biographers, with tantalising snippets from his life, woven into the lives of his characters, but always – or nearly always – changed, adapted, transformed. The one real exception is the disarmingly personal comments that crop up repeatedly in the *History of Earth and Animated Nature*. Even the brief memoir dictated to Thomas Percy in 1773 can in parts be extremely inaccurate or downright misleading; indeed Percy himself underlined many passages that he thought diverged from the truth. We may echo a famous question, and ask what is truth? Clearly, in terms of the infinitely complex nature of human existence, experience and memory, this is a difficult if not impossible question. Oliver Goldsmith, would-be biographer, seems to have been so well aware of this that he fictionalised aspects of his life so effectively that biographers have ever since been trying to extract the truth from his fictions.

Notes

1. I am grateful to Brian Murphy, Robert Welch and Stanley Black for their helpful comments.
2. See W.J. McCormack, 'Goldsmith, Biography and the Phenomenology of Anglo-Irish Literature', in *The Art of Oliver Goldsmith*, ed. Andrew Swarbrick (London: Vision Press; Totowa, NJ: Barnes and Noble, 1984), pp.168–94.
3. John Ginger, *The Notable man: The Life and Times of Oliver Goldsmith* (London: Hamish Hamilton, 1977). The standard Goldsmith biography remains James Prior's *The Life of Oliver Goldsmith, M.B., from a Variety of Original Sources*, 2 vols (London: J. Murray, 1837), and another similar contribution is John Forster, *The*

Life and Times of Oliver Goldsmith (London: Ward, Lock, 1848). A useful collection of autobiographical material was edited by E.H. Mikhail under the title *Goldsmith: Interviews and Recollections* (Basingstoke: Macmillan, 1993).

4. For the most reliable text of *The Life of Richard Nash, Esq; late Master of the Ceremonies at Bath. Extracted principally from his original papers* see the standard edition of Goldsmith's works, *Collected works of Oliver Goldsmith*, ed. Arthur Friedman, 5 vols (Oxford: Clarendon Press, 1966: henceforth *Works*), vol.2, pp.279–398.

5. *The Collected Letters of Oliver Goldsmith*, ed. Katharine C. Balderston (Cambridge: Cambridge University Press, 1928).

6. *The History and Sources of Percy's Memoir of Goldsmith*, ed. Katharine C. Balderston (Cambridge: Cambridge University Press, 1926). The text of the *Memoir* is reprinted in Mikhail, *Goldsmith: Interviews and Recollections*, pp.192–95.

7. Quoted in Prior, *The Life of Oliver Goldsmith*, vol.1, pp.266–7.

8. 21 December 1758: see Prior, *The Life of Oliver Goldsmith*, vol.1, pp.281–2.

9. This was the opinion expressed by Goldsmith's elder sister, Catherine, in 'Mrs Hodson's Narrative' (Mikhail, *Interviews and Recollections*, pp.12–13), and it has been repeated by others. Goldsmith is supposed to have mistaken a private house for an inn, and to have treated the proprietor like an innkeeper. Tickled by the situation, the gentleman in question reputedly amused himself by conniving in Goldsmith's misapprehension.

10. As Friedman observes (*Works*, vol.1, p.336, n.1), a clear indication of this occurs in chapter 13 ('On Universities') of Goldsmith's *Enquiry into the Present State of Polite Learning*: 'Sure pride itself has dictated to the fellows of our colleges, the absurd passion of being attended at meals, and on other public occasions, by those poor men, who, willing to be scholars, come in upon some charitable foundation. It implies a contradiction, for men to be at once learning the *liberal* arts, and at the same time treated as *slaves*, at once studying freedom, and practising servitude' (*Works*, vol.1, pp.335–6).

11. Cf., for example, Goldsmith's gift of his blankets to a poor family, while he was a student at Trinity College (Prior, vol.1, p.94).

12. Richard C. Taylor, *Goldsmith as Journalist* (London and Toronto: Associated University Presses, 1993), provides an extremely useful study of this period.

13. These do not appear in the Friedman edition.

14. Although there has been much discussion about the date of Goldsmith's birth, it is now generally thought to have been 10 November 1728 (Mikhail, *Interviews and Recollections*, pp.ix, xiv).

15. Mikhail, *Interviews and Recollections*, p.193.

16. *Works*, vol.4, pp.107–8.

17. Cf. Ginger, *The Notable Man*, pp.96–9.

18. Mikhail, *Interviews and Recollections*, p.193.

19. Michael Sherringham comments that 'what Serge Doubrovsky has labelled "autofiction"' is 'a species of text where the reader is teased and titillated as the author stages a masquerade in which truth and falsity, authentic recollection and patent fantasy, cease to be distinguishable' (*French Autobiography, Devices and Desires: Rousseau to Perec*, Oxford: Clarendon Press, 1993, p.328).

20. *An History of the Earth, and Animated Nature: By Oliver Goldsmith. In Eight Volumes* [...] 'London: Printed for J. Nourse, in the Strand, Bookseller to His Majesty. MDCCLXXIV' (all references to this edition, except otherwise stated). I wish to express my thanks to Aidan Heavey for his permission to consult this, and the other items, in his magnificent Goldsmith collection (Aidan Heavey Public Library, Athlone).

My thanks also to Andrew Carpenter, for telling me about the collection, and to the librarian, Gearoid O'Brien, for his courtesy, help and encouragement.

21. According to Wardle, 'it went through twenty-two editions [...] the last appearing in 1876' (*Oliver Goldsmith*, Lawrence: University of Kansas Press, London: Constable, 1957, p.286). A fine example is *A History of the Earth and Animated Nature. By Oliver Goldsmith. With Numerous Notes from the works of the most distinguished British and foreign naturalists. Illustrated by upwards of two thousand figures*, 2 vols (Edinburgh and London: Blackie and Son, 1854). The same publishers produced another reprint almost a hundred years after the first edition (*A History of the Earth and Animated Nature, with numerous notes from the works of the most distinguished British and foreign naturalists*, 2 vols, London, 1868–70). As the titles of both editions indicate, substantial efforts have been made to update the work, but the text remains Goldsmith's own. The illustrations in both volumes, especially the colour plates in the former, are magnificent. The 1854 edition was clearly meant to serve as a valuable work of reference. A shortened version of Goldsmith's text, again accompanied by colour plates, was published in 1990, with a foreward by the distinguished naturalist Gerald Durrell (*Oliver Goldsmith's history of the natural world* (London: Studio Editions, 1990).

22. *The Notable man*, p.338.

23. Ibid., pp.337–8. In this Ginger shares the opinion of many critics; as early as 1795 Robert Anderson commented that Goldsmith 'submitted to the drudgery of compiling' the work, 'which procured him more money than fame' (quoted in Mikhail, *Interviews and Recollections*, p.7).

24. Some critics have taken the work more seriously, starting with James Hall Pitman, *Goldsmith's Animated Nature* (New Haven: Yale University Press, London: Oxford University Press, 1924): noteworthy are Ralph Wardle, *Oliver Goldsmith*, pp.281–6, and Graham Parry, '*Animated Nature*: Goldsmith's View of Creation', in *The Art of Oliver Goldsmith*, ed. Swarbrick, pp.51—68). A series of articles by Winifred Lynskey investigates Goldsmith's use of his sources: 'Pluche and Derham, new sources of Goldsmith', *PMLA*, 57 (1942), pp.435–45; 'The Scientific sources of Goldsmith's *Animated Nature*', *Studies in Philology*, 40 (1943), pp.33–57; 'Goldsmith and warfare in Nature', *Philological Quarterly*, 23 (1944), pp.333–42; 'Goldsmith and the Chain of Being' (*Journal of the History of Ideas*, vol.6, no.3, January 1945, pp.363–74).

25. Fontenelle's *Entretiens sur la pluralité des mondes* (1686) spawned a host of imitations, and Voltaire's *Éléments de la philosophie de Newton* crowned his efforts to popularise Newton's scientific ideas in France.

26. 420 subscribers ordered 510 sets of the edition, a total of 4,080 volumes. Subscribers included Baron Lifford (Lord High Chancellor of Ireland), the bishops of Clogher and Derry, the deans of Derry and Kildare, and other important churchmen. The printers and booksellers come from all over Ireland, not only Dublin: from Belfast (John Hay 'senior' and John Hay 'junior', 2 sets each); Clonmell ('Edw. Collins', 3 sets); Cork ('Wm. Flyn', 2 sets; Thomas White, 10 sets); Kilkenny (Edmund Finn, 8 sets); Drogheda (John Fleming, 2 sets); Waterford ('Messrs. Ramsey', 2 sets). 'W. Halhead, Bookseller', and 'B. Leathem, Esq' each subscribed for 20 sets, followed by Laurence Flin 12, Caleb Jenkin, 'Mrs. Eliz. Lynch, Bookseller', Richard Moncrieffe, 'Wm. Wilson, Bookseller', 'Thos.Walker, Bookseller', and 'Wm. Whitestone, Bookseller', all with 12 sets (*An History of Earth and Animated Nature. By Oliver Goldsmith*. In eight volumes [...] 'Dublin: Printed for James Williams, [No.21,] Skinner-Row. M DCC LXVII', pp.v–viii).

27. See Arthur Lytton Sells, *Les Sources françaises de Goldsmith* (Paris: Bibliothèque de la Revue de Littérature Comparée, vol.xii, 1924).
28. *The Notable man*, p.337.
29. An exception is Wardle, who details some of Goldsmith's personal investigations (*Oliver Goldsmith*, p.284).
30. *Animated Nature*, vol.4, p.152.
31. Vol.3, p.55. The same could be true when he states that the 'islands to the north of Scotland, the Skelig islands of the coasts of Kerry, in Ireland [...] abound with them [gannets]' (vol.6, pp.71–2).
32. Vol.3, pp.111–12.
33. Vol.8, p.136.
34. Vol.3, p.365.
35. Vol.3, p.301.
36. Vol.3, pp.292–3.
37. Vol.3, p.320.
38. Vol.3, p.114. The so-called Irish elk was in fact a giant deer (Megaloceros giganteus), found principally in Ireland but also in many other parts of Europe, becoming extinct some 10,000 years ago. Skeletons are to be seen in the National History Museum, Dublin, the Geology Museum, Trinity College Dublin, and in the Ulster Museum, Belfast. See *The Encyclopedia of Ireland*, ed. Brian Lalor (Dublin: Gill & McMillan, 2003), pp.347–8. I am grateful to Kevin De Ornellas for help on this point.
39. *Animated Nature*, vol.3, p.114.
40. Vol.3, p.114.
41. Vol. 4, p.177.
42. Vol.2, p.393.
43. Vol.3, pp.33–4: 'it was shewn under the name of the bonasus', and was said 'to have come from India'.
44. 'We have in the Tower, at present, one of above four feet high, that was brought from Morocco, which is the largest that for some time past has been seen in Europe' (vol.3, p.232).
45. Vol.3, p.256.
46. Vol.3, pp.266–7.
47. Vol.3, p.260.
48. Vol.4, p.516.
49. Vol.3, p.42. Goldsmith goes on to give details about the pipe and the way it is played.
50. vol.5, pp.207–8.
51. Possibly in France and/or Italy, both of which countries he mentions in this connection; 'I have often seen them taken and put into a place of security, exerting all their rage against the sides of the glass vessel that contained them. I have seen them attempt to sting a stick, when put near them [...]' (vol.7, pp.296–7).
52. Vol.7, p.87.
53. Vol. 7, p.254. A long and detailed description follows.
54. Vol.7, pp.392–3.
55. Vol.3, p.205.
56. 'In sending the imagination in pursuit of these, in following them to the chirupping grove, the screaming precipice, or the glassy deep, the mind naturally lost the sense of its own situation, and attentive to their little sports, almost forgot

the TASK of describing them' (vol.6, p.148). I quote only a part of Goldsmith's enthusiastic comments.

57. Vol.3, p.330.
58. Vol.7, p.281.
59. Vol.7, p.282.
60. Cf., for example, vol.1, pp.19–20.
61. Vol.8, pp.171–2.
62. Vol.8, p.199.
63. *Goldsmith as Journalist*, pp.47–56.
64. For one thing, Voltaire was exiled in Switzerland. For detailed analysis of the *Memoirs*, see my 'Goldsmith's *Memoirs of M. de Voltaire* – biography or fantasy' (*British Journal for Eighteenth-Century Studies*, vol.26, no.2 (Autumn 2003), pp.203–16, and 'Oliver Goldsmith et ses *Mémoires de M. de Voltaire*', in *Les Vies de Voltaire: discours et représentations biographiques, XVIIIᵉ – XXIᵉ siècles*, ed. Christophe Cave and Simon Davies, SVEC 2008:04 (Oxford, Voltaire Foundation, 2008), pp.203–22.
65. *Works*, vol.3, p.243.
66. Serge Doubrovsky, *Le Livre brisé* (Paris: Grasset, 1989), p.256.

6
Obstacles Confronting the Literary Biographer*

Dale Salwak

"Whenever you feel passionate about an author," said the biographer Matthew J. Bruccoli, "go ahead and plunge into the research. Don't worry about what other scholars think of your project." This advice, given years ago to a student of his fresh out of graduate school, I have made the cornerstone of my own modest publishing career. Bruccoli's words are pertinent, I believe, because many of us have decided with some anxiety to write our books on living authors. As we soon discover, the challenges are formidable, the discouragements are many – but if we persist we find the results are rewarding for many reasons both personal and professional.

My own consuming interest in the genre goes back to my graduate school years. In the summer of 1972 my father was in New York City to visit with his friend Gordon Ray, president of the Guggenheim Memorial Foundation, and during their conversation he mentioned that I wanted to write my doctoral dissertation on Kingsley Amis, the foremost English comic novelist of the twentieth century. Ray said he knew Amis and would be glad to write to him on my behalf to see whether he could set up an interview. I sent Ray a copy of my proposal, and a few weeks later I received a note from him along with a copy of Amis's response: "I'm sure you can imagine the mixture of tickled ego and slight sinking of the heart with which I read your letter," Amis had written to Ray in November. "Mr Salwak seems, from his dissertation proposal, a sensible enough young man, and he and I may get along together famously: but then again we may not." He agreed to see me for a minimum of a couple of hours' chat followed by lunch, "after which," his proviso stated, "I'm free to disappear from his life, but may well elect (and have the leisure) not do to so." If I was prepared to come all the way from California to London on that understanding, then he'd "very cheerfully" see me and do his best to answer any questions I may devise.

I wrote immediately, and on 18 December he replied with several possible dates and added: "Obviously, the sooner you can let me know which day is best for you, the sooner I can regard the other days as free for other appointments. But, with Santa at our throats, you needn't rush too hard."

We agreed to meet at 11 a.m. on 24 January, in his club, The Travellers', in central London.

His letter came at a crucial time for me. My dissertation proposal had met with some resistance – not surprising, considering that choosing any contemporary writer for such intense scrutiny would have been questioned in those days. One committee member had doubted whether the project was worthy, saying that he found it difficult to justify Amis as a fit subject "in the same breath" as, say, Milton or Chaucer. Another had advised me against writing on still living authors. "It could not soon be completed," he said, "and research material will lead to endless further revision and revision." He suggested that I look for another subject – "the deader, the better."

But owing to the unwavering support of my director (who had led me to the topic in the first place) as well as Amis's positive response and my own consuming interest, I persisted – and two drafts later my proposal was approved unanimously. As I had argued, little of substance had yet been written on the man or his work, and so clearly this was an area wide open for exploration. "It's only a matter of time before someone steps forward to do so," I said. And given that most of his contemporaries were alive and still writing, I envisioned many years of fruitful research into their work as well.

When I left for London and that meeting with a writer who was very much alive indeed, I could not have known where the journey would ultimately take me. We travel outward to grow inward. To this day I can recall every feeling, every sight, every word, every thought from my ten days in the great metropolis on the Thames. I had heard numerous stories about Great Britain's people and culture from my maternal grandparents, who were themselves English, and I had visited the city in the pages of more books than I could count. And so I was in love with London before I ever set foot there. That first trip marked an important turning point for me as a student of the world, and since then I have returned to that great city many times.

I arrived at the Travellers' Club ten minutes early and sat down as directed by the porter (whom I overheard say to an associate, rather indignantly, "He wishes to see Mr Amis."). I did my best to relax, but I didn't know quite what to expect, nor did I know how a writer I so admired would receive me, although he had been cordial in his letters and over the telephone the day before. As I watched two club members pass by, I felt somewhat like the hero of *Lucky Jim* as he sees the notables of town and gown assemble before his public lecture and finds himself "admiring the way in which, without saying or doing anything specific, they established so effortlessly that he himself wasn't expected to accompany them."

Within seconds of Amis's arrival, however, I felt at ease and liked him immediately. He couldn't have been more courteous with his greeting. He stood about five feet nine inches tall, with hair a mixture of gray and sandy blond. He was wearing a dark brown suit, pastel green shirt, green striped tie, and – orange socks. There was no pretense or stuffiness in his behavior and, in fact, after the interview turned out a success, he said one of his chief worries had been that I wouldn't be amiable. Apparently he had had some unpleasant encounters.

We shook hands and he led me upstairs to what had been a television room. He chuckled. "The management would be quite upset if we were caught with a tape recorder," he said. "They frown on things like that." If anyone should come in and see it, he added, "We'll just stare at them and hope they'll go away. Possession is nine-tenths of the law."

When we have the privilege of interviewing an author whom we admire it's essential that we do our homework before we meet. This means reading all that the author has ever published and as much about him or her as we can find and shaping our questions with care. We don't want to waste time during the interview by asking for information already available from other sources. What we're seeking is what is *not* in print – clues to his or her writing techniques or literary philosophy, or central themes, for example – and once we've fallen under an author's spell, we'll want to know everything. And unless there are objections, it is essential to bring a tape recorder and offer to send the subject a transcript of the interview for revisions or corrections before we use it. All this is my way of saying – respect the writer's time and talent. This approach has helped me find and reveal some new insight or understanding through many pleasant, stimulating, and enlightening conversations.

Over the next two hours Amis responded patiently and generously to what I asked. He spoke clearly, without hesitating, almost as if he had seen my questions before I posed them. If I had shut my eyes I would have thought from his tone of voice that William F. Buckley was speaking. I have never met anyone so observant, humorous, and professionally thorough as he talked about his career, his novels and poetry, and closed with his thoughts on science fiction, criticism, and his life as a fulltime writer.

2:30 arrived: I had another hour's worth of questions, but it was time for lunch, and so we walked to the dining room where I enjoyed lamb chops, mashed potatoes, salad, potted shrimp, and a glass of burgundy, while he had ham, kippers, salad, and wine. I was so caught up in our conversation, trying to remember every gesture, every word, and every expression that I almost missed a brief but revealing event. At one point a friend of his came up to the table and asked, "Has the Rachmaninoff record arrived?" The reply was, "No." What I didn't know is that this was a code. Had Amis's reply been "Yes," he explained to me afterward, he would have used the interruption as an excuse to leave immediately – a method of safeguarding against the possibility of being bored by my company.

Conducting an interview is as uniquely rewarding as it is demanding. Given discipline, patience, and a lot of advance work, it may be the only means of really piercing the surface of a subject. It requires a giving out of everything we have and concentrating fully on what's being said and done. We want to make the most of the experience. To have only a few hours with the subject, as I did, makes the time very precious indeed. I didn't want to return home and think to myself, "If only I had asked that, or that ... " The next morning I sat cross-legged on my hotel bed with a rented typewriter and transcribed the tapes. I felt exhilarated because for the first time in my young academic life (I was twenty-five), I was on the verge of making an original contribution to scholarship. During the previous day's lunch, Amis had called me, almost with reverence, a *scholar* – a high compliment indeed. I came to understand it then and know it now as a privileged position, hard-won. I felt legitimized as an academic and a professional.

We met again on 30 January, and I asked him another dozen questions followed by drinks. Before we parted, he promised to send me the proofs of his new novel, *The Riverside Villas Murder*, so that my dissertation would be up to date.

"My dear Dale," began his handwritten letter accompanying the package that arrived the next morning at my hotel. "Hope you get this in time. And that you enjoyed your trip. I certainly enjoyed our meeting, and very much look forward to more of the same when you're back this side. Good luck with the dissertation. Let me know if you find some annoying gap, anything not clear, etc. Or if you have further questions, etc." He signed it, "Warmest personal regards, Yours, Kingsley Amis."

The tone of his letter – friendly, courteous – foreshadowed the letters I would receive from him over the next fifteen years. Amis has written of his friend Philip Larkin that he was "always the best letter-writer" he has known and that "a glimpse of the Hull postmark brings that familiar tiny tingle of excitement and optimism, like a reminder of youth." May I say that I felt some of the same lift in my spirits each time a letter from London appeared in my mailbox with the familiar handwritten or typed return address.

To get a publication out of a dissertation project early in one's career is a significant step forward. After *Contemporary Literature* accepted the interview for publication, I asked Amis for permission to print. A month later he granted it, apologized for the delay in responding ("due to twin pressures of work and laziness"), and sent along seventy pages of his novel-in-progress to be titled *Ending Up*. He concluded: "If I can be of any further help, don't hesitate to let me know; but you're well enough acquainted with me by now to realize that such a request, unless signed in blood, may not bring an instantaneous response. I hope all goes well for you, in your Amis project and in general." The interview appeared in the Winter 1975 issue and I sent him a copy. "I must say I do seem to have gone on and on rather," he wrote, "but you must take the blame for asking so many answerable questions."

Once I was finished with my dissertation, *Kingsley Amis: Writer as Moralist*, I mailed him a copy and asked for his reactions. On 17 October 1974 he wrote: "Please forgive my remissness in not writing to you long ago. I thought your dissertation was very full and very fair, with an excellent sense of relevance and no wasted words. I can detect no substantial errors of fact, nor any material omissions." He concluded: "I remember with great pleasure our meetings in London." Though understandably proud of the work I had done, I knew it wasn't close to being ready for publication (although I did send it to a few publishers after removing any telltale signs that it was a dissertation). Looking back on that early work fifteen years later, I said to Amis that I was embarrassed by it. "I'm glad to hear you say that," he said. "You didn't go far enough." I nodded. I had done my best but also knew that usually it takes many rewrites before a dissertation is ready for publication – if ever.

One of the joys of living contemporaneously with an accomplished novelist is that we never know what a new work will be like. The surprising publication of *The Alteration* in 1976 – a wonderfully wrought what-if novel in which Amis imagines the world as if the Protestant Reformation had never happened – gave me another reason to write him, offering my congratulations and letting him know that I was sending a copy of my just-published annotated reference guide in which I traced the history of the reviews and critical responses to all of his published work. In August 1978, he wrote: "The book is very handsome and amazingly exhaustive. I feel both proud and slightly guilty at having occasioned so much hard work. And *useful*: this very week I must draft a blurb for my collected poems, due in the spring, and your record of the reviews of the earlier volumes will be invaluable. Many, many thanks." That meant everything to me. I had managed to please the one person who mattered.

The year 1980 approached, and I felt it was time for a follow-up interview on the occasion of the publication of Amis's sixteenth novel, *Russian Hide-and-Seek*. The Borgo Press had contracted with me to do a book for their series, Literary Voices, to be titled *Interviews with Britain's Angry Young Men* and to include John Wain, John Braine, Bill Hopkins, and Colin Wilson, all of whom had agreed to be interviewed. In March 1980 Amis wrote: "I would be very happy to see you, update interview, indeed discuss any matter of interest within reason. ... It will be fun to meet again." We chose to meet at his home in July. "Of course," he said, "if you'd care for a modest lunch under this roof my wife and I would be only too happy to have you. You're welcome to inspect the study where I'm writing this and where at the moment there are almost as many bottles as books." He added: "I hope you won't be too shocked at the renewed sight of me. I have put on a bit of weight and my face is a rather pouchy affair. We must arrange things so that you can't possibly mistake me for some relic of the previous generation."

Streets swelled with shoppers in the noontime rush hour at Hampstead Station. Rain speckled the pavement, and as I followed the housekeeper past a high brick wall, down some steep stairs, and into Gardnor House, the man who appeared in the entranceway – wearing a light blue sweater and tan slacks, with hair grayer than before and glasses – was a man I had no difficulty in recognizing. "Well, you look no different than when I last saw you," he said, to which his housekeeper commented, "That's quite a compliment."

Narrow stairs led into a spacious and book-lined sitting room. A small dog nipped at my heels. Ever able to produce the well-turned phrase for any occasion, Amis said, "She recognizes origins of distinction."

Four years previously, after Amis and Jane had moved to Gardnor house, 4 Flask Walk, he had sent me a message: "Note new address; much more fun!" As we sat down I reminded him of that, and he laughed hard. No sound was more satisfying.

The room seemed to reflect its owners: hospitable, comfortable, and unpretentious. Absent was the earlier formality of the club scene; here was a more relaxed, domestic setting. Or so I believed. Through lofty windows I looked onto a pleasant garden, which, together with the house, had the air of being obstinately self-contained. Moments later we were joined by his brother-in-law, Robert Howard, and by Amis's second wife, the novelist Elizabeth Jane Howard – tall, stout, blond-haired. She settled comfortably in a chair, crossed her legs, and busied herself with needlepoint as we talked and sipped our drinks (scotch for Amis and me, vodka for Robert, nothing for Jane).

Thirty minutes later Amis looked at Jane, his light blue eyes shining perceptibly brighter, and asked, "Well, where's this lunch you've been promising us?" To get to the kitchen we had to walk through Amis's study. "I could do a lot of work here," I said. A 1960s Adler office manual typewriter (which would be sold a year after Amis's death in 1995 to a private buyer for £550) sat on his desk with a sheet of paper in its carriage. As I peeked at the words, Amis said he was writing the introduction to a collection of the essays of Peter Simple (a pseudonym used by the London journalist Michael Wharton). Behind his desk were three teetering piles of envelopes and papers and on a shelf a complete set of the *Encyclopaedia Britannica*, a thirteen-volume edition of the *Oxford English Dictionary*, and other reference books.

The life that the Amises seemed to be enjoying in their new home smacked of an earlier, gentler era, and it was very English. The meal was a case in point: watercress soup, lamp chops with mint sauce, roasted potatoes, and red wine. Like my hosts, the housekeeper knew exactly what she had time for. Although I tried, I couldn't catch her serving me. As in a well-orchestrated performance, food appeared before me like magic; my wine glass seemed to refill itself. When faced with the decision of which dessert should come first, the cheese or the ice cream and apricots, the others deferred to the guest. "Let's save the cheese for last," I said. "Good!" Amis said. Then we can have more wine with the cheese!"

In due course we were back in the sitting room. Once again he was an easy man to question, and forthcoming with his answers. He showed me the page proofs for his collected short stories, due out that autumn, and surprised me with a copy of *Russian Hide-and Seek* with the inscription: "A wet but cheerful afternoon, 14 July, 1980. Kingsley Amis." (Its subject – a futuristic dream world turned nightmare – was at the time a far cry from the apparently contented domestic life that the Amises seemed to be enjoying.) And I caught a tantalizing glimpse of his famous talent for impersonations when he imitated a Soviet reviewer's attack on the book. Then Jane joined us and also signed her novel, *After Julius* (the one she had dedicated to Kingsley), with the words: "This is Dale's copy of my book, which I inscribe with my very best wishes." She returned upstairs to work on some letters.

When Kingsley peered out the window, then leafed through a copy of the *London Magazine* "to find something to read," I understood this to be his polite signal that it was time to leave. We agreed to meet at 11:30 a.m. one week later at his new club, the Garrick; he had resigned from the Travellers' some years ago, he explained, because the Garrick, with its membership of lawyers, actors, writers, and artists, was more in tune with his own temperament.

"It was very nice for Jane and me to have you to lunch and we both much enjoyed the occasion," he wrote to me three days later. "You made an excellent impression!" He added that he had been talking with his friend Colin Welch of the *Daily Telegraph* who had said: "I saw a young American at the Kings and Keys who was not drunk with John Braine, who very much was." Amis said, "Dale!" Welch was astounded that Amis was able to identify me.

All seemed well in Amis's domestic life at that time, and I imagined a cozy scene of two fellow novelists working back to back in separate rooms of Gardnor House during the day, then reuniting in the evening and over a drink reading to one another their day's work. But then in 1982 I was surprised to learn that after seventeen years of an often stormy marriage, Amis and Jane Howard had separated painfully. He was now living in Kentish Town with his first wife, Hilly, and her third husband, Lord Kilmarnock, and for the first time in his professional career, he had abandoned a novel in progress. As I was in London at the time, I called him the next day and he invited me to come right over.

Hilly greeted me at the door, showed me in, and then left the room so that I could be alone with Amis. The change in his circumstances and appearance since 1980 couldn't have been more dramatic. One leg was in a cast, he had a beard (which he said he planned to shave off when the cast was removed), and he looked dejected. Listening to him talk, I found myself wondering whether he would ever write a good novel again, a question that he may well have been asking himself. His confidence was understandably at low ebb. I abandoned any prepared questions, and instead listened as he talked about Jane, his club, and his stay in hospital.

We continued to correspond as I moved on to other projects, but the subject wouldn't let me rest. A recurring edginess and anxiety visited me whenever I glanced at my Amis collection or read a new novel of his. When Amis told me in 1985 that Julian Barnes had approached him about writing a book on his life and work, I said with interest and alarm, "Well, there'll be two then – one by an American." I was committed.

And so that year I began in earnest to revise my dissertation with publication in mind and asked for Amis's help. "As regards your dissertation, of course send it to me and I will read it through and comment on it," he wrote. Six more years of work lay ahead, however, before I felt ready to take him up on the offer. By then I was fortunate to have unrestricted access to his archival material, except for the Bodleian Library's collection of letters to Philip Larkin and Bruce Montgomery. Jack Gohn's 1976 bibliography alerted me to the Humanities Research Center's collection of Amis's juvenilia, his rejected Oxford thesis, and the notebooks and typescripts covering his first five published novels. Queries in *PMLA*, the *New York Times Book Review* and the *Times Literary Supplement* helped me to locate letters held at Pennsylvania State, Syracuse, Princeton, and the University of Victoria. And when I learned that the Huntington Library might acquire the Amis archives for its collection, I spoke to the committee in strong support of the plan – successfully, for they bought the entire collection of almost one hundred drafts of Amis's novels, as well as various stories, unpublished plays, essays, notebooks, radio and television scripts, and 250 letters. Together, these materials span the entire course of Amis's career from 1934, when he was twelve years old, to 1990, and tell us much about his education, his evolution as a writer, his methods of composition, his friendships and acquaintances, and his respective tenures at Swansea, Princeton, Cambridge, and Vanderbilt. A gold mine, as it were, in my backyard.

I had no more preparation than this. I continued to exchange daily faxes with my editor at Simon & Schuster International, with whom I had by now signed a contract for the book, and I searched for photos as I completed and then revised a draft of the text. I had selected 1990 as my cut-off date – a pivotal year, to be sure, with Amis's ascension to knighthood in June, the publication of his twenty-second novel, *The Folks That Live on the Hill*, and the completion of his *Memoirs*. Then during the summer of 1990 and with my work nearing completion, I asked Amis over lunch if he would consider reading the first three chapters of my book because of their emphasis on biographical background. "Yes, of course," he said, "send then along and I will comment." I did so, and went on my way, pleasurably anticipating his response.

On October 10, 1990, I received back the chapters along with the following letter:

Dear Dale,
Thank you for letting me see the first three chapters of your book about me and my work, which I have at last read through with the attention they deserve. I return them herewith, marked here and there.

I am very sorry to have to tell you that I consider them altogether unsatisfactory. It is not that I find what you have written offensive in any way, or improper to its subject. It is that the level of your performance seems to me to be so low as not to earn a place on any serious publisher's list.

Please realize that no imaginable rewriting would rectify the situation. The fact that I have left many passages and pages of your typescript unmarked testifies to my weariness and boredom with them, not to their correctness or adequacy.

I think it would be best if the book were to be withdrawn.

Yours, Kingsley.

Imagine receiving that in the mail one morning. I felt baffled and downcast. Amis's response contradicted everything he had communicated to me in person and in letters over the previous seventeen years, and I was somewhat reminded of how I had felt in high school at the end of one semester when I received a couple of C's and one D on my report card, and suffered through the disappointment of my parents. (I brought my grades back up the next semester.) "All we expect of you," they said at the time, "is that you do your best," and I knew deep down that I had not.

But the Amis book was different: I knew that I *had* done my best, that my intentions had been honorable. But my performance had not risen to his standards – and that was a pretty hard knock. (Amis's biographer, Zachary Leader, would later write, "It is not clear whether he understood how brutal he was being in this assessment or if so whether he cared.") At the same time I was sure that Amis's objections were detached, not personal, and aimed at the text, not me – a fact confirmed by his agent, Joanthan Clowes, who wrote in a letter to my editor that the criticisms were "purely professional" and that "Sir Kingsley found Professor Salwak personally very pleasant and amiable." And although there's a very real possibility that my book was simply not as accomplished as I had hoped, in retrospect I believe that my editor and I made the right decision to push for publication despite Amis's objections and those of his agent. "One writes what one can," says Emerson, "not what one ought."

But for a brief exchange a year later, there would be no more letters between me and Amis, and I understood the shock of something being over.

Kingsley Amis: Modern Novelist was released by Harvester Wheatsheaf, a division of Simon and Schuster, in 1992. They published the book in part on the strength of independent readers, including Barbara Everett of Somerville College, Oxford, who called it "a splendidly spacious, relaxed yet shrewd study of Amis' work. Lucid and very informative, it is ideally suited to the general reader." Others saw its merit as well, with several positive reviews, one calling it "mandatory reading for all students of Amis."

Three years after Kingsley Amis died on 22 October 1995, Zachary Leader, a professor of English at Roehampton University, was invited by Amis's son Martin and commissioned by HarperCollins to edit the collected letters from Amis. Over lunch one day I delivered to Leader copies of all my letters from Amis – but one, the last one of October 1990. In July 1999 he wrote to say that he needed to raise a somewhat "delicate matter." Among the papers found in Amis's home was a copy of that letter to me of October 10, 1990. Leader acknowledged that the letter was "shockingly blunt," and although he understood why I had not include it among the collection I had given to him, he thought it should be included. Amis's literary executors had already deposited it at the Huntington Library, and it was available to other scholars. Leader also argued that it showed an important side of Amis – "how ferocious he could be in his later years." The letter, he continued, said "something about his willingness to sacrifice personal feelings for what he seems to have seen as the welfare of his reputation as a writer." Leader added that he had thought "long and hard" about the decision to publish and felt that, especially because of Amis's earlier warm and helpful letters to me, it needed to be included. With some reluctance, I agreed. Scholarship requires integrity – fidelity to the quest for understanding, regardless of where it leads. I suspect that in his own way, Amis was following something like that principle when he wrote that last letter to me (an explanation that Leader would develop in detail in his biography of Amis published in 2006). Most of us face difficult decisions or harsh criticism or vehement disagreement at some point in our research and writing. Painful as these flashpoints might be, they are the sparks that ignite dialogue and inquiry; sometimes disagreement, not accord, advances knowledge.

From this experience, and others, what have I learned? I have learned that writing about authors whose lives are over is itself difficult, but writing about living authors presents its own set of problems, including the subject's understandable anxiety over the biographer's scrutiny, the seemingly endless research necessary to keep current with the primary and secondary works, the possible loss of objectivity, the perils of misinformation and miscommunication, and a lack of closure. Many biographers have experienced the frustration of not being able to consult restricted material because the author, friends, or family are understandably concerned about harmful ramifications. "This is one of the hazards of working in the modern field," one librarian told me, "where most of what one writes on a living author is bound to be provisional."

I have also learned about the limitations and constraints of the chosen form. No matter how many letters, diaries, unpublished manuscripts, earlier biographies, memoirs, photographs, and other sources are available to the researcher, there remain what Victoria Glendenning calls "lies and silences" in the public record. "Biography is the clothes and buttons of the man," wrote Mark Twain, "but the real biography of a man is lived in his head twenty-four hours a day, and *that* you can never know." Unlike the novel, here omniscience is impossible. There's so much that can never be known, and finding those bounds can be both daunting and intriguing.

Other obstacles confronting the biographer stem from the faulty memories of interviewees, the inability to verify facts or documents, conflicting accounts of the same events, problems of copyright, and publishers who increasingly want less rather than more detail. Construction also poses a special challenge. What shape shall the book take? Straight narrative? Topical treatment? Essay? Where should the story begin? And how should it end? What is the biographer's proper relationship with the subject? "Never mind if one has met these questions before, and answered them," says Catherine Drinker Bowen. "Each book one writes is different in content and therefore in form; with each book old problems present themselves in guises new and strange."

Opening the door to private lives clearly raises ethical and legal questions as well. How far should biographers go in respecting the privacy of the subject – or of other people implicated in the lives they describe? Are private lives always relevant to biography? Is it ethical to disregard instructions in documents left by the dead, even more to use those documents as a basis for further diagnosis? Surely the biographer has a responsibility in the selection of evidence: eye-witness *vs* gossip or hearsay, the scrupulous weighing of facts *vs* the preference for conjecture, and so on. "It is the experience of many of my friends," wrote Natasha Spender, "that often their giving witness to an error of fact is greeted by a biographer as an outrageous attempt to interfere with his or her creativity, as if his creation of a legend is more important than the facts of the lives he describes." Such public *vs* private issues become all the more troubling now that many biographers are no longer unwilling to explore intimate questions of gender, race, culture and sexuality. John Updike laments, "The trouble with literary biographies, perhaps, is that they mainly testify to the long worldly corruption of a life, as documented deeds and days and disappointments pile up, and cannot convey the unearthly human innocence that attends, in the perpetual present tense of living, the self that seems the real one." In the Foreword to his memoir, *Self-Consciousness*, he relates the understandable horror he felt upon learning that someone was writing his biography: "to take my life, my lode of ore and heap of memories, from me!" The idea seemed "so repulsive," he writes, that he was "stimulated to put down, always with some natural hesitation and distaste," some elements of an autobiography.

Finally, it will not come as a surprise when I say that the research and writing of this book was not at all as organized, as straightforward, or as well-planned as my remarks suggest. In 1972 Amis wrote in a letter that in general, critics "tend to overestimate the part played in a novelist's career by planning, forethought, purpose ... while underestimating the role of chance, whim, laziness, excess of energy, boredom, desire to entertain oneself, wanting a change for change's sake." My experience has been that some of these words apply to the literary biographer as well.

Note

* A different version of this chapter, from which the present one has been revised and updated, appeared in *Teaching Life: Letters from a Life in Literature* (2008).

7
Hartley Coleridge and the Art of Elf-effacement

Andrew Keanie

> *Because I bear my Father's name*
> *I am not quite despised,*
> *My little legacy of fame*
> *I've not yet realized.*
> *And yet if you should praise myself*
> *I'll tell you, I had rather*
> *You'd give your love to me, poor elf,*
> *Your praise to my great father.*

(Hartley Coleridge: New Poems, 93)

It has been quite a while since the last biography of Hartley Coleridge (1796–1849). Since Earl Leslie Griggs's *Hartley Coleridge: His Life and Work* (1929) and Herbert Hartman's *Hartley Coleridge: Poet's Son and Poet* (1931), our perception of Romanticism has changed dramatically. But with the publication of *Bricks Without Mortar: The Selected Poems of Hartley Coleridge* (2000) Lisa Gee has aimed at putting the remarkable, though overlooked, poet back in circulation.

Taking my cue from Gee, I wish to justify Hartley Coleridge's claim on the modern reader's attention. Inspired by the novelist Louis de Bernières's introduction to Gee's book, I write in the awareness that impressionistic views – in the manner of Hartley Coleridge himself – can often be more revealing than the judgements of academics.

This chapter explores the sense in which Hartley Coleridge, poet, essayist, biographer and letter-writer, lived and worked in his father's shadow; but it also follows Hartley's progression away from his father's shadow to transcend the prevailing modes and concerns of the period.

It is difficult not to think that Samuel Taylor Coleridge's (1772–1834) magnificent mind and intermittent basic decency made him the most peculiar, and powerful, shaper of Hartley's life. When Hartley was 23, Samuel Taylor Coleridge (hereafter STC) evoked – or perhaps *in*voked – the central problem around which Hartley is thought[1] to have found it impossible to reengineer his personality:

> But alas! it is the absence of a Self, it is the want or Torpor of Will, that is the mortal Sickness of Hartley's Being, and has been, for good & for evil, his character – his moral *Idiocy* – from his earliest Childhood ...
>
> (*Letters of Hartley Coleridge* 73)

There is a Self, a unifying force, underneath STC's fragmented output, bringing the heterogeneous matter into a mighty unity, and Thomas McFarland has argued the case compellingly in *Romanticism and the Forms of Ruin: Wordsworth, Coleridge, the Modalities of Fragmentation* (1981). But no such central strength can as easily be seen to assemble into a comparable unity the distresses in Hartley's life, or the digressions in his writings.

The biographer Richard Holmes once said that STC treated his friends and acquaintances in the same way he used books, by getting what he needed from them (often money) before leaving them with annotations and moving on (Holmes, *Early Visions* 99). For STC, his firstborn son was like a living annotation, so lively, yet so little (and lacking in some of the basic skills of emotional self-management) that he was unable to climb off the page and *be*. Hartley's father's restlessness and remoteness are crucially important elements of the atmosphere in which Hartley was formed.

STC originally named his son David Hartley – shortened to Hartley (Griggs, *Life and Work* 4) – because of a temporary enthusiasm for the work of the philosopher of that name. A little later, STC would name his second son Berkeley, when his philosophical enthusiasm veered away from Hartleian necessitarianism towards the idealism of the Irish philosopher and Anglican bishop, George Berkeley (1685–1753). Berkeley Coleridge did not survive infancy. It is intriguing to speculate what might have become of him; but then again, it is intriguing to speculate what might have become of many of STC's literary and philosophical projects, had they survived their early stages. Notoriously, his unfinished projects outnumbered his finished projects. His letter to his Bristol publisher, Joseph Cottle (1770–1835), in April 1797, gives an idea of the tangential tendencies of STC's mentality:

> I should not think of devoting less than 20 years to an Epic Poem. Ten to collect materials and warm my mind with universal science. I would be a tolerable Mathematician, I would thoroughly know Mechanics, Hydrostatics, Optics, and Astronomy, Botany, Metallurgy, Fossilism, Chemistry, Geology, Anatomy, Medicine – then the *mind of man* – then the *minds of men* – in all Travels, Voyages and Histories. So I would spend ten years – the next five to the composition of the poem – and the last five to the correction of it.
>
> (STC, *Letters* I 320–21)

Hartley became (as Berkeley Coleridge might have become, had he lived) a significant piece of STC's personalized metaphysical jigsaw puzzle. Critics have tended to argue that Hartley lived his life in a way that fulfilled his father's poem, "Frost at Midnight" (1798), and Wordsworth's poem, "To H.C., Six Years Old" (1802).[2] STC said to his baby son:

> But *thou*, my babe! shalt wander like a breeze
> By lakes and sandy shores, beneath the crags
> Of ancient mountains, and beneath the clouds,
> Which image in their bulk both lakes and shores
> And mountain crags, so shalt thou see and hear
> The lovely shapes and sounds intelligible
> Of that eternal language, which thy God
> Utters, who from eternity doth teach
> Himself in all, and all things in himself.
> Great universal Teacher! he shall mould
> Thy spirit, and by giving make it ask.
>
> (STC, *Poetical Works* 242)

As if parenting were another form of art,[3] STC expressed himself through his elfin son. In the conclusion to the second (less inspired) part of STC's "Christabel" (1801), Hartley became the effortless poet that STC felt he had been, once:

> A little child, a limber elf,
> Singing, dancing to itself,
> A fairy thing with red round cheeks,
> That always finds, and never seeks ...
>
> (STC, *Poetical Works* 235)

As the following notebook entry illustrates, STC recorded the infant Hartley's development with more of the scientist's detachment than the average father:

1. The first smile – what *reason* it displays ... 2. Asleep with the polyanthus fast in its hand, its bells drooping over the rosy face ... 3. Stretching after the stars ... 5. Sports of infants – their incessant activity, the *means* being the end. – Nature how lovely a school-mistress – A blank-verse, moral poem ... 9. mother directing a Baby's hand. Hartley's love to Papa – scrawls pothooks. 8. reads what he *meant* by them ... 14. The wisdom & graciousness of God in the infancy of the human species – its beauty, long continuance etc etc. Children in the wind – hair floating, tossing, a miniature of the agitated Trees, below which they played ...

(STC, *Notebooks* 330)

STC was not slow to mention the things he did not like about his son's appearance and character. The description of Hartley as "a Poet, spite of the Forehead *'villainous low'*, which his Mother smuggled into his Face" (STC, *Letters* II 847) offers a telling breath of the atmosphere of emotional violence in which Hartley was brought up. Perhaps the very father who noticed a Self-shaped hole in the personality of Hartley Coleridge was the same father who had punched it.

Hartley would never earn enough to support himself, and he would never publish enough to cut the profile of a writer of genuine importance. He was profoundly self-deprecating. As an adult, he could not even hold unto a sovereign without becoming fidgety with the feeling that it threw into greater relief his shabby being:

> OH when I have a sovereign in my pocket
> I cannot sit – my toes extempore dance
> Gay as a limber son of merry France;
> 'Tis like grey hair enclose[d] in gilded locket
> Whose gold and glass by contrast seem to mock it ...
>
> (*Hartley Coleridge: New Poems* 72).

Hartley could solve the problem of the out of place coin by exchanging it for a drink (and drunkenness is no sin if it is whimsical):

> Shall I in ocean take a fatal plunge
> Or shall I with sixpenny worth of ale
> Condole the sovereign spent – or get quite frisky
> And just hibernify myself with whiskey?
>
> (*Hartley Coleridge: New Poems* 72)

He could not, however, attempt to solve the problem of the out of place world – or, rather, his out of place life in it – with the same levity:

> ... Yet could a wish, a thought,
> Unravel all the complex web of age, –
> Could all the characters that Time hath wrought
> Be clean effaced from my memorial page
> By one short word, the word I would not say ...
>
> (*Complete Poetical Works of Hartley Coleridge* 13)

Just as there is no word in English for the back of the knee, so there is no word to use in reference to the ideas, and the expressions, characteristic of Hartley Coleridge: "Coleridgean" refers to the thinking characteristic of his father, and "Hartleian" refers to the thinking of the English philosopher who introduced associationism (the psychological theory that all mental activity is based on connections between basic mental events, such as sensations and feelings). What about Hartley Coleridge? Even at birth the words of his own name were already spoken for, and his work was destined to slide into the interstices of English Romanticism, just as he was left to inhabit the interstices of life. The following little stanza provides an example of Hartley's acceptance of his marginalized status:

> And yet if you should praise myself
> I'll tell you, I had rather
> You'd give your love to me, poor elf,
> Your praise to my great father.

> (*Hartley Coleridge: New Poems* 93)

Limited by the number of words that rhyme with "myself," he presents himself as a mischievous and whimsical little creature of little consequence. Whereas the (now undisputed) major Romantic poets – such as Byron and Shelley – left roadkills behind them as they zipped along the fast-lane, Hartley went easy on everyone – not least on himself – and his single approach to (or avoidance of) the real world was consistent throughout his life:

> I would not have the restless will
> That hurries to and fro
> Searching for some great thing to do
> Or secret thing to know
> I would be treated as a child
> And guided where to go.

> (Plotz, *Children's Literature* 147)

Whereas, say, Byron desired, and in a sense required, warm Mediterranean weather in order to live and write at his best, Hartley needed the unconditional love and sympathy of his family and friends. At first Hartley got it. As a child, he was permitted, and even encouraged, to be very impractical in his everyday habits. Dorothy Wordsworth wrote feelingly on the issue:

> Poor thing! he has been so much accustomed to move about after his own fancies that we find some trouble in checking him ... he is absolutely in a dream when you tell him to do the simplest thing – his Books, his Slate, his pencils, he drops them just where he finds them no longer useful.
>
> (Griggs, *Life and Work* 32)

He was not persecuted at school like Cowper (*Letters of Hartley Coleridge* 9) or Shelley (Christiansen, *Romantic Affinities* 39), but the adults around him monitored the growth of his mind with anxious solicitude. Robert Southey (1774–1843) felt that "such an intellect can never reach maturity [and that] The springs are of too exquisite workmanship to last long" (Griggs, *Life and Work* 20).

However, Hartley the growing child found increasingly that love and sympathy were coming to him alloyed with less and less soothing ideas about self-improvement. His father wrote him a letter, which explained to the 10-year-old Hartley what was wrong with him and what he should do to fix it. If it was a key piece of advice, it was certainly never actioned by the recipient:

> ... this power which you possess of shoving aside all disagreeable reflections, or losing them in a labyrinth of daydreams, which saves you from some present pain, has, on the other hand, interwoven with your nature habits of procrastination, which, unless you correct them in time (and it will require all your best exertions to do it effectually) must lead you into lasting unhappiness.
>
> (STC, *Letters* IV 10.)

STC was (apparently) helping Hartley to see what was "wrong" with him, but nobody would (or could) compel Hartley to fix it. Hartley did not fix himself, either as a child or as a man. He was, as Griggs says, "a queer mixture of shyness and self-satisfaction" (Griggs, *Life and Work* 55). By manhood, he learned the wisdom of resignation to the fits and starts of his own malfunctioning mind; his "irregular passions and [his] intellect, powerful perhaps in parts, but ever like 'a crazy old church clock, and its disordered chimes"' (Griggs, *Life and Work* 163).

Hartley's much celebrated father – "the Da Vinci of literature" (Fruman, *Damaged Archangel* 292) – recorded memorably his longing for the freedom of Paradise:

> If a man could pass through Paradise in a Dream, & have a Flower presented to him as a pledge that his Soul had really been there, & found that Flower in his hand when he awoke – Aye! and what then?
>
> (STC, *Notebooks* 4287)

STC traced his (and helped Wordsworth to trace some of his) intimations of a beauty inaccessible, and yearned after the legendary land which some call Eden, some Erin, some Tibet, and some Zion. STC called it *Xanadu*. *Xanadu*, spoken, sibilates like a whoosh of cosmic energy before leaving its vapour trail, *u*. "Kubla Khan" (which STC wrote in 1797, when Hartley was an infant) is the poem that showcases the never-never-world of *Xanadu*, as if it has just been verbally slung-shot into syncopation with the very pulse of existence. Teeming with ravishing reverberations, the poem has survived literary-critical dissection for more than 200 years.

Hartley would have been beginning to struggle up onto his feet around the time his father caught sight of the vision of *Xanadu*. Despite (or because of) his opium habit, STC's relish of the English language had become peculiarly vascular with life and sensation:

> ... it [opium] leaves my sensitive Frame *so* sensitive! My enjoyments are so deep, of the fire, of the Candle, of the thought I am thinking, of the old Folio I am reading – & the silence of the silent House is so *most* & very delightful.
>
> (STC, *Letters* I 539)

STC was tracing the taproots of his own talent to their antediluvian depths, and heights. He also frequently portrayed himself as a fond father, which he often genuinely was (when he was actually at home), but he had a great deal more in him than domestic aspirations. He told his friend, the political lecturer, revolutionary and poet, John Thelwall (1764–1834):

> We are *very* happy – & my little David Hartley grows a sweet boy – & has high health – he laughs at us till he makes us weep for very fondness. – You would smile to see my eye rolling up to the ceiling in a Lyric fury, and on my knee a *Diaper* pinned, to warm.
>
> (S.T. Coleridge, *Letters* I 308)

"Lyric fury" is the key phrase in the above excerpt. STC had a wife and child in a cottage at Nether Stowey, Somerset, but (as the notebooks show) he was often turning in upon himself and becoming wildly energized by what he found.

Every syllable of "Kubla Khan" is animated by preternatural urgency. The poem's momentum modulates with the untaught, exhilarated control of an animal on the hunt: here, sinewy, feigned indifference;[4] there, rough, rapid pursuit through the undergrowth.[5] "Kubla Khan" was written because it had to be. It quickened in and found its way out of STC with an insatiable craving for a multiplicity of meanings. It has since devoured readers', and listeners', attentions. The language still struggles with an imperishable rudeness of health and violence of appetite: "Could I revive within me / Her symphony and song" expresses a longing new at the time in English literature, a longing which would permeate Hartley Coleridge's lifelong search for something beyond learned books' concepts and insights, and beyond the tangle of sense-perceptions and thought-systems. As an adult, Hartley would ask "What was't awaken'd first the untried ear / Of that sole man who was all human kind?" (*Complete Poetical Works of Hartley Coleridge* 5), but, unlike his father's, Hartley's writing would not become less accessible the more he contemplated the mystery of existence.

René Wellek has argued that the ideas in STC's later prose are "heterogeneous, incoherent and even contradictory which makes the study of [S.T.]

Coleridge's philosophy so futile" (Wellek, *Immanuel Kant in England* 68). Without announcing any intention to formulate a metaphysical explanation of the universe, Hartley delivered extraordinarily condensed insights (and in so doing he matched his father's portrait of him in "Christabel" – always finding and never seeking):

> What is the meaning of the word 'sublime',
> Utter'd full oft, and never yet explain'd?
> It is a truth that cannot be contain'd
> In formal bounds of thought, in prose, or rhyme.
> 'Tis the Eternal struggling out of Time.
>
> (*Complete Poetical Works of Hartley Coleridge* 117)

STC would search again and again, paradoxically stimulated by his own "disabling immersion in the diversity of sense experience" (Perry, *Coleridge and the Uses of Division* 26), looking for union with the mystery.

"Kubla Khan" was not the result of STC's conscientious approach to family life. STC "was rather a flagrant example of Samuel Johnson's observation that 'poets, with reverence be it spoken, do not make the best parents" ' (Hartman, *Poet's Son and Poet* 1). Norman Fruman has found STC's record as a parent wanting:

> It is a mournful fact that after 1823 son [Hartley] and father were never to meet again. Hartley was thirty-eight years old when his father died. In all those thirty-eight years he did not live in his father's presence for as much as five years. Coleridge's brilliant daughter, Sara, who was to do so much for his after-fame, did not see him once between her tenth and twentieth years. The orphanhood which death had inflicted on the young Samuel Coleridge was in effect visited upon all his children.
>
> (Fruman, *Damaged Archangel* 432)

Before marriage and the arrival of children to feed, STC could pronounce a moral/philosophical line of reasoning, while at the same time making it plain that digestion was a process about which he was feelingly appreciative:

> It is each Individual's *duty* [he told Southey] to be Just, *because* it is in his *Interest*. To perceive this and assent to it as an abstract proposition – is easy – but it requires the most wakeful attentions of the most reflective minds in all moments to bring it into practice. – It is not enough, that we have once swallowed it – The *Heart* should have *fed* upon the *truth*, as Insects on a Leaf – till it be tinged with the colour, and show its food in every the minutest fibre.
>
> (STC, *Letters* I 115)

Unfortunately for his family, STC would continue to formulate more moral arguments (of which the above is a representative instance) than he would fund hot dinners. No doubt when hungry Mrs Samuel Taylor Coleridge (1770–1845) and little Hartley would have been more interested in slices of second-rate topside than in the choicest poetic utterances.

The finale of "Kubla Khan" effects the whip and snap of the fabric of STC's *"so* sensitive" (STC, *Letters* I 539) self in a one-off storm of metaphysical insight. Perhaps the poet forgot all about the diaper that he had told Thelwall was pinned to his knee. Perhaps the diaper was not there in the first place.

"Kubla Khan" would not bring the Coleridges in a sixpence until it was actually published in 1816. Meanwhile, Sarah Coleridge (née Fricker) was at a loss what to think or do: why would her obviously brilliant husband who could dream up "Kubla Khan" not simply snap out of non-professional meditation, and get on with the job of looking after his family? Why could he not settle down? His letter to Thelwall, in February 1797, suggest that he was far from uxorious:

> I have society – my *friend*, T. Poole [Hartley's godfather] and as many acquaintances as I can dispense with – there are a number of very pretty young women in Stowey, all musical – & I am an immense favorite: for I pun, conundrumize, *listen*, & dance. The last is a recent acquirement –.
>
> (S.T. Coleridge, *Letters* I 308)

Why could he not be more like the deadline-honouring, mortgage-sensible Southey, to whom Sarah's sister, Edith Fricker (1774–1837), seemed to be more comfortably married? Sarah would always be baffled. She would not always be tolerant:

> If any woman wanted an exact and copious Recipe, 'How to make a Husband completely miserable', I could furnish her with one—with a Probatum est, tacked to it.—Ill-tempered Speeches sent after me when I went out of the House, ill-tempered Speeches on my return, my friends received with freezing looks, the least opposition or contradiction occasioning screams of passion, & the sentiments, which I held most base, ostentatiously avowed—all this added to the utter negation of all, which a Husband expects from a Wife—especially, living in retirement—& the consciousness, that I was myself growing a worse man / O dear Sir! no one can tell what I have suffered.
>
> (STC, *Notebooks* 876)

Poor Hartley.

"Kubla Khan" is one of the most important poems written in English. It is a sudden eruption ("momently ... forced") through a familiar verbal crust: until STC created the poem, it had been the comparatively placid spirit of sensibility that merely dribbled through porous eighteenth-century poetry. Almost every acre of England's arable language had been devoted to the cultivation of descriptive specifics. One thinks of R. Dodsley's essay, "A Description of the Leasowes," which virtually guides the reader through the landscaped estate to the seat of the late William Shenstone (1714–63), or one thinks of Thomas Gray's (1716–71) 'Ode on the Spring' (1748), with its gentle enjoyment of "rosy-bosomed Hours", and "gaily-gilded" insects. The best descriptive poets knew how to ripen such classical conventionalities to their optimum vividness. *The Seasons* (1726–30), by James Thomson (1700–48), and *The Task* (1785), by William Cowper (1731–1800), afford first-rate examples of poetry aglow with mild, placid and confinable exclamations of sensibility. STC's image of "gardens bright with sinuous rills, / Where blossomed many an incense-bearing tree" seems to suggest that the poet is sitting the reader down, in the first stanza, for the usual, cool, sensible recitation. "But oh!," he exclaims unexpectedly, at the beginning of the second stanza, dropping the preparatory, therapeutic first stanza like a coal suddenly gone hot. There is an immediate increase in the intensity of jostling consonants, and then a fiery flash flood of transfigured words, "With ceaseless turmoil seething." The *hss*ing, *fss*ing and *thss*ing suggests the visceral sensation of unprecedented passage. The words left behind, as if to cool, look like the monument to a moment's convulsive consideration of what life actually is:

> ... *all things* appear little – all the knowledge, that can be acquired, child's play – the universe itself – what but an immense heap of *little* things? ... My mind feels as if it ached to behold & know something *great* – something *one* & *indivisible* – and it is only in the faith of this that rocks or waterfalls, mountains or caverns give me the sense of sublimity or majesty!
>
> (STC, *Letters* I 349)

The cold embrace of the literary historian has not reduced STC's "sense of sublimity or majesty," his *Xanadu*, to a funny little thing bathetically belying the mighty throes that brought it into being. The magnificence, the scope, and the irregular aliveness of the vision remain intact.

How then is Hartley's poetic vision not a much diminished and degraded one by comparison? As a 46-year-old man, he sat smoking and thinking about "the truth:"

> If truth had been a vapour still aspiring
> From passive matter's self-consuming brands,
> A smoky something, while we stand admiring,
> But nothing when you take it in your hands;
> Then would I bid you puff the truth away,
> And watch it thinning from your pipe of clay.
>
> (Pomeroy, *Poetry of Hartley Coleridge* 109)

Hartley's poetic art seems to have involved little of his father's "disabling immersion in the diversity of sense experience" (Perry, *Coleridge and the Uses of Division* 26). Perhaps the conclusion to the above poem, "Thoughts While Smoking" (1842), is too lightweight and trite to have been uttered by a truly great poet:

> Where each true man may say unto his brother,
> One thing is true at least, we love each other.
>
> (Pomeroy, *Poetry of Hartley Coleridge* 109)

As a young boy, Hartley had an imaginary country (when many children just have imaginary friends). The juvenile vision may suggest to the modern reader the wooden props of an amateur-theatrical adaptation of one of C.S. Lewis's (1898–1963) *Chronicles of Narnia* more than it calls to mind the magical synthesis of a *Xanadu*. In his *Memoir*, Derwent Coleridge has given an account of his brother's fantasy world, "Ejuxria:"

> Taken as a whole, the Ejuxrian world presented a complete analogon to the world of fact, so far as it was known to Hartley, complete in all its parts; furnishing a theatre and scene of action, with *dramatis personae*, and suitable machinery, in which, day after day for the space of long years, he went on evolving the complicated drama of existence. There were many nations, continental and insular, each with its separate history, civil, ecclesiastical, and literary, its forms of religion and government and specific national character ... The names of generals and statesmen were "familiar to my [Derwent's] ears as household words". I witnessed the jar of faction, and had to trace the course of sedition. I lived to see changes of government, a great progress of public opinion, and a new order of things!
>
> (*Poems by Hartley Coleridge, with a memoir of his life by his brother* xxxvii–xxxix)

During Hartley's childhood, his father's thinking, talking and writing were often about politics – about politicians and power, and the human interactions that take place within the architecture of political organisation and discourse. Hartley's father was, as Peter J. Kitson says,

> a deeply political man ... [whose] writings reveal him as someone who closely followed the contemporary political scene as it unfolded during one of the most turbulent and exciting periods in the nation's history
>
> (Newlyn, ed., *Cambridge Companion to Coleridge* 156).

Still not 10 years old, Hartley did not have to clutter up his writing with correlations to the real political landscape of any actual, identifiable place. Whereas, for example, STC had delivered political lectures in Bristol in the mid-1790s, and was writing insightful political leaders in the *Morning Post* in the early 1800s, Hartley's narratives (all his life) were unfettered by the limitations of the political system familiar in Britain, or, for that matter, in America or France. Hartley's writing remained without the restriction of correctness. STC's poem to his son, "Answer to a Child's Question" (1802), indicates the untrammelled imaginative journey upon which he had already encouraged Hartley to embark:

> Do you ask what the birds say? The Sparrow, the Dove,
> The Linnet and Thrush say, 'I love and I love!'
> In the winter they're silent – the wind is so strong;
> What it says, I don't know, but it sings a loud song.
> But green leaves, and blossoms, and sunny warm weather,
> And singing, and loving – all come back together.
> But the Lark is so brimful of gladness and love,
> That he sings, and he sings; and for ever sings he –
> 'I love my Love, and my Love loves me!'

> (STC, *Poetical Works* 386)

Hartley learned to make things up. Where would it end? In almost total obscurity.

Consider the self-promoting achievement of Shelley's "Defence of [his own] Poetry" (1821) or of Wordsworth's "Preface" to the *Lyrical Ballads* (1805). The major Romantic poets preached from the pulpits of their assumed superiority with relentlessly steely application. Hartley did no such thing:

> I own I like to see my works in print;
> The page looks knowing, though there's nothing in't ...
> ... who'll admire me when, poor barren elf,
> I scarce, with all my pains, admire myself?

> (*Complete Poetical Works of Hartley Coleridge* 64)

It would have felt uncomfortable to Hartley to have anyone goggle learnedly over what he had to say. He felt that it would be wrong to "show what the work is about, not what it is" (*Essays and Marginalia* I 181).

Hartley has excited neither the adulation nor the opprobrium that a writer of great significance tends to excite. He did, for instance, write about sin, but there is no sign of any dark secret lurking beneath the light idiom. No vapours from some central iniquity rise up through any cracks and fissures in Hartley's versification. The utterances may be too persistently apologetic for readers who prefer their mental pabulum to have come from a more ostentatiously backboned being: "When I am unwell, which, I thank Heaven, is much seldomer than I have deserved ..." (*Memoir* xcviii). There is the continual presence in Hartley's writing of an inferiority complex, and the poet has remained undefended by anyone fired up enough on his behalf, despite John Wilcock's incitement to critics in 1898:

> All the critics I have read have lamented upon what Hartley Coleridge *might have been* with his gifts, but none has duly valued what he overcame to be what he was.
>
> (*Manchester Quarterly* XVII 127)

The major Romantics got respect from their readerships. They had exquisite sensitivities, but they also had plenty of the crude insistent passion that one must have in order to achieve anything. Respect is firm and strong, and therefore different from love (or the fond smiles of approbation against which Wilcock has protested, above). Hartley has been – if anything – loved more than respected. Love is erratic and a mere luxury, and most people cannot afford to give it consistently. Hartley became a kind of emotional mendicant, sometimes referring to himself as "Tom Thumb," or even (in a letter to Poole) "your grateful and sincere little friend" (*Letters of Hartley Coleridge* 18). Whereas Shelley could conclude letters until the end of his life with the words

> I am not
> Your obedient servant
> P.B. Shelley,
>
> (Wroe, *Being Shelley* 390)

Hartley would remain humble, writing (in 1848) the last sonnet before his death, which shows his intimate sympathy with a feminine predicament – the penitential love of Mary Magdalene:

> SHE sat and wept beside His feet; the weight
> Of sin oppress'd her heart; for all the blame,
> And the poor malice of the worldly shame,
> To her was past, extinct, and out of date,
> Only the *sin* remain'd, – the leprous state;
> She would be melted by the heat of love,
> By fire far fiercer than are blown to prove
> And purge the silver ore adulterate.
> She sat and wept, and with her untress'd hair
> She wiped the feet she was so blest to touch;
> And He wiped off the soiling of despair
> From her sweet soul, because she loved so much.
> I am a sinner, full of doubts and fears,
> Make me a humble thing of love and tears.
>
> (*Complete Poetical Works of Hartley Coleridge* 359)

The absence of quotation marks around the final couplet, above, says it all. "I" is Hartley.

To many observers Hartley continued all his life to be escapist to a profound and troubling extent. Some time between 1835 and 1849 (when he was well into his decidedly unroaring 40s) he would write "Adolf and Annette," a fairytale which seems to confirm his lifelong avoidance of growing up. In the following "song" from Hartley's parable, there are, typically, echoes of his father's "Kubla Khan," suggesting the inherited pleasure dome that Hartley is loath to leave for good:

> Saw ye ever sight like this?
> Where the broad bright waters flow
> To the shining vale below.
> There are butterflies and lilies,
> And a thousand daffodillies
> Velvet turf beneath your feet
> Berries juicy, ripe and sweet!
> There are joys beyond all measure,
> Mirth, and fun, and sport and pleasure;
> Plunge into the white abyss
> Ye shall win that land of bliss.

> (Plotz, *Children's Literature* 157–8)

He retained his spellbound imagination to which he flew for comfort when the world got the better of him (which was nearly always), and from the shelter of which he often witnessed worldly people react to his behaviour in bewilderment.

Just after his career, as a Fellow of Oriel College, Oxford, went stunningly amiss,[6] he told his father (in October 1820) that he was "the one scabby sheep turn'd out of an immaculate flock" and "the sole jarring note in the concert of the Coleridges." (*Letters of Hartley Coleridge* 153.) In September 1846, when Hartley had just turned 50, even his best apologist, Derwent, was unable to contain his irritation when he heard that Hartley (probably drunk) had set fire to his own bedclothes:

> Would not this be playing a part, justifiable only toward a child, or a lunatic? My dear, dear Brother, there are those who regard you in one or both of these lights – some with kindly feelings, that they may excuse that which they must else condemn ... And would you shelter *yourself*, would you wish *me* to shelter you under such a plea?

Derwent continued the letter by registering a protest on behalf of the Coleridge family against Hartley's strange behaviour:

> Oh my dear Brother, need I remind you what this cruel enchantment has cost you? that it has cut you off from those who yearn to have you with

them ... My circumstances have ever been such that the possibility of your losing your self-respect has put it out of my power to see you ... Not to say that my health would immediately give way under the misery which it w[ould] occasion me.

(*Hartley Coleridge Letters: A Calendar and Index* 19)

During Hartley's childhood and teenage years, his uncle Southey and Wordsworth worried that Hartley would spend his entire life in reclusive preparation for work that would never actually come into being. STC had noted Hartley's boyhood claim about

some Tale & wild fancy of his Brain – 'It is not yet, but it will be – for it *is* – & it cannot stay always *in* here (*pressing one hand on his forehead and the other on his occiput*) – 'and then *it will be* – because it is not nothing." '

(S.T. Coleridge, *Notebooks* 3547)

The portrait of an artist as a boy and then a man eternally engaged in groundwork can be a disturbing one.

The word Hartley invented for his imaginary world ("Ejuxria") seems to represent the received wisdom: Hartley's achievement is inferior to his father's. But the Hartley who invented Ejuxria was only 8 years old. It is just that the way things have since fallen into place in the public imagination, Hartley's reputation as an adult writer has remained as bound up with Ejuxria (initially, the excrescence of an 8-year-old) as STC's reputation has remained bound up with *Xanadu* (the "symphony and song" of an artist at the height of his power). The critic Stanley T. Williams said in 1924:

When the name of Hartley Coleridge is mentioned we dispose of it lightly. We say: "Oh, his sonnets –." Apart from family distinction he survives in hardly any other way ... He has done enough to seem the spiritual son of his father, but very little more.

(*South Atlantic Quarterly* xxiii 73)

Ejuxria is an unwieldy word of four syllables that does not look as if it could fit sweetly into a sentence, let alone into a line of verse. (In contrast, the five syllables of Shelley's "Ozymandias" make up a magical handful of imaginative power.) Ejuxria does not advertise, with any euphoniousness, much aptitude for the gregariousness with which the words summoned by a great Romantic can mysteriously unite (as, for example, the rolling swells and peals of STC's "Kubla Khan," "The Rime of the Ancient Mariner," or "Christabel"). Ejuxria seems too oddly curlicued to contain the rough magic that wins a writer popularity or critical acclaim. The pattern of the vowels and consonants somehow gives the word the appearance on the page of a word turned inside out, as if the threads and fabrics on the underside of an embroidered cloth were on display by mistake. The word might sound better said backwards. Whereas the sound *Zan-a-doo*, in "Kubla Khan," is like the exotic music with which, say, the middle-Eastern vision of "Mount Abora" may be summoned from a basket (mosques and minarets glinting in the background), Hartley's word seems brittle, or self-extinguishing; the sound of each syllable collides with, or even cancels out, the sound of the preceding syllable – perhaps reminding one of the succession of "quickly form'd and quickly broken resolutions" (*Letters of Hartley Coleridge* 62) that would make up much of Hartley's adult life:

> A WOEFUL thing it is to find
> No trust secure in weak mankind;
> But ten-fold woe betide the elf
> Who knows not how to trust himself.
>
> What then remains? Can oath or vow,
> Or formal protest aid me?
> Ah! no, for if I make them now,
> Next week they will upbraid me:
> For what I am, oh! shame and sorrow,
> I cannot hope to be tomorrow.

(Complete Poetical Works of Hartley Coleridge 218)

Ejuxria is an important word to consider when reassessing Hartley's life and work. The word (how on earth is it to be pronounced?) suggests awkwardness more than exoticism. Many readers will have an easier familiarity with STC's water-snakes and his demon-lover than with Hartley's "pipe of clay" (Pomeroy, *Poetry of Hartley Coleridge* 109), his goldfishes (*Complete Poetical Works of Hartley Coleridge* 86), his nightingale (*Complete Poetical Works of Hartley Coleridge* 158), his anemone (*Complete Poetical Works of Hartley Coleridge* 159), and his "daily round of household things." (*Complete Poetical Works of Hartley Coleridge* 23.)

Could it be that Hartley's greatness has been overlooked, and that it lies in his search for the lost lineaments of the most high in the most low? Hartley's observations concerning the vital importance of love to human life remain unappreciated:

> ... The worst –
> The worst of hearts, that hath not ceased to feel,
> Grows soft and childish, when the number'd hour
> Records the moment of a mother's pain –
> When the faint mother lifted first her eyes
> To Heaven in thankfulness – then cast them down
> Upon her babe in love. – Oh, gracious Heaven!
> Thy mighty law – in spite of rebel will,

> Spite of all theories of doubting man,
> Still rules triumphant through the tribes of life,
> Confutes the quirks of calculating pride,
> And o'er the feeblest of all feeble things,
> Sheds the strong potency of love divine:
> For God is stirring in the mother's heart –
> The living God is in her milky breast;
> And God's own image, fresh from paradise,
> Hallows the helpless form of infancy.
>
> (*Complete Poetical Works of Hartley Coleridge* 98–9)

The succession of "quickly form'd and quickly broken resolutions" that constituted Hartley's life constitutes most lives. The reader should readily appreciate the sense (in the above passage) of a life muddled through, a sense underpinned by Hartley's heartfelt consciousness of "the quirks of calculating pride" and how love "Confutes" them.

In Hartley's sonnet, "February 1st, 1842," "the better mind / Puts forth some flowers, escaped from Paradise" (*Complete Poetical Works of Hartley Coleridge* 143), which inclines the reader to speculate sympathetically about the (unmentioned) activity of the worse mind the previous January (the month during which most new year's resolutions are broken). In acquainting himself with the small and the broken, and in cultivating the wisdom to make the best of them (because they are all we have), Hartley made poetic use of his

> humbler spirit [that]
> Hears ...
> A low sweet melody, inaudible
> To the gross sense of worldlings.
>
> (*Complete Poetical Works of Hartley Coleridge* 23)

This is not to portray an exclusively elfin poet, unaware of anything beyond the ken of his personal odds and ends. No,

> Around you, and above you, and within you.
> The stars of heaven (as elder sages told)
> Roll on from age to age their lonely way
> To their own music.
>
> (*Complete Poetical Works of Hartley Coleridge* 23)

In Hartley's poetry the personal gives immediacy to the universal, which in turn gives meaning and eminence to the personal. Who is not familiar with the personal feeling that "every birth-day [is] a new argument / Of hope and pride?" (*Complete Poetical Works of Hartley Coleridge* 98.) Yet who has ever put the idea into words, as Hartley did? It would be as easy to overlook Hartley's achievement in that particular little instance as it would be in many other little instances in his writings. He has expressed the idea so unobtrusively, and with such economy, that one might be enriched by it, but forget where one read it. The quiet brilliance is typical. Whereas his father had been (or so he told Poole) "*habituated to the Vast*" (S.T. Coleridge, *Letters* I 354) by the age of 8, Hartley stood in awe before the minute because it contained the sort of scattered wisdom and power that only he could – or would – assimilate and synthesize:

> Whither is gone the wisdom and the power
> That ancient sages scatter'd with the notes
> Of thought-suggesting lyres? The music floats
> In the void air; e'en at this breathing hour,
> In every cell and every blooming bower
> The sweetness of old lays is hovering still …

> (*Complete Poetical Works of Hartley Coleridge* 6)

The stars in the sky and the smallest particles bear a resemblance that has often been observed. In one characteristic sonnet, the poet John Masefield (1878–1967) has looked at the sky:

> So in the empty sky the stars appear,
> Are bright in heaven marching through the sky,
> Spinning their planets, each one to his year,
> Tossing their fiery hair until they die …

> (Masefield, *Collected Poems* 429).

In another equally characteristic sonnet, Masefield has looked at himself:

> What am I, Life? A thing of watery salt
> Held in cohesion by unresting cells …

> (Masefield, *Collected Poems* 430)

For Hartley (as for his father), the charm of science was aesthetic, and the big philosophical questions often informed equally his contemplation of the vast and the minute. Just as the popular science writers of the twenty-first-century wonder about how exactly it came to pass that chemical activity switched to biological activity (at the molecular level), from which humankind eventually evolved (accidentally?), so Hartley asks:

> Was there a time, when, wandering in the air,
> The living spark existed, yet unnamed,
> Unfixt, unqualitied, unlaw'd, unclaim'd,
> A drop of being, in the infinite sea,
> Whose only duty, essence, was to be?
> Or must we seek it, where all things we find,
> In the sole purpose of creative mind –
> Or did it serve, in form of stone or plant,
> Or weaving worm, or the wise politic ant,
> Its weary bondage – ere the moment came,
> When the weak spark should mount into a flame?

> (*Complete Poetical Works of Hartley Coleridge* 74)

STC had his "Rime of the Ancient Mariner" (1798) in which to explore a profound sense of guilt. The above sonnet, however, is Hartley's rhyme of the ancient molecule, in which he explores a profound sense of uncertainty: is everything we know (or think we know) the result of an accident? Hartley's question has yet to be answered. In the meantime, the insistent sense of wonder in the above sonnet is a powerful lesson in humility.

Hartley Coleridge has not given the Lake District its legend, nor has he led readers to a land of retrospective milk and honey like his friend and hero, Wordsworth, about whom he wrote many glowing lines, such as the following:

> A village lies, and Rydal is its name.
> Its natives know not what is meant by fame;
> They little know how men in future time
> Will venerate the spot, where prose and rhyme
> Too strong for aught but Heaven itself to tame,
> Gush'd from a mighty Poet.

> (*Complete Poetical Works of Hartley Coleridge* 119)

Nonetheless, any idea about writing Hartley off as a stylist, as someone whose talent may be lovely to look at but remains essentially a frippery, or a non-essential luxury, is inadequate, and a mere cliché of misunderstanding.

Beyond the image of the anodyne imp that Hartley is supposed to have been, some inner part of him, thirsting for experience and for self-knowledge, was able to enter into every situation and emotion, while as yet remaining itself cloud-like and without personal identity:

> WHAT is the life of man? From first to last,
> Its only substance, the unbeing past!

(Complete Poetical Works of Hartley Coleridge 73)

Unlike the later Imagist poets – such as T.E. Hulme (1883–1917), F.S. Flint (1885–1960) and Amy Lowell (1874–1925) – Hartley kept his continuity of voice; but, like them, he seems to have realized that keeping the continuity of voice entailed his hanging on to something illusory, since mind itself was illusory:

> So man delights in the wide waste of time,
> The tide of moments ebbing as they flow,
> To set his land-marks; and recording names,
> Pavilions of the pausing memory,
> Historic pillars, quaintly sculptured o'er
> With hieroglyphics of the heart.

(Complete Poetical Works of Hartley Coleridge 97)

In understanding that life is a disputable mirage, yet at the same time holding on to the mirage, Hartley became a poet of quirky and compelling originality, "though he was often regarded as a sort of superior being, left perfectly help-less, in a world unsuited to him" (*Memoir* cxxx). If, in the Wordsworthian sense, Hartley entered the world "trailing clouds of glory," then simultane-ously, in the Coleridgean sense, he trailed also the competing vapours from his own delinquencies: "No man believes in Heaven till he finds something in himself that demands it, or in Hell, till he finds something in himself that deserves it" (Griggs, *Life and Work* 163).

Sometimes Hartley seemed to allow his poems to form and precipitate like little lyrical teardrops, apparently as causeless, incomprehensible and truly obscure as the innocence of a newborn baby:

> To see thee sleeping on thy mother's breast,
> It were indeed a lovely sight to see –
> Who would believe that restless sin can be
> In the same world that holds such sinless rest?

(Complete Poetical Works of Hartley Coleridge 68)

Yet babies grow eventually into "adulthood," having been moulded and given "meaning" first by their families, and later by the world. They eventually become strapping ploughboys, or doctors of philosophy, or inky-fingered misfits. Though undeceived by the outward show of the world, Hartley had the additional wisdom not to despise society's conventional arrangements related to the production of ploughboys, doctors of philosophy and misfits. Everything has its place:

> But who may count with microscopic eye
> The multitudes of lives, that gleam and flash
> Behind the sounding keel, and multiply
> In myriad millions, when the white oars dash,
> Through waves electric, or at stillest night
> Spread round the bark becalm'd their milky white?

> (Plotz, *Children's Literature* 138–9)

Or *has* everything its place? What about the "Pure, precious drop of dear mortality" (*Complete Poetical Works of Hartley Coleridge* 67) that every individual human that has ever lived has first been as an infant – "Unconscious witness to the promised birth / Of perfect good, that may not grow on earth" (*Complete Poetical Works of Hartley Coleridge* 67)? Hartley also knew the validity of the belief that there is much that does not have its place: "Nor to be computed by the worldly worth / And stated limits of mortality" (*Complete Poetical Works of Hartley Coleridge* 67). Wanting to have faith, but wary of nurturing his "Fond ignorance" (*Complete Poetical Works of Hartley Coleridge* 68) in a "work-day" world of "worldly care" and "hard-eyed thrift" (*Complete Poetical Works of Hartley Coleridge* 69), Hartley sometimes felt his spirit "Sinking beneath the base control / Of mindless chance" (*Complete Poetical Works of Hartley Coleridge* 84). Was Hartley (and, for that matter, is any stone, or tree, or reader of this book) a random coalescence of atoms, or a (Berkeleian) construct of mind? He could not resolve the problem in him of the antagonistic answers to life's riddle. In a strangely modern (Modernist?) way, he worked at the riddle too obliquely to be taken seriously by influential, taxonomically rigorous readers, to whom he would have seemed to be engaging in what twentieth-century psychologists would call displacement activity.

His family had wanted him to become a scholar, living a life of learned ease in the firelit studies and libraries of Oxford. Instead, they witnessed him become an alcoholic, and a Lakeland recluse. What Hartley himself witnessed with his imagination is more fascinating. In one instance, he could become a comically violent donkey:

> [The prelate] used to ride me in his full canonicals, which enveloped my body, leaving my four legs to appear like those of my rider, and my hinder parts emerging to complete the Reverend compound, indeed it was impossible to tell where the Prebendary ended and the Ass began … [I] kicked so furiously as to throw the Prebendary over my head into a ditch – this

caused his death, and so grievous as sin it is, that I am now a man, such as you see me.

(Griggs, *Life and Work* 169)

In another instance, he could become an embarrassing, nameless insect:

Don't you know that I was one of the martyrs to Helen's beauty? I was then an insect which in these days is nameless, & having crawled upon her bright yellow hair, I was pointed out to her by Paris, and she crushed me with her pearly nail.

(*Memoir* cxlii)

In these presences of imagined creatures, this "absence of a Self" (about which his father complained so bitterly), he could have been a pair of ragged claws scuttling across the floors of silent seas. Pursuing the metaphor, the great vessels of twentieth-century studies in Romanticism and literary biography (their hulls to become so barnacle-encrusted) would glide far above him, not knowing he was there.

And yet Hartley's thoughts have echoed through the centuries, and into *here* and *now* (despite the noise of his father's impact on literature). Having made the "faery voyage," they have finally arrived, and can tell us what we feel:

> To live without a living soul,
> To feel the spirit daily pining,
> Sinking beneath the base control
> Of mindless chance, itself consigning
> To the dull impulse of oppressive time,
> To find the guilt without the power of crime.

(*Complete Poetical Works of Hartley Coleridge* 84)

We twenty-first-century readers – alienated yet also fully owned in a computerized, post-modern, post-human western world – can hear the aspects of our condition as foretold by our most unsung ancestral voice:

> Such is the penance, and the meed
> Of thoughts that, boasting to be free,
> Spurning the dictates of a practic creed,
> Are tangled with excess of liberty,
> Making themselves sole arbiters of right,
> Trampling on hallow'd use with proud delight.

Complete Poetical Works of Hartley Coleridge 84–5)

Notes

1. Judith Plotz's *Romanticism and the Vocation of Childhood* (2002) and Anya Taylor's *Bacchus in Romantic England* (1999) contain chapters on Hartley.
2. "Thou faery voyager! that dost float / In such clear water, that thy boat / May rather seem / To brood on air than on an earthly stream;/ Suspended in a stream as clear as sky, / Where earth and heaven do make one imagery; / O blessed vision! happy child! / Thou art so exquisitely wild, / I think of thee with many fears / For what may be thy lot in future years."
3. One more to add to the gamut of STC's activities as outlined by Richard Holmes: "... [STC] was much more than a Romantic poet: he was also a journalist of genius, a translator, a matchless letter-writer (six volumes), an incomparable autobiographer and self-interrogator in his Notebooks (over sixty surviving between 1794 and his death), a literary critic, a spectacular lecturer, a folklorist, a philosopher, a psychologist (specialising in dreams and creativity), a playwright and dramatic critic, and – that much disputed word – a metaphysician. He was also a travel-writer, a fell-walker, and amateur naturalist ..." (Holmes, *Early Visions* xv).
4. "So twice five miles of fertile ground / With walls and towers were girdled round: / And there were gardens bright with sinuous rills, / Where blossomed many an incense-bearing tree; / And here were forests ancient as the hills, / Enfolding sunny spots of greenery." (STC, *Poetical Works* 297.)
5. "But oh! that deep romantic chasm which slanted / Down the green hill athwart a cedarn cover!/ A savage place! as holy and enchanted / As e'er beneath a waning moon was haunted by woman wailing for her demon lover! / And from this chasm, with ceaseless turmoil seething, / As if this earth in fast thick pants were breathing, / A mighty fountain momently was forced: / Amid whose swift half-intermitted burst / Huge fragments vaulted like rebounding hail, / Or chaffy grain beneath the thresher's flail: / And 'mid these dancing rocks at once and ever / It flung up momently the sacred river." (STC, *Poetical Works* 297.)
6. "At the close of his probationary year he was judged to have forfeited his Oriel fellowship, on the ground, mainly, of intemperance. Great efforts were made to reverse the decision. He wrote letters to many of the Fellows. His father went to Oxford to see and to expostulate with the Provost. It was in vain. The specific charges might have been exaggerated. Palliations and excuses might have been found for the particular instances in which they were established. A life singularly blameless in all other respects, dispositions the most amiable, principles and intentions the most upright and honourable, might be pleaded as a counterpoise in the opposite scale. It was to no purpose. The sentence might be considered severe, but it could not be said to be unjust ..." (*Memoir* lxxiv–lxxv).

8

'A Horse May Show His Good Intent': Opinionated Protestant Equines from Morocco to Black Beauty*

Kevin De Ornellas

Introduction

It is thought that Anna Sewell's sole publication, 1877's *Black Beauty*, is the sixth best-selling English-language book of all time.[1] Paid a mere forty pounds by her first publishers, Jarrold & Sons, Sewell (1820–78) lived just long enough to see the work become a big-seller in England, but not long enough to enjoy the paradoxical honour of having the book pirated in America by 1890, where more legitimate editions soon broke publishing records. A signed British first edition will cost a buyer over £33,000.[2] A trip to any charity book store, though, will reveal that many of the later editions are available for virtually nothing. Almost everyone in the western world has a copy of the novel. Such ubiquitousness may have made the novel paradoxically invisible to critics. Too often, it goes unremarked that *Black Beauty* succeeds because of Sewell's conceit of constructing her narrative in the vein of an autobiography – an autobiography told by the eponymous horse. Intentionalist critics – when bothered to comment on this best-selling Victorian work – focus generally on Sewell's avowed call for the humane treatment of material horses during the period. However, in this chapter I wish to argue that Sewell's concern for non-human animals is secondary to her overall vision of human decorum, order and moral rectitude. For Sewell's vision is a Quaker-influenced, high church-eschewing vision of personal responsibility and personal self-reflection. The format of the equine pseudo-autobiography facilitates an articulation of a clear belief in a low-Protestant sense of self, a self that flourishes morally away from an intrusive theological hierarchy. There may even be a considerable element of post-Swiftian satire in *Black Beauty*: a horse is able to demonstrate a sense of common sense-based righteousness that is lacking in many of the human mammals that Black Beauty encounters. Furthermore, I seek to demonstrate that there was a tradition of Protestant equine autobiography in England. Centuries before, Anti-Catholic and anti-Anglican propagandists had used the genre of the equine autobiography to satirise the alleged corruption of their enemies.

Speaking through the life-story of a horse enhances the writers' anonymity and perhaps renders more anonymous the human originator of the dangerous satire. In 1595's *Maroccus Extaticus*, I will argue that there is a literary construction of a coarser, more aggressive forerunner of Sewell's horse. In this superficially bizarre 1590s text, an Elizabethan celebrity horse is given a voice with which he castigates many of the vices of the Church of England-dominated London of the day – his invective against landlords will find sympathy with any put-upon tenant of this century. In 1645's *Dialogve Betwixt a Horse of Warre, and a Mill-Horse*, the steadfastness of the humble, profoundly Protestant mill horse is contrasted tellingly with the vainglorious extravagance of the amoral, crypto-Papist, Royalist war horse. Although it is improbable that Sewell would have ever encountered these obscure texts, I argue for a generic, political and spiritual connection between them and *Black Beauty*. Sewell's purpose is as direct as the early pamphleteers – and her first-person speaking horse is as politically outspoken (albeit more subtle and more mannered) as Morocco and the mill horse. *Black Beauty* needs to be treated not as a picturesque children's book about a cute horse, but rather as a subtle outlining of Sewell's belief in the capacity of humans to act with discretion and dignity: it is a belief that is consistent with the more acerbic pamphleteers who were writing equine autobiographies centuries before Sewell's 'innovation' in the genre – and consistent with Sewell's own devotion to a low-Protestant spirituality.

Morocco: assertions of equine vituperation against vice

In his autobiography, Black Beauty retains a discourse characterised by ingenuous humility. But he observes a range of human vices. The vices are often perpetuated by moneyed men and women, persons of high class and wealth. Sewell ventriloquises her attack on higher-order decadence through the mouth of her pious quadruped. In a 1595 pamphlet, a talking horse of the 1590s attacks vices similar to the vices attacked by Black Beauty three centuries later. Unlike Black Beauty, Morocco was a real, documented horse – and a very famous one. Ricky Jay has claimed that William Banks and his horse, Morocco, are 'the most mentioned entertainers of Elizabethan times'.[3] He may be right. The first report of this famous animal comes in 1591; in 1656 he is still being referred to (by Samuel Holland) as 'the four-legg'd wonder of the world'.[4] The animal and its trainer are cited in much literature of the English Renaissance: there are at least seventy instances of the horse's act being described or alluded to. These references have been collected by a number of scholars over the years – a tradition beginning with J. O. Halliwell-Phillips in an 1879 account. Halliwell-Phillips and S. H. Atkins (1934) have produced long lists of allusions to Morocco, augmented with generous quotations.[5] Such an approach is fitting for their essentially bibliographical projects. But it would not be possible discursively to account for all of the early modern allusions to Banks and his horse in a single article: there are too many references to cover. A discussion that attempts to account for the power of the Morocco myth must be selective.

Little is known about the horse's owner, Banks, and the ultimate fate of the horse itself. Holland goes on to say that horse and master travelled to Rome where 'they were both burned by the commandment of the Pope' (Holland, sig. I1v). This notion of Inquisition martyrdom is not credible: Banks himself is known to have lived well into the 1630s, and the horse and he died separately.[6] In John Marston's play of 1601, *Iacke Drums Entertainment*, Planet mocks the amorous pretences of Brabant Junior: the would-be lover's move on Camelia 'shall be Cronicled next after the death of Bankes his Horse'.[7] There was certainly a horse called Morocco that performed all manner of stunts. But the reports of the actions are confused and often obviously representational rather than mimetic. Despite Planet's jibe and Holland's relation of a slaughter, Morocco defies straightforward chronicling. In 1598, the animal was familiar enough to be referred to as 'the dauncing Horse' in Shakespeare's *Love's Labour's Lost*.[8] Thomas Bastard tells us, in another 1598 publication, that Morocco 'can fight, and pisse, and daunce, and lie'.[9] The improbable litany of unerring abilities is added to by Richard Braithwait in a 1615 text: the horse can 'know an honest woman from a whoore'.[10] All these qualities are non-normative. Human-like abilities are being claimed for this exotic horse. Honesty, probity and sexual continence are all judged by this animal. That it takes a horse to establish guilt or otherwise is implicitly satirical, for this conveys an impression that early modern society does not feel fit to judge itself. There is little real mystery regarding the abilities of the horse. A colourful, 1926 account of *Ben Jonson's London* by N. Zwager asserts that any 'modern trained circus-horse might do the same' tricks as the one trained by Banks; and a historian of *The English Circus*, Ruth Manning-Sanders, writes in a 1952 book that Morocco's 'tricks were not beyond the achievement of any little pony in the smallest of tenting circuses to-day'.[11] So, explainable retrospectively or not, Morocco was a well-known, real horse. He was famous enough to 'speak' in a satirical 1595 work.

In a satirical duologue between horse and master, *Maroccus Extaticus, or Bankes Bay Horse in a Trance*, Morocco speaks 'in person', bemoaning many abuses of late-Elizabethan London. Basically, the pamphlet is a sort of interview: Banks asks Morocco questions: the horse answers them fully and thoroughly. He tells us just about enough about himself for us to think of the text as a sort of pre-Sewell equine 'autobiography'. Morocco, arrogant and well-fed, but sympathetic to the suffering of many of his fellow Londoners, tells us that he who 'will thrust his necke into the yoke, is worthy to be vsed like a iade [poor horse]'.[12] Morocco is, then, no slave. He is assertive and opinionated, unafraid to spit out his coruscating damnations of vice in London. On the frontispiece, it is claimed that the author is one John Dando. Of course, Dando does not exist: the piece was written and published anonymously. The horse facilitates the publication of acerbic comments that may have landed a named author in serious trouble in the litigation-swamped era of Shakespeare's London. Morocco's main attack is on what we would now call 'slum landlords' – men who accumulate money by renting out poor accommodation to undesirable tenants. It is my view that the author uses Morocco not just to criticize outwardly law-abiding but inwardly corrupt landlords, but to criticize particularly their false professions of religious devotion. False, Anglican-like social and moral rectitude is attacked by Morocco, as it would be attacked by Sewell in *Black Beauty*.

In the pamphlet, Morocco's fictional, talking counterpart attacks rogues ranging from dishonest merchants and tradesmen to beggars and disease-infested prostitutes. In a rather modern way, though, Morocco presents the low-life prostitutes – real-life versions of Shakespeare's Doll-Tearsheet – not exactly as victims of vice but rather as unfortunate participants in a wider social malaise. London in the 1590s is corrupt, asserts this self-appointed equine commentator: the main cause of the corruption is the greed of landlords. With aggressive, alliterate spite Morocco declares that 'the couetous landlord is the caterpillar of the common-wealth' (*Maroccus Extaticus*, sig. C2v). So, a landlord who seeks to earn money through renting out properties is like a destructive insect, a cancer within society as a whole. He goes on to lament the alleged fearlessness of the multi-property-owning classes. The landlord:

> Neither feares God nor the deuill, nor so he maye racke it out [charge a tenant excessively], cares not what Tenant he receieues ... hee sits warme at home, and sets downe his accounts, and saies to himself, my houses goe nowe but for twentie poundes by the yeere. Ile make them all baudie houses, and they will yield mee twice as much
>
> (*Maroccus Extaticus*, sigs C2v–3r).

In short, the landlord fears no deity or demon, has a cosy home and doesn't care who resides in his other properties. If the fearless landlord can make more money by allowing brothels to be established in his properties then he will do so, despite its impact of such vice on metropolitan society. Implicitly, Morocco's comment attacks the authorities of London because they are unable or unwilling to combat the abuses perpetuated by the moneyed landlords. Also, if the landlord does not fear God or the Devil, then, again implicitly, established religion is failing because sinners are not being made to fear the eternal consequences of their sins. As the only legal church in England was the episcopal Church of England, then the horse may be seen to be attacking that hierarchy-enforced mode of theological responsibility for England's collective conscience. To understand the full venom of Morocco's attack on the way that landlords allow vice to flourish, we need to return to the very start of the duologue. There, a cheery Banks finds his horse in a downbeat mood and, light-heartedly, asks him 'whose mare is dead that you are thus melancholy' (*Maroccus Extaticus*, sig. B1r). Banks assumes that the lusty Morocco is pining for some female horse (the fact that the real horse was apparently a gelding is passed over in this fantasy-enshrined text). Morocco ignores the insinuation, relates a few anecdotes about troubled marriages and then states, seriously, that he has been 'brought vp' to be 'an vnderstanding horse' (*Maroccus Extaticus*, sig. B1v). So, right from the beginning of the interview, Morocco constructs himself as a sober commentator on current affairs, a cerebral horse who has the capacity to analyse society as a whole – he is not some lusty jade who seeks pleasure.

Morocco cares about unlucky members of society, even imagining a typographical impoverished person called 'Nicol Neuerthriue' (*Maroccus Extaticus*, sig. C3v). Nicol will never thrive because the lower sorts are manipulated ruthlessly by landlords, Morocco continues to insist. His most venomous portrait of a typically malign landlord appears towards the end of the short pamphlet. Here, Morocco again rants about the 'vnreasonable rent' charged by landlords and their desire to overlook 'all the roguerie committed in his houses' (*Maroccus Extaticus*, sig. C4r). But now, in the same exposition and on the same page of the pamphlet, Morocco goes on to make a new charge: these landlords not only profess to be religious but ostentatiously participate in displays of vacuous religious devotion. The horse, continuing to use alliteration that conveys disdain, stresses further his disgust for a typical landlord who is castigated as a 'filthie felow'. This unsavoury individual, despite his covetousness nature, will 'sit at his doore on a sonday in the high street and my mistres his wife by him'. With his silent (embarrassed or supportive?) wife by his side, the landlord will 'forsooth talke so saint-like of the sermon that day, and what a good peece of worke the young man made, and what a goodly gift of utterance he had'. Keen to be seen to support the Church of England, the established church, the landlord loudly commends its officers. Of course, however talented the clergyman is, he won't receive any financial assistance from the landlord: 'not the value of a pound of beefe wil a [he] giue him, were his gift of vtterance comparable to S[aint] Augustines eloquence'. It is significant, I think, that the landlord praises only the efficacy of the oratorical, presentational skills of the clergyman. The landlord is, tellingly, failing to do what Protestant theologians of the Renaissance urged worshippers to do: to engage with the substance of the religious discourse delivered at services. He is anxious to be seen to be at once servile and obsequious to the clergyman and simultaneously elevated enough socially to feel able to comment critically if superficially on the performance. But he fails to *think* about the details and substance of the Christianity preached.

The landlord goes to church to be seen, and is keen to be seen as someone who respects and lauds the clergy. His focus on the performance of a churchman places an emphasis on the clergy and by extension on the importance of an earth-based church that enthusiastic Protestants sought to limit.

Unarguably, the talkative Morocco – or, rather, the writer of the understandably anonymous pamphlet – betrays his dubiousness about those who go to church services to be seen. There is no inherent merit in churchgoing, Morocco seems to suggest. This, I feel, is a very Protestant, very sixteenth-century scepticism. One characteristic of the complicated phenomenon of the English Reformation was a visceral cynicism about the merits of gaudy churches and showy religious display. Such alleged gaudiness and showiness, once the preserve of Romanism, was retained by the Anglican church. Puritans, those who felt the Reformation had not gone far enough, were dismayed by the failure of England to establish a more private culture of religious devotion.[13] It is not unreasonable to link the fictional landlord's enthusiasm for public declarations of his church-based worship with the supposedly superficial, Papist-like charades that so enraged enthusiasts for non-established, lower types of Protestantism. The churchgoing that the stereotypical landlord revels in is useless because it has no moral impact on him nor any meaningful impact on the London that he lives off. His sort of public worship is as empty as a shrine or a statue or a crucifix. Ultimately, Morocco at the very least articulates a scepticism about churchgoing that Anna Sewell would betray in her subsequent construction of a talkative horse.

The mill horse: virulent propaganda spoken by a horse

On the title page of *Maroccus Extaticus*, prospective purchasers of the pamphlet are assured that the horse will offer a mere 'merry Dialogue'. Instead, of course, readers of the text itself are subjected to acerbic rants from a Morocco who is not at all 'merry'. A title-page of a pamphlet of 1645 similarly promises to be innocuous, but instead delivers virulent propaganda of a hugely unsubtle nature, in a tone that jars greatly with the title-page's promise of 'harmlesse Mirth'.[14] Written anonymously at the height of the Civil War period, *A Dialogve Betwixt a Horse of Warre, and a Mill-Horse* appropriates the trope of the talking horse and exploits it for narrow political and sectarian purposes. As the title suggests, the short pamphlet dramatises in rhyming couplets a conversation between two enemies: an arrogant cavalier horse and a humble mill horse. Simply, the cavalier horse represents the Charles I, Royalist, Anglican side of the conflict; the mill horse represents the Parliamentarian, low church, anti-Laudian and anti-Catholic side. As well as disingenuously promising 'harmlesse mirth', the title page also fails to declare the anonymous pamphleteer's propagandist intentions. It is suggested that the dialogue inside will persuade the reader that 'an humble and painfull life, is preferred above all the Noyse, the Tumults, and Trophies of the Warre'. The reader may then anticipate a sort of paean to a pastoral, retired existence, a quiet, contented articulation of a preference for the quiet life – or maybe even a pacifist, anti-war discourse. Such discourse does not materialise in the pamphlet at all – the mill horse asserts no pacifism but, rather, vociferous criticism of Charles I's supporters.

We see the mill horse before we hear him, on the woodcut illustration on the title page. As with many Civil War pamphlets, the woodcut is crude but full of semiotic resonance. In the illustration, the mill horse's body language – in the superficially bizarre genre of equine autobiography it is legitimate to read an illustrated horse's body language – does suggest a desire for quietness and humility. To cite a very basic structuralist point, humility means nothing unless it is compared with its opposite – arrogance. The mill horse is only humble in contradistinction to the haughtiness of the cavalier horse. The mill horse has a bowed head and is somewhat weighed down by the flour sack that he carries dutifully: dedicated to work and service, the mill horse is as much an ancestor of Orwell's Boxer as he is of Sewell's Black Beauty. Despite its simplicity, the woodcut is effective in manipulating the viewer: because of the woodcutter's perspective control, the cavalier horse is nearer to us than the mill horse, so the cavalier horse simply appears to be larger and more 'full' than the mill horse. The cavalier horse's head is held disdainfully high: he literally looks down on the mill horse; in class terms, the cavalier horse is the rich, gilded beneficiary of Royalist extravagance whereas the mill horse is the salt-of-the-earth labourer. The cavalier horse actually seems to be laughing at the patient, meek mill horse. Not surprisingly, though, we soon hear a conversation where the sensible, instinctive religion of the mill horse exposes the vainglorious, ultimately self-defeating posturing of the cavalier horse. The obfuscatory, deliberately perplexing dishonesties of the title-page are forgotten as we hear the dialogue. There it becomes apparent very quickly that the pamphleteer is ventriloquising his dedication to the Parliamentary cause through the mill horse. The mill horse, despite the woodcut's iconography of humility and acceptance, proves to be as acerbic as Morocco. And, in a time of national crisis, is even more pointed and urgent about the target of his vitriol: rich, pampered jades like the cavalier horse – in other words, all supporters of Charles I and all self-serving political and religious hierarchies.

The cavalier horse is constructed as an embodiment of a Charles I supporter. He is demonised as a crass, selfish, haughty, rich scoundrel. The mill horse has little need to abuse the cavalier horse directly: the Royalist beast makes his own egoism clear. He cares little for others:

> And with the simple clowne [poor person] I do say still
> If I do well I care not who doth ill,
> For with the Cavalliers I keep one course,
> And have no more Religion than a Horse

> (*A Dialogve*, sigs A2v–3r).

Speaking callously and selfishly, the cavalier horse states bluntly that he does not care for any poor man. He knows to stick with the Royalists because that is the lucrative thing for him to do. The use of the word 'course' may allude to the Stuart kings' enthusiasm for horse racing at Hyde Park and Newmarket, an activity seen by Puritans as extravagant, sinful and wasteful.[15] The nervous, satiric energy of the pamphlet is encapsulated by the uncomfortable, merely assonant rhyming of 'course' and 'Horse'. The jarring half-rhyme conveys an awkwardness that undermines the stridency of the Royalist horse's self-centred sense of certainly. Ungainly as the cavalier horse's poetic discourse is, the writer's satiric point is clear: Royalists are selfish and ungodly, and have the same devotion to God as horses – i.e., none.

The *Dialogve* is a crucial piece of cultural history for many reasons. One of these many reasons is its allusion to the emerging culture of the propagandist newspaper – a phenomenon unheard of before the tight censorship laws of the late-Tudor and early-Stuart administrations broke down in the early 1640s. Significantly, the cavalier horse asserts that he never heeds reported stories: he does not want to hear about cavalier losses – in other words, he does not want to face up to the fact that the King is on the losing side of these upheavals. With language that is at once aggressive and scornful, the cavalier horse rejects any suggestion that he should heed military and political reports:

> Leave tales, there are too many tales already,
> That weekly flye with more lies without faile
> Then there be haires within a horses taile;
> And if the writers angry be I wish,
> You would the Cavalliers horse arse both kisse,
> Not as the Miller thy back doth kisse with whip,
> But as a Lover doth his Mistresse lip;
> For know the Cavalliers brave warlick horse
> Scornes vulgar Jades, and bids them kisse his arse
>
> (*A Dialogve*, sig. A3v).

The cavalier horse witlessly confirms a range of the charges made against Cavaliers by the radically Protestant Parliamentarians: they fail to heed the truths of earthly news, they use vulgar language which is often allusive to loose sexuality and they scorn all those 'below' them on the economic chain. Writers of newspapers are to be derided: the suggestion that the mill horse and the writers of news should kiss the rump of the cavalier horse is followed by the suggestion that all poor jades should do likewise. This attitude towards the poor is conveyed in language that alludes to sodomitical dominance. The mill horse is, the cavalier horse suggests snidely, effectively buggered by the Miller who uses the whip on him to assert his dominance and puissance.[16] This is sexualised because it is compared to the normative eroticism of two heterosexual lovers. The decadent message asserted by the cavalier horse is that while impoverished sots like the mill horse are symbolically screwed by their masters the elitist cavaliers demand, albeit rhetorically, that those lower than them express their humility through revolting sexual acts of submission. Put simply, the cavalier horse cares not for truth nor for people: Royalism, then, is a mentality that is defined by callous disregard for others. It is an attitude that is countered triumphantly by the morally righteous mill horse.

The mill horse asserts a humble, patient devotion to duty that uncannily anticipates the dedication to work that Black Beauty argues for in Sewell's novel. The cavalier horse can mock all he wants, but salt-of-the-earth workers will get on with their work:

> And if a horse may shew his good intent,
> Some Asses raile thus at the Parliament.
> Scorn is a burthen laid on good men still,
> Which they must beare, as I do Sackes to Mill
>
> (A Dialogve, sig. A3v).

The straightforward fullness of the mill horse's rhymes contrast with the occasional jarring awkwardness of the cavalier horse's half-rhymes. The mill horse's attitude towards work is as simple and as effective as his largely monosyllabic mode of speaking. The Parliamentarian is configured as a worker, someone who builds productively, ignoring the jeering scorn of the elitists who consider themselves to be too privileged for work. Getting on with the job, the righteous opponent of the king will carry scorn wilfully, just as the mill horse carries sacks: this is a strikingly Christian image of conscientiousness, obedience and indifference to the caterwauling mockery of non-believers. The mill horse goes on to hyperbolically lambast Cavalier decadence and the political consequences of having an England run by a selfish, work-shy elite:

> Besides I heare your Cavaliers doe still,
> Drinke sacke [wine] like water that runs from the Mill;
> We heare of Irish Rebels coming over,
> Which was a plot that I dare not discover [reveal].
> And that the malignant Army of the king,
> Into this Land blinde Popery would bring
>
> (A Dialogve, sig. A4r).

Here, a range of serious charges are made against the King and his supporters. The mill horse's disdain for excessive alcohol consumption anticipates Anna Sewell's depiction of the ruinous effects of drink in Black Beauty. Drinking is irresponsible: if the ruling classes succumb to alcohol-sodden hedonism, then atrocious things can happen – Irish men could even invade England in a grotesque, topsy-turvy parody of traditional English dominance over Ireland. When the mill horse states that he dare not reveal the Irish plot, he is, I think, mocking the cavalier horse who has stated previously that he does not want to hear bad news: the mill horse will not reveal the Irish threat lest the sensitive cavalier horse gets perturbed. Most worryingly of all, the on-the-run Charles I could return to power if an Irish plot is successful – and Catholicism would return to establish Romanist hegemony in England once more. Crucially, the mill horse conflates Royalism with Irishness and Anglicanism with Catholicism. The Cavalier phenomenon is a foreign one, an alien aberration in a Protestant England. For the low church, non-conformist Protestant mill horse, all hierarchical, ritual-based religions are one. At the *Dialogve's* conclusion, the mill horse discards his humble mode of discourse, mocking the cavalier horse for belonging to a cowardly army. The Cavaliers, those who 'seek the blood of Protestants to spill' are 'undone'. They – now totally demonised as non-Protestant, despite their Anglican heritage – are serviced by yellow-bellied horses:

> And yet the Cavalliers horse as I heare
> At Kenton field beshit themselves for feare.
> And the Cavalliers being kill'd, they ran about
> The field to seek another master out
>
> (*A Dialogve*, sig. A4r).

The scatological virulence of the mill horse at this point echoes quite consciously the anal fixation betrayed by the cavalier horse previously. The mill horse's lapse into vulgarity is necessary for him because it affords him an opportunity to make a crucial sociological observation. The cavalier horse self-fashions himself as someone who transcends earthly and heavenly servitude: he is his own egocentric unit, caring for nobody. But when cavalier horses (and their riders – horse and rider are pointedly amalgamated by the mill horse) are on the losing side they lose control of their bowels and flee, looking for 'another master'. In other words, the Cavaliers are, ultimately, more desirous of subjugation than the Roundheads. In fact, with his self-assured dedication to duty, the mill horse is more self-contained and sturdy than any cavalier horse. Controlled, orderly, disdaining alcohol and quietly assured about his own low-Protestant righteousness, he is, surely, an uncannily relevant literary ancestor of Black Beauty.

Black Beauty's good equine intentions

Quakerism links Anna Sewell directly to the time of the English Civil Wars. The origin of the Society of Friends lies in the mushrooming of radical Christian sects during the administrative discombobulation of England between

1642 and 1660.[17] Sewell herself gave up the Quakerism on which she had been raised when she was eighteen (*ODNB*), but she retained the movement's basic mode of self-sufficient moral ethics. Sewell's family had a long involvement in the radical tradition: the writer's biographer, Susan Chitty, points out that Quakers called Sewell were jailed in the late 1650s.[18] Anna Sewell is a human descendent of Quaker pamphleteers of the Civil War period as her fictional horse is a descendent of the mill horse. Quakerism was much more respectable (and moneyed) in the 1870s than in the period of Cromwell, but the Society of Friends remained (and remains) a much-misunderstood, minority activity. The opinions espoused by the eponymous Black Beauty are Quaker opinions: the horse is dutiful, laments the abuse of alcohol, is a pacifist and – most significantly, I insist – sceptical about Sunday religious services. So, Black Beauty is a mouthpiece for a sectarian view of society as were Morocco and (more obviously) the mill horse of centuries before. Before I argue for the polemical edge of Black Beauty's autobiography, I must underline the major difference between Sewell's work and the work of the early modern creators of talking horses: *Black Beauty* is, to an extant, a piece of literature that is actually *about* horses. Morocco, the cavalier horse and the mill horse are mouthpieces for the opinions of their pamphlet's authors, as is Black Beauty – but Sewell was partially motivated by a passionate urge to improve equitation and the general treatment of horses by their human handlers. The writers of *Maroccus Extaticus* and *A Dialogve* had no interest in animal cruelty: they had other issues to focus exclusively on. Sewell has been the subject of almost hagiographic praise in this regard. Sewell's niece (the childless Sewell never married) wrote many years after her aunt's death that 'the sight of cruelty to animals ... roused her indignation, almost to fury, and wherever she was, or whoever she had to face, she would stop and scathe the culprits with burning words'.[19] Here, Sewell is constructed as a fearless prototype of the animal rights activist, before such activism was seen as a way of life for many in later years. This is relevant here because this putative energy in Sewell's personal life can be linked easily with the satiric energy directed against animal abuse in Sewell's novel. The power of Sewell's sarcasm about the unnecessary brutality used by some horse trainers has been undervalued, even by those few scholars who read the novel in a fully critical way. Early in his autobiography, when talking about his early life, Black Beauty tells us about the horrors a horse experiences during breaking:

> When his harness is once on, he may neither jump for joy nor lie down for weariness. So you see this breaking in is a great thing.[20]

Disparagingly, Gina M. Dorré – who is otherwise sensitive to Sewell's social critique – cites this passage as being exemplary of 'the text's ungainly form and strained didacticism'.[21] This is unfair, because it ignores the generic specificity and innovation of the 'translated from the equine' novel.[22] I'm not even sure that the passage is, as Dorré claims, ironic. Dorré assumes that the word 'great' is ironic or sarcastic. But I take 'great' here to mean significant, weighty. Broken horses go through a brutal, substantial, 'great' hardship. Sewell's sarcastic yet humorous denigration of human lack of consideration for horses becomes more pronounced later in the novel. With vituperation that Morocco would be proud of, Black Beauty almost misanthropically damns human laziness:

> These people never think of getting out to walk a steep hill. Oh no, they have paid to ride, and ride they will! The horse? Oh, he's used to it! What were horses made for, if not to drag people uphill? Walk! A good joke indeed!
>
> (Sewell, p. 104).

Here, Sewell's mastery of free indirect speech – where the author impersonates a horse impersonating and caricaturing the thoughts of callous people – surely is sophisticated in a way that Dorré does not acknowledge. So, *Black Beauty* is undoubtedly *about* horses to an extent, but other controversies matter to the horse – and to Sewell.

On the home page of the British Society of Friends, it is stressed that Quakerism differs from mainstream Christianity:

> Quakers share a way of life rather than a set of beliefs. Quakers seek to experience God directly, within ourselves and in our relationships with others and the world around us. We meet together for silent worship in local meetings which are open to all.[23]

Quakerism, with its effective removal of any sort of conventional clergy and its focus on community, may then be seen as a sort of ultimate low-church Protestantism. Quakers are a disparate bunch of people, but you will rarely find a Friend who craves physical combat, who drinks, or who orders people to attend ritualistic, priest-dominated religious services on Sundays or on any other days. Like a good Quaker, Black Beauty is pacifistic and abstemious by instinct and by rearing. He was taught by his mother to accept work patiently – as the mill horse would have been taught by its mother. 'Grow up gentle and good', she tells her son. 'Do your work with a good will' and 'never kick or bite' (Sewell, p. 4). This is a clear Protestant work ethic but it is also a rallying cry for a pacifism that leads on to a more serious satiric thrust. Black Beauty tells us about a conversation with an old retired horse called Captain. This now-elderly beast had fought in the Crimean War. Black Beauty, young and untutored, asks what the war was about. The Captain doesn't know: 'that is more than a horse can understand, but the enemy must have been awfully wicked people, if it was right to go all that way over the sea on purpose to kill them' (Sewell, p. 129). The key word is 'if'. For a pacifist, there is no 'if'. War is wrong. The satiric point is that the war is fought by horses – and men – who do not know what they are fighting for. War is a waste, as is hunting with horses, which Sewell derides with a mocking of 'men [who] are so fond of this sport' that anticipates the famous Oscar Wilde aphorism about the unspeakable chasing after the inedible (Sewell, p. 7). Black Beauty also sees the destructiveness of alcohol: this is a very low church focus because, to this day, extreme Protestants (Baptists, Free Presbyterians, Methodists, Quakers) campaign against alcohol abuse more vocally than Anglicans or Catholics. The mill horse condemns the Cavaliers for ruinously drinking excessive sack. Black Beauty likewise notes the catastrophic effects of drink on one Reuben Smith, who falls off the wagon occasionally, becoming 'a disgrace to himself, his wife and a nuisance to all' (Sewell, p. 90). Drinking does not just damage the liver – it is a menace that threatens all of society, the horse asserts. The social commentary here is so obvious that explication is scarcely necessary. But it is in a cheeky scepticism about Sunday churchgoing that Sewell, unconsciously but instructively, brings us back full-circle to Morocco and the sixteenth-century origins of radical English Protestantism.

Conclusion: subjectivity and instinctive spirituality

Morocco was lacerating in his contempt for a landlord who went to church in order to pontificate about his piety. In *Black Beauty*, the opinionated horse notes with disapproval a husband who wants the horse to be used to ferry his wife to church every Sunday. Jerry, one of Black Beauty's better masters, refuses the work, despite losing out financially. He refuses on religious grounds: his simple monosyllables recall the simple, dogmatic moral rectitude of the mill horse:

> I can't give up my Sundays, sir, indeed I can't. I read that God made man, and He made horses and as soon as He had made them, He made a day of rest and bade that all should rest one day in seven
>
> (Sewell, p. 137).

Mrs Briggs does not need the horse to go to church – she is a woman who also wastes time and money 'shopping for hours, or making calls' (Sewell, p. 137). The horse is simply a tool of ostentation, a display of status. Her ambition is merely to be seen to arrive pompously at church with a horse-drawn carriage. It is an empty ritual, a conspicuous consumption of horse power, one that is as futile as it is pointless. Figuratively speaking, the Briggs family are descendents of the posturing landlord and his wife from *Maroccus Extaticus*. By questioning the motives of men and women who attend Sunday services, the writers of both pamphlets are calling into question the validity or purpose of institutionalised, high church Christianity as a whole. For a 1590s satirist and for a nineteenth-century woman, these suggestions are dangerous and revolutionary. They are opinions that needed the fantastic, superficially bizarre conceit of talking horses to be delivered. We don't read autobiographies to follow the chronological progress of the factual developments in a person's life. We read autobiographies, I'm sure, to understand the mentalities and the perspectives and subjectivities of the writer. The three texts that I have discussed here mimic autobiographies because they all contain to some degree the illusion of the 'development of personality' that Philippe Lejeune considered necessary for any 'autobiography'.[24] The 'personalities' of the ultra-Protestant horses created by Sewell and her predecessors are shaped by their specific historical circumstances. Autobiography, as Linda Anderson has reminded us, is 'always a complex matter involving both the subject's discursive position *and* material/historical position'.[25] Morocco railed against landlords, the mill horse lambasted Cavaliers and Black Beauty condemns drunks, hunters, warmongers and wasteful women. All three horses narrate their autobiographies in a way that cunningly, ingeniously protects the authors of these works. Although divided by 'material/historical location', each piece conveys a 'good intent' that is characteristic of a strident sense of Protestant self. And no genre of writing is better at constructing a sense of self than autobiography – whether or not it is translated from equine.

Notes

* For help with this chapter and with the conference paper on which it is based, I thank Richard Bradford, Katherine Byrne, Maria Campbell, Graham Gargett, Jan Jedrzejewski, James Ward and Rachel Willie.

1. Adrienne E. Gavin, 'Anna Sewell', *Oxford Dictionary of National Biography*, online edition. 2004 (www.oxforddnb.com), accessed 22 July 2008.

2. 'First edition sells for £33,000', BBC News, 2006 (http://news.bbc.co.uk/1/hi/ england/norfolk/5053402.stm), accessed 22 July 2008.

3. Ricky Jay, *Learned Pigs and Fireproof Women: a History of Unique, Eccentric and Amazing Entertainers* (London: Robert Hale, 1987), p. 105.

4. Samuel Holland, *Don Zara Del Fogo: a Mock-Romance* (London, 1656; Wing H2437), sig. I1v.

5. S. H. Atkins, 'Mr. Banks and His Horse', *Notes and Queries*, 167 (1934), pp. 39–44; J. O. Halliwell-Phillips, *Memoranda on 'Love's Labour's Lost', 'King John', 'Othello' and on 'Romeo and Juliet'* (London: James Adlard, 1879), pp. 21–57. Other useful pieces include a chapter on 'The Dancing Horse' in Jan Bondeson, *The Feejee Mermaid and Other Essays in Natural and Unnatural History* (Ithaca: Cornell University Press, 1999), pp. 1–18; Emma Phipson, *The Animal Lore of Shakespeare's Time* (London: Kegan Paul, Trench and Co., 1883), pp. 108–11; and Raymond Toole Stott, ed., *Circus and Allied Acts: a World Bibliography*, 5 vols (Derby: Harpur, 1958-92), I, pp. 30–1.

6. The obscure Banks is known to antiquarians simply because of his owner-ship/training of Morocco. The *ODNB* piece on Banks focuses more on the horse than on Banks himself. Eva Griffith, 'William Banks', *Oxford Dictionary of National Biography*, online edition. 2004 (www.oxforddnb.com), accessed 22 July 2008.

7. John Marston, *Iacke Drums Enter-tainment* (London, 1601; STC 7243), sig. B3r.

8. William Shakespeare, *A Pleasant Conceited Comedie Called Loues Labors Lost* (London, 1598; STC 22294), sig. B2v. A lengthy footnote to the allusion is provided in Horace Howard Furness, ed., *A New Variorum Edition of 'Love's Labour's Lost'* (Philadelphia: J. B. Lippincott, 1904), p. 45.

9. Thomas Bastard, *Chrestoleros: Seuen Bookes of Epigrames* (London, 1598; STC 1559), p. 62.

10. Richard Braithwait, *A Strappado for the Diuell: Epigrams and Satyres Alluding to the Time* (London, 1615; STC 3588), p. 159.

11. N. Zwager, *Ben Jonson's London* (Amsterdam: Swets and Zeitlinger, 1926), p. 49; Ruth Manning-Sanders, *The English Circus* (London: Werner Laurie, 1952), p. 23.

12. *Maroccus Extaticus, or Bankes Bay Horse in a Trance* (London: 1595; STC 6225), sig. B3v. A ballad about Morocco, *A Ballad Shewinge the Strange Qualities of a Yonge Nagge Called 'Morocco'*, was registered by Edward White at the Stationers' Company in November 1595 – a month before the registration of *Maroccus Extaticus* – but it is lost. See Edward Arber, ed., *A Transcript of the Registers of the Company of the Stationers of London*, 5 vols (Birmingham: Privately Published, 1875–94), III, p. 5.

13. A very precise and, I feel, very useful definition of early British Puritanism can be found in Pauline Croft, *King James* (Basingstoke: Palgrave, 2003), pp. 155–7

14. *A Dialogve Betwixt a Horse of Warre, and a Mill-Horse* (London: 1645; Wing D1347).

15. On Stuart-supported racing at Hyde Park and at Newmarket, see Elspeth Graham, 'Reading, Writing, and Riding Horses in Early Modern England: James Shirley's *Hyde Park* (1632) and Gervase Markham's *Cavelarice* (1607)', in Erica Fudge, ed., *Renaissance Animals: Of Animals, Humans, and Other Wonderful Creatures* (Urbana and Chicago: University of Illinois Press, 2004), pp. 116–37, especially pp. 118–24.

16. On the early modern symbolic association between horses and transgressive human sexuality, see Bruce Boehrer, 'Shakespeare and the Social Devaluation of the Horse', in Karen Raber and Treva J. Tucker, eds, *The Culture of the Horse: Status, Discipline, and Identity in the Early Modern World* (Basingstoke: Palgrave, 2005), pp. 91–111, especially pp. 102–4.

17. For a brief overview of the rise of Civil War and Protectorate-era sects, see Jim Daems, *Seventeenth-Century Literature and Culture* (London: Continuum, 2006), pp. 30–3.

18. Susan Chitty, *Anna Sewell: The Woman Who Wrote 'Black Beauty'* (Stroud: Tempus, 2007), p. 13.

19. Anna Sewell and Margaret Sewell, *Black Beauty: An Autobiography of a Horse by Anna Sewell, with Reflections of Anna Sewell by Margaret Sewell* (London: Harrap, 1938), p. 3.

20. Anna Sewell, *Black Beauty*, ed. by Peter Hollindale (Oxford: Oxford University Press, 1992), p. 9. All further quotations from the novel are taken from this edition.

21. Gina M. Dorré, *Victorian Fiction and the Cult of the Horse* (London: Ashgate, 2006), p. 109.
22. Lopa Prusty is much more appreciative of Sewell's aesthetic merits, praising the writer for her 'delight in words and written form'. Lopa Prusty, 'Anna Sewell', in Meena Khorana, ed., *Dictionary of Literary Biography, 163: British Children's Writers, 1800–1800* (Detroit: Gale, 1996), pp. 259–66, especially p. 263.
23. www.quaker.org.uk, accessed 14 August 2008.
24. Philippe Lejeune, 'The Autobiographical Contract', in Tzvetan Todorov, ed., *French Literary Theory Today* (Cambridge: Cambridge University Press, 1982), pp. 192–222, especially p. 193.
25. Linda Anderson, *Autobiography* (London: Routledge, 2001), p. 104.

9
Literary Biography: The Elephant in the Academic Sitting Room

Richard Bradford

Of all the various professions and recreations undertaken by figures in recent, recorded history, literary writing seems to exercise the most compulsive fascination for biographers. Consult reference works on every significant author in English from Chaucer onwards and you will encounter someone's 'Life' of them. The attractions for literary biographers are obvious. Poems, plays and novels function in two dichotomous ways: magnetically, as stories or projections of a particularly intriguing state of mind; and also duplicitously, given that they have little, if anything, to do with truth and unalloyed facts. As a consequence we feel, sometimes despite ourselves, compelled to locate something real and trustworthy behind the fabric of effects. We do so because the questions posed and left unanswered by our encounters with literature can we suspect be clarified if not satisfactorily answered by a clearer perception of the figure behind the work.

Literary biography has a long and fairly respectable history. It began, in English, with Izaack Walton's lives of his near contemporaries of the late 16th and 17th centuries, notably John Donne (1641), George Herbert (1670) and Richard Hooker (1665). Soon afterwards Aubrey's *Brief Lives* involved a raucous assembly of unattributable facts, first and second hand gossip and pure speculation disguised as record and chronicle; literary writers, famous and nondescript featured. The genre came of age in the 18th century, its best-known practitioner being Samuel Johnson whose *Lives of the English Poets* (1779–81) set the standard for combining a picture of the writer's background and circumstances with an evaluation of their work. Johnson did not patronise the reader by tracing explanatory links between his portraits of these figures and the character of their writing but he assembled his evidence with the ruthless calculation of a barrister: the parallels and causes were self-evident. The acknowledged classic of the period was the life of Johnson himself, assembled with hound-like acuity and attention to detail by James Boswell, his companion. Boswell's *The Life of Samuel Johnson* (1791) is a magnificent and curious piece of work and can be seen as contributing significantly to the skewed, uncertain status thereafter of literary biography.

Few subsequent commentators have questioned the probity and accuracy of Boswell's account, and here we encounter a problem. Boswell's perspective was unique. He was himself a writer and had direct unhindered access to his subject's moods, habits and predispositions. Boswell, a gifted literary critic, did not need to rely upon a fabric of records and his own speculations to link the man with his work; his knowledge of both was intimate and comprehensive. Rarely can literary biographers make claims upon such opportunities, and indeed the only similar, and controversial, literary biography to be produced within a century of Boswell's work was borne out of almost identical circumstances, Elizabeth Gaskell's life of her friend Charlotte Brontë (1857). It is, by today's standards, a work of cautious discretion but Gaskell's albeit euphemistic, respectful account of Bronte's private world – involving on some occasions 'men' – unsettled reviewers and self-appointed representatives of the reading public. They were affronted, one suspects, less by the nature of Gaskell's disclosures, which could only have shocked those who were blind to the human condition, than by the unnerving spectacle of a literary artist being brought unsparingly and unapologetically to life.

Literary biography endured during the 19th century mainly because most if its subjects were long dead, safely protected both by the sacred autonomy of their work and the fact that recorded details of their lives and circumstances were unlikely to include anything remotely embarrassing. At one end of the spectrum we have Godwin's four-volume *Life of Geoffrey Chaucer* (1804) a gargantuan, doorstop size account of a man about whom hardly anything was known. In his preface Godwin proclaims that 'it is undoubtedly pleasing, in a subject which in many particulars is involved in obscurity, to be able to seize some points which are free from the shadow of doubt' (p.xxi). Relief, if not exultation, informs this statement which refers to two facts, the dates of Chaucer's birth and death, records of which were, as subsequent scholars would point out, available but manifestly unreliable. Godwin, heroically, attempts to resurrect Chaucer from every scrap of historical and contextual information that might, even remotely, have affected his life. Sometimes among the vast bulk of historical detail a small glimmer of the poet's actual existence appears. His name is recorded among the sixty-two 'scutiferis camere regis' (or esquires of the King's chamber) of 1371–73. He served in the early 1380s as Controller of Customs in London and after his move to Kent was appointed as a Justice for the Commission of peace, himself summoned by the bench as a debtor on two occasions in 1389 and 90. He had defaulted, so the records inform us, of monies due to one Henry Atwood, innkeeper. Details such as this are intriguing mainly for their scarcity. If placed end-to-end as a list of verifiable facts regarding Chaucer's existence they would fill no more than three pages, roughly 0.4 per cent of Godwin's four volumes.

There is a fine line between impression and invention and while Boswell, through his private acquaintance with his subject, could enjoy an abundance of the former Godwin made use of neither. He speculated on what Chaucer might have done or felt but only so far as historically authentic knowledge of the period would allow. The paucity of evidence regarding Chaucer was matched, in the case of John Milton, by a profusion. Had Milton been notable only as a poet little more would have been known of him than of his sixteenth and seventeenth century peers. But because of his involvement in politics – specifically the Civil War and the Cromwellian Protectorate – he became the earliest example of a writer whose life and experiences and indeed his opinions were thoroughly chronicled. In this respect he presents us with a useful index to the mutations in the nature of literary biography during the two centuries following his death. Johnson in his 'Life of Milton' pretends to impartiality but the fact that he does not like his subject becomes persistently evident. Johnson bases his study on what was even then a considerable amount of evidence in print on Milton's politics and activities and constructs from this an embodiment of querulous unorthodoxy, an image he buttresses with unsympathetic readings of his poems. Johnson's prejudices reflect the mood of his epoch; the Augustan preference for order over contingency did not as a rule permit for radicalism. By the same token the Romantics treated Milton as their glorious antecedent. De Quincey's *Life of Milton* (1838) and *On Milton* (1839) are the only book-length studies of the man by one of the first or second generation of Romantics, but Shelley, Coleridge, Wordsworth and Blake reconstruct in their writings an image of Milton based upon somewhat biased readings of his work. The Romantics were affiliated to the Enlightenment ethos of unorthodox, often revolutionary thinking (albeit with varying degrees of sincerity and commitment) and they elected Milton as the precursor of their intellectual condition: he was a rebel in that he allied himself with a cause which effectively ended monarchical totalitarianism as a form of government and he had produced an epic poem which, as they interpreted it, challenged the Old Testament myth upon which Christianity was based. Were they disclosing the real John Milton or allocating to him elements of themselves? This is a question which attends the writing of literary biography today, but in the post-Romantic period of the 19th century it was effectively sidelined.

The radical energy that had fuelled Romanticism and inspired the Romantics' veneration of Milton was replaced in the mid-19th century by a less energetic brand of empiricism, one which valued truth and fact above the reprobate impulses that might inform them. David Masson's magisterial biography of Milton bespeaks the contemporaneous mood. His *Life of Milton* is made up of seven lengthy volumes which appeared gradually from 1859 until its completion in 1894. It is a masterpiece of scholarship. All recorded facts, relevant texts and contextual details – or at least those available to Masson – are included. It tells us everything but it says virtually nothing. Controversy, particularly religious controversy, is accounted for in a manner which more than implies that Milton is a no longer relevant historical curiosity. The living Milton who spoke so eloquently to Blake, Shelley and De Quincey has been displaced in Masson by an assembly of dusty evidence.

The Victorian tendency to present that life as it ought to be rather than as it is informs this reluctance to search for the living presence behind the books: dry documentation seemed safer than experience. John Forster's life of Charles Dickens testifies to this. Forster was Dickens's contemporary and while not a particularly close acquaintance was part of the same social and literary circuit. He knew of Dickens's estrangement from his wife, of his mistress Ellen Ternon, his manic depressive temperament and his bouts of vituperative bitterness and anger. There were no rules on censorship or libel that would have forbidden a muted account of Dickens as he really was – a state that many readers suspected was distributed among some of the more disturbing figures of his novels – but what we get is an exemplar of decency and Christian probity, the equivalent of presenting Byron as a version of Gerard Manley Hopkins.

Lytton Strachey's *Eminent Victorians* (1918), though including only a small number of literary writers, broke away from Victorian convention in that Strachey asked questions about the mental condition and even the more visceral impulses that lay behind verifiable facts. Shortly after its publication one of the most peculiar and fascinating exercises in literary biography was begun and while there is no evidence that one influenced the other the parallels are, nonetheless, fascinating. Florence Hardy's *The Life of Thomas Hardy* was published in 1933, its nominal author being Hardy's second wife. In truth the book had been written largely by Hardy himself during the 1920s and the original draft is thought to have been completed approximately two years before his death in 1928. It is, then, an autobiography disguised as a biography, an act of calculated incompetence that sheds some light upon the complexities and tensions that surround literary biography, particularly as perceived by its potential subjects. While Florence could hardly be regarded as an entirely impartial witness to her husband's life and achievements she could, simply by not being him, make some claim to having observed rather than experienced these matters. Through her Hardy reconstructs himself as he wishes to be perceived – and it's clear that he is motivated by the fear of some Strachey-inspired scrutineer chasing through documents, and interviews with surviving witnesses toward a portrait of himself that is not entirely inauthentic yet equally not what he would wish for as the enduring monument to his career. As he was aware his writings would live on but readers' perceptions of them would inevitably be biased by their opinions of him. The image of Hardy that emerges from this hybrid of biography, autobiography and fiction is of a man preoccupied almost exclusively with poetry. Even in the 1920s fiction was regarded as a somewhat vulgar latecomer to the literary court while poetry was the genre from which all other literary writing originated, something to be undertaken as a purely artistic endeavour. Hardy, through Florence, presents his career as a novelist almost apologetically. He is honest about his modest background and treats his fiction as a necessity, something which, through its popularity, would guarantee him an income and provide him with the time to pursue his true vocation as a poet. Subsequent researchers would gaze with astonishment upon the vast number of cautiously revised drafts that preceded each of his novels as testaments to the fact that he actually gave more care and attention to the style and trajectory of his fiction than he did to his verse.

Also, Hardy takes great care to disguise any connection between the characters and occurrences of his fiction and what was known, or might subsequently become known, of his life. For example, he censors his account of his meeting with and courtship of Emma Gifford, later to become his first wife, carefully excluding anything that might prompt comparisons between their relationship and that between Stephen Smith and Elfrida Swancourt in *A Pair of Blue Eyes* (1873). In truth the novel was inspired and shaped almost exclusively by Hardy's relationship with Emma. It could, and has, been treated as daring exposure of a society obsessed with class and status – Stephen's humble background causes him to be regarded as the least suitable of Elfrida's suitors – but if it were known that Stephen was a version of his author then, Hardy suspected, admiration might turn to pity or even derision: what embittered Hardy in the real world had caused him to pursue vengeful retribution in a world he created and controlled. It might have been seen as a skilfully executed gesture against an iniquitous society, but hardly one that qualified as high art – or so he feared.

Hardy's self-ghosted account of his life points up a number of issues which confer upon literary biography a popularity and unique status within the broader genre of biographical writing, and also explains its rather precarious classification as a branch of literary criticism. All forms of biography incorporate by necessity the biographer and their subject but the literary version involves a third party, the subject's writing. One might argue that a comparable situation obtains with painters, sculptors, composers, philosophers, even rock stars. They too merit the attention of the biographer and the reader because of things they have produced, but literature is different. There is something in the lyrical speaking presence of a poem, the compelling narrative of a piece of fiction or the magnetic quality of its principal characters that prompts the question: where do they come from? More specifically we are caused to wonder if creations which hold our attention so urgently can be inspired by anything other than private experience, observed or endured. Hardy was determined to obviate such questions and his reasons for doing so are I think self-evident. It was not that he was fearful of his life being opened to public scrutiny; in that respect he, like Florence, is cautiously, selectively honest. What horrified him most of all was the prospect of the disclosure, or even the suspicion, that his work was built upon real people, private experiences, actual events. Even today the exalted status of a work of literary 'art' becomes slightly tarnished by the knowledge that it is not driven by the creative or imaginative spirit of the writer, and is instead borrowed from life.

Examples abound of writers who deny that their work is autobiographical. Kingsley Amis in a 1973 article for the *TLS* called 'Real and Made Up People' states that a few parallels are obvious and hardly worth comment, such as the fact that Jim Dixon of *Lucky Jim* was, like his creator, a young, poorly paid academic in a provincial university. Only one other of his novels 'by common consent my worst … *I Like it Here*' is 'out of laziness or sagging imagination' based upon actual people and events. He adds that 'the writer whose direct experience gives him one satisfactory novel (as opposed to a short or very short story) in fifty years is very lucky'. (*The Amis Collection*, p.3).

One begins to suspect that he protests too much, and the example he gives of how life can rarely provide enough material for fiction is, to say the least, suggestive.

> If in life, his marriage breaks down, he takes off with somebody else, has difficulties with her and with his children and finally returns home, or stays away, he has little hope of writing about that experience and these people and coming through with a novel. (p.3)

This is a candid summary of the life of Kingsley Amis from 1963 to 1973, from which he 'came through' not with 'a novel' but four. He worked hard and quite successfully at obscuring the autobiographical thread that runs through these books, deflecting the truffle-hunter's attention with narratives and scenarios that could only have been invented – in *The Green Man*, for instance, the main character's marital problems are sidelined by visits from God and an agent of Satan. At the same time, in each novel a particular relationship, sometimes an unsteady one, underpins the more prominent themes and plotlines, and this relationship is a version of his own with his second wife, Elizabeth Jane Howard.

In *Lucky Him* (2001) I treat Amis's fiction as one of the most entertaining and thought-provoking autobiographies ever produced. It would have been possible to raise all manner of questions about whether or not the reader should be left to come to his or her own conclusions about the relationship between the life and the work of a writer, but in this biography I did not, because in Amis's case the answers were self-evident. It was not my intention to treat his writings as a kind of diary in code. That, inevitably, would diminish their purely literary value, compromise their deserved status as original and brilliantly crafted contributions to post-war English fiction. Paradoxically, Amis's fears regarding the disclosure of his blend of autobiography and invention were not only unfounded but counter-extensive to his reputation as a writer. As I show, there is a dynamic relationship between what he did, thought, experienced and what he wrote. He did not use his personal world, internal and external, as a substitute for imaginative effort;

quite the contrary. His literary skills were tested and extended in their dealings with the confounding, puzzling panorama of his life. At the same time it is impossible to offer a comprehensive picture of Amis the man, as husband, philanderer, friend, father, jester, son, boozer, agnostic, pseudo-socialist and club-land Tory, without considering the relationship between what we know and that private world in which what he knew was re-examined, remodelled and written.

I think that I succeed in this but one of the more fascinating aspects of my research for the book was my encounter with Eric Jacobs who, five years before, had published the authorised biography of Amis. Jacobs was an investigative journalist who had got to know Amis at their club, The Garrick, and it soon became clear to me why he had been chosen as a modern counterpart to Boswell. He was a clever resourceful man, a scrupulous researcher and persuasive interviewer possessed of an engaging pithy prose style but he had never previously written anything about literature. While he dutifully absorbed himself in his subject's work he remained convinced, with the assistance of Amis himself, that the books had little to do with the life. Jacobs informed me that over the two years he worked on the biography Amis had treated him as his confessor. They might take lunch at The Garrick or meet for drinks at the house in Primrose Hill which Amis shared with his ex-wife Hilly and her husband Lord Kilmarnock. During these exchanges Amis played an ingenious game. He never, according to Jacobs, seemed particularly contrite regarding his behaviour during the 1950s and 60s, when celebrity brought him an apparently endless supply of female admirers, but nor did he appear proud of his exploits. 'He was' Jacobs told me 'commendably honest. We kept more or less to the chronology of his life and he made sure that I knew everything. The list of his ... well, his liaisons, was enormous and he was equally candid regarding his long-term relationships with Hilly and Jane Howard. He certainly made no excuses for himself.' (Interview with Bradford, April 1999.) Did he not, I asked Jacobs, say anything about his work, about how he developed as a writer? 'There was no need to. All that is in the public realm and I'd read the novels.' Amis was blinding his biographer with an abundance of truth. Week by week he would disclose a little more of his career as a serial adulterer, along with superbly authentic profiles of individuals he variously loved, hated, mocked and admired. For Jacobs it was rather like being offered a novel by the likes of Fielding; rollicking, shameless and dispensed in monthly episodes to keep the reader hungry for the next chapter. He can hardly be blamed, therefore, for not paying sufficient attention to the fiction itself; the life seemed far more exciting.

Hardy wrote his own biography, published posthumously, and Amis similarly 'ghosted' his, using Jacobs as his unwitting accomplice. Both pursued the same objective of obscuring the parallels between their lives and their fiction because of their understandable, if slightly misguided, even neurotic, fear that that imagination might appear soiled by actuality.

I will return in due course to the tendentious relationship between the writer, their work and the biographer, but I shall now consider the somewhat nebulous status of literary biography as a relative of literary criticism. By the latter I refer mainly to criticism produced by academics, but it must be said that it is difficult to imagine anything written during the past fifty years about literature that is not in someway influenced by English as a university discipline. Even critics who make their living as journalists, novelists or from some other branch of *belles lettres* have usually, at some stage in their career, felt the effects of academia upon them, even if only as undergraduates.

The history of English studies is well documented and most chroniclers seem to agree that it went through three principal stages. There were the early years when its advocates, such as Saintsbury and Bradley, treated it as much as a respectable hobby as a serious academic discipline, followed by what might be termed the period of anxious maturity when the so-called New Critics of the US and their more disparate British counterparts attempted to graft a methodological framework onto the pursuits of aesthetes and scholars. Finally – and I use the term with resignation, given that aside from internal skirmishes no further cataclysmic change can be envisaged – English was overrun by a horde of interpretive and contextual ideas borrowed mostly from other disciplines and known collectively as Literary or Critical Theory.

The traditionalists – that is, those whose affiliations predate the influx of Theory – and the Theoreticians of various types have over the past forty years or so nurtured a mutual and abiding contempt, but in one respect this is matched by an unspoken consensus. Literary biography is treated by most with what can only be regarded as tolerance: it exists, is indeed sometimes practised by peers and colleagues, but it owes rather too much to the vulgar undisciplined practises and tastes of the book world outside the academy.

No academic has, as yet, prepared a systematic condemnation of literary biography but it has by various means been ostracised from the mainstream. Certainly during the nascent years of 'English' in the university some literary biographies were produced by academics but given that until the 1950s the curriculum closed at around the same time that the Romantics burst onto the scene, they were made up largely of dry scholarly detail; the equivalent of a thousand footnotes to the Collected Works, sewn together as a chronology. George Sherburn's *The Early Career of Alexander Pope* (1934) is a commendable example. Note 'Career': it was about Pope, but almost exclusively about Pope-the-writer, with little attention given to his religious affiliations, relationships with women or diminutive stature. Enterprises such as Sherburn's were tolerated principally because they buttressed the strengthening belief that the literary text should be the predominant subject for academic scrutiny.

Early, influential works by New Critics, such as Brooks's and Penn Warren's *Understanding Poetry*, John Crowe Ransom's 'Criticism Inc.' and W.K. Wimsatt's and M. Beardsley's 'The Intentional Fallacy' (1946) and 'The

Affective Fallacy' (1949), systematically and very effectively dislodge the notion of the author – as someone with actual experiences and perhaps unreliable predilections – from the procedure of literary interpretation. Ransom will not permit of 'Personal registrations' (tears, humour, desire, excitement) on the part of the reader; these are the stuff of the vulgar arts, such as film, where the uneducated so easily suspend disbelief. To read through a poem to the assumed state of mind of the poet indulges a similarly philistine ignorance of art as art. 'Historical Studies', in Ransom's view, tell us about the author and their circumstances but are of no real relevance to the specificity of the poem. Wimsatt and Beardsley in their two essays draw a line between what we might encounter in the literary text and our collateral desire to telescope this into an assumption about real emotional factors that might have influenced the author. In general, the idea that the text allows us access to a living individual and their preoccupations is disallowed. Similarly I.A. Richards of the Cambridge English Faculty argued in *Principles of Literary Criticism* (1924) that while literature might rehearse or reconstruct the emotional tensions that crowd our existence 'the question of belief, or disbelief, never arises' (1966, p.277) by which he means that the issue of authenticity or of whether the text is an accurate index to the author's mental condition is irrelevant.

William Empson's *Seven Types of Ambiguity* (1930) and Cleanth Brooks's *The Well Wrought Urn* (1947) consider, respectively, ambiguity and paradox as inherent, even definitive characteristics of poetry. They also, however, make it clear that while in non-literary exchange these effects are generally the result and cause of uncertainty, fraud, deliberate falsification, misapprehension or indecision, in literature they are purely aesthetic and stylistic devices, unincriminated by the cause and effect relations of the actual world. Though not necessarily intended as such both books contributed significantly to the working maxim in academic criticism that while the author exists, his/her preoccupations and experiences should not be allowed to intrude upon the exclusively scholarly and evaluative domain of textual scrutiny.

With the arrival of Theory the ideal of 'literature' as an autonomous discourse, with characteristic, defining features was systematically undermined. Emphasis was given instead to issues such as the state of mind, background, or gender of the reader and the socio-historical circumstances of the act of reading. The literary text was treated not as an aesthetically privileged artefact but rather as one of many competing discourses. Its author, as a consequence, was all but extinguished. Many of the otherwise diverse sub-strata of Theory – Structuralism, Poststructuralism, Feminism, Psychoanalysis, New Historicism *et al.* – share the presumption that language is a sign system which enables us to construct our sense of subjectivity. As a consequence the idea of the author as a real individual, influenced by and existing in a world comprised to a large part of prelinguistic emotions and experiences, as someone capable of projecting these into literary texts, is treated as a preposterous delusion. Roland Barthes's famous essay 'The Death of the Author' (1977) could stand as a manifesto for this school of criticism.

> The Author, when believed in, is always conceived of as the past of his own book: book and author stand automatically on a single line divided into a *before* and an *after*. The Author is thought to *nourish* the book, which is to say that he exists before it, thinks, suffers, lives for it, is in the same relation of antecedence to his work as a father to his child. In complete contrast, the modern scriptor is born simultaneously with the text, is in no way equipped with a being preceding or exceeding the writing, is not the subject with the book as predicate; there is no other time than that of the enunciation and every text is eternally written *here and now*. ...
>
> We know now that a text is not a line of words releasing a single 'theological meaning (the 'message' of the Author-God) but a multi-dimensional space in which a variety of writings, none of them original, blend and clash. The text is tissue of quotations drawn from the innumerable centres of culture .....
>
> Once the Author is removed, the claim to decipher a text becomes quite futile. To give a text an Author is to impose a limit on that text, to furnish it with a final signified, to close the writing. Such a conception suits criticism very well, the latter than allotting itself the important task of discovering the Author (or its hypostases: society, history, psyche, liberty) beneath the work: when the Author has been found, the text is 'explained' – victory to the critic. Hence there is no surprise in the fact that, historically, the reign of the Author has also been that of the Critic, nor again in the fact that criticism (be it new) is today undermined along with the Author. In the multiplicity of writing, everything is to be *disentangled*, nothing *deciphered*; the structure can be followed, 'run' (like the thread of a stocking) at every point and at every level, but there is nothing beneath: the space of writing is to be ranged over, not pierced; writing ceaselessly posits meaning ceaselessly to evaporate it, carrying out a systematic exemption of meaning.
>
> (Lodge, 1988, p.283)

Crucial to Barthes's thesis is the notion of the literary text as open, even unfinished. It is not something securely anchored to a specific creator but rather a network of possibilities mobilised by the reader. While Barthes and subsequent Poststructuralists might seem to have little in common with the New Critics and their orthodox confederates both parties are, albeit for different reasons, hostile to the presence of the author in the ceremony of interpretation. Barthes's presentation of the traditional classification of an author as the 'father' of the text is accurate to the extent that the latter was, and for many still is, treated as unquestionably the originator of the words on the page; but as we have seen the New Critics often found the author's presence unnerving, something that might contaminate the science of analysis with intuitive, subjective registers. Barthes and his successors might have confessed to bringing about the demise of the author but their otherwise inimical predecessors were in truth accomplices in the act.

Even after Barthes, biographies of authors continued to appear with metro-nomic regularity. Hostility towards them, in the exalted sphere of Theory, intensified but this had little if any effect upon the sub-genre itself because it had always been the bastard child of academic criticism; self-evidently a blood relative but with an equally close genetic kinship to the unregulated world in which the promise of disclosure sold books. A classic case of this twin affiliation is evidenced in the career of one of the most exalted literary biographers of the 20th century, Richard Ellmann. Ellmann's first significant publication was *Yeats. The Man and the Masks* (1948). Ellmann was a Yale grad-uate whose academic career was interrupted by war service with the OSS (the forerunner to the CIA) in London, a posting which enabled him to make tentative contacts with the late poet's relatives, friends and acquaintances and to follow up on these as soon as the war in Europe ended. The resulting book is a magnificent hybrid. On the one hand it reflects Ellmann's training and skills as an academic researcher and indeed his shrewdness as a literary critic but at the same time it quietly undermines virtually all of the ongoing attempts to establish a methodological programme for English Studies in the University. For example, Ellmann's account of Yeats's first encounters with Maud Gonne and her effect upon him is speculative only to the extent that he transforms a fabric of interviews, details from correspondence and undis-puted facts with regard to time and place into a narrative and a portrait of a man who seems at once compulsive and pitiably naïve. Ellmann goes further than this, however, and describes how Yeats's 'dreamy ineffectual' state was telescoped into his verse where the pseudo-mystical treatment of sexuality is in truth aesthetic collateral for his private sense of vulnerability (see pp.80–1).

Ellmann would go on to hold senior academic posts in English at Yale and Oxford. No-one questioned the significance and quality of his work, while at the same time nor did anyone point out the glaring inconsistencies between his practice and the desperate attempts by his peers to transform English from the status of a belletristic diversion to a discipline at least the equal of the social sciences. His interpretative acumen is comparable with that of Empson, Richard, Brooks, or Wimsatt but unlike them he 'close reads' and evaluates Yeats's verse while raising, and indeed answering, questions as to why this curious enigmatic man was caused to create the beguiling effects of his words on the page. He does not treat Yeats's poems, as might a psychoanalytic critic, as an involuntary index to his troubled state of mind or as some precious reflection of his unsteady political affiliations. At all times he respects their autonomy, and varying qualities, as works of art, but he also refuses to place them in an interpretive vacuum, demonstrating that a profile of the poet, his experiences and temperamental condition can co-exist with, indeed enlighten, our appreciation of his verse.

Ellmann consolidated his reputation as the most eminent literary biographer within academe with his life of Joyce (1959), a more detailed, lengthier work than the Yeats volume but involving the same technique of balancing an appreciation of the work against an epistemological survey of how it was formed in the experiences, decisions and consequences that made up its author's life. The biography was published just prior to the exchange of power from New Criticism to Structuralism and Poststructuralism. By 1983 the ideas of the former were perceived as dated curiosities; the author was not only an unwelcome presence in serious critical practice but banished completely from the jamboree of theories; dead and buried. This was the year that the enterprising Christopher Sinclair-Stevenson, Chief Editor of the mainstream publishing house that carried his surname, sensed among the reading public a new interest in the once rather specialised sub-genre of literary biography. Michael Holroyd's two-volume life of Lytton Strachey (1967–68) had attracted favourable reviews in the broadsheets, as had Robert Gittings's studies of Keats and Hardy and Richard Holmes on Shelley. More significantly they were popular; self-evidently aimed as much at the ordinary reader as the academic. What intrigued Stevenson most of all was the publication in 1983 of Peter Ackroyd's *The Last Testament of Oscar Wilde* written as Wilde's autobiography. The audacious gesture of having the long dead writer tell his own story was embedded in a scrupulously researched fabric of detail. The voice of Wilde, his emotional and reflective register, might have been pure invention but everything else was fact. Ackroyd won the Somerset Maugham Award and his book was a minor bestseller. Despite Ackroyd's avant-gardist technique Sinclair-Stevenson suspected that his success was guaranteed by a less elevated register of interest on the part of his many readers; Wilde as the cynosure of gossip, scandal and secrecy, each with the cache of debauched sexuality. Why not, then, he thought, a book which offers a seamless, comprehensive and uncensored account of Wilde's life, or to be more accurate his lives. With this in mind he made overtures toward the most eminent literary biographer of the day, Professor of English at Oxford, one Richard Ellmann. The advance was £35,000. By today's standards – taking into account the cost of living, salary increases, the massive explosion in property prices and of course the recent epidemic of publishing largesse with regard to six-figure-plus advances – it would be reasonable to calculate the equivalent as £200,000. Sinclair-Stevenson's peers in the profession thought this a somewhat rash, indulgent gamble, involving a subject that was still enshrouded by highbrow respectability – albeit touched by loucheness in Wilde's case – and a writer who while eminent was still after all an academic. When the book appeared in 1987, however, it sold 90,000 copies at £15 per 632-page door-stopping hardback. I mention these statistics because they point up the bizarre, one might almost say unwittingly farcical, division between literary academia and the world outside. A member of the former had, to the exhilaration of his accountant and family, stepped into the latter.

1977 saw the first translation into English of Michel Foucault's *What is an Author?*. The question mark is rhetorical and disingenuous since Foucault is certain of what an author is, or rather is not.

> One can say that the author is an ideological product, since we represent him as the opposite of his historically real function. (When a historically given function is represented in a figure that inverts it, one has an ideological production.) The author is therefore the ideological figure by which one marks the manner in which we fear the proliferation of meaning. ...
> ... I think that, as our society changes, at the very moment when it is in the process of changing, the author-function will disappear. (p.372 from reprint in Lodge, 1988)

The translation into English reflected the gradual shift from Theory as the highbrow sustenance of academics themselves to its maturing function within teaching and the curriculum. How odd it was then that six months later Heinemann had published *The Nature of Biography* (published in the US by University of Washington Press, 1973) a short book by Robert Gittings based upon a series of lectures he had been invited to give at the University of Washington, Seattle. Their subject was literary biography, specifically how biographers treat the authors of literary works, based upon Gittings's own experience as a practitioner of this branch of biographical writing.

Imagine the discipline of Theology, or in more modern terms Religious Studies, comprised mainly of radical post-Nietzschen philosophers who take it for granted that God is very long dead. Elsewhere in the profession one encounters Spiritualists who claim to have direct contact with God, in an advisory and congenial manner on an almost daily basis. This might sound ludicrous but it is a reasonably accurate analogy for the status of literary biography in relation to English Studies.

I must confess that my own interest in literary biography was fuelled in part by this Swiftian separation of academic thinking from what might be termed the general consensus. What intrigued me most was the fact that some writers, generally contemporary figures, seemed capable of obviating the debates on the precarious relationship between the text and its author. Most critics, academic and non-academic alike, treated the works of Kingsley Amis as supporting evidence for their almost entirely hostile perception of the man, but it was Amis's friend Philip Larkin who prompted the most blatant instances of interpreting literature as an abutment to temperament and personality.

According to Tom Paulin, Larkin might seem to speak for 'the English male, middle class, professional, outwardly confident, controlled and in control', which Paulin implies is bad enough, but this demeanour masks deeper repressions and complexes. Larkin 'writhes with anxiety inside that sealed bunker which is the English ethic of privacy', a collective mood of loss and failure, the end of Empire. In Paulin's view even Larkin's reluctance to get married partakes of this psychological fear of losing sovereignty. Larkin's political counterpart is Norman Tebbit. 'Larkin's snarl, his populism and his calculated philistinism all speak for Tebbit's England and for that gnarled and angry Puritanism which is so deeply ingrained in the culture' (*Times Literary Supplement*, 20–26 July 1990, pp.779–80). The hint that there is a connection between England's national decline and sexual disappointment, both apparently evident in Larkin's verse, became something of a cliché. Neil Corcoran: 'Larkin's idea of England is as deeply and intimately wounded by such post-imperial withdrawals [*sic*] as some of the personae of his poem are wounded by sexual impotence' (*English Poetry Since 1940*, London: Longman, 1993, p. 87). Both men are sophisticated literary critics but each appears to be only in part control of some deeper instinct – ideological, puritanical or whatever – which overrides whatever opinions they might have about the poems themselves. Irrespective of the quality, or otherwise, of the latter, they are treated as symptomatic of something very nasty indeed. When Thwaite's edition of the *Letters* was published in 1992 and Motion's biography came out a year later Larkin's enemies seized upon these new disclosures with a frenzy hardly witnessed since the McCarthy era.

The letters themselves provided a number of fascinating examples of what had hitherto been regarded only as potential inclinations evidenced by Larkin's poems. He complained to Amis in 1943, for example, that 'all women are stupid beings' and remarked in 1983 that he'd recently accompanied his partner Monica Jones to a hospital 'staffed ENTIRELY by wogs, cheerful and incompetent' (31 July). His views on politics and class seemed to be pithily captured in a ditty he shared again with Amis. 'I want to see them starving,/The so-called working class,/Their wages yearly halving,/Their women stewing grass …'. For recreation he apparently found time for pornography, preferably with a hint of sado-masochism: '… I mean like WATCHING SCHOOLGIRLS SUCK EACH OTHER OFF WHILE YOU WHIP THEM.'

Tom Paulin had had his suspicions confirmed but managed to curb his elation. He found the letters to be 'a distressing and in many ways revolting compilation which imperfectly reveals and conceals the sewer under the national monument Larkin became' (*Times Literary Supplement*, 7 November 1992). So there. One suspects that Paulin's metaphor lodged in Andrew Motion's mind because a sanitised version of it resurfaced in the preface to his biography of Larkin little more than a year later. Motion wrote of 'the beautiful flowers of his poetry … growing on long stalks out of pretty dismal ground'.

Others disagreed with Motion's maintenance of a separation between the man and his art. Lisa Jardine of the English Department, Queen Mary and Westfield, University of London, stated that while they would not go quite so far as to ban the study of Larkin his poems would be removed from the core curriculum and dealt with only to disclose 'the beliefs which lie behind them' – presumably according them a status similar, say, to *Mein Kampf* in a course on political philosophy. How, asked Jardine, could Larkin continue to be presented as a 'humane' writer when the student who consults the *Letters* is met with 'a steady stream of obscenity, throwaway derogatory remarks about women and arrogant disdain for those of different skin colour or nationality?' (*Guardian*, 8 December 1992). How indeed. One feels confident that parents throughout Britain remained grateful for Professor Jardine's concern regarding the innocent, fragile sensibilities of their undergraduate offspring.

Jardine was not alone. Otherwise sane and judicious critics seemed almost overnight to take on the role of arbiters of public morality. Peter Ackroyd judged Larkin to be 'essentially a minor poet who acquired a large reputation'. Bryan Appleyard: 'a minor poet raised to undeserved monumentality'. James Wood: 'a minor registrar of disappointment, a bureaucrat of frustration'. Apart from their exhaustive use of a single adjective these registrars of Larkin's minority had one other thing in common. They did not bother to ground their judgements in anything resembling evaluation. Larkin's poetry had not changed, and since none of these figures had previously claimed membership of the anti-Larkin camp of Paulin *et al.* one can only assume that after reading the letters they had decided that Larkin was a bad man and as a consequence his work no longer deserved approbation.

Contra Motion I argue in *First Boredom, Then Fear* (2005) that to pretend his work 'floats free of its surrounding material' undermines a proper understanding of Larkin both as a writer and as a man. Anyone who has read 'Sunny Prestatyn', particularly if that person is male, is attended by twin feelings of empathy and guilt. The 'girl on the poster' in the swimsuit is advertising the seaside resort and her image has been defaced.

> Huge tits and a fissured crotch
> Were scored well in, and the space
> Between her legs held scrawls
> That set her fairly astride
> A tuberous cock and balls

The most troubling aspect of the poem is not so much its mood of quiet indifference as an implied sense of approval. The original image of the girl 'In tautened white satin' was visited by what it provoked, aggressive male sexuality. As art, 'Sunny Prestatyn' is excellent. It combines a superb control of language with an incautiously honest demonstration of male uncontrol. How then is our estimation of it as a poem affected by the knowledge that Larkin very much enjoyed pornography and was as concerned with the words accompanying the images as with the pictures themselves? Indeed less than a year before the poem was finished he had written to his occasional pornography supplier Robert Conquest that the author of a piece in *Swish* should be recommended for the Somerset Maugham Award and had done so with only a degree of irony. Feminists and psychoanalytic critics would have a field day, of course, but for less sanctimonious readers the poem becomes even more intriguing as a poem. Larkin has always been celebrated as a writer whose verbal craftsmanship grafted significance on to the mundane and caused informality of speech to carry a muted elegance – a Dutch Master of modern verse and life. The mental image of him reading a particularly gratifying edition of *Swish* while the plan for 'Sunny Prestatyn' forms in his mind is neither prurient nor aesthetically reductive. It is like watching an artist at work and, more unusually, like sharing the spaces that divide up the components of his life.

The writers who so vigorously condemned Larkin were motivated by a combination of impulses – predominantly envy and political self-righteousness – but for all of them the factor that underpinned their outbursts was aesthetic prejudice. Larkin is a traditionalist who undermines the longstanding mantra of the academic and literary establishment that without innovation writing is hidebound, indebted to the past. Thwaite's and Motion's volumes triggered an impulse amongst them which had previously been suppressed by the protocols of critical writing: suddenly they had an excuse to unleash their pent up feelings for a man and what in their view he represented. The whole episode dismantled, unwittingly ridiculed, decades of theorising on how the somewhat vulgar notion of the real author might be excised from the elevated practises of textual scrutiny. Larkin, thanks to the attention of his rancorous scrutineers, became very real indeed.

Bibliography

Amis, Kingsley (1990), *The Amis Collection*, London: Hutchinson.

Bradford, Richard (2001), *Lucky Him. The Life of Kinglsey Amis*, London: Peter Owen.

Bradford, Richard (2005), *First Boredom, Then Fear. The Life Philip Larkin*, London: Peter Owen.

Ellmann, Richard (1948), *Yeats. The Man and the Masks*, Oxford: Oxford University Press.

Ellmann, Richard (1959), *James Joyce*, Oxford: Oxford University Press.

Ellmann, Richard (1987), *Oscar Wilde*, London: Sinclair Stevenson.

Godwin, W. (1804), *Life of Geoffrey Chaucer, The Early English Poet*, 2nd edn., 4 Vols., London: Richard Phillips.

Lodge, David (1988), (ed.), *Modern Criticism and Theory. A Reader*, London: Longman.

Richards, I.A. (1924), *Principles of Literary Criticism*, London: Routledge and Kegan Paul, (referenced from 1966 edn).

Wimsatt, W.K. (1954), *The Verbal Icon*, Lexington: University of Kentucky Press.

Part II
Various Selves, Different Discourses: The Broader Contexts of Life Writing

10

Reflections on the Timing of Juan Goytisolo's Autobiographies

Stanley Black

Juan Goytisolo's experiment in life-writing, two volumes of memoir produced in the mid-80s, has by now attracted considerable attention. When the two books were published as a single volume in 2002, the prologue gave an intriguing insight into the timing:

> After I had finished the novel *Landscapes after the Battle*, I read a handful of memoirs by older or contemporary Spanish writers, then put aside a narrative project that was already fermenting and began to write *Forbidden Territory*.[1]

He then goes on to state two reasons for undertaking his own version of the genre. One is that what he understands as autobiographical writing, which he associates with 'personal reflection' and sees as common in the English tradition, is unmatched by Spanish writers who, he claims, 'maintain a cautious silence in respect of the most intimate aspects of their own lives and, above all, avoid like the plague any examination of their consciences and recognition of mistakes which might call them to account'. The one exception is that of José María Blanco White whose work Goytisolo had translated from English 'into the mother tongue of the man who described himself as a "self-banished Spaniard"' in the early 70s.[2] Hence, the aim was 'to plug one of the many gaps in Spanish literature' and so corresponds to Goytisolo's familiar aspiration to add new branches to the 'tree of Spanish literature'. The second reason is the need 'to explain the wherefore of a literary vocation, shared with my two brothers, and the change this underwent after *Count Julian*'.[3]

It is not clear why Goytisolo was immersing himself in autobiographical writings at the time, though it seems reasonable to assume it was preparation for his own planned attempt, and certainly the two reasoned motives that he outlines here differ from the more dramatic, subjective and visceral motives outlined in the actual autobiographies themselves. Here their genesis is located in two near-death experiences, one a car accident and another a near-goring at a bullfight in a Spanish village, both in the early 80s.[4] This leads to:

> *the urgency and need to write, express yourself, not to allow all that you love,*
> *your past experience, emotions, what you are and have been, to disappear with*
> *you, determination to fight tooth and claw against oblivion [...] to order your*
> *impressions and feelings, shape them on the blank page, abridged reminiscences,*
> *like waves breaking, subject to your wandering memory, imperative to tell others*
> *and yourself what you were and are not, whom you might have been and have*
> *not become, to clarify, correct, complete the reality elaborated in your successive*
> *fictions.*[5]

This urgency to write, in response to a succession of personal traumas, seems at odds with the more clear-headed decision related in the 2002 prologue:

> If I had been a British author I would not have tried to compete with so many distinguished predecessors or I would have done it differently, through recourse to parody, as in the autobiographical fiction of *Landscapes after the Battle*, or, more recently, *A Cock-Eyed Comedy*.[6]

Curiously, the 'narrative project that was already fermenting' mentioned above is hard to identify since the prologue to volume IV of the Complete Works (published in 2007) tells us that the novel which followed his autobiographies, *The Virtues of the Solitary Bird*, was begun in February 1986, prompted by a health scare that occurred two months earlier, and coinciding with the correction of the galley-proofs of *Realms of Strife*. The result was a creative impulse to write inspired by the theme of AIDS and the mystical writings of Saint John of the Cross.[7] Where the earlier near-death experiences had led to an autobiographical urge to recount the past, the later one had prompted a fictional preoccupation with future transcendence.

As we see from the evidence of the autobiographies themselves and the subsequent prologues, the motivation and timing of the former within the chronology of Goytisolo's life and especially his work are complex and fascinating, as is the relationship with the surrounding novels and the varying approaches to the author's life, ranging from parodic autobiographical fiction to literary memoir. A large part of the criticism of the memoirs relates to the extent to which it conforms or not to the archetypes of the genre. One critic has noted that 'it seems almost *de rigueur* to question the validity of Goytisolo's autobiographies as life-writing' before going on to side with those who regard them as unequivocally autobiographical.[8] In this essay I aim to examine the significance of the timing of the autobiographies within Goytisolo's work as a whole and, hopefully, cast some light on the matter of their generic status.

First, a word about their timing: Goytisolo produced two volumes of autobiographical writing, *Coto vedado*, (Forbidden Territory), in 1985 and *En los reinos de taifa* (Realms of Strife) in 1986. The two works were then combined in a single volume entitled *Memorias* ('Memoirs') in 2002 and similarly published in English as a single volume the following year. In the recently published edition of Goytisolo's complete works, they occupy Volume V, entitled 'Autobiografía y viajes al mundo islámico' ('Autobiography and travels in Islamic countries') along with two of his works on Turkey, one a study of Istambul (*Estambul otomano*) and the other a book of essays *Aproximaciones a Gaudí en Capadocia* ('Approximations to Gaudí in Capadoccia') each published in 1989 and 1990 respectively.[9]

Goytisolo has produced fiction and essays concurrently throughout his career, starting in the early 50s. In terms of his fiction, after an early period of social realism, he underwent a radical change in the 60s and produced a trilogy of aesthetically challenging and experimentalist novels between 1966 and 1975. In spite of its formalism, this trilogy, usually called the Mendiola Trilogy, was also heavily autobiographical and its central character, Alvaro Mendiola, was a clear transposition of Juan Goytisolo, right down to the conjunction of common Spanish forename with Basque surname, although by the later more metafictional instalments, the concept of character had given way to that of author-narrator. As Labanyi has noted 'his novelistic output since *Señas de identidad* [Marks of Identity](1966) has set about blurring the boundary between fiction and autobiography, proposing a series of narrators and characters that are explicit linguistic constructs at the same time as projections of the author's personal history and obsessions'.[10]

The trilogy is widely seen as Goytisolo seeking and finding a new literary style and identity. After it, in 1980, he produced what many consider one of his finest novels, *Makbara*, followed by *Landscapes after the Battle* in 1982. It is at this point that he pauses – he calls it an 'autobiographical parenthesis' – and produces the two volumes of memoir, then resumes in 1987 his novel writing with *The Virtues of the Solitary Bird* followed by five more novels until in 2003 he produced what he claimed was his 'last' novel, *Telón de boca* (Blind Rider).[11]

In the 2008 prologue to volume V of the Complete Works, Goytisolo begins by reiterating the motivations outlined in 2002:

> A desire to relive the past through writing; to establish and clarify, in my case, the circumstances that contributed to the formation of my early vocation as a writer and the subsequent change of direction; returning to the genesis of my adult work. [12]

only to move on to others which one senses he sees as more important, one which he refers to as relinquishing the divine freedom of the novelist in order to 'circumscribe the creative imagination to the limits of lived experience and confirm at the same time the existence of an unsalvageable distance between ungraspable reality and the text which in vain attempts to capture it' (ibid.).[13] The second reason concerns the difference, recognised as far back as Plato, between writing and the reality it describes: 'la ambigüedad inherente al relato en su conexión con la realidad (the ambiguity inherent in the story's connection with reality)'. Autobiography, he claims, like historical writing, has a status which is 'more confusing and uncertain' (p.10). This link is referred to within the autobiography itself:

> When I read history books, the intrepid sureness with which their authors establish what happened thousands of years ago produces in me an insuperable sensation of incredulity. How is it possible to reconstitute a remote past if even the most recent past appears to be sown with doubts and uncertainties? The darkness over the destiny of a good part of my family illustrates perfectly to me our powerlessness to discover and exhume after a few years the tangible reality of what happened.[14]

Thus, Goytisolo's autobiography alternates, though not in a wholly systematic way, between apparently straightforward memoir, in standard roman type, and more self-conscious italicized sections. Much of the italicized sections casts doubt on the process of memory and the ability to recapture the past with any stability.[15] Quite early in the first volume the author speaks of the 'complete inanity of the enterprise: amalgam of your motivation and inability to make up your mind about your aim and would-be destination'. He questions some of the other motivations:

> *a lay substitute for the sacrament of confession?: an unconscious desire to justify yourself?: to make a statement that nobody asks you for?: a statement for whom, from whom?: for you, everybody else, your friends, enemies?: the wish to make yourself better understood?: to awaken feelings of affection or pity?: to feel yourself accompanied by future readers?: to struggle against the oblivion of time?: purely and simply an exhibitionist impulse?*[16]

Forbidden Territory charts a process of change of identity, a shedding of a former self to which Goytisolo had come to refer, in Cavafian terms as an 'unwelcome guest', an inauthentic self that concealed his sexuality and accepted a certain political allegiance (in this case, to the Communist cause) with which he no longer felt happy.[17] The change happened in the early 60s. Thus, contrary to the traditional essentialist concept of autobiography which tends towards integration and representation of a unified self,[18] Goytisolo's intends to highlight division in the self – 'putting your life on the drawing board, the unmentionable material reality of your body, not the one hidden by masks and disguises in daily ritual farce, projection of a false image aimed at the gallery, inopportune guest who usurps your voice [...] no, the other one ...' (p.25). Much of this process will concern the author's assumption of his homosexuality. The painful price of such intimate revelations will be the guarantee of the moral worth of his writing:

> To concentrate on what is most painful and difficult to express, what you haven't yet said to anybody, an odiously vile or humiliating memory, the bitterest blow in life: to find in the internal resistance to laying it bare the moral canon of your writing.[19]

Goytisolo's autobiography, therefore, rather than a process of reconstitution is one of destruction; recuperating the past all the better to consign it to oblivion. Remembrance of the past is the path to a clean slate, memories evoked the better to part with them, like the hated village of Viladrau in which the family took refuge during the Civil War, 'clear in your memory, reconstructed in your imagination while you write, square inch by square inch, house by house. Beyond dream, memory, oblivion: a simple page in this book that once printed, torn from you – will not enter your thoughts again' (p.56). Undoubtedly this is autobiography as self-therapy.

What surprises most critics about Goytisolo's memoirs is the degree to which they are conventional.[20] Some commentators therefore have criticized Goytisolo's half-hearted postmodernism, seeking on the one hand to undermine and destabilise notions of the self and identity as unacceptably oppressive, while in their place erecting an equally stable identity. For these critics, Goytisolo seems to want to posit his autobiography as performatively postmodernist but ends by conforming to the conventional format of autobiography as a cognitive appraisal of one's past self, an attempt to recuperate a past essence, pin down an elusive truth. Loureiro says that 'for all his awareness of the shortcomings of epistemic autobiography, Goytisolo cannot forego the pull to enunciate the truth'.[21] Nonetheless, Loureiro locates the limitations of the task in the genre itself and claims Goytisolo to be aware of it:

> In its yearning for self-knowledge and its desire to control self-representation, autobiography betrays its unavoidable insufficiencies, which the most lucid autobiographers (Goytisolo among them) thematize as self-consciousness about the limitations of the genre.[22]

Jo Labanyi has observed how Goytisolo 'will opt for a self-conscious literariness and theatricality'. Contrasting his autobiography with the more conventional one of Neruda, she notes how the 'alternation of his [Goytisolo's] narrative with passages in italics reflecting on the (impossible) act of writing draws attention to the artificial nature of his text as a cultural product'.[23] Clearly Goytisolo's approach to autobiography is a mixture of the traditional (need for veracity and chronological structuring) and the ironic awareness of limitations (the vagaries of memory). If his opening words ironize on the aim of establishing a family tree:

> The writing of genealogies, according to the ironic narrator of Biely's *Petersburg*, comes down to tracing the origins of well-to-do families right back to Adam and Eve.[24]

by half way through the second volume of memoirs his aim was to: 'forge a genealogy to fit and include therein all those accused of rejecting the fatherland [...] thieves and deserters, heretics, sodomites, the proscribed' (FTRS 275). Edward Said's distinction between an author's filiation (his ties by birth, nationality, profession) and his affiliations (new relations by social and political convictions) is recalled in his comment 'your writerly affinities let you compensate precarious blood ties' (FTRS p.275).[25]

The positioning of Goytisolo's autobiography in the mid-80s when he was in his mid-50s (he was born in 1931) is partly explained by the fact that it forms part of what Laura Marcus calls 'conversion narratives', written from a standpoint beyond a spiritual or secular crisis and 'from which the pattern and meaning of the life can be discerned'.[26] Thus, one is led to ask how it fits in with his literary project. The question has been asked before but usually elicits the rather obvious, though no less untrue, response that Goytisolo himself had offered, which is that the autobiographies explain the background to the fiction.[27] Likewise, Randolph Pope queries why, after novels that challenged identity in a more radical fashion, should he then revert to a more conventional analysis of the self:

> Why then does he come back in 1985 to facts he has told before in different versions in his novels? Why assert the unifying factor of one individual's experience when the individual has dissolved into unrelated networks of disparate information and all narrative has been made suspect? When Ihab Hassan affirms that 'autobiography remains an impossible – and deadly form'?[28]

Pope's conclusion is: 'Over the gaping mouth of Death Goytisolo feels an urge to write his self, to reproduce himself' (97)

Marks of Identity (1966) is essentially a *künstlerroman* with a scenario remarkably similar to that in *Forbidden Territory*. The protagonist, in his early 30s (Goytisolo was 35 when the novel was published) returns home after a heart attack in Paris. Faced with what he sees as inevitable and possibly imminent death, he tries to reconstitute his identity by sifting through family albums and documents, but ends the novel in a poetic and dramatic denunciation of his homeland, effectively rejecting his old self and taking on a new identity represented by authoring the text just read. The concluding lines 'cultivate everything that separates you from them/glorify whatever in you bothers them', is a deliberate echo of the exiled, homosexual poet Luis Cernuda, one of Goytisolo's new affiliations.

Both the 1966 novel and the 1985 memoir have death as an internal motive for writing and self-enquiry. Externally, at the level of authorial intention, the motive appears to be more strategic and literary, as the two prologues, at least in the case of the memoirs, have indicated.[29] While it seems clear that Goytisolo has always suffered from a preoccupation with death[30] and writing is clearly a constant need to make sense of his life prior to imminent demise[31] it seems likely that we are dealing less with a repetition of a similar dread of death twenty years on but rather a coincidence on a different level of a literary strategy. Indeed, *Marks of Identity* and *Forbidden Territory* are like mirror-images of each other, the former is autobiographical literature and the latter literary autobiography and the autobiography's aim is not simply to respond to a real-life trauma but to renew and invigorate a literary project. In the Trilogy, Goytisolo sought to unsettle and provoke the reader by undermining literary realism through progressively self-reflexive metafiction. In this phase, the autobiographical base was both a means of endowing the process with personal authenticity[32] but also of providing a tension that highlighted the ontological issues at stake and prevented the fiction from veering off into pure textuality.[33] By the 80s Goytisolo's unsettling of the ontological boundaries is conducted increasingly through a play on the figure of the real author. Thus in the first novel after the Trilogy, *Makbara*, the central authorial figure lurking in the text, particularly the final chapter is no longer a semi-autobiographical persona but, though unnamed, Goytisolo himself, the denizen of Djemaa-el-Fna, the halaiqui nesrani or Western storyteller caught between two worlds. In *Landscapes after the Battle*, the person and name of Juan Goytisolo is explicitly played with at several levels.[34]

In the autobiography, Goytisolo simultaneously explores and undermines the process of memory: 'In spite of the atmosphere of disruption and agitation, my memories which are confused until then, seem to get clearer and settle down at the beginning of 1936'(p.32). And again: 'In spite of the fact that there are dark spots and gaps in my memory of how this episode developed, I well remember the moment after the intruders left ...'(p.35). Yet another:

> Although I know the tricks that memory and its fictitious recreations play, I retain a clear memory of looking out my bedroom window while that woman, soon to become unfamiliar, walked with her coat, hat and bag, toward the definitive absence from us and from herself.[35]

The seeming security of the latter memory may be explained by its momentousness. It recounts the last image the seven-year old Goytisolo has of his mother as she sets out on the shopping trip in Barcelona from which she would not return, falling victim instead in the bombing of the city by the supporters of Franco, an autobiographical detail that becomes a constant in his novels.

At times he seems to want to adhere to the chronological constraints of pure autobiography but avoiding the teleological approach of the biographer:

> In the light of my past experience it would be very convenient to endow what happened with some prophetic sense and establish a perfect chain of causes and effects from then on. But that is not my aim. I intend to narrate events as I perceived them when they happened. (p.128)

But this inauthentic posture is quickly undercut:[36]

> Awareness of the dangers and snares of the enterprise: futile attempt to erect a bridge over the discontinuity of your biography, to grant coherence after the event to a mere accumulation of ruins:[...] a deceitful precision of detail, unconscious anachronisms, presumptuously clear outlines [...] transmuting uncertain reality into the faked structure of a book. (p.133)

The memoirs end on an apparent admission of failure:

> Memory, writes Walter Benjamin, cannot transfix the flow of time or encompass the infinite dimension of space: it is restricted to recreating set scenes, encapsulating privileged moments, arranging memories and images in a syntactic order that word by word will shape into a book. The unbridgeable distance between act and written word, the laws and requirements of the narrative text will insidiously transmute faithfulness to reality into artistic exercise, attempted sincerity into virtuosity, moral rigor into aesthetics. No possibility of escape from the dilemma; the recon-struction of the past will always be certain betrayal as far as it is endowed with later coherence, stiffened with clever continuity of plot. Put your pen down, break off the narrative, prudently limit the damage: silence, silence alone will keep intact a pure sterile illusion of truth. (pp.404–5)

However, even this self-conscious instance of narrative exhaustion is con-trived as the second volume of memoir has ended at a pre-ordained point, the moment when the writer was in a position to write *Count Julian*. The final chapter of *Realms* links in with the opening sections of that 1970 novel. As explained in the 2002 prologue, where he claims the reasons for his change of literary direction in the 60s is 'clarified by a reading of *Realms of Strife*, especially the final pages, focused on my stay in Tangier, when the idea of the betrayal of Count Julian took seed'.[37] He goes on to say that from that point his novels speak for themselves and require no 'autobiographical com-plement'. Thus, in spite of his struggles with the autobiographical mode,

Goytisolo has very artfully carried off a cleverly ambiguous version of it, one which allowed a traditional recounting of the past while casting doubt on it throughout. His autobiography fits Starobinski's dual function in 'establishing a relation between the "author" and his own past; but also, in its orientation towards the future, of revealing the author to future readers'.[38] Starobinski makes the point that the teleology of the autobiographer means 'it becomes necessary to retrace the genesis of the present situation, the antecedents of the moment from which the present "discourse" stems' (p.79). Strictly speaking the 'present situation' of Goytisolo's autobiography is the 60s, the point when he shrugs off the former identities (Marxist, heterosexual, social realist) and assumes the new identities that find expression in the literature from *Count Julian* onwards, something recognised in Goytisolo's reference to 'returning to the genesis of my adult work' cited earlier. But, again one is led to ask why the twenty year gap.

At the time of the autobiographies, Goytisolo made a speech on winning the Europalia prize in 1985 in which he argued for the need to play down the public figure of the author. This was not a variation on the 'death of the author', simply a plea not to let the public figure of the author get in the way of a proper appreciation of his work, to let the work speak for itself. In the Europalia speech he repeats a phrase that re-appears *Realms of Strife*:

> The writer's physical presence obstructs a proper evaluation of his work by introducing factors outside specific literary criteria. (p.261)

Ironically, the production of a highly successful and controversial memoir might seem destined to have precisely this effect. For a writer who had become something of an elite, avant-garde taste, the mid-80s saw Goytisolo at the top of the bestseller lists with *Forbidden Territory*, which became a *succès de scandale*, partly because of the sexual revelations. Paradoxically, the author as a 'figura', i.e. a public figure, is enhanced by the memoirs which seek to eliminate the empirical author and focus on the emerging figure of the writer, synonymous with his books.

Henry Porter Abbott, attempting a taxonomy of autobiographical writing, identifies three different approaches to the genre. One is the traditional approach of 'those who not only define autobiography but find in it [...] repeatable narrative shape'. This version of autobiography is classically written from a perspective of final stability, after a life of difficulty, when the past self is seen with perspective and a sense of wholeness. A paradigm would be St. Augustine's *Confessions*. As Porter Abbott says, the 'discourse, then, is transparent, or at least semi-transparent; it is featured not as part of the life but as a medium through which the life is seen'.[39] Opposed to this is the view, most identified with Paul de Man, that autobiography is impossible. As a compromise, Porter Abbott cites those, like Elizabeth Bruss, Paul Jay and Janet Varner Gunn, for whom autobiography is seen as an action, as performative. 'These writers stress the drama that takes place in the writing when the self seeks to write about itself', says Porter Abbott, and cites Jay's comment that autobiographical writers confront the 'dissimilarity between identity and discourse [...] the ever-present ontological gap between the self who is writing and the self-reflexive protagonist of the work'.

Porter Abbott refers to the concept of 'suspicion'. Whereas with some autobiographies the reader sympathizes with the author and therefore accepts him or her as an authoritative source, there are those where the author is viewed less sympathetically or with downright hostility by the reader, and as a consequence, these narratives are read with suspicion, or *autographically*, that is, the reader is aware of the 'author present in the text, pushing and shoving the facts, coloring the events, in short, doing something for himself' (p.601). Autographies are characterized then by a 'demystified, analytic awareness of the author in action' and some authors actually cultivate this attitude in the reader.[40]

Goytisolo's autobiographies show him to do precisely that. For example, when recounting the poignant episode of his mother's departure for Barcelona where she would be killed in an Italian air bombardment, he says:

> It no doubt seems suspicious that I should wake up precisely on that day and that, forewarned of my mother's departure by her footsteps or the noise of the door, I should have got up to watch her leave.[41]

Later,

> Although the ease with which this whitewashing operation was carried out may seem suspicious (p.42)

Goytisolo's autobiography partakes of the same unsettling of expectations as his fiction. In his fiction of the 80s he is still exploring the same tensions, but now the realism/metafiction boundary, has been enriched by the fiction/autobiography border. Hence the importance of the novel that preceded this 'autobiographical parenthesis', *Landscapes after the Battle*. Where previous novels had undoubtedly had an implicit autobiographical base, this novel engaged in a more explicit postmodernist way with the (real) author figure; the central writing protagonist was someone who inhabited Goytisolo's flat in Paris and shared many of his characteristics (some mentioned in almost identical terms in contemporaneous non-fiction essays or the memoirs – e.g. his aversion to museums and art galleries, his love of cities and unease with the countryside, his lack of manual dexterity, etc). In a note at the start of the novel the author, as well as thanking the DAAD for the grant that allowed him to finish the novel in Kreuzberg, thanks 'his seeming homonym, the remote and invisible writer "Juan

Goytisolo" for the right to reproduce his dubious scientific excogitations originally published in the Madrid daily *El País*. Towards the end of the novel, the narrator gives us his 'literary ideal', that of the wandering Sufi dervish:

> A man who shuns vanity, scorns the rules of decorum and social convention, seeks no disciples, tolerates no praise [...] Beneath its masks and veils the aim of writing is disdain: the proud rejection of the sympathy or admiration of others as the indispensible requisite for the attainment of that inner alchemy practiced beneath the guise of mocking and sarcastic chronicle, of incidents and adventures in a deliberately grotesque autobiography.[42]

Clearly the autobiography is integral to cultivating that literary ideal as recognised in *Realms of Strife*: 'Set oneself the Genetian ethic of the malamatí as a difficult literary and human ideal' (FTRS p.275). *Landscapes'* postmodernist play with the author figure seems intent on luring the reader into a biographical reading only to mock such an interpretative strategy. The attack on the author-narrator-protagonist by two Lacanian feminists is both an autobiographical[43] as well as a playful jibe at those that see the author as the key to the work. His attackers ransack his apartment for clues and, not finding any, oblige him to write a 'autocriticism, the full story of your real vices and secret inclinations, your fantasies and frailties, your most venial sins' (LB pp.143–4), a task not unlike the one Goytisolo sets himself in the autobiographies.

As the narrator, under instructions from his literary terrorists, drafts his autocriticism, he rereads what he has so far written:

> A rereading of the 170 pages of his manuscript reveals the existence of a fragmented being: ideas, feelings, libido pull in different directions, and the wretched chronicler of his life has been unable to put them together again.[...] in the end he no longer knows if he is the distant individual who usurps his name or if that goytisolo is creating him. (LB p.148)

The metafictional play and destruction of the self in *Landscapes* is predicated on the notion of a stable author which the autobiographical dimension provides. Hence it is not so unusual that Goytisolo should turn afterwards to a genre such as autobiography which while ostensibly focused on the referential, has in recent decades constituted an arena for contemporary critical debate.[44]

Viewed thus, Goytisolo's autobiography emerges as a highly self-conscious and strategically planned work that forms part of a literary continuum that includes the novels, 'the single book, the Book you have been creating and re-creating for twenty years and as you invariably note, at the end of each of its chapters, that you still have not written' (FTRS p.17). As autobiography, it fits the pattern of a dual portrait outlined by Starobinski in his analysis of Rousseau's autobiography insofar as it gives 'not only a reconstruction of his history but also the picture of himself as he relives his history in the act of writing'. But it is the latter that really counts, what Goytisolo had referred to as a 'desire to relive the past *through writing*' (my emphasis).[45] For Starobinski this was the authenticity of autobiography, described as a move 'from the realm of historical *truth* to that of *authenticity* (the authenticity of *discourse*)'.[46]

Authenticity was central to the change brought about by *Marks of Identity*. The generic unsettling of expectations that the play with the autobiography/fiction boundary elicits in the reader is crucial to the effect of the autobiographical fictions from *Landscapes* onwards, either in the more parodic form of the latter and *Carajicomedia* (A Cock-Eyed Comedy, 2000/2002) or the more serious forms of works like *La cuarentena* (Quarantine, 1991/1994) or *Telón de boca* (Blind Rider, 2003/2005). This explains the temporal gap. The autobiography, at the level of the content (*énoncé*) may merge temporally and stylistically with *Count Julian* in the late 70s but, at the much more important level of writing (*énonciation*), its location between *Landscapes* and the autobiographical fictions that follow is crucial. For one, it enacts that shunning of vanity essential to the new literary ideal. For another, it exploits that ambiguity of the autobiographical text in terms of its connection with the real and its capacity to unsettle the reader and which has so powerful a role in the subsequent fictions.[47] The passing reference in the 2002 prologue to the 'personal facts, facets and circumstances [that] appear in filigree in the fictions', alludes to an aspect which far from incidental is actually central to the novels' meaning and effect.[48]

Notes

1. Juan Goytisolo, *Forbidden Territory and Realms of Strife: the Memoirs of Juan Goytisolo*, trans. Peter Bush (London: Verso, 2003), p.vii. All references will be from this translation of the Spanish *Memorias* (2002). I have chosen here to use the terms autobiography and memoir interchangeably despite the existence of critical debate on the definitions. See Sidonie Smith and Julia Watson, *Reading Autobiography: A Guide for Interpreting Life Narratives* (Minneapolis: University of Minnesota Press, 2001), p.198.
2. Goytisolo, *Forbidden Territory*, pp.vii–viii. He cites Pepys, Wilde and Frank Harris as exemplars. Later, in the prologue to volume V of his Complete Works, he would add Henry Spencer Ashby, and Rousseau, and mention the other exception from the Hispanic tradition, José Vasconcelos, indicated to him by Octavio Paz after the latter's reading of *Forbidden Territory*. Cf. *Obras Completas* (Barcelona: Círculo de lectores, 2008), vol.V, p.11.
3. The original Spanish says 'a partir de *Don Julián*' and the meaning is more that of 'commencing with *Count Julian*'.

4. We can work out the date of the near-goring as page 17 tells it coincided with the death of an *espontáneo* (someone who jumps into a bullring in a desperate search for fame) in Albacete. The espontáneo in question was undoubtedly Fernando Villarroel who died in this way on 14 September 1981 during the Festival of Albacete. The car accident happened fifteen months earlier (p.15) and the author claims he started to write the memoirs 'almost two years later', i.e. around the summer of 1983.
5. *Forbidden Territory*, p.17.
6. *Forbidden Territory*, p.viii.
7. *Obras completas IV: Novelas 1988–2003* (Barcelona: Círculo de Lectores, 2007), p.9.
8. Alison Ribeiro de Menezes, *Juan Goytisolo: the Author as Dissident* (Woodbridge: Tamesis, 2005) pp.11–12, note 11. The title of Sixto Plaza's essay is illustrative in itself: '*Coto vedado ¿autobiografía o novela?*' in *Actas del IX Congreso de la Asociación Internacional de Hispanistas*, I-II, ed. Sebastian Neumeister (Frankfurt: Vervuert, 1989), pp.345–50. Gonzalo Navajas refers to the memoirs as 'fictive autobiographies', 'Confession and Ethics in Juan Goytisolo's Fictive Autobiographies', *Letras Peninsulares*, Fall/Winter, 1990, pp.259–278, and Brad Epps tellingly calls them 'the two most overtly autobiographical texts by Juan Goytisolo', 'Thievish Subjectivity: Self-writing in Jean Genet and Juan Goytisolo', *Revista de estudios hispánicos*, 26, 2 (1992), p.164.
9. Juan Goytisolo, *Obras completas*, vol.V 'Autobiografía y viajes al mundo islámico', Edited by Antoni Munné. Prologue by Juan Goytisolo (Barcelona: Círculo de Lectores, 2008)
10. Jo Labanyi 'The Construction/Deconstruction of the Self in the Autobiographies of Pablo Neruda and Juan Goytisolo', *Forum for Modern Language Studies*, Vol.XXVI, no.3, 1990, p.219.
11. This has proved not to be the case with the appearance of the novel *El exiliado de aquí y allá* (Barcelona: Círculo de lectores, 2008) which is an explicit 'update' on the novel *Landscapes after the Battle*.
12. *Obras completas*, vol.V, p.9. The English translations are my own.
13. For Labanyi Goytisolo's attempt to obey the constraints of autobiography actually leads to a more persuasive re-casting of the self than the freedom of fiction. Cf. 'The Construction/Deconstruction of the Self ...', p.220.
14. *Forbidden Territory*, p.21.
15. Indeed Goytisolo was involved in a very public polemic with his younger brother, Luis, also an acclaimed novelist, in the pages of the Spanish daily *El País*, when Luis, clearly aggrieved at what he saw as Juan airing his family's dirty linen so publicly, questioned some details of his bother's account, with a view to undermining the most serious and scandalous revelation, that Juan was molested as a child by their maternal grandfather. As Juan said in his public response to Luis, autobiography is subject to errors, unconscious reconstruction of events, giving a retrospective coherence to events, and in *Forbidden Territory* at several junctures he had warned the reader against the 'possible tricks and failures of his memory'. The difference between the two is evident from the titles of their responses to each other. Juan talks of 'dos memorias (two memories)' – implying a single experience but with different memories or interpretations. Luis speaks of 'Dos equívocos (two mistakes)' suggesting the importance of a stable truth that can be misinterpreted. In the course of his piece Luis makes a comment which is key in understanding the two authors. He notes that while all authors' works, including his own, are influenced by their own biography, in the case

of Juan, especially in his mature period, it is a case of an author whose 'self assumes the principal role, final objective rather than point of departure' (*Dos equívocos*).

16. *Forbidden Territory*, p.25.

17. The reference is to the poem, 'As much as you can'. See C.P.Cavafy, *Selected Poems* (London: Penguin, 2008), p.35. Inger Enkvist speaks of an 'autothanatography' at work: 'Goytisolo very conscientiously "kills" first his bourgeois self, then his left-wing self', 'Autobiographical Intertextuality in Juan Goytisolo's Trilogy' *Readerly/Writerly Texts*, 4.1, (Fall/Winter 1996), p.181.

18. Linda Anderson, *Autobiography* (London: Routledge, 2001), p.5.

19. *Forbidden Territory*, p.25. Ribeiro maintains, not without reason, that the autobiographies are 'texts which pivot between a performative notion of identity and an essentialist one' but doubts Goytisolo is 'engaged in a post-structuralist refutation of the very possibility of selfhood', suggesting rather he succumbs to a new and debilitating essentialism both at a personal level in his newly assumed homosexual identity and at a literary level, his adoption of a dissident voice. Both identities, although apparently constructivist, i.e. existential choices, mask an essentialism: the former by being 'uncovered – ultimately not fabricated, but revealed' (p.27) and the latter by by virtue of its rigid binary oppositionality, a feature she claims only overcome in the 1988 novel *The Virtues of the Solitary Bird* (p.25). David Vilaseca on the other hand reads Goytisolo's 'coming out' as the result of a 'series of anti-essentialist movements (or interpellations from the Other) [...] not the subject's inner self-experience'. ' "Waiting for the Earthquake": Homosexuality, Disaster Movies and the "Message from the Other" in Juan Goytisolo's Autobiography', *Paragraph*, 22/1, 1999, p.66. I, however, would agree with Gonzalo Navajas for whom 'in Goytisolo sexual preference is not seen as an essential and definitive fact' but 'subject to evolution and change' 'Confession and Ethics', p.263. Labanyi similarly, and rightly in my opinion, maintains that the 'self constructed in Goytisolo's text is imperfect, always in the process of construction, manifesting itself through discontinuity' (p.213).

20. In Robert Richmond Ellis's view the autobiographies observe a conventional approach: 'Like a traditional autobiographer, Goytisolo, in fact, aims to reconstruct his past as accurately as possible'. 'Cutting the Gordian Knot: Homosexuality and the Autobiographies of Juan Goytisolo', *Anales de la Literatura Española Contemporánea* 19, 1–2 (1994), p.51. Ribeiro notes '[d]espite the formal innovation of his texts, Goytisolo's motive for writing is a surprisingly traditional self-analysis and self-justification' (p.12).

21. Loureiro, *The Ethics of Autobiography* (Nashville: Vanderbilt UP, 2000), p.124.

22. Loureiro, p.129.

23. Jo Labanyi 'The Construction/Deconstruction of the Self', p.214.

24. *Forbidden Territory*, p.5.

25. Said, 'Secular Criticism' in *The World, the Text and the Critic* (Cambridge Massachusetts: Harvard University Press, 1983), pp.19–20.

26. Laura Marcus, *Auto/biographical Discourses: Theory.Criticism. Practice.* (Manchester: Manchester UP, 1994), p.168. Ribeiro has observed how the autobiographies appear to be written 'not from the perspective of someone reflecting back at the end of a life lived, but someone reflecting from a place of achievement on how that point was reached' (p.12).

27. Cf. Olga Bezhanova '*En los reinos de taifa* de Juan Goytisolo: análisis del proceso creativo' in *Memorias y olvidos: autos y biografías (reales, ficticias) en la cultura hispánica*,

eds. J. Pérez Magallón, R. de la Fuente Ballesteros and KM Sibbald (Valladolid: Universitas Castellae, 2003), pp.25–31.

28. 'Theory and Contemporary Autobiographical Writing: the Case of Juan Goytisolo', *Siglo XX/20th Century*, Vol.8, 1–2, 1990–91, p.91. The reference is to Hassan, *The Postmodern Turn: Essays in Postmodern Theory and Culture*, (Columbus: The Ohio State University Press, 1987), p.147.

29. The literary strategy behind *Marks of Identity* is noted by Miguel Dalmau when he reminds us that the 'need to reconcile oneself with the past and with the reality of the rapidly changing present [which] constitutes the essence of the book' [my translation] was common in 'numerous more or less autobiographical narratives, poems and texts' of other members of Goytisolo's generation in the early 60s as a response to the consolidation of the Franco regime. *Los Goytisolo* (Barcelona: Anagrama, 1999), p.430.

30. His partner Monique Lange in her semi-autobiographical novel, *Les cabines de bain*, has the fictional wife speak of the Goytisolo figure as follows: 'Now he has that peace, that relative peace of those who write, but when they met he was suffering from the frenzy of death. He wanted to die because he had not found himself' [my translation from the Spanish edition, *Las casetas de baño* (Barcelona: Círculo de lectores, 1997), p.52. The original was published in 1982]. Enkvist also mentions evidence in the novels of a 'death wish' 'Autobiographical Intertextuality ...', p.176.

31. See *Telón de boca* for reference to fear of dying before being able to make sense of existence.

32. Goytisolo took this idea from Michel Leiris. Cf. *El furgón de cola* (Barcelona: Seix Barral, 1976), p.58, n.2.

33. Ontology is used here in the sense of the ontology of the literary text itself or of the world which it projects as outlined by Brian McHale in *Postmodernist Fiction* (London: Methuen, 1987), p.10.

34. *Landscapes after the Battle* (London: Serpent's Tale, 1987). Referred to as LB.

35. *Forbidden Territory*, p.39.

36. See John Sturrock: 'An autobiography written without hindsight [...] would be a curious document certainly, but also a perverse one'. 'The New Model Autobiographer', *New Literary History*, vol.9, no.1, Autumn 1977, p.56.

37. *Forbidden Territory*, p.viii.

38. Jean Starobinksi, 'The Style of Autobiography' in Olney *Autobiography: Essays Theoretical and Critical* (Princeton: Princeton UP, 1980), p 74.

39. Henry Porter Abbott, 'Autobiography, Autography, Fiction: Groundwork for a Taxonomy of Textual Categories', *New Literary Review*, 1988, p.599.

40. Julián Ríos in an inventive review of *Landscapes* referred to it as an autography: 'Esa autobiografía del autor escribiendo es ante todo una *autografía* (That autobiography of the author writing is above all an *autography*)', quoted in Andrés Sánchez Robayna, *Paisajes después de la batalla* (Madrid: Espasa Calpe, 1990), p.25.

41. *Forbidden Territory*, p.39.

42. *Landscapes after the Battle*, p.149

43. Goytisolo was often criticised by feminist critics for his supposed misogynism, a feature he satirized with the introduction of the figure of Professor Lewin-Strauss in *The Marx Family Saga*.

44. Anderson, *Autobiography*, pp.5–6.

45. See note 12 above.

46. Cited in Marcus, p.196.
47. The famous 'whirligig' of 'undecidability' that for Paul de Man was so troubling about autobiographical writing. 'Autobiography as De-facement', *Modern Language Notes*, vol.94 (1979), pp.919–30.
48. Note how the autobiographical texts become a crucial intertext in *A Cock-Eyed Comedy*. See my 'Autobiography and Intertextuality in *Carajicomedia* by Juan Goytisolo', *NUI Maynooth Papers in Spanish, Portuguese and Latin American Studies*, 2, February 2001.

11

Wild Realism: The Fresh Air of the Real or the Changing Face of the European Novel

Alexis Grohmann

This chapter is an attempt to rehearse briefly certain ideas about a number of recent full-length European prose narratives, arguably novels.[1] These ideas began to take shape through an interest, in the first instance, in a number of Spanish works published since 1998. It gradually became clear to me that many of the particular features these works had in common were to be found in quite a few contemporary European narratives and that, therefore, the phenomenon transcended the Spanish context. This is a first and schematic endeavour to trace the European outline of this trend. The development observed is the following: since around 1990, a strand of full-length prose narratives that seem to be novels appears to have a taken a definite turn towards empirical reality; in addition, many of them seem to be devoid of what we understand by plot; a considerable number are digressive in a range of ways and are concerned with the multiplicity of the things of this world or their interconnectedness. It appears, therefore, that the form of the European novel, or at least part of it, is changing.

In his introductory essay to the collection entitled *Allegories of Reading*, Paul de Man, discussing the divide between form and content in literary criticism, asserts that "critics cry out for the fresh air of referential meaning".[2] It is not my intention to discuss this or de Man's rhetorical (tropological) readings, I hasten to add, although we may return to the related statement made towards the end of the book in his reading of Rousseau, in which he asserts that "language is entirely free with regard to referential meaning and can posit whatever its grammar allows it to say";[3] rather, for now, I wish merely to highlight the truth of this statement and to point out that nowadays things have gone a bit further than in the late 1970s: critics, publishers and readers alike seem to by crying out for the fresh air of the real in the novel or prose narrative form more generally.[4] This apparent incorporation, representation or re-creation of empirical reality in full-length prose narratives or novels comes in the form of, broadly, two strands, which I shall discuss in turn: (1) the biographical novel and (2) a much more digressive or errant, and even more generically ambiguous form.

I

With regard to the former, there have been published in recent years a number of works of this nature, such as J.M. Coetzee's *The Master of Petersburg* (1994), Malcolm Bradbury's *To the Hermitage* (2000), David Lodge's *Author, Author* (2004), Alberto Manguel's *Stevenson Under the Palm Trees* (2004), Colm Tóibín's *The Master* (2004) and Julian Barnes's *Arthur & George* (2005), which have been called biographical novels or fictive biographies. They are all re-imaginings of a period of the life of a famous writer (Fyodor Mikhailovich Dostoevsky, Denis Diderot, Henry James, Robert Louis Stevenson, Henry James and Sir Arthur Conan Doyle are the writers, respectively). "Fictive biography" is the term D.J. Taylor uses to refer to these works in his review of another narrative of this nature (albeit with a mathematician as the model), David Leavitt's *The Indian Clerk* (2008):

> *The Indian Clerk* is the latest adornment of an increasingly fashionable literary sub-genre: what might be called the fictive biography. At least half a dozen of them have appeared in the last half-decade, from David Lodge's *Author! Author!* [sic] (chapters in the later life of Henry James) to Julian Barnes's *Arthur & George* (Conan Doyle and the Edalji affair) and Benjamin Markovits's ongoing Byron trilogy. In most cases the reader's interest in these real lives, painstakingly set out in the pages of something advertised as a novel, is trailed by a mild anxiety about the form. Even with the Lodge, for example, one of the very best of the bunch, I found it difficult to get over the idea that I was reading a straightforward historical recreation and kept going off in search of the illustrations
>
> (Taylor 2008: 16).

Taylor's anxiety is the result of a certain generic indeterminacy attending these works: the novel form displaces biography in the exploration of a person's life, but in an imaginative way; indeed, this may be one of the ways in which the traditional genre of biography is given new impetus. The facts presented are rigorously researched in all cases (as publishers are at pains to point out on back covers and elsewhere), but they are woven into a narrative of an imaginative, novelistic form.

In an essay that David Lodge wrote on the curious coincidence in the subject matter – Henry James – and year of publication – 2004 – in the case of his *Author, Author* and Colm Tóibín's *The Master*, he confirms that the "biographical novel [...] has become a very fashionable form of literary fiction in the last decade or so, especially as applied to the lives of writers" and defines this subgenre of the novel in the following way:

> The novel which takes a real person and their real history as the subject matter for imaginative exploration, using the novel's techniques

for representing subjectivity rather than the objective, evidence-based discourse of biography.[5]

For Lodge, although there have been one or two works of this nature in the more remote past, "what is notable about the last decade or so is the number of novelists who have taken up the biographical novel at a relatively late stage of their careers, and their focus on *writers* as subjects".[6] His list of such texts includes the ones I have mentioned and a number of others.[7] Lodge distinguishes the biographical novel from the romantic biography (a "discredited" genre which "purports to be history but insinuates a good deal of authorial invention and speculation into the narrative"); the biographical novel, too, fuses empirical reality and fiction, but "makes no attempt to disguise its hybrid nature, though each writer sets himself or herself different rules about the relationship of fact to fiction", with some adhering more closely to historical record than others, some inventing in a limited way and others more freely.[8]

Lodge cites his own *Author, Author* as an example of the former. And he is scrupulous in detailing in a section appended to that novel (entitled "Acknowledgments, etc.") the instances in which, in the absence of any historical record, he imagines details, such as the invention of the personal appearance of Minnie Kidd in the absence of any description or photograph of her, or conjectures possible truths, such as Minnie Kidd's unrequited love for Burgess Noakes, which is speculation based on circumstantial evidence.[9]

What is interesting in the case of *Author, Author* and other biographical novels, is that a certain amount of such paratextual information is appended to determine its (hybrid) generic status. So, not only is the narrative followed by the extensive list of the sources of information consulted – extensive for a novel, that is – and elements imagined, but it has as a subtitle a clear marker for the reader as to the type of narrative it ought to be "taken" as: *A Novel*. Moreover, it is prefaced by an unusual statement, the opposite of the disclaimer used occasionally in the case of works of fiction:

> Sometimes it seems advisable to preface a novel with a note saying that the story and the characters are entirely fictitious, or words to that effect. On this occasion a different authorial statement seems called for. Nearly everything that happens in this story is based on factual sources. With one insignificant exception, all the named characters were real people. Quotations from their books, plays, articles, letters, journals, etc., are their own words. But I have used a novelist's licence in representing what they thought, felt, and said to each other; and I have imagined some events and personal details which history omitted to record. So this book is a novel, and structured like a novel. It begins at the end of the story, or near the end, and then goes back to the beginning, and works its way to the middle, and then rejoins the end, which is where it begins...[10]

The subtitle, appendix and this authorial statement informing us that the story and the characters are not fictitious but real, and that it is a novel structured like a novel with a discernible plot, all form part of the necessary paratext which attests to the generic status of the work as a biographical novel and tells readers how to read it. All of these texts are surrounded in one way or another by such exergues, by such paratextual information on the blend of fact and fiction, on the mixture of "intense research and vivid imagination", as we are told for example on the inside cover of Julian Barnes's *Arthur & George*. The exergue constitutes the illocutionary dimension of these texts and it is required to determine the particular relationship between the novel and the real and between text and reader, their pact, how we as readers are expected to read the text, the genre it belongs to. This is, in part, a "referential pact", to use Philip Lejeune's terminology as developed in *Le Pact autobiographique*; for Lejeune, biography and autobiography stand in opposition to fiction since they are referential texts, in that they aim to provide information on a reality exterior to the text, and the same could be said of these biographical novels, even if at the same time they also pursue novelistic aims in producing the structured, coherent, "rounded" stories that Lodge speaks of.[11]

David Lodge ventures four possible explanations of why the "biographical-novel-about-a-writer has recently acquired a new status and prominence as a subgenre of literary fiction": postmodernism ("incorporating the art of the past in its own processes through reinterpretation and stylistic pastiche"); a way of coping with the anxiety of influence; "a sign of decadence and exhaustion in contemporary writing"; and "a declining faith or loss of confidence in the power of purely fictional narrative, in a culture where we are bombarded from every direction with factual narrative".[12] All of the above may form part of the explanation; the last two are particularly compelling and plausible causes. He adds that he would not have conceived of writing a novel of this kind twenty years previously, because his concept of what constituted a novel, "did not then include the possibility of writing one about a real historical person".[13] The fact that nowadays the novel form does encompass this possibility, for Lodge and many others, is further evidence that the novel has changed.

Let us dwell briefly on one more narrative, before turning our attention to the other type of "new" novel. The 2006 edition of Leonid Tsypkin's *Summer in Baden-Baden* also comes with its exergue: it, too, carries the subtitle *A Novel* and is preceded by an introduction by Susan Sontag that tells us what kind of narrative the work is and orients the reader. The reason I did not list this Russian work above is that it was first published in 1981, so it is not a recent work. However, the publisher's decision to re-issue it in 2006 is directly related to the recent rise of the biographical novel outlined above and also the type of work I will discuss below, into which category fall W. G. Sebald's novels. The publication of Tsypkin's work by Penguin (the English-language publishers of Sebald's last work, *Austerlitz*, in 2001) is modelled on the Sebald novels published in the UK: the font, font size, page margins and generous line-spacing are identical; in addition, this edition of the Russian writer's novel "is the first to be published in book form with the author's original photographs" interspersed throughout the text (as the "Publisher's note" informs us on page viii), something that had by then become a Sebald trademark.[14]

Again, there are ample references to the interplay between fact and fiction, between the research and imagination that have produced this work. Sontag speaks of the "years of preparation consulting archives", of the novel being "scrupulously researched", indeed, of it being "a matter of honour for Tsypkin that everything of a factual nature be true to the story and the circumstances of the real lives it evokes"; at the same time, the narrative is a re-imagining, a re-creation of Dostoevsky's life and "a mental tour of Russian reality", in which "Nothing is invented. Everything is invented".[15] The lives evoked are not only Dostoevsky's (and his wife's) during a particular period, but also the author's own, so this novel, unlike the other biographical novels discussed, has a significant autobiographical strand, making it more akin in this respect to Sebald and other narratives of a similar kind. However, although it may constitute an example of "para-fiction", this narrative is not a "docu-novel" according to Sontag; rather, it

> belongs to a rare and exquisitely ambitious subgenre of the novel: a retelling of the life of a real person of accomplishment from another era, it interweaves this story with a story in the present, the novelist mulling over, trying to gain deeper entry into, the inner life of someone whose destiny it was to have become not only historical but monumental.[16]

What distinguishes *Summer in Baden-Baden* from the other recent biographical novels is not only the fact that it incorporates a substantial autobiographical strand, but the way it does so, its form. The narrative constantly moves from the biographical to the autobiographical and from time past (both Dostoevsky's and the narrator's) to present, and thus shows how past and present interpenetrate. So, its originality, as Sontag puts it, lies "in the way it moves, from the autobiographical narrative of the never-to-be-named narrator [...] to the life of the peripatetic Dostoevskys".[17] And the particular way this forward and backward movement is effected is through a digressive style. So, each paragraph of the novel is made up of a single sentence in each and every case, with some of them ranging over a number of pages (eleven, in one notable instance).[18] These "protracted paragraph-sentences", as Sontag calls them,[19] can therefore encompass both pasts and present, in a backward and forward eddying between the Dostoevskys' and the narrator's lives, between Germany and Russia, between biographical and autobiographical writing. The sentences have something of the obsessiveness of Sebald's in their apparent pursuit of the way things are or were, or of the real (Sontag likens their "incessantness" to Thomas Bernhard's prose), and they are also free in the same way; "the long sentence", argues Sontag, "bespeaks inclusiveness and associativeness".[20]

So, the form, the long sentence and concomitant digressive style, facilitate the genre-switching and the permeability of diachronic contexts, disrupting a diachronic syntax of narrative and interconnecting past and present,[21] whilst striving for a comprehensiveness that allows us to glimpse the interrelated multiplicity of the world. This digressive form works, to some extent, against the coherence, structure and "roundedness" that the biographical novels mentioned earlier seek to attain, and against a coherent plot emerging, however subtly traced. And through its digressiveness Tsypkin's errant work connects with the second kind of emerging narrative form I would now like to turn my attention to.

II

Digressiveness and the "evidence of the real" characterise this other, related strand of writing.[22] The "evidence of the real" as a determining factor is what this set of novels or full-length prose narratives has in common with the biographical novel. But the "real" is not made evident in them merely through biographical writing, but, as in Tsypkin, also through a pronounced autobiographical vein, as well as through travel writing or travelogue, the diary, epistolary and essay forms, amongst others. Into this arabesque are sometimes woven also fictional modes of writing, but only as one of many threads, and all together they make up the amalgam of these hybrid works, which seem to have turned away from fiction as the dominant mode of the novel form and have espoused a seemingly "unveiled" representation of reality. All of these works or "false novels", as one of the authors in question described his narrative,[23] are at the same time formally considerably digressive or errant texts, plotless and seemingly wandering aimlessly or moving without appearing to go in any one particular direction, but with great effect, laying bare the processes of the creative imagination and often performing a certain amount of self-theorising along the way, thus pertaining to a type of narrative that has been termed aptly "loiterature" (Chambers 1999). Moreover, they are all, without exception, imbued with a distinctly European sensibility and subject matter.

Indeed, as the Spanish filament began to emerge with Javier Marías's *Negra espalda del tiempo* (*Dark Back of Time*, 1998) at the vanguard, it became evident that, apart from the fact that they are all referential texts in Lejeune's terminology, remitting us to a reality exterior to the text, namely, to empirical reality, they are highly digressive narratives, to such an extent that through a reading of *Dark Back of Time* in particular I have abstracted four closely related and overlapping levels of digressiveness. This has developed into a very appropriate schema or theoretical framework with which to examine such narratives.[24] Put simply, all such narratives are not only (1) generically and (2) stylistically digressive, they are also (3) plotless and (4) they enact, thematise and often theorise the errant processes of the creative imagination. Let me add that when I say such works are "plotless" what I mean simply is that they are narratives with no main incidents, or no distinction made between main and secondary ones, thus without a clearly traceable outline of events and situations; any incidents narrated do not really add up to a structure of any kind, and certainly not one characterizable in terms of Freytag's pyramid (there is no inciting moment rising in term of action through exposition and complication to a climax that falls by way of reversal to a catastrophe or resolution and a moment of last suspense).[25]

This type of novel has blossomed in Spain since 1998, beginning with Marías's work; some of the other texts in question are (I cite the original title, followed, in brackets, by the title in English – I give the title of the text in a published translation when a translation exists – and the original date of publication of the work): Antonio Muñoz Molina's *Sefarad* (*Sepharad*, 2001) and *Ventanas de Manhattan* (*Manhattan Windows*, 2004), Enrique Vila-Matas's *Bartleby y compañía* (*Bartleby & Co.*, 2000), *El mal de Montano* (*Montano's Sickness*, 2002), *París no se acaba nunca* (*Paris Never Ends*, 2003) and *Doctor Pasavento* (2005), Rosa Montero's *La loca de la casa* (*The Madwoman of the House*, 2003), and Vicente Molina Foix's *El abrecartas* (*The Letter Opener*, 2007).[26] The wider, European context includes, in particular, works by the German Winfried Gottlieb Sebald – *Schwindel. Gefühle* (*Vertigo*, 1990), *Die Ausgewanderten. Vier lange Erzählungen* (*The Emigrants*, 1992), *Die Ringe des Saturn. Eine Englische Wallfahrt* (*The Rings of Saturn*, 1995) and *Austerlitz* (2001) – and the Italian Claudio Magris, especially *Microcosmi* (*Microcosms*, 1997), but, arguably, also *Danubio* (*Danube*, 1986). I would now like briefly to draw attention to some of the main features of such narratives with particular reference to Magris, Marías and Sebald, probably the three major exponents of this "new" novel.

One of the things that could be said of these texts is what Elide Pittarello has observed of Javier Marías's *Dark Back of Time*, namely, that they do not belong to any one customary genre of writing but partake of all of them.[27] Through autobiographical, biographical, fictional, essayistic and other modes of writing, Javier Marías loosely explores the effects of one of his novels, *Todas las almas* (*All Souls*, 1989) on his own life, thus, the effects of (a) fiction on reality, and in the process surveys the lives of a number of others, mainly writers, who had existed, whilst revealing how the inclusion of a seemingly fictional character in *All Souls* lead to him eventually inheriting a literary kingdom. This he attempts, despite the fact that words, as he tells us in the introductory section, cannot represent reality, despite the knowledge that

the time-honoured aspiration of any chronicler or survivor – to tell what happened, give an account of what took place, leave a record of events and crimes and exploits – is, in fact, a mere illusion or chimera, or, rather, the phrase and concept themselves are already metaphorical and partake of fiction. "To tell what happened" is inconceivable and futile, or possible only as invention;[28]

despite this, he continues,

> in these pages I'm going to place myself on the side of those who have sometimes claimed to be telling what really happened or pretended to succeed in doing so, I am going to tell what happened, or was ascertained, or simply known – what happened in my experience or in my fabulation or in my knowledge.[29]

This is why he later insists that *Dark Back of Time* "is not a fiction".[30] Both Sebald and Magris attempt the same thing or something akin, even if they do not preface their narratives with such explicit theoretical considerations; instead, they are scattered throughout the texts, as in the following quotation from Sebald's *Austerlitz*, which, like Marías's words, expresses the impossibility of representing the world through language, a fact that shows that all these writers thus demonstrate an awareness of late-twentieth-century scepticism regarding the possibility of language to represent the real (summed up by de Man's formulation cited at the beginning of this chapter):

> All of us, even when we think we have noted every tiny detail, resort to set pieces which have already been staged often enough by others. We try to reproduce the reality, but the harder we try, the more we find the pictures that make up the stock-in-trade of the spectacle of history forcing themselves upon us [...] the truth lies elsewhere, away from it all, somewhere as yet undisclosed.[31]

It is this truth, bound up with memory and the remembering and recounting of the past in particular, past lives, past events, which narratives such as Sebald's, Marías's and Magris's seek to allow us to glimpse, in the knowledge, paradoxically, that ultimately language is only "something which we use [...] to grope blindly through the darkness enveloping us", as Austerlitz tells the narrator.[32]

Autobiographical, biographical and essayistic modes of writing, to which should be added travel writing, also make up W. G. Sebald's prose narratives. Both Sebald and Marías also intersperse in their narratives photographic reproductions, which seem to aspire to an accurate representation of reality while at the same time casting doubt on it. Anne Fuchs argues Sebald's photographs regularly raise the question of how they are to be taken as the reader often cannot decide and is not told what the relationship of the image to the text is; this gives rise to a certain "undecidability" ("die Unentscheidbarkeit

der Frage").[33] For Elide Pittarello, Marías's use of photographs and reproductions provides, on the one hand, faithful yet spectral proof of a reality
the result of chance, and on the other, following Philippe Dubois's theory
of "the photographic act", it constitutes an "image-act", whose pragmatic
production becomes indissociable from the moment of its interpretation or
reception.[34] Both Marías's and Sebald's narratives constitute in this and other
ways, such as through the inclusion of fictional elements alongside the real,
an ontological hide-and-seek game, not infrequently challenging the reader
to ask whether something is or is not "real" or "true". Claudio Magris, again
through biographical, autobiographical, essayistic, diary and travel writing,
surveys certain Central European regions and lives, their histories or micro-
histories, borders and identity with specific references to the cultures and
literatures of those areas.

All three European writers weave highly digressive narratives and their novels include an awareness of their digressiveness; this is how they represent or
re-enact reality. Because, in a nutshell, this is a "natural" style, as Ross Chambers refers to such digressive writing, "more in tune with the complexity of
things and the tangled relations that join them".[35] Such digressive writing
can wean readers away from a narrative of " 'events' ", Chambers writes –
and I will quote his account because it will take us to the heart of the matter
(and it will do so much more eloquently than I ever could) –

> and onto another, more "nonchalant", style, one that takes its time,
> makes no beelines, is always ready to turn away from a given direction in
> order to explore something other. Such a style, always ready to interrupt
> itself, is inevitably episodic [...] and, veering easily (i.e. without a sense
> of discontinuity) from topic to topic, following associative drifts or the
> promptings of memory, it is digressive: it is organized, that is, by relations
> of resemblance and contiguity, metaphor and metonymy rather than the
> formal unity required by argument or the narrative of event. Such a style
> is often concerned with the, often obscure, "coherence of experience" [...]
> than it is respectful of patterns that are more strictly designed and thus
> "cohesive".[36]

These are the reasons why Chambers then adds that such a style seems
"somehow natural – or at least more natural than disciplined argument or
the tightly controlled narratives that we nonetheless tend to get so caught
up in";[37] because, not conditioned by a goal, by a structure, it has the freedom to drift and follow paths opened up by associations, by memory, by
the contiguous, mentally or otherwise, it appears to be concerned "with the
coherence of experience". It is not at pains to make coherent what is not
coherent; hence, it is *naturally* more "in tune with the complexity of things
and the tangled relations that join them", because the things of this world
are complex and the relations that join them tangled, and the world would

not be recreated appropriately otherwise. Hence, also, the ease with which such digressive texts switch genres, move from the autobiographical to the biographical, from the concrete to the more abstract sphere of the aphoristic and essayistic, and back, etc.; these moves happen digressively, naturally, dictated by the matter at hand and the mind thinking as it goes and establishing, seeing, following links that emerge "without a sense of discontinuity".[38] This is what leads us to the generic indeterminacy and the resistance to contextualization and categorization so characteristic of this type of extensively digressive literature or *loiterature*.

So, Magris, in the first chapter of *Microcosms* entitled "Caffè San Marco", in which he introduces us to his narrative, its nature and preoccupations, discusses the nineteenth-century memoirs of one Giuseppe Fano and highlights and praises certain of its features, shared by Magris's own work (his considerations constitute metanarrative statements on his own narrative): he draws attention to the fact that Fano's text is "too honest to attempt any synthesis of the random multiplicity of what is real – this would be too presumptuous" (later he echoes this view of the world when he speaks of the "scattered multiplicity of things" and refers to the "erratic fractal multiplicity of a certain valley", "the tortuous plurality of all feudal macro- and microcosms"); he extols Fano's unconcern for the lack of coherence of his memoirs, the fact that he does not remove elements that are incoherent or contradictory or lead one astray; "His autobiography", he concludes, "has the coherence of its fragmentary nature, there is no pretence at a conclusion and it interrupts itself in homage to reality, which remains unfinished and unconclusive".[39] This is why Magris has an interest in stories that are "rambling, digressive, constantly breaking off before picking up the thread".[40] Reality is incoherent, hence narrative cannot entirely be coherent if it attempts to represent it; "Whatever happens, respect for others, even for things, remains paramount".[41]

Chambers adds that "in literature there is always time to explore a byway and often it is not clear which road is a byway and which represents the beeline – the main road, the most direct route – since [...] there is no particular goal to attain and no schedule for achieving it".[42] This digressive journey, both in narrative and in real terms, is what interests Magris. In *Microcosms* he tells us, closely echoing Chambers's description: "All straight journeys, with a precise point of arrival, *are* brief [...]. The evening stroll with no precise destination loses itself, caught up on half-buried wrecks that trip one up, sends one down paths that have been erased".[43] It is such erased paths that Magris pursues errantly, also in his *Danube*, where a similar engagement with digression emerges from the very first paragraph, in which he resists the ordering of the errant paths in an invitation extended to him because

> It aims to reduce the unpredictability of travel, the intricacy and divergence of paths, the fortuity of delays, the uncertainty of evening and

the asymmetrical quality of any journey, to the inexorable order of a treatise.[44]

Throughout *Danube*, Magris praises digression. He praises the Austrian tradition of defending the "tangible detail" against ideological totalitarianism; he admires the virtues of the nineteenth-century Austrian poet Franz Grillparzer's opposition to the brutal dogmatism (of Napoleon and others) that sidelines "what appears minor and secondary":

> Grillparzer accuses Napoleon of aiming straight for the 'Hauptsache', the main point, while ignoring the 'Nebensache', the outwardly marginal and secondary but which nonetheless, in the eyes of the Austrian poet who is the defender of 'minute particulars', has its independent dignity and must not be sacrificed to a tyrannical overall scheme of things.[45]

The straight line disrespects the nature of things; Napoleon, in his frantic haste, personifies the "modern frenzy that annihilates the otiose and the ephemeral", "without being able to dally even in love or in pleasure", whereas baroque-inspired, history-transcending or post-historically fragmented Austrian culture "rejects the yardsticks according to which we bestow importance on phenomena and arrange them in order of greatness"; Austrian culture "defends what is marginal, transient, secondary, the pause and respite from that mechanism which aims at burning up such things in order to attain more important results".[46] The cohesive, goal-oriented, single-mindedness, end-directedness of the (Napoleonic) beeline is opposed to the pleasures of errancy, which strives for time out and regard for the seemingly unimportant, negligible element. To neglect the apparently negligible would be negligent. Loiterature represents an enactment of the epistemology of the seemingly unimportant and unsystematic.[47] "The musuem of traditional and systematic knowledge", argues Magris in *Microcosms*, "makes for rigidity and eludes the drama of existence, inserting and neutralizing all phenomena in catalogues and classifications".[48] It is out of respect for existence, the things and the people of this world, that such narratives are digressive; digressivenes is the result of the consideration shown towards lives and objects that people the world. Such works are digressive in homage to reality.

All this is precisely why in *Dark Back of Time* Javier Marías narrates, as he says in the novel, "for no reason and in no particular order, without making an outline or seeking coherence", without his narrative corresponding "to any plan" or being "ruled by any compass", without any "reason to make sense or add up to an argument or plot, or answer to some hidden harmony", or even making up "a story with its beginning and its expectation and its final silence", and also why *Dark Back of Time* is "a book of digressions, a book that proceeds by digression", as the narrator Javier Marías exclaims through an interpolated clause at the very beginning of the fifth chapter or section when he says that he must "make a digression",[49] reminding us implicitly of the same narrative movement described in another narrative and metanarrative reflection, Tristram's famous explanation of the nature of his narrative in Chapter Twenty-two of Volume I of *The Life and Opinions of Tristram Shandy, Gentleman* (a work very dear to Marías and of which he produced a prize-winning translation into Spanish):

> For in this long digression which I was accidentally led into, as in all my digressions (one only excepted) there is a master-stroke of digressive skill, the merit of which, has all along, I fear, been overlooked by my reader, – not for want of penetration in him, – but because 'tis an excellence seldom looked for, or expected indeed, in a digression; – and it is this: That though my digressions are all fair, as you observe – and that I fly off from what I am about, as far and as often as any writer in Great Britain; yet I constantly take care to order affairs so, that my main business does not stand still in my absence. [...] By this contrivance the machinery of my work is of a species by itself; two contrary motions are introduced into it, and reconciled, which were thought to be at variance with each other. In a word, my work is digressive, and it is progressive too, – and at the same time.[50]

These are the two motions at work – digression and progression, progression through digression – in Sterne, Marías, Magris and Sebald.

It is for all the above reasons why Sebald's narratives and *Austerlitz* in particular, digressively roam "all over the place figuratively as well as geographically", as one critic put it.[51] In fact, this particular critic's objections to Sebald's digressive roaming are enlightening, precisely because they construe Sebald's digressiveness as a problem, an obstacle. Discussing a certain object reproduced in *The Emigrants* (the "*teas-maid*", a tea-making alarm clock whose photograph is included in the work during the relation of the narrator's arrival in Manchester in the section entitled "Max Ferber"),[52] the critic argues that the story of the *teas-maid* is inconsequential, an "incidental curiosity", that will soon be forgotten, vanish "without a trace"; however, she is puzzled by such (seemingly) marginal, unimportant parts in Sebald and their relevance; how do they relate to the whole?, she asks; "Sometimes, as with the teas-maid only quite peripherally", she answers. However, a larger problem emerges and the critic's rhetoric of difficulty is revealing (the italics are mine):

> This *problem* is at its most extreme in the *dense* labyrinths of Sebald's last completed novel, *Austerlitz*, which *roams all over the place* figuratively as well as geographically, *overloading* readers with an abundance of frequently technical details in sentences pages long (one extends over nine pages), *details that pose a tough challenge to the reader's capacity to process, let alone to accommodate them in the totality by means of interpretation.* This is a realism

gone wild. Things are juxtaposed associatively, in an apparently *random* manner as a reflection of a universe full of *bewildering* objects and chance encounters, a world governed in the last resort not by any comprehensible order but by a *disconcerting contingency*. And this is where Sebald differs fundamentally from Flaubert for whom the world did have an order, albeit a negative one [...].[53]

Obviously one of the difficulties Furst faces is the fact that she is, naturally, compelled to establish hierarchies of importance, between what is relevant and what is irrelevant or peripheral; such an approach will indeed compel her to raise these issues in the way that she does, because, not least, everything is peripheral or everything is relevant in such a digressive narrative, since all elements form part of the mosaic constructed, which allows us to glimpse that of the real. And the *teas-maid* and its photograph is just as important as, say, the forged photograph of a mass burning of books in Würzburg in 1933 (reproduced later on in the same section) and the concomitant new order being heralded at the time in Germany. The *teas-maid*, as the narrator himself explains, stands in a metonymical relationship to Manchester's industrialization and the 1960s post-industrial wasteland it has left behind (the bizarre combination of functions is the result of the optimism of a process of industrialization gone wild; to the narrator it "looked like a miniature power plant"),[54] which the narrator will subsequently have occasion to observe. In addition, through the glowing, phosphorescent lime-green light it emits, it affords him a protection that he remembers associated with his childhood, to such an extent that in hindsight it seems to the narrator that the presence of this weird and wonderful contraption kept him "holding on to life at a time when I felt a deep sense of isolation in which I might well have become completely submerged".[55] So, to say that the *teas-maid* is merely peripheral, that it is of little consequence, is clearly not accurate; it saved the narrator's life, to put it crudely; it is as important or as unimportant as all the other elements.

"Criticism", says Chambers, "depends, like social order itself, on the possibility of discriminating or hierarchizing, determining what's central and what's peripheral (this is more important that that, the point is such-and-such, the theme is so-and-so; the rest is 'just plot' or 'descriptive detail')";[56] but suppose there is no center, as Chambers asks, and, therefore, no periphery? We do not need to process or accommodate Sebald's details in a way other than they are presented. What Marías says in *Dark Back of Time* is valid for all these texts: "Unlike those of truly fictional novels, the elements of the story I am now embarking upon are entirely capricious, determined by chance, merely episodic and cumulative – all of them irrelevant by the elementary rule of criticism".[57] Such digressive literature involves "the transvaluation of the trivial"; any sense of estrangement it produces, as in the case of the *teas-maid*, is, in Chambers terms, "due to the reversal of conventionally hier-archical values";[58] it becomes a practice that calls into question the very distinctions on which classifications depend.

These eminently digressive narratives do not roam all over the place for the sake of it or because the writers do not care to structure them; as Marías put it in *Dark Back of Time*: "If the reader should wonder what on earth is being recounted here or where this text is heading, the only proper answer, I fear, would be that it is simply running its course and heading toward its ending, just like anything else that passes through or happens in the world".[59] The course of this literature is like the course things take in life or the world.

Of course, in a way, Furst is not entirely wrong to say that Sebald's is a realism "gone wild", though she is wrong to formulate it as a criticism; it is an attempt, akin to Magris's, to provide a critical historiography, "to see that it wasn't just the great events of the past that determine our lives", as Sebald said in an interview;[60] and so, in this *Weltanschauung* the little things matter just as much as the seemingly important elements, sometimes more. And, yes, things are indeed juxtaposed associatively, in an apparently random manner, and they do reflect a universe full of bewildering objects and chance encounters, a world governed in the last resort not by any comprehensible order but by a disconcerting contingency, precisely beacause we are thereby given a glimpse of the bewildering, casually interrelated, array of elements that makes up the random multiplicity of the world. This is how the writer portrays "the quintessential, insoluble enigma of human existence", as Furst rightly concludes.[61]

Both the biographical novel and these exceptionally digressive novels strive to show us that "life is a mystery", as Henry James says in the last major scene in Tóibín's book;[62] the "wild realism" of digressive, errant or loiterly novels, which sacrifices coherence in homage to reality, out of respect for the scat-tered multiplicty of the things of this world, further affords us a glimpse of the real in all its intricate complexity, its potentially limitless comprehensiveness and interconnectedness, a "globality that, in the end, resists inventory".[63]

Notes

1. I say "arguably" because, as we will see, they deviate to some extent from the norm; but the fact that most – if not all – are presented as novels suffices in my mind to classify them as such. The novel form has always been notorious for its promiscuity, for admitting, incorporating, practically any mode of writing.
2. De Man (1979: 4).
3. De Man (1979: 293).
4. Confirmation of this can be found not only through the mere observation of the various manifestations of this phenomenon and the number of such works published, but also, explicitly, in what a few authors have said; so, for example, Colm Tóibín, following the success of his biographical novel *The Master*, which re-creates a period in the life of Henry James, asserted that this is now the dominant literary fashion and the type of work that publishers actively wish authors to

produce (in a conversation on the occasion of the opening of the new Cervantes Institute in Dublin on 20 February 2007). Other, Spanish, authors, such as Enrique Vila-Matas and Vicente Molina Foix have made statements attesting to the rise of the novel incorporating the "real".

5. Lodge (2006: 8).
6. Lodge (2006: 8).
7. The other works cited by Lodge are: Penelope Fitzgerald's *The Blue Flower* (1996), Lynn Truss's *Tennyson's Gift* (1996), Michael Cunningham's *The Hours* (1999), Beryl Bainbridge's *According to Queeney* (2001), Emma Tennant's *The Ballad of Sylvia and Ted* (2001) and *Felony* (2002), Edmund White's *Fanny: A Fiction* (2003), Kate Moses's *Wintering* (2003), C. K. Stead's *Mansfield* (2004) and Andrew Motion's *The Invention of Doctor Cake* (2004).
8. Lodge (2006: 9).
9. Lodge (2004: 387–8).
10. Lodge (2004; the ellipsis is in the original).
11. Lejeune (1975). As is well known, the notion of "illocutionary force" was famously developed by Searle, who in "The Logical Status of Fictional Discourse" argued that there is no textual property *per se* that will identify a text as a work of fiction and that what makes it a work of fiction is the author's illocutionary stance (Searle 1979: 65–6); the concept of the illocutionary stance or force was expanded, with reference to the genre of autobiography, by Elizabeth Bruss, who argued that a text's illocutionary force is derived from the context surrounding the text, which contextual information tells us how we should expect to receive the text; all literature has its illocutionary dimension (Bruss 1976); in "The Law of Genre", Jacques Derrida took this discussion one step further by arguing that this force, the paratext or exergue, is "absolutely necessary for and constitutive of what we call art, poetry, or literature", since there is no work of art that can be identified if it does not bear the "mark of a genre" (Derrida 1981: 51–77). In a sense a text's illocutionary force, its exergue, is less a clearly defined category than a flexible space surrounding the text and not strictly speaking forming part of it; this is more or less what Gérard Genette has defined as the "paratext" (or "paratexte"): "All the marginal and supplementary data around the text. It comprises what one could call various thresholds: authorial and editorial (i.e., titles, insertions, dedications, epigraphs, prefaces and notes); media related (i e , interviews with the author, official summaries) and private (i.e., correspondence, calculated and non-calculated disclosures), as well as those related to the material means of production and reception, such as groupings, segments, etc."; crucially, in Genette's discussion of Proust's text and also generally, the paratext has a pedagogical objective: "namely, the instruction of the public, so as to guard against eventual misunderstanding, and to orient the reader to the kind of reading which Proust considered the most faithful and the most pertinent" (Genette 1988: 63).
12. Lodge (2006: 9–10). In an interview published in the Spanish newspaper *El País* in 2004, Lodge puts forward this last explanation as the only one, when he says that fiction has lost the authority, the conviction, it had in the past since readers have lost faith in its powers (Lodge 2004b).
13. Lodge (2006: 11).
14. Sontag makes the "Sebald-effect" thus sought explicit in her introduction: "Tsypkin may have imagined that if *Summer in Baden-Baden* were ever to be published as a book it should include some of the photographs he had taken, thereby anticipating the signature effect of W. G. Sebald, who, by seeding his books with photographs,

infuses the plainest idea of verisimilitude with enigma and pathos" (Sontag 2006: xxii).

15. Sontag (2006: xx, xxii, xxiii, xxv, xxviii, xxxiii).
16. Sontag (2006: xi, xxv).
17. Sontag (2006: xxiii–xxiv).
18. Tsypkin (2006: 247–57).
19. Sontag (2006: xxxi).
20. Sontag (2006: xxxiii). This digressiveness is also why she refers to the narrative as "a kind of dream novel, in which the dreamer, who is Tsypkin himself, conjures up his own life and that of Dostoevsky in a streaming, passionate narration" (2006: xvi).
21. I am borrowing here some of the terms Ross Chambers employs in his book on digressive writing and its implications entitled *Loiterature* (1999).
22. "La evidencia de lo real" is what Spanish critic and author José María Guelbenzu says distinguishes this emerging type of European novel in an essay entitled "¿Otro camino para la novela?" ("Another Direction for the Novel?"; Guelbenzu 2001).
23. This is what Javier Marías termed his *Negra espalda del tiempo* (*Dark Back of Time*, 1998).
24. I have rehearsed this in three contributions and am currently completing a full-length study in which I examine the digressiveness of the key Spanish texts of this phenomenon (Grohmann 2005a, 2005b, 2006)
25. I am referring to Gerald Prince's definitions of plot in his *Dictionary of Narratology* (2003).
26. To this list could be added novels such as *Soldados de Salamina* (*Soldiers of Salamis*, 2001) and *La velocidad de la luz* (*The Speed of Light*, 2006) by Javier Cercas, and *Las esquinas del aire* (*The Corners of the Air*, 2000) by Juan Manuel de Prada, which have discernible plots and are less digressive but which, through their quest to reconstruct the life of a person who had once existed and events pertaining to it and constituting a mystery, the protagonists seek to solve in each case, include a pronounced layer of the "real" (of a biographical nature, in particular).
27. Pittarello (2001).
28. Marías (2001: 8); I have taken all quotations from the published English translations of these texts.
29. Marías (2001: 8–9).
30. Marías (2001: 74).
31. Sebald (2001: 101).
32. Sebald (2001: 175).
33. Fuchs (2004: 138–42); on Sebald's use of photography see also Jonathan Long (2003) and Lilian Furst (2006), among others.
34. Pittarello (2005).
35. Chambers (1999: 31).
36. Chambers (1999: 31).
37. Chambers (1999: 31).
38. This digressive style has a number of features in common with the anti-Ciceronian style of the seventeenth century, as discussed by Morris Croll: Croll observes, for example, that the progression of the sentence of the loose style (which together with the curt style constitute the two types of anti-Ciceronian style) "adapts itself to the movement of a mind discovering truth as it goes, thinking while it writes" (1972: 109); equally, both forms of anti-Ciceronian period are meant to portray the natural or thinking order, and both express the prejudice against the

formality of procedure, although it is the loose style that is associated with the more sceptical phases of seventeenth-century thought, appearing in writers who are "professed opponents of determined and rigorous philosophical attitudes", such as Sir Thomas Browne, whose work Croll cites most often as an example of both styles in his article (1972). The reasons for this link between the anti-Ciceronian sentence of the seventeenth century and the present author are the digressive nature of the styles of both the past and present authors, and the fact that Browne, who cultivated a particularly digressive style of writing, is an author dear to both Marías (the latter has translated some of his work and Browne has influenced his prose by Marías's own admission) and Sebald (see Sebald's professed admiration and discussion of Browne's style in *The Rings of Saturn*; 1998: 18–19; I have not been able to ascertain whether he has also had a similar influence on Magris). For a discussion of the implications of Sebald's treatment of Browne in his narratives and their affinities see Fuchs (2004: 99–107); for a consideration of Browne's impact on Marías see Grohmann (2002: 55–88).

39. Magris (1999: 124, 205, 25–6, respectively).
40. Magris (1999: 179).
41. Magris (1999: 26).
42. Chambers (1999: 31).
43. Magris (1999: 219).
44. Magris (1989: 15).
45. Magris (1989: 90).
46. Magris (1989: 81).
47. See Chambers (1999: 10).
48. Magris (1999: 251).
49. Marías (2001: 335, 47).
50. Laurence Sterne (1985: 94–5).
51. Furst (2006: 224–5).
52. Sebald (1996: 153–5).
53. Furst (2006: 224–5).
54. Sebald (1996: 154).
55. Sebald (1996: 154–5).
56. Chambers (1999: 9).
57. Marías (2001: 9).
58. Chambers (1999: 34).
59. Marías (2001: 287).
60. Sebald (2006: 24).
61. Furst (2006: 225).
62. Tóibín (2004: 355).
63. Chambers (1999: 13).

Bibliography

Andres-Suárez, Irène and Casas, Ana, eds 2005. *Cuadernos de narrativa. Javier Marías*, Madrid: Arco.

Babb, Howard, ed. 1972. *Essays in Stylistic Analysis*, New York: Harcourt Brace Jovanovich.

Barnes, Julian. 2005. *Arthur & George*, London: Jonathan Cape.

Bradbury, Malcolm. 2000. *To the Hermitage*, London: Picador.

Bruss, Elizabeth. 1976. *Autobiographical Acts: The Changing Situation of a Literary Genre*, Baltimore: Johns Hopkins University Press.

Cercas, Javier. 2001. *Soldados de Salamina*, Barcelona: Tusquets.

———. 2005. *La velocidad de la luz*, Barcelona: Tusquets.

Chambers, Ross. 1999. *Loiterature*, Lincoln: University of Nebraska Press.

Coetzee, J. M. 1994. *The Master of Petersburg*, London: Secker & Warburg.

Croll, Morris. 1972. "The Baroque Style in Prose", in Babb 1972, 97–117.

De Man, Paul. 1979. *Allegories of Reading. Figural Language in Rousseau, Nietzsche, Rilke and Proust*, New Haven: Yale University Press.

Denham, Scott and McCulloh, Mark. 2006. *W. G. Sebald. History –Memory – Trauma*, Berlin: Walter de Gruyter.

De Prada, Juan Manuel. 2000. *Las esquinas del aire. En busca de Ana María Martínez Sagi*, Barcelona: Planeta.

Derrida, Jacques. 1981. "The Law of Genre", in Mitchell 1981, 51–77.

Fuchs, Anne. 2004. *Die Schmerzenschpuren der Geschichte. Zur Poetik der. Erinnerung in W. G. Sebalds Prosa*, Köln: Böhlau.

Furst, Lilian R. 2006. "Realism, Photography and Degrees of Uncertainty", in Denham and McCulloh 2006, 219–29.

Genette, Gérard. 1988. "The Proustian Paratexte", *SubStance*, Vol. 17, No. 2, Issue 56: *Reading In and Around*, 63–77.

Grohmann, Alexis. 2002. *Coming into one's Own. The Novelistic Development of Javier Marías*, Amsterdam: Rodopi.

———. 2005a. "Literatura y digresión: La errabundia de Negra espalda del tiempo", in Andres-Suárez and Casas 2005, 135–144.

———. 2005b. "Literatura y errabundia", in *Antes y después del* Quijote. *En el. cincuentenario de la Asociación de Hispanistas de Gran Bretaña e Irlanda*, eds. Robert Archer, Valdi Astvaldsson, Stephen Boyd, Michael Thompson, Generalitat Valenciana: Valencia, 373–81.

———. 2006. "Errant Text: *Sefarad*, by Antonio Muñoz Molina", in *Travelling Texts. Journal of Iberian and Latin American Studies*, eds. Claire Lindsay and Montserrat Lunati, vol. 12, nos 2–3, August/December, 233–46.

Guelbenzu, José María. 2001. "¿Otro camino para la novela?", in *Claves de la razón práctica*, No. 115, September, 61–5.

Leavitt, David. 2008. *The Indian Clerk*, London: Bloomsbury.

Lejeune, Philippe. 1975. *Le Pacte autobiographique*, Paris: Seuil.

Lodge, David. 2004a. *Author, Author*, London: Penguin.

———. 2004b. "La ficción ha perdido autoridad y poder de convicción", *EL PAÍS, Babelia*, 1 May, 1–2.

———. 2006. *The Year of Henry James or Timing is All: the Story of a Novel*, London: Harvill Secker.

Long, Jonathan. 2003. "History, Narrative and Photography in W. G. Sebald's *Die Ausgewanderten*", *The Modern Language Review* 98, 117–137.

Magris, Claudio. 1986. *Danubio*, Milan: Garzanti.

———. 1989. *Danube*, London: Harvill.

———. 1997. *Microcosmi*, Milan: Garzanti.

———. 1999. *Microcosms*, London: Harvill.

Manguel, Alberto. 2004. *Stevenson Under the Palm Trees*, Edinburgh: Canongate.

Marías, Javier. 1989. *Todas las almas*, Barcelona: Anagrama.

———. 1998. *Negra espalda del tiempo*, Madrid: Alfaguara.

———. 2001. *Dark Back of Time*, London: Chatto & Windus.

Mitchell, W. J. T., ed. 1981. *On Narrative*, Chicago: The University of Chicago Press.
Molina Foix, Vicente. 2007. *El abrecartas*, Barcelona: Anagrama.
Montero, Rosa. 2003. *La loca de la casa*, Madrid: Alfaguara.
Muñoz Molina, Antonio. 2001. *Sefarad*, Madrid: Alfaguara.
——. 2004. *Ventanas de Manhattan*, Barcelona: Seix Barral.
Pittarello, Elide. 2001. "*Negra espalda del tiempo*: instrucciones de uso", in Steenmeijer 2001, 125–34.
——. 2005. "Haciendo tiempo con las cosas", in Andres-Suárez and Casas 2005, 17–48.
Prince, Gerald. 2003. *Dictionary of Narratology*, Lincoln: University of Nebraska Press.
Searle, John R. 1979. *Expression and Meaning: Studies in the Theory of Speech Acts*, Cambridge: CUP.
Sebald, Wingried Georg. 1990. *Schwindel. Gefühle*, Frankfurt o. M.: Eichborn.
——. 1992. *Die Ausgewanderten. Vier lange Erzählungen*, Frankfurt a. M.: Eichborn.
——. 1996. *The Emigrants*, London: Harvill.
——. 1997. *Die Ringe des Saturn. Eine Englische Wallfahrt*, Frankfurt a. M.: Fischer.
——. 1998. *The Rings of Saturn*, London: Harvill.
——. 1999. *Vertigo*, London: Harvill.
——. 2001. *Austerlitz*, Munich: Hanser; London: Penguin.
—— and Gordon Turner. 2006. "Introduction and Transcript of an interview given by Max Sebald", in Denham and McCulloh 2006, 21–9.
Sontag, Susan. 2006. "Loving Dostoyevsky", in Tsypkin 2006, xi–xxxiv.
Steenmeijer, Maarten, ed. 2001. *El pensamiento literario de Javier Marías*, Amsterdam: Foro Hispánico/Rodopi.
Sterne, Laurence. 1967. *The Life and Opinions of Tristram Shandy, Gentleman*, London: Penguin.
Taylor, D. J. 2008. "Adding up to a life", *The Guardian Review*, 26 January, 16.
Tóibín, Colm. 2004. *The Master*, London: Picador.
Tsypkin, Leonid. 2006. *Summer in Baden-Baden*, London: Penguin.
Vila-Matas, Enrique. 2000. *Bartleby y compañía*, Barcelona: Anagrama.
——. 2002. *El mal de Montano*, Barcelona: Anagrama.
——. 2003. *París no se acaba nunca*, Barcelona: Anagrama.
——. 2005. *Doctor Pasavento*, Barcelona: Anagrama.

12

Autofiction: A Brief History of a Neologism*

E. H. Jones

Coined by French academic and writer, Serge Doubrovsky in the 1970s, the term 'autofiction' has since passed into common usage. The major impact that the notion has had in just four decades is clear: it has proliferated in usage and expanded in meaning. Not merely more frequently cited within the world of French literary criticism, its significance has travelled well beyond the hexagonal boundaries of its conception to the English, Spanish and German-speaking literary critical communities. So widespread is its usage that it would be easy to believe that after the initial storm generated in the late 80s and early 90s, autofiction has settled into a comfortable niche within the life writing world, that it has outgrown the moniker of neologism and developed into a fully-fledged literary critical tool. Closer scrutiny, however, reveals that whilst there is frequent usage, there is actually little consensus about either the term's real meaning or its validity. Indeed, the theoretical rigours that underpinned its conception – in particular Philippe Lejeune's ground-breaking work in the 1970s to define autobiography and establish a taxonomy of literature– have certainly not been translated into the emergence of an uncontested, consistently applied definition for this neologism: the characteristics outlined as defining features by the term's instigator, M. Doubrovsky, have been variously contested, flouted or – most regrettably – ignored. The term is celebrated by some, disparaged by others, and carelessly appropriated by yet more.

It is a contribution to the debate about 'autofiction' and the theoretical ambiguity that surrounds it that the current study seeks to achieve, seeking in particular to refute the all too common careless and unthinking appropriation of the term. Turning upon its head the argument of some critics that the most crushing weakness of 'autofiction' is the historical amnesia upon which the notion is based, this paper will begin by briefly revisiting the terms and conditions of autofiction's own genesis, before reviewing the more recent developments in the field. I will argue that over the last four years, the amorphous and sometimes ill-tempered viewpoints generated by this literary phenomenon have at last begun to coalesce into a number of clearly distinguishable if often conflicting and contradictory schools of thought. I will suggest that whilst confusion and opacity of meaning might be acceptable or even inevitable in relation to a neologism, it is desirable for the debate to be established on firmer ground before 'autofiction' reaches its fifth decade. As Jean-Louis Jeannelle points out, whilst Lejeune was able in 1992 to sum up the history of autofiction as a neat 'pièce en cinq actes' (five act play) complete with beginning, development, identifiable characters and clear outcome, the field has begun to resemble something more akin to 'a theoretical soap opera comprising numerous episodes and many twists and turns' (Jeannelle, 2007: 18).[1] Clearly there is great need for clarification and rigorous investigation. Moreover, as this study aims to demonstrate, close study of the phenomenon of autofiction raises issues that are of greater importance than might at first be obvious. Jeannelle's work is again useful as he asserts that: 'it is rare to be able to witness the different steps in the life of a genre from birth to legitimacy, condensed into little more than three decades' (Jeannelle, 2007: 19).[2] From this point of view, the study of autofiction provides a useful case study which is revealing in relation to generic evolution and change in a wider sense. In addition, as David Duff points out in the introduction to 'Modern Genre Theory', 'the problem of genre is always liable to open into larger questions about the organisation and transmission of knowledge and the dynamics of cultural change' (Duff, 2000: 2). Situated as it is on the cusp of fiction and fact, on the edge of one literary genre and another, discussion of autofiction seems particularly prone to invoking wider questions about literature and life. The paper will seek to elucidate the complex relationship of genre and the wider social context of production, before concluding by looking at the very viability of genre itself.

The now familiar story of autofiction's conception begins with the work of Philippe Lejeune in the 1970s to establish a definition of autobiography and a taxonomy of literary genres. Inspired perhaps by the growing influence of the autobiographical, and the implicit questioning of the Aristotelian belief that referentiality precludes literarity, Lejeune has continued to write extensively and influentially on the subject. Building his arguments around the importance of nominal identity and the establishment of a pact, or contract, between author and reader, Lejeune scrutinised the possible scenarios within the literary spectrum ranging from pure fiction to conventional autobiography. According to his schema, if the narrator-protagonist of a work shares the same name as the author, and this is established within the text, then a work can be classified as 'autobiography'. If nominal identity is not established, irrespective of the compelling nature of other indicators, a work can only be classed as 'autobiographical'. Displayed in tabular form and then systematically unpicked within his discussion, Lejeune's classification suggested that two possibilities did not exist: the one that concerns us here is, of course, that of a text in which author and protagonist bear the same name, but in which there is an overt attempt to fictionalise. Working on the manuscript that was to become *Fils*, his first significant work of autofiction, Doubrovsky tells us that he was hit by the realisation that it was exactly this impossibility that he was currently undertaking: a work in which author, protagonist and narrator all bore the same name, but which did not make the simple truth claims of conventional autobiography.

The motivation for adopting this unorthodox format has been argued by Doubrovsky himself to stem primarily from the need to evade the particularly stringent and exclusive social norms within which traditional autobiography was constrained. Revisiting the story of his coming to autofiction in *Le Livre brisé*, Doubrovsky's intratextual avatar tells us that: 'A-great–man-in-the-twilight-of-his-life-and-in-an-elegant-style. Can't fill those shoes. [...] I DON'T HAVE THE RIGHT TO. Not a member of the club, I'm not allowed in. MY LIFE DOESN'T INTEREST ANYONE' (Doubrovsky, 1989: 256).[3] He adds: 'I'm not allowed into the pantheon of funeral parlours that is autobiography. Ok. But I can smuggle myself in. I can sneak in, with the help of fiction, under the cover of the novel (Doubrovsky, 1989: 256).[4] In fact, Doubrovsky's clear sense of the impossibility of entering into the literary world of life writing without renegotiating its fundamental conventions can be argued to be a far from isolated impulse. Within the Francophone literary arena, the emergence of the term 'la nouvelle autobiographie' over the last few decades attests to a general challenge to many aspects of the rules that had previously constrained autobiography and a desire to mirror literary innovation with social democratisation. According to Mounir Laouyen, the editor of a special edition of the journal *L'Esprit créateur* dedicated to this very topic, 'new autobiography' is marked by experimentation with pact, story and mode of narration (Laouyen 2002: 3). He goes on to argue that 'the new autobiographer tries to grasp the meaning of a life that is still in progress, in a fragmented state, whilst avoiding the temptation to fall into any totalising representation, since any attempt to recapitulate is in vain'[5] (Laouyen 2002: 6). It is clear to see that there is a very strong correspondence between the characteristics that Laouyen sketches out and the characteristics of Doubrovsky's own autofiction.

In fact, Doubrovsky's autofictional impulse can be seen to be in tune not merely with other contemporary literary developments, but also with the wider socio-cultural context, a factor to which the runaway success of 'autofiction' can be at least partially attributed. To cite Doubrovsky again, we learn that:

> Unlike autobiography, which explains and unifies, which wants to get hold of and unravel the threads of someone's destiny, autofiction doesn't perceive someone's life to be a whole. It is only concerned with separate fragments, with broken-up chunks of existence, and a divided subject who doesn't coincide with him or herself.
>
> (Doubrovsky, 1999: back cover)[6]

Autofiction, as opposed to autobiography, then, is highly attuned with an age in which the subject is no longer accepted to be a unified, simple whole. Moreover, the admission of fiction is a clear recognition of the extent to which memory is fallible and a move away from the mythical figure of an omniscient writer looking back and taking stock of his life, many decades after it began. Indeed, this relationship with time is a key characteristic of Doubrovsky's own definition of autofiction. In an interview with Michel Contat he tells us: 'autofiction can be defined by one clear thing: everything is written in the present' (Contat, 2001: 126),[7] words that he reinforced by arguing that 'this presence of the present is, I believe, the very signature of autofiction' (Contat, 2001:126)[8]. Moreover, as is clear in Doubrovsky's auto-fictions, the relationship with language also bears marks of a detotalising, more disjointed view of selfhood. Again in interview, Doubrovsky has told us that whereas classic autobiography tends to be written in a relatively for-mal style, in which the author seeks to tightly control the precise nuances of everything the narrator–protagonist says, this is not the case for autofic-tion. He tells us: 'in autofiction there is a much more immediate relationship with the violence of words, scenes and memories' (Contat, 2001: 119).[9] Doubrovsky's own use of language is what he himself calls 'l'écriture con-sonantique' or 'consonantal writing', a way of playing with language in such a manner as to remain very close to the subconscious. This close relationship with both the literary context and the wider socio-critical context of writing are one way in which the study of autofiction proves illuminating in relation to the classic debates of genre theorists. In particular, this 'case study' adds weight to the arguments of Russian and Polish formalists that 'every liter-ary trend – or phase of it – has underlying it certain defined socio-historical factors' (Opacki, 2000: 119).[10] Far from inhibiting individual creativity as some genre critics have claimed, we see from the case of autofiction that a close relationship between genre and socio-historical context is a source of innovation and experimentation.

Perhaps more fundamentally, the notion of autofiction also clearly inter-pellates the contested topic of the nature of change within the literary genre system. Should the characteristics of autofiction be interpreted as represent-ing a clear shift away from the genre of autobiography and the emergence of a new genre, or something more subtle? To put the question another way, does the emergence of autofiction represent the decline of the 'royal' genre of autobiography, perhaps as a result of a natural process of literary evolu-tion and the inevitable automation of a well-established genre, or some more complex kind of shift?[11] In order to respond to this question, it is helpful to turn to Doubrovsky's own, clear view of the place that autofiction and his own writings should occupy in the literary spectrum. The author himself has strongly refuted accusations that he is a pioneer of 'anti-autobiography'.[12] In 1999, he argued that: 'I am not at all anti-autobiography. What I've tried to do is a different type of autobiography [...] I would place myself amongst the sub-categories of autobiography' (Hughes, 1999).[13] *Autofiction*, at least as Doubrovsky defines it, should not be conceptualised as directly opposed to autobiography, but rather as one of autobiography's many variations. Doubrovsky goes on to tell us that 'at the end of the 20th Century, you don't do things the way you could at the end of the 18th' (Hughes, 1999).[14] *Autofiction*, then, is seen by this writer as a late twentieth-century form of autobiographical writing and is one that seems to represent a gradual evolution of literary form rather than a sharp break with tradition and the replacement of a dominant form with its opposite.

The notion of autofiction, as elaborated by Doubrovsky, can then, be seen to be an innovative form that corresponds clearly with some of the key elements of contemporary thinking. Why has the notion caused controversy and what new light have critics thrown on the subject in recent years? Perhaps the most vocal theorist of autofiction in recent times has been Vincent Colonna. In a thesis completed under the tutorship of Gérard Genette which remains unpublished, and in his 2004 monograph, *Autofiction et Autres Mythomanies Littéraires*, Colonna at once testifies to the importance of the term whilst simultaneously calling into question the most fundamental aspects of Doubrovsky's definition of autofiction. He argues that 'unfortunately, his theory isn't up to his verbal inspiration: in his explanations [...] autofiction is completely confused with the 'nominal' autobiographical novel' (Colonna, 2004: 196).[15] Indeed, the kernel of Colonna's argument seems to be found in the assertion that 'the phenomenon of fictionalising the self is universal. [...] We would do well to restrict the neologism 'autofiction' to authors who invent a personality and a literary existence for themselves'(Colonna, 2004: 198).[16] Whereas for Doubrovsky, autofiction represents the fictionalisation of a framework through which to represent a 'deeper' truth of selfhood, Colonna advocates the same word being used for those literary texts in which the writer imagines a different life for him or herself. The contrast between the two definitions is both striking and of considerable importance. Indeed, Colonna's criticism is not restricted to alleging the limitations of Doubrovsky's thinking, but goes as far as to construct a complex scenario to explain why literary critics might have gone along with the use of this term. In this alarming scenario, Colonna suggests that literary critics first threw their weight behind the neologism in the belief that it would allow them to avoid the long-disliked term 'roman autobiographique', or 'autobiographical novel', but were then forced into a position of more extreme rejection once the deceit was uncovered:

> Alas, when a faction of the literary community realised the deception, it turned against the term and accused autofiction of all the wrongdoings previously associated with the autobiographical novel: navel-gazing, lack of modesty, exhibitionism, creative impotence etc. Frightened by this reaction, certain scholars gave up using the term because of its ability to

attract controversy, rash judgements and name-calling. (Colonna, 2004: 199)[17]

Indeed, Colonna's argument, then, that 'autofiction' should be used to refer to incidences of 'the fictionalisation of the self' rather than the Doubrovskian 'fictional scene setting', would attribute a much more extensive past to the notion. Furthermore, Colonna goes on to elaborate his own complex taxonomy of autofictional types, ranging from 'fantastic autofiction' to 'specular autofiction' and claims that critics should rein in their desire to limit the genre too much just because certain texts appear incongruous and would make the genre 'messy'. Clearly, this raises serious questions about the validity of generic classifications at all.

An additional layer of complexity is added to the picture when the arguments of Philippe Gasparini are considered. In a substantial monograph of admirable quality entitled *Est-il je? Roman Autobiographique et autofiction* (2004), Gasparini argues that autofiction is to the writing self what science fiction is to science (2004: 26). That is to say that one is a kind of imaginary projection, inspired by, or taking as a starting point, the other. Going some way towards concurring with the thesis of Colonna, Gasparini argues autofiction to be a recent development within the longstanding but critically neglected tradition of the autobiographical novel. Adding to the well-known accusations that autofiction might represent little more than a marketing tool, Gasparini implies that the use of the label 'novel' to what is essentially an autobiography might, in some cases, represent little more than a cheap way in which to assert a text's literariness and to address lingering Aristotelian prejudices that that which is referential cannot also constitute sophisticated literature (Gasparini, 2004: 70 and 235). The crucial element of Gasparini's argument, however, is his insistence that although important, the establishment of nominal identity between author, narrator and protagonist is not crucial. On the contrary, Gasparini goes to great lengths to examine the myriad of other ways in which an identitarian relationship can be suggested between author and intratextual characters, including correspondences in age, sociocultural background, occupation and aspirations (Gasparini, 2004: 24–5). Moreover, moving beyond Colonna's arguments, Gasparini suggests that the most significant distinguishing feature between an autobiographical novel and an autofiction is to be found in its *vraisemblance*. The autobiographical novel, according to Gasparini, retains an appearance of credibility, of possibility. Autofiction is what results when the realms of the impossible, of the more than possible, are entered into. Doubrovsky's response to these criticisms and alternative theories is succinct. Responding directly to Colonna's arguments he tells us: 'I completely oppose Vincent Colonna's argument that autofiction consists of giving your name to a character and inventing an imaginary life for him...No' (Louette, 2000–2001: 217).[18] Indeed, only further examination of Doubrovsky's autofictional writings, as well as his metatextual commentary upon them, allows us to move beyond the critical stalemate in which the debate about autofiction finds itself. Gasparini's argument that autofictions are less 'vraisemblable' is certainly not sustainable with reference to Doubrovsky's own autofictions. In fact, as has been pointed out by numerous critics, the occasions upon which the authorial voice seems to intrude into the diegesis and to question the veracity of the account, thus shattering vraisemblance, may have the reverse effect of allowing the reader to suspend disbelief more comfortably.

Moreover, Colonna's argument seems to suggest that Doubrovsky has failed to realise the fact that fiction is a long-standing element of life writing. Examination of Doubrovsky's comments reveals that this misses the nuance of his argument. In an interview with Michel Contat, Doubrovsky argued that even the most classical autobiography is full of the writer's fantasies and elaborated upon this with reference to Rousseau's idealised portrayal of his mother and father (Contat, 2001: 119). In an interview with Jean-François Louette, Doubrovsky makes the point even more clearly, stating that: 'even classic autobiographers knew that they were writing fiction. In Rousseau's work it's very clear: he recognised the role of the imagination in filling in the gaps in memory' (Louette, 2000–2001: 217).[19] Doubrovsky's argument, then, is not that he is the first to have produced a text in which there is nominal identity between author, narrator and protagonist and yet there is clear evidence of fictional elements, but rather that in his writing, the play with non-referential elements is overtly signalled to the reader. Furthermore, the insistence with which some critics have focussed on the importance of tracing the history of 'autofiction' and the glee with which they chronicle those examples which pre-dated Doubrovsky is also questionable. The most justifiable claim to originality of Doubrovsky's notion of autofiction is not, I would argue, to be found in some kind of radical break with the traditions of the autobiographical novel in France, or even with the tradition of autobiography. It is to be found, rather, in the ways in which this literary impulse is influenced by the dominant socio-critical developments of the late twentieth-century. Autofiction thus represents a way of acknowledging the constructed nature of selfhood, particularly those selfhoods which have undergone the twentieth-century experience of psychoanalysis. Rather than stuffing narratives with wordy explanations of contexts and situations in their full and impossible detail, Doubrovsky's autofictions simply acknowledge the impossibility of memory and allow themselves the luxury of sketching an imaginary framework through which a truth can be told. Moreover, displacing the time of narration and often narrating things in the present avoids giving the impossible illusion of a whole, unflawed memory. Colonna's argument that autofiction is no more than a particular form of the autobiographical novel, represents a rejection of Lejeune's taxonomy that few critics, I believe, are ready to make. In Lejeune's classification, the nominal identity between author, narrator and protagonist means that Doubrovskian autofiction is not the same as the autobiographical novel.

In fact, perhaps it is to Lejeune that we should turn in the hope of finding an arbiter to rule on this critical stalemate? Well, in a 2002 interview, Lejeune stated that 'the word [autofiction] now refers to the space between an autobiography which doesn't want to give itself that name and a work of fiction which won't separate itself from its author' (2002: 23).[20] Clearly, this response does not clear up the ambiguity but rather seems to fall foul of Elizabeth Bruss's long established assertion that the only useful definition of literary genre is one that is neither too broad to explain nor too rigid to cope with change and development (Bruss, 1975: 1). More fundamental, perhaps, are Paul John Eakin's questions:

> Why, we might well ask, with its pretensions to reference exposed as illusion, does autobiography as a kind of reading and writing continue and even prosper? Why do we not simply collapse autobiography into the other literatures of fiction and have done with it? (Eakin, 1992: 27)

Perhaps it is the very attempt to draw clear lines between genres that is the problem?

A thorough examination of the contemporary polemic regarding autofiction does indeed indicate that the notion has prompted some of the most classic debates about literary genre to resurface. Autofiction is, perhaps, the ultimate terrain on which the competition between author theory and genre theory can be played out: it is a genre in which the uniqueness of the author is foregrounded not only in the form but also in the very content of the work, but which simultaneously has sought to locate itself within the genre system and thus exploit what Duff (2000: 16) terms 'the power of genre' from its very outset. Rather than inhibiting innovation and self-expression, in Doubrovsky's case, it seems that literary genre and the classificatory niches through which it finds meaning have proved a stimulus to literary creativity. Far from separate from this is the relationship of the genre of autofiction with its socio-historical context, another long-standing source of debate. Again, rather than stripping such texts of agency, in the case of Doubrovsky's writing, correlation with the context of writing seems to make these texts speak particularly strongly to contemporary readers.

Perhaps the real answer to the conundrum of autofiction is to be found in Derrida. In *Parages*, he tells us that 'a text can't belong to any genre. All texts participate in one or in several genres, there's no text without genre, there's always a genre and genres but this participation is never the same thing as belonging' (1986: 264).[21] If the contemporary world teaches us anything, we must at least acknowledge that no boundary can exist without inviting transgression, no category without inviting rupture and no separation without inviting contact. In the case of autofiction, it seems that the very existence of generic categories and boundaries were stimuli for literary production and, perhaps no less importantly, for scholarly discussion and study. In sum, it seems that we must acknowledge that however imperfect, genres not only have a practical role to play, but also a psychological one in inviting questioning, in soliciting innovation. As Gasparini himself argues, 'in societies that are constantly changing, static genres become fossilized and die, as do the processes that they're made up of. Evolving genres, on the other hand, stimulate creativity' (2004: 286).[22] If we accept the positive nature of continual change within the field of literature, then it is only logical that we should also recognise the importance of continually re-evaluating the categories and classification systems through which we understand literature, and Gasparini goes on to emphasise the danger of not at least reflecting upon the role and purpose of genre. He tells us: 'such an abdication of intellectual responsibility would leave the way clear for others to exploit the term, through cultural prejudice, through the laws of business and marketing' (2004: 333).[23] Whilst it is clear that no definitive conclusions can be drawn at this stage in autofiction's evolution, what is clear is that the crime lies not in questioning the definition of autofiction, but in failing to do so, and in the careless appropriation of the term with which I began my piece.

Notes

* Where no official translation of a text exists, I have translated it myself. The original French citations will be given in corresponding footnotes.

1. 'un feuilleton théorique aux épisodes foisonnants, riches en rebondissements' (Jeannelle, 2007: 18). [pl. Add full stops at ends of all Notes]

2. 'il est rare que l'on puisse assister aux différentes étapes de la vie d'un genre, ramassées en à peine trois décennies, de sa naissance jusqu'à sa légitimation. De ce point de vue, l'autofiction apparaît comme un véritable cas d'école' (Jeannelle, 2007: 19)

3. 'grand-homme-au-soir-de-sa-vie-et-dans-un-beau-style. Peux pas prendre la pose. [...]. J'Y AI PAS LE DROIT. Pas membre du club, on me refuse l'entrée. MA VIE N'INTÉRESSE PERSONNE' (Doubrovsky, 1989: 256).

4. 'l'autobiographie, ce panthéon des pompes funèbres, l'accès m'en est interdit. D'accord. Mais je puis m'y introduire en fraude. Resquiller, à la faveur de la fiction, sous le couvert du roman' (Doubrovsky, 1989: .256).

5. 'le nouvel autobiographe cherche à maintenir le sens d'une vie en suspens, dans un état fragmentaire, à l'abri de toute postulation totalisante, car toute tentative de récapitulation est vaine' (Laouyen 2002: 6)

6. 'À l'inverse de l'autobiographie, explicative et unifiante, qui veut ressaisir et dérouler les fils d'un destin, l'autofiction ne perçoit pas la vie comme un tout. Elle n'a affaire qu'à des fragments disjoints, des morceaux d'existence brisés, un sujet morcelé qui ne coïncide pas avec lui-même' (Doubrovsky, 1999: back cover)

7. 'ce qui fait l'autofiction, c'est un fait très précis: tout est écrit au présent' (Contat, 2001: 126).

8. 'cette espèce de présence du présent est, je crois, la signature même de l'autofiction' (Contat, 2001: 126)

9. 'dans l'autofiction il y a un rapport beaucoup plus immédiat à la brutalité des mots, des scènes, des souvenirs' (Contat, 2001: 119).
10. Opacki's work is argued by Duff (2000: 14,118–26) to belong to the 'Polish Formalist' school of literary criticism which stresses the importance of the context of creation.
11. The theory of 'royal genres' which inevitably become 'automated' or taken for granted and passé is to be found in Opacki's 'Royal Genres' (Translated and discussed in Duff 2000:118-126). Discussion of the way in which in the dynamic system of literary evolution, dominant genres inevitably become automated and give rise to the creation of an opposite can be found in Tynyanov (Reprinted and discussed in Duff 2000: 29–49).
12. Paul John Eakin, for example, accuses Doubrovsky of having written an 'anti-autobiography' in *Fils*, that tests the boundaries of generic definition. See Eakin: 1992: 26.
13. 'je ne suis pas du tout anti-autobiographique. Ce que j'ai essayé de faire, c'est un type différent d'autobiographie. [...] Je me range parmi les sous-catégories de l'autobiographie'.
(Hughes, 1999)
14. 'à la fin du vingtième siècle, on n'en fait plus comme on pouvait faire à la fin du dix-huitième' (Hughes, 1999).
15. 'malheureusement, sa «théorie [...] ne fut pas à la mesure de son inspiration verbale: dans ses explications [...] l'autofiction se confond entièrement avec le roman autobiographique nominal' (Colonna, 2004: 196).
16. 'le phénomène de la fictionalisation de soi [est] universel, [...] le néologisme autofiction gagnerait à être restreint aux auteurs qui s'inventent une personnalité et une existence littéraires' (Colonna, 2004: 198).
17. 'las, quand une faction du monde des lettres se rendit compte de la supercherie, elle se retourna contre le vocable et accabla l'autofiction de tout les méfaits, associés naguère au roman personnel: nombrilisme, impudeur, exhibitionnisme, impuissance créatrice etc. Effrayés par ce reflux, certains lettrés renoncent maintenant à utiliser le mot, qui appelle la polémique, les jugements à l'emporte-pièce et les noms d'oiseaux' (Colonna, 2004: 199)
18. 'je suis tout à fait opposé à la thèse de Vincent Colonna: l'autofiction consisterait à donner son nom à un personnage, et à lui inventer une vie imaginaire...Non' (Louette, 2000-2001: 217)
19. 'même les autobiographes classiques savaient qu'ils écrivaient de la fiction. Chez Rousseau c'est très évident: il a très bien vu le rôle de l'imagination, qui se substitue à la mémoire' (Louette, 2000–2001: 217)
20. 'le mot [autofiction] désigne maintenant tout l'espace entre une autobiographie qui ne veut pas dire son nom et une fiction qui ne veut pas se détacher de son auteur' Philippe Lejeune interviewed by Michel Delon in *La Magazine littéraire* (2002: 23).
21. 'un texte ne saurait appartenir à aucun genre. Tout texte participe d'un ou de plusieurs genres, il n'y a pas de texte sans genres, il y a toujours du genre et des genres mais cette participation n'est jamais une appartenance' (Derrida, 1986: 264).
22. 'dans des sociétés en constante mutation, les genres statiques se fossilisent et meurent, tout comme les procédés qui les composent; les genres évolutifs, au contraire, stimulent la créativité' (Gasparini, 2004: 286).
23. 'une telle démission intellectuelle laisserait en effet le champ libre à d'autres formes d'instrumentalisation, par les préjugés culturels, par les lois du commerce et du marketing' (Gasparini, 2004: 333)

Bibliography

Elizabeth Bruss (1976), *Autobiographical Acts: the Changing Situation of a Literary Genre* (Baltimore and London: Johns Hopkins University Press).

Vincent Colonna (2004), *Autofiction et Autres Mythomanies Littéraires* (Paris: Tristram).

Michel Contat (2001), 'Quand je n'écris pas, je ne suis pas écrivain' in *Genesis*, 16, 119–35.

Jacques Derrida (1986), *Parages* (Paris: Galilée).

Serge Doubrovsky (1977), *Fils* (Paris: Galilée).

—— (1989), *Le Livre brisé* (Paris: Grasset).

—— (1999), *Laissé pour conte* (Paris: Grasset).

David Duff (ed.) (2000), *Modern Genre Theory* (Harlow: Longman).

Paul John Eakin (1992), *Touching the World: Reference in Autobiography*, (Princeton: Princeton University Press).

Philippe Gasparini (2004), *Est-il je? Roman Autobiographique et autofiction* (Paris: Seuil).

Alex Hughes (1999), 'Interview with Serge Doubrovsky'. Online at: http://artsweb. bham.ac.uk/artsFrenchStudies/Sergedou/intervw .htm

Jean-Louis Jeannelle (2007), Catherine Viollet and Isabelle Grell (eds), *Genèse et autofiction* (Paris: Academia-Bruylant).

Mounir Laouyen (2002), 'Introduction: les nouvelles autobiographies', *L'Esprit Créateur*.

Philippe Lejeune (1975), *Le Pacte Autobiographique* (Paris: Seuil).

Philippe Lejeune (2002), interviewed by Michel Delon in *La Magazine littéraire*, p.23.

Jean-François Louette, 'Je ne cherche aucune absolution, mais un partage' in *Les Temps modernes* 611–12 (2000–2001) pp. 210–18.

Ireneusz Opacki (2000), 'Royal Genres' in David Duff (ed., *Modern Genre Theory* (Harlow: Longman), pp.118–26.

Yury Tynyanov (2000), 'The Literary Fact' in David Duff (ed.), *Modern Genre Theory* (Harlow: Longman), pp. 29–49.

13
Sick Diarists and Private Writers of the Seventeenth Century

David Thorley

When I first took this task in hand, *et quod ait ille, impellente genio negotiu suscepi* [and, as he saith, I undertook the work from some inner impulse], this I aimed at, *vel ut lenirem animum scribendo,* [or] to ease my mind by writing; for I had *gravidum cor, fœdum caput*, a kind of imposthume in my head, which I was very desirous to be unladen of, and could imagine no fitter evacuation than this.

(Robert Burton, *Anatomy of Melancholy* 'Democritus to the Reader)[1]

Introduction

Literary historians tend to associate the seventeenth-century diary with the methods of the burgeoning experimental science. Summarising these arguments, Stuart Sherman writes that, 'Early diarists often absorbed their sense of both form and purpose from the techniques and practices of bookkeeping, bringing them to bear on questions other than – but still including – cash. Writers began to track self, health, soul, salvation, as though those too were question of debit and credit.'[2] I do not dissent from this theory, but in what follows, I wish to argue that personal illness, in particular, presents a set of formal and linguistic problems which test the boundaries of this framework.

I began by quoting Burton, not in order to draw a theoretical paradigm for my discussion, but in order to give it a more urgent, personal and physical context. For Burton, the decision to write was almost visceral: he felt (or so he claims) compelled to perform a fit evacuation of the 'imposthume' in his head. Inspired by 'some inner impulse,' he seeks 'to ease my mind by writing.' Burtonian writing is the lancing of boils, an intellectual form of curettage or cauterization. Like the early diarists described by Sherman, Burton seek to achieve something specific: he is suffering a specific physical condition, and he seeks to understand, and ultimately, to excise it by producing an Anatomy. 'He claims to be expelling '*clavum clavo* [a nail with a nail]'; to 'comfort one sorrow with another, idleness with idleness, *ut exvipera theriacum* [as an antidote out of a serpent's venom], make an antidote out of that which was the prime cause of my disease.'[3]

Though Burton is not a diarist, the overwhelming size and complexity of his *Anatomy* demonstrates quite clearly the difficulties with taking stock of one's health in this way. The story of its evolution and expansion is well known, but worth repeating. Its first edition in 1621 was a small but stout quarto volume of nearly 900 pages and 350,000 words. Over nineteen years and another four folio editions, it continued to grow until the author's death. By the time of the sixth edition, published in 1651, the text had swelled to over half a million words.[4] Jonathan Sawday has correctly rejected the idea that the *Anatomy* is an 'intellectual aberration.' It 'is absolutely of its age,' he claims, supporting his argument that 'The Renaissance culture can be termed the culture of dissection".'[5] This may be so. *The Anatomy* may very well be a product of its time, but it is also the product of an obsessive mind, using the prevalent discourse of his time, to enquire deeper and deeper into his illness, and producing a vast, expanding answer, dissecting not only his melancholy, but a million tangential other subjects as well, all competing for investigation and explanation.

Perhaps, even by attempting to 'make an antidote out of that which was the prime cause of my disease', Burton got what he was asking for. But, if illness is to be understood autobiographically, as a physical and personal experience – rather than one which is socially construed and theorised under the heading of "The Body" – then its rhetorical presentation needs attention. How is the diarist or the private writer to analyse the self and the body, in a discourse which is liable to spill out of his control?

Walter J. Ong had puzzled out some of the peculiarities of writing a diary, which he suggests is a curiously unnatural mode of writing. 'We do not normally talk to ourselves', he points out, 'certainly not in long involved sentences and paragraphs.' And what is more, ' the diarist, pretending to be talking to himself has also, since he is writing, to pretend he is somehow not there.' What appears to remain is a paradox under which the ailing diarist is forced to deny his symptoms (or at least their physicality) in order to make an assessment of them.

In the case of seventeenth-century self-writing, the problem is exacerbated. When the popular habits of news recording and record keeping described by Sherman intrude on the form, inevitably they begin to reintroduce the type of social generalisation which a personal diary ought to dispel. Smart linguistic work is then required in order to keep the diarist from sinking into complicity with the received wisdom about his own body. I will consider examples from the diaries of Robert Hooke and Samuel Pepys, as well as the philosophy of Anne Conway, and the "autobiography" of Alice Thornton, hoping to show up their formal and linguistic difficulties in transcribing and rationalising illness.

Hooke: the diarist as scientist?

Hooke's diary seems to bear out the arguments described by Sherman. In the main, it is a catalogue of his physical condition, a record of complaints and symptoms endured, medicines and preparations taken, and, frequently, of waste substances expunged. He noted down, how well he slept each night, when his perspiration was more than usually heavy, even every time he had an orgasm. Lotte Mulligan argues that Hooke's 'diary keeping was an integral part of his scientific vision reflecting the epistemological and methodological practices that guided him as a student of nature'. She notes that 'he chose to chose to record a self that was as subject to scientific scrutiny as the rest of nature and that he though that such a record could be applied to producing, in the end, a fully objective "history" with himself as datum.'[6] Astute though this observation is theoretically, if it is to be applied to the text rather than the principles of Hooke's diary, I think it needs to be refined. I too wish to present Hooke's diary as certainly 'an integral part of his scientific vision', but I think that the project of 'recording a self' was not simply biological (or, in Mulligan's term, natural-historical). The experiment is confused: its method and result stages are conflated. Hooke's diary is inevitably more than an enquiry into the self; it is an enquiry into the self writing a diary.

That is not to deny that it has its practical purposes. Keeping a diary allowed Hooke to supplement his weak (according to Aubrey)[7] memory and to cross-reference his symptoms and treatments, as well as his behaviour and psychological state. In this, the diary is far more than a set of medical notes, though it remains very different from a more "conventional" diary such as that of Pepys. Even a first glance at Hooke's manuscript reveals an unusual and convoluted document. The early part begins as a series of weather tables with personal notes confined to a column on every right hand page. The later diaries are recorded in a much smaller notebook, and although the scientific tables have been dropped, the peculiar, shorthand style of record keeping remains (and, if anything, is briefer still). The relative size of these notebooks in itself suggests that their author conceived of them as two quite different types of text. In both, fragments of sentences and recollections collide and overlap in order to fit onto the available space.[8] They bring to mind Freud's observations on the similarities between writing and memory, an attempt to find a method of writing that would provide a much more precise analogue with the dense and fragmentary nature of memory than the simple transferring of ink to page. His more sophisticated system was 'The Mystic Writing Pad' which proposed a children's 'writing tablet from which notes can be erased by an easy movement of the hand', but which also 'can provide both an ever-ready surface and permanent traces of the notes that have been made upon it.'[9] Of course, nothing of the sort can have been deliberate, but Hooke's diary also provides a more sophisticated analogy than either a simple catalogued record or a conventional narrative account. His abbreviated (cryptically so) style is obviously not designed to be read by anyone other than the diarist himself, and often has the effect of leading the reader along tangential trails of thought. His habit of recording his orgasms, for instance, (noted by the symbol of Pisces, and often registered next to a name – usually, his maid, Nell, or his niece, Grace) suggests more than a mere register of discharged semen. It appears to be the skeletal frame of a narrative as well. (For example, 7 April 1673: 'Slept little. Nell orgasm. sweat. Drank Anniseed cordiall. better next day.')[10] For a man whose memory was already poor, this series of prompts, though perhaps recorded with the most scientific of intentions, seem to give the diarist a guarantee that, when returned to, they will rekindle the diarist's psychological and perhaps even physical state at their transcription. The dense authography of the manuscript entries, despite the systematic intentions suggested by their layout, does little to assist this process of cross-referral.

For Hooke memory was a physical organ and could therefore be assisted prosthetically. 'The Soul can no more remember without the Organ of Memory', he wrote, 'than it can see without the organ of Sight, the Eye, or hear without an Ear.'[11] And he evinces a concern for suggestive details which might be expected to assist the memory by stimulating the imagination. In amongst the variably meticulous accounts of his physical health and physic taking, Hooke includes tall stories, gossip he happens to pick up, and recipes, and he is always careful to note the source of the rumour or advice. For instance, on 31 January 1775, he recorded, 'Hewk told me the recipt of the aldersgate cordiall. Sena, coriander seeds, Elecampane, Guacu, Liquorice, brandy and white wine, Raisins.'[12] The effect of this mixture of detailed note keeping, punctuated by personal observation is to create a manuscript which is very difficult indeed to read, and a narrative thread which, even in its twentieth-century transcriptions, is hard to follow. The cramped layout and anti-rhetorical, short-hand style often lend themselves to density, instead of clarity, vagary instead of precision. Insignificant things are retained, and important ones fragmented; records run into one another and become confused. And like the human memory, Hooke's diary often makes a better record of trivial details which appeal to his scientific mind, than it does of important life events. Early in 1772, Hooke noted down the circumstances of his friend John Wilkins, Bishop of Chester's illness and eventual death from a kidney stone. He seems less moved by the loss than fascinated by the details of Wilkins' condition:

Lord Chester dyed about 9 in the morning of a suppression of wine. At Jonas Mores,sick, he was cured of a sciatica by fomenting the part for an hour with hot steames for one hour afterward chafing in oyles with a rubbing hand and heated firepans which gave him a suddain ease.

Sir Theodore Devaux told me of Sir Th. Meyerns cure of the stone in the kidneys by blowing up the bladder with bellows etc.[13]

The interest of these details to Hooke is purely scientific, but not entirely academic. That is, from the death of his friend, he has learned two things: a method of curing sciatica, and one of curing kidney stones, which can be kept for his own use whenever necessary. This is the nature of Hooke's diary: lessons are learned, and by being recorded, protect Hooke against incurring this danger to his health later on. Where his memory fails, writing endures but this writing cannot entirely immunise Hooke against a recurrence of all medical complaints from his previous encounters. The convoluted nature of the manuscript, and the terseness of the entries often render the diary confusing and devoid of context – similar flaws to those deliberately built into Freud's "Writing Pad" model of memory.

In order to present a truly full case history, Hooke's 'General Scheme' for the improvement of Natural Philosophy argues that rhetorical control must be dispensed with. Words, he recommends, should be handled with utmost care and suspicion:

> In the choice of which, there ought to be great Care and Circumspection, that they be such as are shortest and express the Matter with the leat Ambiguity, and the greatest Plainness and Significancy, not augmenting the Matter by Superlatives, nor abating it by Diminutives, not inclining it to this or that Hypothesis, or accomodating it to this or that Autor's opinion; avoiding all kinds of Rhetorical Flourishes, or Oratorical Garnishes and all sorts of Periphrases, and Sayings, or 1the like ...[14]

This is from a general schema for writing up scientific observations and comparing Hooke's diary to these prescriptions shows a fairly clear correlation with the first stage of scientific record keeping, by which observations are taken down quickly, in short-hand in an attempt to register every salient detail before it becomes lost to or distorted by the memory. Only later, as Hooke ordains it, should the evidence be transcribed onto 'a very fine piece of paper' and entered 'in the most compendious manner of writing.'[15] From the state of Hooke's manuscripts for the early diaries at least, it may therefore be presumed that its author intended it as a rough and immediate hand list of experience, rather than the completed composition. Interestingly, the manuscript for the late diary is written in a much more careful hand, and its entries are more obviously distinct, suggesting it to be a far more polished and edited record, perhaps one more rhetorically calculated. Even for the early diary to have abandoned rhetoric is a suspicious claim from any sort of writer (even a compiler of meteorological tables), and though Hooke does not condescend to any prefabricated rhetorical schemes, occasionally, he even has recourse to a linguistic sleight of hand:

> Yesternight, I woke with an intollerable pain in head which I found to be from having cut my hair a week before and not put on a thicker cap, but upon keeping my head warmer recovered.[16]

This entry bears out Mulligan's notion of Hooke's diary as 'a fully objective "history" with himself as datum.' His commitment to trial and error continues, as he discovers a problem (headache) and invents an experiment to establish a diagnosis, proceeding from hypothesis (that it was caused by a cold head) to proof (putting on a thicker cap relieved the pain). Of course, this is purely an empirical proof, only scantly supported by scientific theory,[17] but nevertheless, it demonstrates the effectiveness of Hooke's method. The language of the entry is by no means merely a by product, however. There is a key word upon which the whole thesis hinges: 'found'. This simple past tense verb is shorthand in Hooke's dairy for some other scientific jargon, such as, "tests have proved", or "all the evidence demonstrates". In other words, by presenting his observations as "findings" Hooke lends his diary the credibility of scientific data. But such language is not always exactly appropriate:

> Eat Dinner with good stomack and pannado at night but drinking posset upon it put me into a feverish sweat which made me sleep very unquiet.[18]

Whereas in the entry above, Hooke proceeds from hypothesis to conclusion, here, he proceeds merely by assumption. Again, it is his choice of verb which is crucial. His claim that 'drinking posset' with dinner 'put me into a feaverish sweat which made me sleep very unquiet,' professes an objectivity which, without the rigour of experiment, is not obvious to other readers. 'Put' suggests a certainty that effect ('feverish' sweating and interrupted sleep) proceeds from a particular cause (a surfeit of drinking). However more plausible this may sound to readers now, it is important to remember that this diary was composed for Hooke's benefit alone.[19] The rhetorical use of the verb 'put' to impute his fever to his drinking can then be analysed in psychological terms. Rather than admitting to uncertainty about the cause of his symptoms – which in turn might reveal at least paranoia and hypochondria, and, at worst, some more sinister malady – a linguistic short-cut dismisses any suggestion of medical doubt.

Pepys: a rhetorical dilemma

Seemingly by contrast, the prose of Pepys's diary is cohesive and conversational. The particulars it records often seem scarcely worth the noting. In describing the day of Charles II's coronation (23 April 1661), Pepys leaves to posterity the detail that, throughout proceedings, he needed desperately to relieve his bladder,[20] as well as the following account from his celebratory antics that night:

> But no sooner a-bed with Mr. Sheply but my head begun to turn and I to vomit, and if ever I was foxed it was now – which I cannot say yet, because I fell asleep and sleep till morning – only when I waked I found myself wet with my spewing. Thus did the day end with joy everywhere; and blessed be God, I have not heard of any mischance to anybody through it all, but only to Sarjeant Glynne, whose Horse fell upon him yesterday and is like to kill him …[21]

Unlike Hooke's notes, this record enjoys (and appears to revel in) the qualities of grammatical cohesion and comic juxtaposition. The subject turns from a description of Pepys' drunken vomiting to an exhortation of the universal joy of the city, where the adverbial connection ('thus') seems to imply that the vomiting is the reason of the joy. And again, an observation that nobody was as hurt in the carousing is qualified immediately by a rumour that a man's life is in danger after he was crushed by a horse. Pepys contradicting himself twice in quick succession, begins to sound as if his prose is a deliberate rhetorically contrived with a deliberate comic purpose. It cannot be argued that Pepys' perceptions are drunken and therefore unreliable, because the diary gives evidence that he wrote up his entries from memory several days at a time. In this case, he records that, the following evening, Pepys set himself 'down to write down these three days' diary.[22] He was perhaps still hung over, but, having already eaten dinner that night, and only drunk one draught of ale, not intoxicated beyond coherence. The technique then begins to sound like a purposeful device, one which rhetoricians would perhaps call "antanagoge by *non sequitur*" (balancing a favourable aspect with an unfavourable one, in this case, in a manner which is wilfully illogical). And that Pepys contrives to use such sophisticated rhetoric in his private jottings to himself suggests that, far from being the prosthetic bodily extension of Hooke's diary, his diary is conceived of as a source of entertainment, a companion who requires to be discoursed with intelligently.

When it comes to his health, however, Pepys demonstrates something in common with Hooke's practices of diary-keeping. Like Hooke, Pepys is fascinated – apparently to the point of paranoia – by his body and its condition. Certainly, Pepys had more reason for paranoia than his Royal Society colleague, having undergone highly dangerous surgery to remove a kidney stone in 1658. This operation was a controversial one at the time:[23] excruciatingly painful and life-threateningly intricate. The conventional method of removing the stone required the patient to be strapped to a table and held in position by four strong men. 'Then', according to, Ambrose Paré's account of the proceedure, 'the surgeon shall thrust into the urenary passage even to the bladder, a silver or iron and hollow probe, annoynted with oyle, and opened or slit on the out side, that the point of the knife may enter thereinto, and that it may guide the hand of the workman, and keep the knife from piercing farther into the bodies lying there-under.'[24] Using this tool, the stone is dislodged from its situation and moved into a position from where it can be removed by forceps passed through an incision in the *perineum*. Of course there was no anaesthetic: the patient simply had to hope that the pain of surgery would make him faint at an early stage. Possible (and indeed, likely) complications were urine leakage, leading to infection, irreparable scar damage caused by the instruments, and internal haemorrhage. Sir D'Arcy Power suggested that the reason for Pepys' never fathering a child was 'due to the left ejaculator having been divided at the time of he operation, whilst the right one was so bruised by the system of dilation then employed that it afterwards became occluded.'[25] Pepys' diary demonstrates an understandable relief at having survived such a dangerous and unimaginably painful ordeal, as well as an equally understandable fear of the stones recurring,[26] and of having that pain and terror revisited upon him.

Each year, on the anniversary of his operation (26th March), Pepys held a celebration of its success, and normally used his diary entry to take stock of his health. The entry for the seventh anniversary in 1665 found Pepys in particularly jubilant mood:

> This is the day, seven years, which by the blessing of God, I have survived of my being cut of the stone. And am now in very perfect good health and have long been. And though the last winter hath been as hard as any hath these many years, yet I never was better in my life, nor have not, these ten years, gone cooler in the Summer then I have done all this winter – wearing only a doublet and a waistcoat cut open at the back – abroad, a cloak; and within doors a coat I slipped on. Now I am at a loss to know whether it be my Hares-foot which is my preservation against wind, for I never had a fit of the Collique since I wore it – and nothing but wind brings me pain; and the carrying away of wind takes away my pain – or my keeping my back cool; for when I do lie longer then ordinary upon my back in bed, my water the next morning is very hot – or whether it be my taking a pill of Turpentine, which keeps me always loose – or all together. But this I know, with thanks to God Almighty, that I am now as well as ever I can wish or desire to be – having now and then little grudgings of wind that brings me a little pain, but it is over presently. Only do I find that my back grows very weak, that I cannot stoop to write or tell money without sitting but I have pain for a good while after it.[27]

What is important to consider here is that only eighteen days before, Pepys had seen concrete evidence that more kidney stones had gathered. On 8th

March, he recorded that 'in pissing there came from me two stones'[28] and noted a concern that 'I hope my disease of the stone may not return to me.'[29] This paragraph may suggest that the disease had, as Pepys hoped, voided 'itself in pissing' and that its excitable, jubilant tenor is merely an expression of relief. But simply to accept this explanation, it seems to me, would be to overlook the something in the style of Pepys' writing here. Unlike in his recounting of the coronation celebrations, here, the diarist seems to have lost control of his sentences and his punctuation. Here, is not calculated rhetoric, but rather an exaggerated torrent of generally promising signs. The exaggeration is palpable from the second sentence.[30] 'Very perfect' may have been a construction familiar to seventeenth-century drama,[31] of which Pepys' was a devotee, and a likely phrase to fall from his pen; but, given the diary's own evidence, a claim to have '*long* been' in this type of health cannot be credited. In contrast to the passage quoted from 1661, Pepys seems here to be losing control over the information he is presenting. Extra detail is given in a series of parentheses; there are four sets of dashes in the space of three sentences. What is more, these parentheses are not always able to contain all the information that Pepys wishes to convey. By way of an initial support of the claim to 'very perfect health', he notes down how cool he has been all winter, breaking off to provide an inventory of a typical outfit: ' only a doublet ...'. However, when he attempts to return to his main clause, the partner dash does not return him to a discussion of the climate, or his well-regulated temperature. Instead, he comes to a further detail of his dress habits which he had overlooked ('abroad a cloak'), after which yet another permutation of costume ('within doors a coat I slipped on') is introduced in the guise of a semi-colon. The subject moves on to the business of the medicinal hares' foot (and here Pepys sounds most like Hooke, who constantly experimented with unorthodox therapies). This brings up the subject of colic, which sustains him through the next two sentences. There are two successive semi-cola which each have the same form ("and" + adjectival phrase + "wind" + verb phrase + "pain"), but even if these were a rhetorically calculated scheme, their effect is spoiled by their failure, again, to contain all the information Pepys wished to convey. The dash again fails to bring him back to his main subject (the hare's foot) and leads into a qualification of the parenthesis which he has supposedly just left ('or my keeping my back cool'). The conjunctive "or" then becomes a favourite for introducing information which Pepys is keen should not be left out, and two further alternative theories (a pill of Turpentine, and a combination of factors) are suggested. This loss of linguistic control represents not only a similarity between Hooke and Pepys' attitude to their own bodies, but also a desire on Pepys' part that his diary should tell the full truth, albeit sometimes given a slightly optimistic spin. As much as the raw and unrefined nature of this passage denotes an anxiety about Pepys' condition, it also suggests a curious psychological antagonism. That is, whilst attempting to persuade himself of his good health – almost to write himself into good health – Pepys also appears determined that he should not deceive himself. Perhaps an explanation for the apparent fragments of rhetorical schemes which seem to haunt this passage might be (tentatively) suggested by this psychological interpretation – persuasive writing edited for accuracy, but without wishing to sacrifice its optimistic character.

In this way, Pepys' diary begins to seem less like a sort of spreadsheet of the self on the model described by Sherman, and more like a dialogue – an argument even – between competing needs to analyse and to encourage himself. But a diary can only provide a certain amount of therapy. Pepys eventually felt forced to give his up because of its ominous implications for his health. The final part of his final entry is formal and devotional:

> And so I betake myself to that course which [is] almost as much as to see myself go into my grave – for which, and all the discomforts that will accompany my being blind, the good God prepare me.[32]

Leaving off his diary in this manner, Pepys makes a tantalising suggestion about his relationship to God and about the significance of his writing the diary. It is tempting to hear an echo of Job in this entry: 'If I wait, the grave is mine house: I have made my bed in the darkness.'[33] But the 'course which is almost as much as to see myself go into my grave' is not a reference to Pepys' encroaching blindness. The preceding sentence is Pepys resolution 'from this time forward to have [the diary] kept by my people' and his resignation to 'be contented to set down no more then is fit for them and all the world to know.'[34] He knew that things could never be the same again, and as his editors note, 'he never again kept a personal diary for any length of time.'[35] It is the prospect of not writing, rather than the fear of blindness, which he compares to seeing himself go the grave. Not to write a diary seems to have become a kind of blindness of its own. And what is more, he sees this death as a waking death: 'to see myself go into the grave,' intimates a curious notion of being present at his own funeral. This rather eerily makes the same point as Ong, that the diarist has 'to pretend he is somehow not there'. As his body begins to fail him, he finds himself edited and divided. The argument between encouragement and analysis has not so much been won as eclipsed by cold physical fact. And, having ceded editorial control the only available option to Pepys is submission to the will and mercy of God.

But Pepys raged against the dying of the light. The resolution to let an amanuensis take down his diary for him was an absolute last resort. The entry for 11 October 1666, records that,

> I had taken my journal during the fire and the disorders following in loose papers until this very day, and could not get time to enter them in my book till January 18th in the morning, having made my eyes sore by frequent attempts to do it.[36]

These are unusual circumstances but the fire is not the only hindrance to Pepys' diary-keeping. Even at three months' distance, he feels the compulsion to record each day chronologically almost without omission. What is more, the failed attempts to update the diary must have taught him the increasing price of his continued practice of straining his eyes in poor-light. But Pepys was a Fellow of the Royal Society and an acquaintance of Hooke, that pioneer of optical microscopy. He would have known about the scientific developments which could assist him. In 1911, D'Arcy Power made a study of Pepys' eyesight as recorded in the diary and reached a diagnosis of hypermetropia (long-sightedness) with astigmatism, caused by eyestrain.[37] Power recreated an episode of 1667 in which Pepys attempted to seek ophthalmologic help, but unfortunately his spectacle-maker 'was clearly recommending [him] to use concave glasses when in reality he needed convex ones.'[38] Power concluded that the spectacles were tried but never purchased, noting that an entry a fortnight later records, 'so home to supper and to bed, my eyes being bad again; and so by this means the nights nowadays do become very long to me, longer than I can sleep out.'[39] The tenuous connection to Job seems to become more palpable. 'I have made my bed in the darkness' now bears a far closer resemblance to Pepys' condition. A vicious circle is developing whereby Pepys' restricted lifestyle diminishes the fullness and vividity of the diary, but then keeping the diary contributes directly to the restrictions on his lifestyle. The eyestrain suggested by Power and his further assertion 'that his fear of becoming blind was wholly unfounded'[40] indicate that a significant part of Pepys' visual trouble was artificially provoked. Although Pepys' could not possibly have known this,[41] he recognised that the only response to the problem could be an experimental one:

> Up and to my office awhile, and thither comes Lead with my vizard, with a Tube fastened within both eyes; which he prompts me to, of a glass in the Tube, doth content me mightily. So to church, where a stranger made a dull sermon, but I mightily pleased to look upon Mr. Buckworths little pretty daughters; and so home to dinner, where W How came and diner with us; and then I to my office, he being gone, to write down my journal for the last twelve days; and did it with the help of my vizard and Tube fixed to it, and do find it mighty manageable; but how helpful to my eyes this tail will show me.[42]

Power makes an interesting observation on this: that 'astigmatism can only be relieved by allowing the rays of light to pass through only a single meridian of the irregularly curved cornea or lens', adding that 'it is tantalising to think that Pepys might accidentally stumbled upon this method if anything had caused him to read through a slit whilst he was wearing his glasses.'[43]

This is tantalising indeed especially given the company of experimental scientists which Pepys kept. However, the inference I wish to draw from this example is that, for a time, Pepys considered his habit of diary writing to be a more valuable commodity than his sight. He was willing to alter his habit of looking and seeing, but not of writing. This suggests something acutely vital about his practice of keeping a diary. Hooke thought that by doing so, he could prosthetically extend what he considered to be the physical organ of his memory; Pepys, on the other hand seems to view his sight as the commodity which allows him to perform the essential function of writing his journal.

For the reasons Power identifies, however, the tubes did not work and only five weeks later, Pepys was writing his final entry. His diary writing was causing him severe eyestrain, and interestingly this eyestrain was the result of his physical adaptation to working in poor light. Robert M. Stecher explains that, 'man is unable to judge accurately the level of illumination by his senses alone, though he may learn to do so with experience by indirect means. Inability to judge light is due in part to the adaptability man has for this sense.'[44] The innate ability of Pepys' body to adapt to his environment and behaviour in fact became the reason for his having to alter that behaviour so radically. It's a thought which brings an uncanny literalness into Robert Burton's formulation that in writing Pepys was making the antidote out of that which was the prime cause of his disease.

Lady Anne Conway: philosopher-sufferer

A more meaningful example of therapeutic writing is that of Lady Anne Conway. Her life-story is one of isolation. Suffering fearful headaches from the age of twelve until her death at 47, she remained (and remains) undiagnosed, and was often too unwell to bear company. It is particularly worth noting that in Conway's case it was essential that her writing be private because of the anti-social nature of her condition. Although a more specific diagnosis of the root cause would be reckless, the symptoms described by Willis are largely consistent with current medical categorisation of migraine: 'Migraine sufferers typically have unilateral headache (but it may be bilateral) and complain of throbbing headache (but equally it may be constant). They usually have some degree of nausea and often have sensitivity to light (photophobia) or sound (phonophobia). They often find normal physical activity that involves movement of the head aggravates the pain.'[45] This characterisation does not precisely fit Willis' remark that the sickness was limited to 'no one side of the head,'[46] but at least it lends credibility to her apparent impatience 'of light, speaking, noise, or of any motion.'[47] It might be speculated, then, that a significant therapeutic quality of Anne Conway's writing is its ability in some way to act as a substitute for the human company of which she is so physically intolerant.

Conway's writing moves still further away from the notion of diaries-as-bookkeeping, and this is strictly because she did not write a diary. But neither did she write her philosophical treatise with the intention of publishing. In the main, it is a justification, in dispute with a significant body of contemporary mechanistic philosophy, of the essential purposiveness of God's creation. Towards the end, however, she comes to a philosophical rationalisation of pain:

> But if is be said, it [the Creature of God] goes into Eternal Torments, I answer, if by Eternal thou meanest an Infiniteness of Ages, which shall never cease, that is Impossible; because every Pain and Torment excites or stirs up an operating Spirit and Life in every thing which suffers; as we observe by continued Experience, and Reason teacheth us, that of necessity it must be so; because through Pain, and the enduring thereof, every kind of crassitude or grossness in Spirit or Body contracted is attenuated and as the Spirit captivated or detained in that grossness or crassitude is set at Liberty, and made more Spiritual, and consequently more Active and Operative, through suffering.[48]

It is noteworthy that a key idea in this theory of pain is also a key idea in the Burtonian theory of writing with which I began: the purgative capacity, the need for 'fit evacuation.' But for Conway, writing was not an instinctive response to her condition, but a measure of last resort (albeit a highly-serendipitous one) after medicine failed her. Thomas Willis, who gave the most complete account of her symptoms, diagnosed some ill-matter which required expunging. 'It appears by the history', he wrote, 'that the distemper at first arose from a Morbific matter, which was translated into the Head, after an ill cured Feavour.'[49] Willis records that, in 1656, Conway had travelled,[50] at William Harvey's suggestion, to Paris with the intention of undergoing trepanning (whereby a hole is drilled into the skull to give access to the dura matter). Apparently, she was unable to go through with the drastic operation. Whatever 'crassitude or grossness' had got into her head, it remained there, notwithstanding the efforts of the greatest medical experts of the day. If Thomas Willis – Sedleian Professor of Natural Philosophy at Oxford – could not treat the disease, all that remained was the personal, private remedy of explanation and exposition.

The passage above bears one similarity to the entry from Hooke's diary in which he claims that medication caused his illness rather than overindulgence. Both are speculative rather than positively assertive (although Anne Conway is more ready to admit to speculation that Hooke is). Conway introduces her rationale of pain with successive conditional clauses ('*if* it be said …'/ '*if* […] thou meanest …'). As with her disease, she is fighting an illusive opponent. She give no indication who might claim that a creature of God goes into eternal torments, but her use of the nominative singular pronoun ('thou') suggests she has a particular addressee (real or fictional) in mind. Like Hooke, she demonstrates a desire to deploy both theoretical and empirical proofs in expounding her theory. By the beginning of her main clause, the pronoun has changed to the first person plural ('we') suggesting a new objectivity, a common grounding from which both writer and reader can proceed. That grounding is 'Reason and Experience' (the theoretical and the empirically tested). Here, the supposed comradeship between Ann Conway and her reader seems to fall away. The pronoun, 'we' is ambiguous to begin with in that it is unclear whether or not it is used in the specific sense (me the writer, and you the imaginary addressee), or in a more general one. OED[51] suggests this general usage has been deployed 'by a speaker or writer in order to secure an impersonal style and tone' since the time of Ælfred. 'We', in that case, might simply indicate "scholars". The shift of pronoun glosses over a more significant rhetorical movement. That is, 'Reason and Experience teacheth *us*'. Now, as much as pain might be theorised by anyone, the case of Lady Ann Conway, as far as is known, was singular and the pain intense. Experience could only have taught *her* any meaningful lessons about her particular pain, and the enforced collectivity of her pronouns begins to seem inadequate. But private writing can envisage it own audience, one which can be tailored exactly to the writer's requirements, and it promises at least a manageable record of disease, understandable by others, even if those others are imaginary.

It is also important to note that her first person plural pronouns establish a different type of discourse from that which Conway would have be able to achieve discussing her symptoms with doctors such as the eminent Willis. From this observation, it is possible to develop a theory of why Anne Conway chose to explore her illness in this short passage towards the end of a philosophical treatise, rather than by keeping a diary of her symptoms. Conway was highly educated and, famously, a close correspondent with the Cambridge philosopher, Henry More. She became something of a protégé of More's, and their close relationship induced her to write the *Principles*. More regarded her very highly, claiming that he had, 'scarce ever met with any Person, Man or Woman, of better Natural parts than Lady Conway.'[52] Here, at last, was a discourse in which she was not an outsider. It is scarcely surprising, then, that coming to the conclusion of her opus, she should seek to incorporate herself into the work. Neither is it surprising that her grammar should imply (faintly) the camaraderie which she enjoyed in intellectual life but was missing from her physical life. It seems that, far from keeping an empirical record of herself, Anne Conway final resort was to fictionalise her illness – placing it within an imagined public context, she couldn't possibly achieve. In order to rationalise her pain, she makes it another topic for academic discussion amongst peers.

Alice Thornton: devout rebel

Of course, there is an alternative to analysing and rewriting an illness. Instead of providing a taxonomical breakdown of causes and symptoms, Alice Thornton explores (or appears to explore) the option simply to accept illness, and pray for recovery. A devoted royalist and Anglican, her *Autobiography* seems to exemplify a tendency to turn to God with the pen as well as through the more conventional methods of prayer. Thornton refers to the book herself as 'the collections of all God's dealings and mercies to me and all mine till my widowed condition.'[53] This writing is not entirely private – it was designed to be circulated among friends in mitigation of the Thornton family's decline of status. But it remains a work with a strictly controlled audience, and one which must of necessity have been written in secret. And paradoxically, one of the most fascinating aspects of the devotional *Autobiography* is its author's resistance to authority, both medical and spiritual. Pen service is paid to conventional duty of female subservience. For example, on one bout of sickness, Thornton recalls, 'I was deprived of seeing or doeing my faithful duty to my beloved husband, through the Lord's hand upon myselfe in exteamity.'[54] But the private arena of writing gives her a bolthole from which to mount a challenge against this convention. On her condition following the miscarriage of her first child she wrote:

> I continued ill in panic by fitts upon this journey, and within a fortnight fell into a desperate fever att Hipswell. Upon which my old doctor Mr. Mahum, was called, but could doe little towards the cure, because of beeing with childe. I was willing to be ordered by him, but said I found it absolutely necessary to be lett blood if they would save my life, but I was freely willing to resigne my will to God's ...[55]

As her account of the episode develops, Thornton's willingness to submit to the will of God and the judgement of her physician wanes:

> The doctor came post the next day, when he found me very weake, and durst not lett me blood that night, but gave me cordialls, etc., till the next day, and if I gott but one hour's rest that night. he would doe it the morning following. That night the two doctors had a dispute about the letting blood. Mr Mahun was against it, and Dr. Witte for it; but I soon desided that dispute, and tould them, if they would save my life, I must bleed.[56]

It is significant that, unlike the entries of Pepys and Hooke, above, Thornton is writing with the benefit of some years' hindsight (the manuscripts date from 1668, while the *Autobiography* begins with the year 1626), and is able to advance a more considered prose. It is perhaps not surprising that she should have felt she knew better than her doctor. Margearet Pelling has explained the curious overlap between a physician's role and the perceived duties of a woman at this time:

> Physicians had privileged access to bodies as well as the minds of their elite patients but although they could make economic gains, they were largely unable to make public use of this knowledge, which contemporaries tended to equate with the forms of access more commonly available to women.[57]

The doctor was surely encroaching on her territory; but, in private writing, Thornton is able to stand her narrative ground. As in the example from Ann Conway's philosophy, Thornton's grammar transforms the dispute from a medical to a moral one. Her conditional clauses insist on her theoretical and physical centrality to the tale: she is its protagonist, and her life is at risk. The recurrent phrase from the first passage to the second – 'if they would save my life' – overrides any medical disputes the doctors may have been engaged in, presenting them with a practical question. This demonstrates not so much Thornton's medical expertise over that of her physicians, nor a pugnacious browbeating character, but rather an ability to shift the discourse into an area in which she can be empowered alongside the supposed experts. She was bled and records, 'I found a change in my sight, which was exceedingly dime before ...'.[58] Although this seems like a miraculous recovery, it is hardly surprising that its record shows the patient to be unequivocally cured. Having reclaimed the case history from the specialised medical narrative of her doctors, Thornton has the rhetorical equipment at her disposal to reclaim responsibility for her own health.

It is worth pausing here to reflect more closely upon another potential benefit of a woman writing a diary. Diaries are a form in which women could take control of rhetoric (which was an important part of the tool-kit of power, and particularly, male-dominated parliamentary power). Thereby in private writing, mistresses become masters. Such insurrection becomes all the more powerful in a pseudo-diary such as this, which, although composed in secret, is in fact written to be shown to other people. At the same time as explaining how efficiently she dispensed her wifely duties, Thornton is able to express her dominances of her patrons:

> Neverthelesse, after the use of great meanes, which God directed me in by Dr. Wittie, etc.,as leaches, and gentle courses of physick, Spring and fall, as there was occassion ever since we weare married, those were much abated, and he oftener was in a more chearefull frame of spiritt then formerly, as both he and his friends have oftentimes acknowledged, whoes utmost endeavours and caire was ever to study his good and sattisfaction in whose life and wellfaire my owne did subsistt.[59]

The most convincing upheaval of the power of her male masters of which Thornton was capable was to put her husband in her debt for his life, and then, after his death, to record and propagate this fact. As Pelling points out, it was traditionally a woman's job to be the physician to her household, and her medical knowledge and skill would have greatly surpassed that of her husband. Indeed, Pelling suggests that more than demonstrating superior expertise to their husbands in matters of physic, such wives and nurses were often heavily influential on some of the most renowned doctors of the seventeenth century.[60] Far from simply writing herself into good health, as Pepys and Hooke tended to, Thornton elevates herself in writing to the rank of a healer. The sentence begins and ends with a declaration of subservience, to God and to her husband, but it also is careful to record that the effectiveness of Thornton's efforts was acknowledged by Mr. Thornton and his friends. I have already suggested that she had a tendency to erase (or at least downplay) God's providence and male authority from certain episodes of her *Autobiography*, and this incident is no exception. Thornton deliberately plays on the traditional female role of household physician, relegating all authorities to the background. Male assistance is purely theoretical and intellectual, whereas, again, her influence is applied, involving physical contact.

It was all too convenient for Thornton to write God out of her report, but she does not overlook this, returning to her faith after the event (and others like it) with a direct prayer of thanksgiving:

> And as I did not foolishly or lightly put myself upon itt, without begging Thy direction, in which my desires was unfeinedly to serve Thee, and trusting and relieing upon Thee my guide so, deare Lord leve me not, but lett me still find Thy goodnesse and clemency in comforting me in all crosses, afflictions, sicknesses, and calamities, in soule and bodie, giveing me faith, patience, humility, chastity, charity, hope, and fortitude; with fixed resolutions to love serve, and follow Thee to my live's end, that soe I may receave the end of my hope in the salvation of my poore soule.[61]

'Unfeinedly' seems to me to be a curious word in this exhortation. It is significant that she separates her prayers (written directly to God, although presumably included to make some impression on her friend-readers) from the rest of her prose, suggesting that an act of contrition is necessary for her failure to trust in and rely upon her dear guide. It almost sounds like an admission that her "resignation" 'to the will of God' in her illness was feigned (last time: "feinedly"; this time: "unfeinedly"). In the face of bodily 'afflictions, sicknesses, and calamities' her faith may have failed her. Thornton did not begin writing the *Autobiography* until after the death of her husband in 1668, and the detail recalled in her narratives suggest that some care had been taken over them.[62] Nevertheless, that the prayer is separated from narrative suggests a genuine piety, in contrast with the stylistic polish of her story-telling. In this, Thornton differs from Pepys who (with no audience in mind) incorporates his appeals and exaultations to God into his daily narrative:

> After dinner I writ a great many letter to my friends at London; and after that, the sermon begin again, all which time I slept, God forgive me.[63]

This is not to say that Thornton does not incorporate reminders of her faith into body of her prose too, but the specific difference is that Pepys addresses God directly; he talks to him. From Pepys' private world, the diary, God is very rarely absent. It is almost an instinct of Pepys' pen to remember God, both in direct prayer and in his rhetorical manoeuvres.

If Thornton does appear to address him directly, her parentheses to God do not seem to have quite the same integrity as the devotional asides of Pepys. The primary reason for this is that with her friends prospectively in mind as an audience, Thornton's writing does not have the authenticity of private prayer. A good example is the narration of her wedding day:

> That very day on which I was married, haveing bin in health and strength for many yeare's before I fell sodainly soe ill and sicke affter two a'clocke in the afternoon, that I thought, and all that saw me did believe, it would have bin my last night, beeing surprised with a violent paine in my head and stomacke, causing a great vomitting and sicknesse at my heart, which lasted eight houres before I had my intermition; but blessed be the Lord our God, the Father of mercies, Which had compassion on me, and by the meanes that was used I was strengthened wonderfully beyond expectation, beeing pretty well about ten a'clock at night.[64]

Given that one of the scandals which prompted Alice Thornton to write the *Autobiography* was her husband's financial ruin, it is difficult not to read something portentous into this episode. The first semi-colon, here, resembles that sentence of Pepys' in which he attempted to assert his good health in the face of a recurrence of his kidney disease. Technically speaking, it is a complex sentence (two main clauses in the form "X that Y"), but it is a complex sentence which is convoluted by parentheses and series of qualifying verb phrases. These qualifications, suggest a need to fit a certain amount of information into a sentence with an inadequate rhetorical frame. Where in the case of a wholly private diary, this may be seen as a loss of (or disregard for) rhetorical control, in the case of Alice Thornton, the psychological explanation has to be a concern to do herself justice: to forward her case thoroughly (normally a masculine luxury). In this light, it is implausible to read the (again parenthetical) affirmation of faith, as denoting genuine gratitude for and satisfaction with her lot. She makes a statement about God, rather than speaking directly to him. It is a formality, almost a phatic gesture, in the midst of an assertion of Thornton's independence and control over her own body. Her devotional remarks are no more than a preamble to the main clause of final semi-colon, in which she asserts that, 'by the meanes that was used I was strengthened strengthened wonderfully, and beyond expectation.' It sounds like a miracle, but, like the *Autobiography*, it is a miracle of her own making: 'by the meanes that was used'.

Conclusion

In conclusion, it is worth recapping my arguments so far.

Conceiving of the seventeenth-century diary as an exercise in bookkeeping is probably consistent with the thinking of the diarists with whom I have been dealing in this discussion. I argue, however, that whatever the intentions of these diarists, in practice the texts they produce throw up formal problems, especially in the diarist's approach to personal illness. Illness is not easy to pin down: it is not always easy to be precise in attributing symptoms to their causes, or even – a problem exemplified by Burton – to make a full and accurate record of symptoms, much less diseases. And for a diarist (whose status, Ong identified as ambiguous – "pretending he's not there") the difficulty of being objective in analysing illness is compounded. I argue that the difficulties of giving a balance-sheet account of health and illness in a diary can be observed by close attention to its linguistic character.

Hooke's diary, I argued, appears to correspond most closely to the model of the diary as a scientific table of health. But I am instinctively suspicious of Lotte Mulligan's assertion that the diary presents 'a fully objective "history" with himself as datum.' Or more accurately, I am suspicious of such a project's ability to produce insights into the self, which are anything other than insights into the self writing a diary. What Hooke's diary reveals, in spite of his mistrust of rhetoric, is that Hooke, sometimes loads the terms of his experiment.

If Hooke's diary appears at first glance to be no more than a catalogue of medical detail, Pepys' is immediately different. It is conversational and digressive, and seems to be envisaged by Pepys as a companion with which he has to make intelligent conversation. But, even so, in the diary he takes his health very seriously. There emerges in Pepys' diary, therefore, a rhetorical dialogue between the wish to analyse himself accurately, and the wish to encourage or comfort himself. Inevitably, then, feeling that he has to give up the diary for health reasons is to Pepys a personal tragedy.

Conversely, it is Anne Conway's personal tragedy (as well as a philosophical triumph) that she has to resort to writing. Private writing is all that remains for her after medicine has failed. She attempts to rationalise her pain, as part of God's creation, but it leads her to no conclusions about herself other than that she must submit to the will of God. Writing and scholarship, however, is a sort of proxy for company, and one which paradoxically, affords her admittance to the establishment.

Likewise, Alice Thornton's devotional *Autobiography* appears to represent a devotional deference to the will of God, but there is a lingering sense that the respect that she pays authority is merely pen service. Indeed there are times, at which she directly confronts authority and, I argue that the quasi-secret nature of her *Autobiography* prompts her to do so. In spite of her pious Anglican tendencies, clear to read on every page, the tendency to challenge authority extends as far as Thornton's questioning the terms of her submission to God.

What I hope emerges is a narrative which moves the diary away from simply being an exercise in record-keeping, and demonstrates some of the formal (and thereby psychological) difficulties diarists faced by embarking on such a project. By definition it is impossible to be objective in writing about the self, but I do not wish to suggest that failure on this score is at all a defect of these varyingly concerted attempts to do so. They prove Aubrey's observation in his life of Hooke, that "tis such a hard matter to get people to doe themselves right,"[65] and it is because they do that they are able to disclose rich personal stories of tragedy and rebellion. Hooke's is the story which I have developed the least, and it seems appropriate to close with an observation from his diary. On 3 September 1672, Hooke recorded that he, 'Purged 7 times. eat dinner well. Disordered somewhat by physick, urine had a cloudy sediment but brake not. Slept pretty well.'[66] As his editors remark, Hooke 'was a weakly child from birth,'[67] and chronic ill-health plagued him throughout his life. But rather than remarking, as most readers of his diary do, that 'Hooke regarded his body as a laboratory and experimental subject combined,'[68] I wish to close by reflecting – given the increasingly physic-addled state of Hooke's body – on his tragic impossibility that he should 'doe himself right.'

Notes

1. *Anatomy of Melancholy*, ed. by Holbrook Jackson (New York: New York University Press, 1932; repr., 2001) 'Democritus to the Reader,' p.21.
2. 'Diary and Autobiography' in *The Cambridge History of English Literature 1660–1870*, ed. by John Ritchie (Cambridge: Cambridge University Press, 2005), p.651.
3. *Anatomy of Melancholy*, 'Democritus to the Reader,' p.21.
4. See, "Textual Introduction," in Robert Burton, *The Anatomy of Melancholy*, ed. by Thomas C. Faulkner, Nicholas K. Keissling, and Rhonda I Blair, VI vols (Oxford: Clarendon Press, 1992) I, xxxvii–lx.
5. Jonathan Sawday, *The Body Emblazoned: Dissection and the Human Body in Renaissance Culture* (London: Routledge, 1995) p.3.
6. Lotte Mulligan, 'Self-Scrutiny and the Study of Nature: Robert Hooke's Diary as Natural History', *The Journal of British Studies*, 35:3 (July, 1996), 311–42 (p.312).
7. *Aubrey's Brief Lives*, ed. by Oliver Lawson Dick (London: Secker and Warburg, 1949) p.165.
8. The early diaries are in the Guildhall Library (MS 1758) and the later ones in the British Library (Sloane MSS 4024).

9. Sigmund Freud, 'A Note Upon the Mystic Writing Pad', in *The Standard Edition of the Complete Works of Sigmund Freud*, ed. by James Strachey, 24 vols (London: Hogarth, 1953–73) XIX, 227–32 (p.228).

10. Robert Hooke, *The Diary of Robert Hooke 1672–1680*, ed. by Henry W. Robinson and Walter Adams (London: Taylor and Francis, 1935) p.38.

11. *The Posthumous Works of Robert Hooke*, ed. by Richard Waller (London: Smith and Walford, 1705) p.140.

12. *The Diary of Robert Hooke*, p.145.

13. *Diary of Robert Hooke*, p.13.

14. Robert Hooke, 'A General Scheme of Idea of the Present State of Natural Philosophy', in *The Posthumous Works of Robert Hooke*, ed. by Richard Waller (London: Smith and Walford, 1705), p.63.

15. Ibid., pp.63–4.

16. *The Diary of Robert Hooke*, p.36.

17. There is a proven link between coldness and illness, but it should only really have serious implications for the health of elderly people. See, P.J. Neild, D. Syndercombe-Court, W.R. Keatinge, G.C. Donaldson, M. Mattock and M.Caunce, 'Cold-induced Increases in Erythrocyte Count, Plasma Cholesterol and Plasma Fibrinogen of Elderly People Without a Comparable Rise in Protein C or Factor X.' *Clinical Science*, 86 (1994), 43–48.

18. *The Diary of Robert Hooke*, p.26.

19. A revision was planned for public consumption. According to Mulligan (1996), Hooke 'later intended to use his diary as a source for an autobiography' (p.316).

20. *The Diary of Samuel Pepys*, ed. by Robert Latham and William Matthews, 2nd edn., XI vols (Berkely and Los Angeles: University of California Press, 1995; repr., 2000) ii. p.84.

21. Ibid. ii. p.87.

22. Ibid. ii. p.88.

23. There were two methods of removing kidney stones: one conventional, described by Ambrose Paré *The Works of that Famous Chirugion, Ambrose Paré* (London: Cotes, 1634) pp. 664–82, and the newer, experimental method, by which the lower belly was cut, described by John Douglas, *Lithotomia Douglassiana* (London: Woodward, 1720).

24. Paré, *Works*, p.674.

25. D'Arcy Power, 'An Address on the Medical History of Mr. and Mrs. Samuel Pepys', (Reprinted from the Lancet, 1895), p.8.

26. Medically speaking, there is a strong chance that the stone would have recurred. 'Once a kidney stone forms, the probability that a second stone will form within five to seven years is approximately 50%.' Malvinder S Parmar, 'Kidney Stones', *BMJ*, 328 (2004), 1420–24 (p.1420).

27. *Diary of Samuel Pepys*, vi. pp.66/7.

28. Ibid. vi. p51.

29. Ibid. vi. p.52.

30. (The first sentence, here, is a variation on a set piece which Pepys uses to recognise every 26 March).

31. The phrase crops up in plays by George Villiers, George Chapman, John Denis, Thomas Dilke, Ben Jonson, Thomas Jordan and George Wilkins.

32. *Diary of Samuel Pepys*, ix. p.565

33. Job 17:13.

34. *Diary of Samuel Pepys* ix. p.564.

35. Ibid. p.565 n.1.
36. *Diary of Samuel Pepys* vii. p.318.
37. D'Arcy Power, 'An Address on Why Samuel Pepys Discontinued his Diary' (Reprinted from the Lancet, 1911).
38. Power (1911), p.8.
39. *Diary of Samuel Pepys* viii. p.528.
40. Power (1911), p.12.
41. OED gives 1790 as the earliest citation for 'long-sighted' and 1868 for hypermetropia (OED suggests the coinage is Darwin's).
    See also, Daniel M. Albert and Diane D. Edwards, *The History of Ophthalmology* (Cambridge, M.A.: Blackwell Science, 1996), p.107, 'Despite the writings of Maurlyco and Kepler, hypermetropia was poorly understood until the 18th century.'
42. Diary of Samuel Pepys ix. p.533.
43. Power (1911) p.14.
44. Robert M. Stecher, 'Let There Be Light – At Least Enough for Reading in Libraries', Bulletin of the Medical Library Association, 33:2 (April, 1945), p.224.
45. Peter J. Goadsby and Jes Olesen, 'Fortnightly Review: Diagnosis and Management of Migraine', *BMJ*, 312 (1996), p.1280.
46. Willis, *Two Discourses Concerning the Souls of Brutes*, trans. by Samuel Pordage (Oxford: Davies, 1683) p.121.
47. Ibid.
48. Anne Conway, *The Principles of Most Ancient and Modern Philosophy*, ed. by Peter Lopston (The Hague: Martinus Nijhoff, 1982) p.193.
49. Thomas Willis, *Two Discourses*, p.122.
50. Ibid. p. 119.
51. Sense 2b.
52. Richard Ward, *The Life of the Learned and Pious Dr Henry More* (London, 1710) p.193.
53. Alice Thornton, *The Autobiography of Mrs Alice Thornton*, ed. by C. Jackson (Durham: Andrews, 1875) p.259.
54. Ibid, p.149.
55. Ibid., p.86.
56. Ibid., p.87.
57. Margaret Pelling, 'Public and Private Dilemmas: the College of Physicians in Early Modern London' in Steve Sturdy, ed., *Medicine, Health and the Public Sphere in Britain, 1600–2000* (London: Routledge, 2002) p.32.
58. *Autobiography*, p.87.
59. Ibid, p.132.
60. Margaret Pelling, 'The Women of the Family? Speculations Around Early Modern British Physicians', *Social History of Medicine*, 8:3 (1995), 383–401.
61. *Autobiography*. pp.89–90.
62. For further discussion of the manuscripts' dates, see, Raymond A. Anslement, 'Seventeenth-Century Manuscript Sources of Alice Thornton's Life', *Studies in English Literature 1500–1900*, 45:1 (Winter, 2005) 135_55.
63. *Diary of Samuel Pepys* i. p.97.
64. *Autobiography*, p.83.
65. *Brief Lives*, p.167.
66. *Diary of Robert Hooke*, p.6.
67. Ibid. p.xiv.

68. Lucinda McCray Bier, 'Experience and Experiment: Robert Hooke, Illness and Medicine,' in Michael Hunter and Simon Shaffer, eds., *Robert Hooke: New Studies* (Woodbridge: Boydell Press, 1989) p.240.

Bibliography

Albert, Daniel M., and Diane D. Edwards (1996), *The History of Ophthalmology* (Cambridge, M.A.: Blackwell Science).

Anslement, Raymond A. (2005), 'Seventeenth-Century Manuscript Sources of Alice Thornton's Life', *Studies in English Literature 1500–1900*, 45:1 (Winter) 135–55.

Aubrey, John (1949), *Aubrey's Brief Lives*, ed. by Oliver Lawson Dick (London: Secker and Warburg).

Bier, Lucinda McCray (1989), 'Experience and Experiment: Robert Hooke, Illness and Medicine,' in Michael Hunter and Simon Shaffer, eds., *Robert Hooke: New Studies* (Woodbridge: Boydell Press) pp.235–52.

Burton, Robert (2001), *Anatomy of Melancholy*, ed. by Holbrook Jackson (New York: New York University Press, 1932; repr.).

Burton, Robert (1992), *The Anatomy of Melancholy*, ed. by Thomas C. Faulkner, Nicholas K. Keissling, and Rhonda I Blair VI vols, (Oxford: Clarendon Press).

Conway, Anne (1982), *The Principles of Most Ancient and Modern Philosophy*, ed. by Peter Lopston (The Hague: Martinus Nijhoff).

Douglas, John (1720), *Lithotomia Douglassiana* (London: Woodward).

Freud, Sigmund (1953–73), 'A Note Upon the Mystic Writing Pad', in *The Standard Edition of the Complete Works of Sigmund Freud*, ed. by James Strachey, 24 vols (London: Hogarth) XIX, p.228.

Goadsby, Peter J,. and Jes Olesen (1996), 'Fortnightly Review: Diagnosis and Management of Migraine', *BMJ*, 312, 1279–83.

Hooke, Robert (1705), *The Posthumous Works of Robert Hooke*, ed. by Richard Waller (London: Smith and Walford).

Hooke, Robert (1935), *The Diary of Robert Hooke 1672–1680*, ed. by Henry W. Robinson and Walter Adams (London: Taylor and Francis).

Mulligan, Lotte (1996), 'Self-Scrutiny and the Study of Nature: Robert Hooke's Diary as Natural History', *The Journal of British Studies*, 35:3 (July), 311–42.

Neild, P.J., D. Syndercombe-Court, W.R. Keatinge, G.C. Donaldson, M. Mattock and M.Caunce (1994), 'Cold-induced Increases in Erythrocyte Count, Plasma Cholesterol and Plasma Fibrinogen of Elderly People Without a Comparable Rise in Protein C or Factor X.' *Clinical Science*, 86, 43–8.

Paré, Ambrose (1634), *The Works of that Famous Chirugion, Ambrose Paré* (London: Cotes).

Parmar, Malvinder S (2004), 'Kidney Stones', *BMJ*, 328, 1420.

Pepys, Samuel (2000), *The Diary of Samuel Pepys*, ed. by Robert Latham and William Matthews, 2nd edn., XI vols (Berkely and Los Angeles: University of California Press, 1995; repr.).

Pelling, Margaret (1995), 'The Women of the Family? Speculations Around Early Modern British Physicians', *Social History of Medicine*, 8:3, 383–401.

Pelling, Margaret (2002), 'Public and Private Dilemmas: the College of Physicians in Early Modern London' in Steve Sturdy, ed., *Medicine, Health and the Public Sphere in Britain, 1600–2000* (London: Routledge) pp.27–42.

Power, D'Arcy (1895), 'An Address on the Medical History of Mr. and Mrs. Samuel Pepys', (Reprinted from the *Lancet*).

Power, D'Arcy (1911), 'An Address on Why Samuel Pepys Discontinued his Diary' (Reprinted from the *Lancet*).

Sawday, Jonathan (1995), *The Body Emblazoned: Dissection and the Human Body in Renaissance Culture* (London: Routledge).

Sherman, Stewart (2005), 'Diary and Autobiography' in *The Cambridge History of English Literature 1660–1870*, ed. by John Ritchie (Cambridge: Cambridge University Press), pp.649–72.

Stecher, Robert M. (1945), 'Let There Be Light – At Least Enough for Reading in Libraries', *Bulletin of the Medical Library Association*, 33:2 (April), 220–30.

Thornton, Alice (1875), *The Autobiography of Mrs Alice Thornton*, ed. by C. Jackson (Durham: Andrews).

Ward, Richard (1710), *The Life of the Learned and Pious Dr Henry More* (London).

Willis, Thomas (1683), *Two Discourses Concerning the Souls of Brutes*, trans. by Samuel Pordage (Oxford: Davies).

14

Trans-genre Confusion: What Does Autobiography Think It Is?

Claire Lynch

> In talking about autobiography, one always feels that there is a great and present danger that the subject will slip away all together, that it will vanish into thinnest air, leaving behind the perception that there is no such creature as autobiography and that there never has been – that there is no way to bring autobiography to heel as a literary genre with its own proper form, terminology and observances
>
> (Olney 1980 4).

Autobiography is arguably the most underhand of all literary genres, consistently avoiding the definitions fashioned for it and eluding the genre boundaries expected of it. As James Olney laments above, this can be frustrating for those who find that every reasonable definition of the genre is evaded by writers. To some extent this situation is simply logical, as lives are unique, so too are the texts which represent them. Uniqueness and originality are frequently admired both in people and writing, and yet an incentive to label and classify persists. In literary terms, this is manifested in the gathering together of individual texts into groups, using labels which often inadequately describe them. As Olney points out, some types of writing, and indeed some types of people, do not fit comfortably into this system. The term 'trans-genre' is used here to describe this problem and to suggest that the definitional issues Olney identifies are a result of autobiography's position between or across genres. It is impossible to apply the same methods of classification to autobiography because of a disparity between its apparently simple appearance and its complex identity. Although it appears to be comprised of facts, it is very often mainly fictional; it claims to be about the individual but very often focuses on the group, and in various other ways, mocks the concept of genre. The 1974 Autobiography *Conundrum*, re-published in 2002 with some additional material, provides a useful framework in which to discuss this concept as both the text and author reject the use of limited and limiting definitions. Born James

Humphrey Morris in 1926 the author recalls an early awareness of identity confusion:

> I was three or perhaps four years old when I realized that I had been born into the wrong body, and should really be a girl. I remember the moment well, and it is the earliest memory of my life (1).

The autobiography charts the emotional, physical, and legal process by which James became Jan and her 'tragic and irrational ambition, instinctively formulated but deliberately pursued, to escape from maleness into womanhood' (7). In a sense, autobiographical theory has mirrored this process of cautious evolution, moving from the denial of its complexity, through to a contemporary acceptance of a less reliable, but more accurate identity. For many, this conundrum presents an irresistible challenge and as Linda Anderson notes, 'many literary critics have turned to definitions as a way of stamping their academic authority on an unruly and even slightly disreputable field' (2001 2). Just as James Morris experimented with identity, becoming Jan and reaching the conclusion that none of the available identity terms were applicable to her experience of selfhood, so too is autobiography repeatedly faced with an identity crisis when placed alongside other literary genres.

Definitions of autobiography are frequently formed by comparing it with the novel, because the two forms are, as Laura Marcus notes 'morphologically similar as continuous prose discourses' (1998 237). This likeness is based on appearances, rather than more significant factors and as a result, autobiography is often unfavourably compared to its more glamorous fictional counterpart. Similarly, Morris considers her physical appearance as a man to be a misleading and incorrect representation of her true self; in autobiography, things are very rarely what they appear to be. Hannah Arendt links these dilemmas, reminding us that 'the moment we want to say *who* somebody is, our very vocabulary leads us astray into saying *what* he is' (1958 181). We are limited in this respect not only linguistically but also imaginatively, formulating the identities of people and texts through a series of established conventions not exclusive definitions. In *Conundrum*, Morris applies her experience of transgressing such limits to the act of writing, using a form which depends upon subversion for its existence, autobiography.

Whilst writers may thrive as a consequence of this freedom, theorists are inclined to control this 'unruly' genre by reclassifying it as 'life writing', a broader category which includes autobiographies, biographies, case studies, diaries, memoirs, autobiographical novels, ethnography, blogs, profiles and numerous other forms. To an extent, the concept of life writing is synonymous with thinking of autobiography as a trans-genre due to the ease with which it acknowledges the links between subtly different categories. Trans-genre is different, however, because it also allows for the inclusion of other texts which fall beyond the remit of life writing. *Conundrum*, for example, overlaps into the genre of travel writing, not only because its author describes the significance of locations such as Oxford, Wales and Casablanca to her life-story, but also because the theme is extended by describing the ultimate autobiographical journey from one identity to another. The inclusion of travel narratives therefore, is not an irrelevance but a vital means of capturing the author's experience. It is as much a part of the text's identity as the more traditional autobiographical elements such as the use of the first person, or the reminiscences of schooldays. In both content and form then, Morris avoids the restrictions of definitions to represent a trans-gender self in a trans-genre text.

Autobiography stands out amongst its life writing siblings through its level of implicit intentionality. Unlike diarists, for example, an autobiographer writes with the objective of publication. Producing a text in order to make public, or even 'publicise' the 'self' is an act of declaring difference and as a consequence, proclaiming a public identity. According to Linda Anderson this places a responsibility on autobiography to become a standard-bearer as the experiences of one person 'which may be representative of a particular marginalised group' become a source of empowerment and public recognition (2001 104). Ironically, in presenting a supposedly 'unique' life, the autobiography necessarily becomes the blueprint for others. As Morris admits, 'acquaintances often treat me as a sounding board for their own neuroses, just as many readers will doubtless have read this book hoping for sidelights on their own confusions' (144). In its capacity to be representative, autobiography oversteps the line which separates literature and reality by referring to the reader's involvement and considering the implications of the text upon lived experiences. Autobiography often disrupts this division between the textual world and reality, with the author's repeated emphasis of her own existence supporting Philippe Lejeune's case that the autobiographer has 'one foot in the text and one outside, he is the point of contact between the two' (1989 4). In the trinity of author/subject/narrator that Lejeune promotes, the autobiographer is expected to be more candid than a novelist need be within their force field of fiction. Readers look to autobiography with an assumption that (some) truth will be told and that the text is essentially different from other genres because its origin is confession. However, as Estelle Jelinek observes, contrary to the theory which links autobiography and exposé, 'the admission of intense feelings of hate, love, and fear, the disclosure of explicit sexual encounters [...] are matters on which autobiographers are generally silent' (13). In *Conundrum*, Morris explicitly links these two obligations by noting her readers' disappointment when they have 'looked for lust' in the text and not found it. Morris' honesty in regard to one aspect of her life leads her reader to expect it throughout the text. Their disappointment is the inevitable response to autobiography in which revelations rarely satisfy readers' curiosity. Lejeune's description of the author's omnipresence is significant nonetheless because it highlights auto-biography's central identity crisis as it moves constantly between fact and fiction.

The inclusion of verifiable facts and the sub-title autobiography encour-age the assumption that the narrative is a 'true' account of a life, devoid of the fictitious elements on which a literary text usually functions. Paul John Eakin's eminently sensible point that 'it is as reasonable to assume that all autobiography has some fiction in it as it is to recognise that all fiction is in some sense necessarily autobiographical' neatly undermines this idea (1988 5). From the perspective of trans-genre this allows the intermingling of two supposedly incongruous forms. For Morris, the concepts of truth and fiction take on a further significance as she recalls: 'my life was one long protest against the separation of fact from fantasy: fantasy *was* fact, I reasoned, just as mind was body, or imagination truth' (100). As a consequence, whilst her autobiography purports to be an uncomplicated account of a complex life, fiction is repeatedly evoked, as she admits, 'if I consider my story in detach-ment I sometimes seem, even to myself, a figure of fable or allegory' (147). As Morris' life is dominated by an awareness of her difference, the text in which she recounts her life inevitably differs from the expectations of late twentieth-century British autobiography. The core structure is highly con-ventional in fact, with the subject evolving from choir boy, through Oxford, into the army and then a career at *The Times*. However, as this entire process takes place with the underlying knowledge of the trans-gendered subject, fic-tion lies behind every fact. Morris draws attention to her use of 'images of magic' 'wizards and wise women' to emphasise that if not in form then in style, traditional autobiography is insufficiently able to represent her lived experience.

Conundrum extends the concept of trans-genre writing at the matrix between fiction and non-fiction by subverting precise genre tropes, most overtly the *Bildungsroman*. The representation of childhood in the genre is defined by Jerome Buckley as follows:

> A child of some sensibility grows up in the country or in a provincial town, where he finds constraints, social and intellectual, placed upon the free imagination …His first schooling, even if not totally inadequate, may be frustrating insofar as it may suggest options not available to him in his present setting (2002 23).

In the classic *Bildungsroman*, a difficult or exceptional childhood is followed by the individual overcoming adversity resulting in a major achievement. From this point, the narrator describes the progress of life and career, adult success and the development of the sense of self and personal philosophy. Often the subject is able to rise to a higher position in society where his success can be attributed to his own hard work and effort. In *Conundrum* the process of childhood ambitions culminating in adult satisfaction is magnified as Morris explains:

> I have interpreted my journey from the start as a quest, sacramental or visionary, and in retrospect it has assumed for me a quality of the epic, its purpose unyielding, its conclusion inevitable (2002 144).

The correlation between the *Bildungsroman* and autobiography is thus doubly emphasised in *Conundrum* both through the journey motif and the philosophical implications of the conclusion. By combining the traditional passage from childhood to adulthood with the more unexpected route from manhood to womanhood, *Conundrum* maintains an important link with the fantasy of the happy ending more commonly found in other literary genres. When comparing the genres of autobiography and *Bildungsroman* Laura Marcus argues that in both forms 'fictions are often seen as more important, and revealing, than facts' noting further that 'autobiography like the *Bildungsroman*, is a privileged site' for representing the process by which a gendered individual is formed (214). In Morris' case, the supposedly simple process by which the individual gains maturity is disrupted by the child's ambiguous starting point as she wonders:

> Perhaps one day, when I grew up, I would be as solid as other people appeared to be: but perhaps I was meant always to be a creature of wisp or spindrift, loitering in this inconsequential way as though I were intangible (5).

Inevitably then, the form in which such a self could be represented must be equally nebulous. Part generic novel of development in its *Bildungsroman* style and part highly stylised autobiography in its aims, *Conundrum* is unfaithful to the expectations of both genres as both are inadequately supple to accommodate the shape of Morris' life. Nevertheless, for all of the identity crises on which the narrative is built, it is ultimately the formal definition of a fictional genre which comes closest to describing Morris's personal journey, reinforcing the value of genre-crossing.

Morris self-defines her quest for identity as a simple one stating: 'all I wanted was liberation, or reconciliation – to live as myself' (91). To capture this in textual form, however, is far from straightforward. Like any other form of writing, an autobiography must be constructed and shaped within the limits of a publishable, textual form. Consequently, the process of writing it is no more 'essential' than the process of writing fiction as James Olney clarifies, 'the self, then, is a fiction and so is the life, and behind the text of an autobiography lies the text of an "autobiography": all that is left are characters on a page' (22). Autobiography is 'a fiction' certainly, but it is not classifiable as a form of fiction in the way that novels or short stories are. The inadequacy of genre labels to describe the process and the product of autobiography leads to Olney's original fear that 'no such creature as autobiography exists'. Like many autobiographers, Morris highlights the constructed nature of her text by referring to the writing process, including the editors, proof readers, and in a note to the second edition. This emphasis of *Conundrum's* artificiality parallels the life-changing process it describes; the gradual and painful process by which the autobiography is written, mirrors her own life with both reaching a conclusion which is ultimately incomplete. Focusing on the process rather than the product is common in autobiography, with numerous writers extending their life stories into sequels or re-editing the original after publication, suggesting dissatisfaction with the textual version of the self. The failure of autobiography to adequately distinguish itself from fiction which this implies adds to the confusion about its status and forces the genre as a whole into a state of denial.

For some, autobiography's ability to overlap with other genres is a defining characteristic. Eakin for example claims that twentieth century autobiographer's 'readily accept the proposition that fictions and the fiction making process are a central constituent of the truth of any life that is lived' (1988 5). Whilst Eakin's idea of acceptance suggests that fiction is a naturally occurring element in autobiography, it is the author's conscious and deliberate use of other literary genres which ultimately provides its trans-genre status. The over-identification with fictional forms in an autobiography provides an opt-out clause for the author who wants to withhold the ultimate truth of the self from the reader. When in young adulthood Morris seeks to counteract her awareness of a female identity with the adoption of hyper-masculine activities she is concealing the whole truth from herself as she will later do with her readers. Far from resulting in a reconfiguration of gender identity, these roles reinforce her sense of difference; when in the army, for example, she recalls: 'far from making a man of me, it only made me feel more profoundly feminine at heart'(2002 23). Attempts to force the self into a conventional gender role fail, however extreme the measures taken; when on an expedition to Everest for instance she recalls that the experience 'taught me new meanings of maleness' but also that it 'emphasized once more my own inner dichotomy' (75). Autobiographical theorists who attempt to surmount ambiguous definitions find themselves similarly dissatisfied; the appearance and behaviour of the text is always concealing another identity beneath the surface. For Morris, the experiments with maleness do not simply provide evidence of her femaleness, but also devalue the question of gender as a whole:

> I had reached the conclusion myself that sex was not a division but a continuum, that almost nobody was altogether of one sex or another, and that the infinite subtlety of the shading from one extreme to the other was one of the most beautiful of nature's phenomena (42).

In recounting a personal acceptance of trans-gender identity, a trans-genre autobiography allows Morris to reconstruct the process through which the self evolved in both content and form as she claims: 'it was only in writing this book that I have delved so deeply into my emotions' (143). The cathartic benefit autobiographers often refer to again emphasises its distinction from other genres in which the author's presence is consciously obscured. Whereas readers of the novel ceased grieving for Barthes' dead author long ago, New Criticism has forced readers of life-writing to remain in purgatory as autobiographies and biographies insist on maintaining a connection with real (living) people. In biography in particular the existence of the subject is insisted upon with photographs, facsimiles of correspondence and interviews. In autobiography, the standard association between the name of the author on the cover and the name of the narrator who guides the reader through the text cuts a ghostly figure in Barthes' formulation. Whereas removal of the author's authority has led to broadening the potential interpretations of the novel, the same approach is prohibited in autobiography and biography by the author's obvious presence. In this sense Morris endlessly subverts the expectations of autobiographical form, moving across personal pronouns, subject names, and moving in and out of gender roles like a self-conscious Orlando.

In autobiography, the relevance of the author is unassailable in a way that it is not in the novel, indeed publication does not eradicate the author but rather awards a form of immortality; in autobiography the author is the text. This connection, some have argued, is not simply bound up in ideas of genre theory, but is a consequence of human experience more broadly. Adriana Caverero argues that 'every human being, without even wanting to know it, is aware of being a *narratable self* – immersed in the spontaneous auto-narration of memory' (2000 3). The proposal that memory inflicts upon all of us an internal autobiography which only some choose or are able to transfer into a written form challenges many of the key ideas of autobiography's status amongst other genres. Morris is confident in the interest her story will evoke, stating: 'it seems to me that what has happened to me, and what I have tried to describe in this book, is one of the most fascinating experiences that ever befell a human being' (2002 128). The originality of the experience results in a responsibility to write it up, upgrading the experience to representative status as she claims: 'many people believe that what has happened to me reflects more than a rare predicament, but in some way illustrates *la condition humaine*' (145). This transfer of meaning between the author and the reader represents the real difficulty when attempting to allocate autobiography to any literary genre. The uncomfortable presence, in however limited a form, of the 'real' in autobiography maintains the necessity for human as well as objective critical reactions from readers. Leigh Gilmore has described 'the paradox that the autobiographer be both unique and representative' which the author must face in representing their own life amidst the lives of others noting that when writers take the opportunity to 'promote themselves as representative subjects [....] legitimation or shaming is always possible' (2001 8). To write autobiography is to choose to be representative, both of oneself and those with whom one is associated and as Morris' example demonstrates, the representative potential of the life is not always realised:

> Few people understood it. I did not expect them to understand the cause, since it was a mystery even to me, but I had supposed more people might understand the compulsion (2002 140).

In crossing between types of life and types of life writing, Morris also discovers the potential impact of autobiography to be seen not as inspirational in its representative capacity, but alienating.

Traditional autobiographers are linked by common motivations and therefore similar uses of the autobiographical genre. In its most essential form, autobiography is equally concerned with confession and self-promotion, with the author's ultimate intention to provide a self-censored record of their own life. For a great deal of its history the contributors to the genre have also shared broadly similar lives so that 'classic' examples have been considered together to form standards upon which new texts are judged. Authors who exist beyond the traditional expectations of autobiography must overcome these barriers in order to produce their text. Julia Swindells has described how autobiography 'now has the potential to be the text of the oppressed and culturally displaced, forging a right to speak both for and beyond the individual', highlighting the accessible nature of the genre (1995 7). Autobiography is both an attractive and profitable form of writing as Swindells notes, precisely because it provides the individual with the opportunity of 'forging a right to speak'; it allows the author to reassert his or her individual legitimacy as well as defending the reputation of the group. In contemporary studies of autobiography approaches familiar in feminist criticism and post colonialism are invoked in which the texts of the 'oppressed and culturally displaced' are recovered. Indeed, it is now commonplace to think of autobiography in exactly this way, not as the preserve of the lives of great men, but as active in the promotion of untold life stories. The groups which have previously been excluded from autobiography are determined to reclaim their place in it by writing their own lives and it is with these different expectations and motivations that new and influential autobiography is produced. The profit for authors who exist outside of the traditional autobiography is in the freedom to produce a text based on their own personal potential. Equally, distance from the tradition allows autobiographers to redefine the genre in relation to more fluid concepts. As Mary Evans argues, the genre is 'in urgent need of reclassification' and that 'its place on the library shelves is not with non-fiction but very much closer to fiction' (1999 143). Nonetheless, autobiographers continue to insist upon their presence in the text and the implied accuracy and revelation of the genre as a whole. When Morris shares her 'yearning' for a solid identity (2002 4) and confides in the reader her sense of being 'non-human' or a 'monster' (99) a form of empathy is called for which is greater than that applied to fictional characters. Autobiography is a trans-genre form of writing not only for the ways in which authors construct it amidst other forms of writing, but also in the ways in which it is read.

The greater detachment an autobiographer has from the traditional life experiences that define the genre, the greater their opportunity to create a revolutionary text. Just as an individual's identity may be dependent on belonging to a number of different and potentially incongruous groups, so too can a text function through a variety of genre combinations. Autobiography can be seen as trans-genre in a very clear sense then as comprising of an infinite combination of elements of other genres. For Morris the moment of completion occurs when 'identity is achieved', when external and internal selves converge. Autobiography cannot exclude itself from the concepts of genre which describe and define types of writing nor can individual texts re-fashion definitions for their own means. What they can do, however, is stand astride the 'terminology and observances' Olney points to. When authors recognise this they are able to produce a textual format as ambiguous as the life they seek to represent. Through this approach in which fact and fiction are applied in equal measure and styles and forms are welcomed from across the literary spectrum, the troublesome 'creature' autobiography continues to thrive. Morris concludes her personal journey, not with an acknowledgement of her life's success, but rather, with the acceptance that such journeys are inevitably incomplete:

> So I do not mind my continuing ambiguity. I have lived the life of a man, I live now the life of a woman, and one day perhaps I shall transcend both – if not in person, then perhaps in art, if not here, then perhaps somewhere else (14)

When Morris explains that conceptions of sex and gender 'obviously over-lap' but are 'far from synonymous' she echoes the place of autobiography on the spectrum of life writing; differences are understood, but difficult to clearly describe. The blurring of apparently distinct gender categories which Morris' journey moves towards similarly provides a way of understanding that many of the definitions of autobiography are based on the impossibility to define it. When defining genres (and for that matter genders), we emphasise difference, defining the subject by what it is not. In the case of autobiography, other genres are not only conceived of as opposites, but also as close relations. This is problematic for genre purists as autobiography demonstrates an aptitude for ranging across disciplines. Laura Marcus captures this expertly when describing how autobiography 'lies between "literature" and "history" or perhaps philosophy, and between fiction and non-fiction' (1998 229).

It is located 'between' multiple genres, in the same way that Morris' autobiography is written by both a man and a woman and simultaneously neither. As a 'trans-genre' type of writing, autobiography echoes the analogous state of trans-gender people in which physical appearance and self-image are incongruous, avoiding binary distinctions through a simultaneous connection to more than one category to undermine rigid classifications.

Bibliography

Arendt, H. (1958), *The Human Condition*. Chicago: University of Chicago Press.

Anderson, L. R. (2001), *Autobiography*. London: Routledge.

Buckley, J. H. (1974), *Season of Youth: The Bildungsroman from Dickens to Golding*. Cambridge, Mass: Harvard University Press.

Caverero, A. (2000), *Relating Narratives: Storytelling and Selfhood*, trans. by Paul A. Kottman. London: Routledge.

Eakin, P. J. (1988), *Fictions in Autobiography: Studies in the Art of Self-Invention*. Princeton: Princeton University Press.

Evans, M. (1999), *Missing Persons: The Impossibility of Auto/Biography*. London: Routledge.

Gilmore, L. (2001), *The Limits of Autobiography: Trauma and Testimony*. London: Cornell University Press.

Jelinek, E. C. (1980), *Women's Autobiography: Essays in Criticism*. London: Indiana University Press.

Lejeune, P. & Eakin, P.J. (1989), *On Autobiography*, Minneapolis: University of Minnesota Press.

Marcus, Laura (1998), *Auto/biographical Discourses: Theory, Criticism, Practice*, Manchester and New York; Manchester University Press.

Morris, J. (2002), *Conundrum*. London: Faber & Faber.

Olney, J. (1980), *Autobiography, Essays Theoretical and Critical*. Princeton: Princeton University Press.

Swindells, J. (1995), *The Uses of Autobiography*. London: Taylor & Francis.

15

The Art of Losing: The Place of Death in Writers' Memoirs

Timothy C. Baker

From the first loss,
we begin naming.
Mark Doty, "A Replica of the Parthenon"[2000 3]

The acceptance of a text as autobiographical often rests on what Laura Marcus terms the intention of totality and sincerity. As she writes, "If the autobiographer is 'sincere' in the attempt to understand the self and to explain that self to others, then the 'autobiographical intention' becomes accepted as a serious one" (1998 3). Yet given the necessary impossibility of a living subject's presenting his or her life as totality, the full realization of this possibility remains untenable: while the distinction between autobiography and memoir is traditionally understood to be one of relative completeness, in which the former recounts the subject's whole life and the latter focuses on a particular aspect or moment, it is difficult to imagine how any self-account could be other than partial or anecdotal. However sincere the attempt, the autobiographical work is always predicated on a death or a completion that is yet to come. If autobiography assumes the subject's death, it is necessarily problematic; as Philippe Lacoue-Labarthe states: "If all autobiography is an autothanatography, autobiography as such is, rigorously speaking, strictly impossible" (1998 193). The question of how a subject can write a retrospective account of a life that is still ongoing remains both central and unanswerable. For Paul de Man, any claims to totality arise not from the life that is being documented, but from the documentation itself: "can we not suggest", he writes, "that the autobiographical project may itself produce and determine the life and that whatever the writer *does* is in fact determined, in all its aspects, by the resources of his medium" (1984 69). For de Man, it is not the writer's intent that creates the possibility of autobiographical interpretation, but the very act of writing itself.

De Man goes on to suggest that autobiography cannot be seen as a genre in itself, but should instead be approached as a "figure or reading or understanding that occurs, to some degree, in all texts" (70). Linda Peterson takes a similar approach in suggesting that, even as it has historically been figured in terms of the continuity of a generic form, autobiography can also be seen as a literary act "that interprets experience and thus creates a self by working within (and sometimes against) the formal conventions of the genre" (1986 33). The autobiography can thus be seen to be born of conflicting demands: the desire to present a totalized life is opposed by the subject's own ongoing consciousness, while the ability to interpret individual experience is only made possible through reference to writing itself. It is insufficient to argue that the autobiographical subject employs a fiction of her own death in order to write the account of her life, for such an argument fails to explain how this double vision comes to pass. It is instead in Jacques Derrida's concept of the ghost that autobiography can be revealed as an account of: "Neither life nor death, but the haunting of the one by the other" (2003 41). The ghost, for Derrida, allows for the recognition of both alterity and death in autobiographical writing; it is "the concept of the other in the same [...] the completely other, dead, living in me" (2007 272).

This haunting, Derrida argues, underlies all autobiographical writing. Indeed, "the most 'autobiographical' books [...] begin with death" (2007 297). The experience of "haunting", understood not only as the movement between the actual life and presumed death of the autobiographical subject but also as the haunting of the living subject by the missing or absent other, is brought to light in a wide variety of autobiographical works, but can be seen most clearly in writers' memoirs and autobiographies. In both life histories and comprehensive family chronicles, as well as in more explicit accounts of immanent grief and mourning, the death of a loved other is presented as both a narrative framework and an explanatory principle. In order for an autobiographical subject to confront her life as a totality, she must first come to terms with the death of the other. An understanding or a witnessing of the other's death makes the premonition of one's own death possible: it is only through this act of witnessing that the writer of an autobiography or memoir can begin to approach her own life. This death of the other is the event that underlies all claims to both totality and interpretation. The death of a parent or a lover, especially, permits a life-within-death in which the writing subject can begin to understand at least one portion of his or her life as past or complete. It is a familiar commonplace that the death of a parent brings a recognition of the child's own mortality, but just as importantly it also permits a reappraisal of the subject's life, up to that moment of the other's death, as something that has now ended. As Peter Handke writes in *A Sorrow Beyond Dreams*, his brief account of his mother's death: "When I write, I necessarily write about the past, about something which, at least while I am writing, is behind me" (2002 7). The autobiographical project is made possible only through a recognition of a self that is historicized in relation to the other. Additionally, accounts of a subject's life that begin with the death of an other prevent the subject from being seen only in an artificial isolation; as

Marcus writes: "Recounting one's own life almost inevitably entails writing the life of an other or others" (1998 273). Writing the life of others necessitates a re-evaluation of one's own history, and writing one's own history requires an engagement with the life, and death, of others.

The centrality of a relation with the other in any account of an individual life is made clear in Derrida's own elliptical autobiographical document *Circumfession*, published as a counterpart to Geoffrey Bennington's more traditional philosophical biography. Derrida stresses in his self-account that: "I confess my mother, one always confesses the other, I confess (myself) means I confess my mother" (1999b 147). Without first detailing the way in which the self stands in relation to the other, specifically the deceased or absent other, the autobiographical project could not be completed. Derrida's work is especially pertinent to an exploration of totality and interpretation, both in terms of his theoretical reflections on these issues and his own autobiographical acts. Just as *Circumfession* explicitly relates his life to his mother's death, many of Derrida's most interesting autobiographical statements can be found in *The Work of Mourning*, a collection of obituaries and memorial speeches. For Derrida, as for the other writers discussed below, the self can only be understood in relation to an other, and more precisely, to an other who is now dead. To write an autobiography is not only to write the life of an other or others, but also to write their death. Writers as diverse as Jean-Jacques Rousseau (1953) and John Lanchester (2007), as Jonathan Franzen (2007) and Andrew Motion (2007), begin their memoirs with an account of their mother's death, just as John Burnside (2006), Philip Roth (1991), Michael Ondaatje (1982) and Blake Morrison (2006) present their fathers' deaths as the motivation for their autobiographical accounts. Such a foregrounding of parental death suggests that without an originary understanding of the relationship between the self and the other in the context of that other's death, nothing that follows can be properly understood. The death of the other is presented as uprooting all previous knowledge of the self, and indeed of language itself. As Franzen writes of his experience of his mother's death: "What lived on – in me – was the discomfort of how completely I'd outgrown the novel I'd once been so happy to live in" (2007 25).

Just as Franzen foregrounds the written aspect of his life in the context of this death, for Derrida the death of the other is productive of, even as it is a challenge to, writing itself. At the start of *Circumfession* he contextualizes his own confessions in the light of Augustine's, arguing that for Augustine to make his confessions to a God who already knows their content: "he has to do so in *writing*, precisely, after the death of his mother" (1999b 18). This connection is made clear in autobiographical documents ranging from William Wordsworth (1995) to Mary McCarthy (1987). In revising *The Prelude* from the two-book poem of 1799 to the longer version of 1805, Wordsworth moves his account of his childhood experiences with the deaths of others from a central position – closing the first book – to the discussion of "Books" in book five. The death of Wordsworth's mother, the drowned man in Esthwaite's Lake, and the child of "There was a boy" are mingled with early readings of Milton, Shakespeare, and *Arabian Nights*. Similarly, in *How I Grew* McCarthy (1987) introduces her parents' deaths in a discussion of the influential books of her childhood. For both authors, the death of others is situated as part of a narrative of personal and intellectual development. In these texts, the death of others is presented as a necessary aspect of the development of the literary self: the intersection of the self, the death of the other, and the demands of writing creates the autobiographical environment.

The work of mourning

Although the impact of the other's death on an individual's conceptualizations of self and writing has been explored in a wide variety of autobiographical contexts, it is most readily apparent in a recent spate of books detailing writer's experiences with immanent grief. Memoirs of death both sudden, as in Joan Didion's *The Year of Magical Thinking* (2005), and long-expected, in the case of Donald Antrim's *The Afterlife* (2005) and Mark Doty's *Heaven's Coast* (1996), explore the ways in which a re-thinking of the self is necessitated in light of the death of the other. Antrim's account of his mother's death begins with this assertion: "The story of my mother's lifelong deterioration is, in some respects, the story of her life. The story of my life is bound up in this story, the story of her deterioration. It is the story that is always central to the ways in which I perceive myself and others in the world" (2006 4). It is only as Antrim is able to identify his mother's sickness and death as, in retrospect and in actuality, the central principle of her life, that he is able to define his relationship both to her and to himself. As he writes a few pages later: "I could not imagine life without my mother. And it was true as well that only without her would I feel able to live" (15). Like Handke before him, Antrim is only able to frame the stories of his own youth in the larger story of his mother's death: it is that death which makes his writing possible. It is only as the autobiographer sees himself in relation to an absent other that he can begin to account for his own life. As is the case with Franzen's *The Discomfort Zone* (2007), many of Antrim's stories in *The Afterlife* have little to do with his mother, at least on a superficial level. Yet it is only through his mother's illness and dying that he is given access to these aspects of his life: her death provides a narrative he can use to understand his own life. In both Handke and Antrim's texts, it is only through the prism of the other's death that the self can begin to be known: there is no autobiography without biography. Only by recounting their mothers' lives as now-completed wholes can they begin to approach their own lives. The self that emerges in these accounts is elliptical and incomplete, certainly, but it is nevertheless a self that survives and moves forward.

As Emmanuel Levinas makes clear, the death of the other is neither second-hand knowledge nor firsthand experience, but affects the very identity of the "I". While it cannot be equated with the death of the self, the death of the other is our true experience with death. As he writes: "The death of the other who dies affects me in my identity as a responsible 'me' [*moi*]; it affects me in my nonsubstantial identity which is not the simple coherence of various acts of identification, but is made up of an ineffable responsibility" (2000 12). Death locates what Levinas calls "the other in the I" (2006 145): it is the way in which the self is made responsible for the other by having to answer for his death. The death of the other cannot be approached as an empirical fact, but as an uneasiness in regards to the "unknown", an unknown that, as Derrida makes clear in a commentary on Levinas, is not "the negative limit of knowledge [... but] the infinite distance of the other" (1999a 8). For Levinas, death is the "most unknown of all unknowns", yet also that which "awakens me to the other" (1999 153, 161). The other, in death, is simultaneously revealed as infinitely distant and as the locus of one's ethical responsibility. It is through death that alterity itself is revealed. Witnessing the death of the other – whether, as for Levinas, the death of "the-first-to-come-along" (1999 167), or for many of the autobiographical subjects discussed here, the death of a singular and greatly-loved other – demands a confrontation with the self at the limits of the unknown. As Jorge Semprun makes clear in his own autobiographical work, the other's death is significant precisely because it is the only death that the "I" can experience: "personal death" cannot be experienced, but only determined (1997 155). One's relation with death can only be seen through the death of the other. The inclusion of responsibility for the other, including that other's death, in an account of one's own identity is a significant focal point for many of these autobiographical works. In both Handke and Antrim's memoirs, the self is initially presented through various acts of identification, through remembrances of particular, unconnected moments in their past. It is only as the authors come to terms with their responsibility to the other, as they begin to understand their lives as ultimately relational, that their greater autobiographical project becomes clear. What wholeness or totality these texts present is only made possible through a reflection on responsibility for the other.

This space of reflection and responsibility is the space that mourning opens. Mourning, which Didion defines in *The Year of Magical Thinking* as "the act of dealing with grief" (2005 143), can be seen as the coming-to-terms with the otherness of the deceased. As in Freud's pivotal definition, mourning entails the adjustment of "each individual memory and expectation" connected to the other (2006 312): it is a complete rethinking of the self predicated on the other's death. If grief is the emotional response to a particular death, mourning is the way that response is understood in relation to death as such. It is, in Stanley Cavell's phrase, "the path of accepting the loss of the world" (1994 172). As Derrida writes: "mourning is the phenomenon of death and it is the only phenomenon behind which there is nothing" (2003 148). Mourning is simultaneously productive and destructive, a reckoning with the other as they were that is always coupled with the fact that they are no longer. As in Antrim's claim that he cannot live through his mother's death, nor without it, mourning is the recognition of death as both impossible and necessary, as both separation and relation. Mourning separates the self from the world, a separation that is essential if the self is to understand her own relation to the world. Yet mourning cannot be understood solely as a response to a particular event, or as a particular course of action with definable limits. For Derrida, mourning is both what "institutes my relation to myself" (1993 76) and at the same time "not one kind of work among others. It is work itself, work in general, the trait by means of which one ought perhaps to reconsider the very concept of production" (1994 121). While Derrida is establishing a Marxian account of production here, for the purposes of autobiography mourning is also the work through which we reconsider the production of the self. For Derrida, mourning as production in general is recognized by its interminability: it is "Inconsolable. Irreconcilable. Right up until death" (2003 148). Mourning is not only the way in which we approach the other's life, but is itself the endless work of living, the very production of the self.

One of the clearest recent accounts of mourning as the work of separation and production can be found in Leon Wieseltier's *Kaddish* (1998). The book consists of a history of the Jewish prayer of mourning, said three times a day for the eleven months following a parent's death, interspersed with Wieseltier's occasional commentaries on his own coming-to-terms with his father's death. At the end of his period of mourning, Wieseltier comes to realize that: "I am a man who will die, the son of a man who has died, and I can exceed myself. I am the gap in the world, since I can exceed myself" (572). It is only by leaving the world, here achieved by a religious practice committed to the exclusion of all else, that Wieseltier can identify his place within it. It is only in engaging with the continual work of mourning that the self can be produced. Wieseltier thus comes to self-recognition through a willful act of separation from himself and from the world. Earlier in his work of mourning he writes of his fear that "the rest of my life will interfere with my mourner's life" (131). This initially jarring statement demonstrates that mourning is both a necessary aspect of the life of the self and yet wholly separate from it. Mourning is all-consuming work. Through this work, the mourner comes to learn both that he will die and that the dead continue to live in him through acts of remembrance and responsibility: even as he separates himself from the world, he also interiorizes and makes permanent his own relation to the dead. It is only through the act of saying this one rote prayer that Wieseltier comes to the realization that: "I am not a man without a father. I will never be a man without a father. He will not die until I die" (368–9). This sense of continuance when everything has been ruptured defines the work of mourning. The ability to see both the self and the other as mutually defined, always separated yet always inherent in each other, is at the heart of mourning.

In each of these memoirs, the author comes to an understanding of his relation to the world through an understanding of parental death. The parent continues to live through the child's responsibility for him or her, yet the child is only able to understand him or herself as a totality by means of the parent's death. As such, the relationship between the deceased parent and the self is both highly particular and also representative of the relationship between the self and the other: a reflection on parental death becomes a reflection on alterity itself. For both Levinas and Derrida, albeit in very different ways, the recognition of alterity is at the centre of all self-conception. For Levinas, "I am 'in myself' through the others" (1998 112), while for Derrida, conversely, there is "no alterity without singularity" (1994 37). Although they approach the question of alterity from opposed perspectives, for both thinkers the self and the other are mutually defined. There is no self without the other, and no other without the self. As the works of mourning by Handke, Antrim and Wieseltier show, however, an understanding of this relation is only made possible through the witnessing of the other's death. It is only in that moment of death, always coming and always yet to come, that these relations can be made clear. Death, then, is both the limitation of possibility and its totality: death both removes the other from the world and defines the other's relationship to it. This complex relationship underpins all autobiography, for each autobiographical text must at once answer to the death of the self and the other, and yet be written as if those deaths were impossible.

Immanence, mourning, and narrative

Didion's *The Year of Magical Thinking* (2005) has gained her a new, much larger audience, at least in part because of its perceived universality. Yet the book is grounded in the particular; its focus on the minutiae of grief and mourning is itself extraordinary. Where Handke (2002) moves his account of his mother's death into the most general terms possible, and Wieseltier (1998) focuses his account primarily on particularities of Talmudic interpretation, Didion frames her account of her husband's death, coupled with her daughter's illness, in the familiar details of medical examination. Times, dates and names of drugs are all central to her account; she quotes extensively from medical manuals and interviews with doctors. No memory of the other has any greater import than another: discussions of apparently important decisions are given an equal footing to descriptions of a particular china pattern. What Didion foregrounds throughout the book is the specificity of memory that grief demands, and her own ability to record it.

As in the accounts discussed above, the balance between separation from and internalization of the other explicitly comes from writing. Didion uses a familiar journalistic style as a bulwark against doubt and uncertainty. As she introduces her text:

> This is my attempt to make sense of the period that followed [her husband's death], weeks and then months that cut loose any fixed idea I had ever had about death, about illness, about probability and luck, about good fortune and bad, about marriage and children and memory, about grief, about the ways in which people do and do not deal with the fact that life ends, about the shallowness of sanity, about life itself. I have been a writer my entire life. As a writer, even as a child, I developed a sense that meaning itself was resident in the rhythms of words and sentences and paragraphs, a technique for withholding whatever it was I thought or believed behind an increasingly impenetrable polish. (2005 7)

The necessity of writing what is almost impossible to write underlies each of these memoirs, even as the authors often explicitly condemn or ridicule their attempts to use familiar methods to encapsulate the unfamiliar. Wieseltier laments that: "One of the most dreaded eventualities in a man's life has overtaken me, and what do I do? I plunge into books! [...] It is what I know how to do" (1998 172), while Handke frames the failure of his writing even more clearly:

> I am only a *writer* and can't take the role of the *person written about*, such detachment is impossible. I can only move myself into the distance; my mother can never become for me, as I can for myself, a winged art object flying serenely through the air. She refuses to be isolated and remains unfathomable; my sentences crash in the darkness and lie scattered on the paper.
>
> (2002 33, Italics in original)

Each of these authors thus operates in the space where writing is clearly inadequate and nevertheless essential. As Mark Doty puts it in his recent volume *Dog Years*, the death of the other is an "unassimilable fact" which nevertheless must be written (2007 8): "What does a writer do, when the world collapses", he asks in an earlier memoir, "but write?" (1996 263). Similarly, for Martin Amis writing is the necessary response to death: "Why should I tell the story of my life? I do it because my father is dead now, and I always knew I would have to commemorate him. He was a writer and I am a writer; it feels like a duty to describe our case" (2000 6–7). Again, for Paul Auster writing about his father's death is: "an obligation that began to impose itself on me the moment I was given the news. I thought: my father is gone. If I do not act quickly, his entire life will vanish along with him" (2003 4). Writing is what remains when everything else has been stripped away. To write the other is to recognize him as separate from yourself, but also, in a tangible way, to memorialize him as someone deeply and intimately connected to you.

Didion writes, in the closing pages of her memoir, that "This will not be a story in which the death of the husband or wife becomes what amounts to the credit sequence for a new life, a catalyst for the discovery that [...] 'you can love more than one person'" (2005 197). This statement is telling both in its assertion that the work of mourning produces a "story" and in its equal insistence that this story is not the account thus far provided, but remains yet to come. Earlier in the volume she has written about the "vortex", a state in which unconnected memories appear without her will: "If by accident I remembered the morning we drove down to St.-Tropez from Tony Richardson's house in the hills and had coffee on the street and about the fish for dinner would I also need to remember the night I refused to swim in the moonlight because the Mediterranean was polluted and I had a cut on my leg" (132). Death removes the notions of linearity and causality from lived experience, notions that are often central in the biographical project. In a quote such as this, even the structure of a sentence is problematised: ideas and images emerge almost at random, removed from any sense of narrative order. This emergent timelessness is one of the key aspects of the work of mourning: a self-knowledge that is established in an experience of the death of the other must work in all times and in all experiences. The death of the other does not merely account for who one will be in the future, but for who one was in the past.

The death of the other can thus be seen not only as a factor in the self-recognition of the autobiographical subject, but also as a structural element in the texts produced. Roth (1988), Morrison (2006) and Motion (2007) all begin their memoirs with an account of the moment at which they realised that their mother or father would die, and culminate with that death. For Motion, the news of his mother's decline brings with it a sudden end to childhood: indeed, he is only able in his memoir to detail his life up until the point of her death. Writing about his childhood decades later is not only a way of keeping his mother's memory active in the present, but of recapturing "everything as it was, when I saw the world for the very first time" (2007 16). Framing his memoir with this initial depiction of imminent death allows him to maintain a dual perspective, in which his adult experience and childhood innocence are given equal space. Morrison (2006) uses this structural element even more dramatically, juxtaposing a chronological account of his father's death with scattered, non-linear memories of his life until that point. By using parental death as an explanatory structure, the autobiographical subject is free to develop new interpretations of their lives that are not dependent on historical or linear narratives.

If these memoirs are relatively explicit, the knowledge of death, derived through the experience of the death of the other, appears to similar explanatory effect in more ruminative texts such as John McGahern's *Memoir* (2005) and Paul Auster's *The Invention of Solitude* (2005). Both authors consciously problematise the notion of the self in their autobiographical work: Auster uses the initial "A" in place of an "I", arguing that he "must make himself absent in order to find himself" (132), while McGahern claims that he has only written about his own "separate life" in the memoir in order to show the people around him, "in their time and landscape" (261). Yet for both authors, the death of a parent changes the self's relation both to the self and to time. When the other dies, Auster writes, "Life becomes death, and it is as if this death has owned this life all along" (3). At the moment of this death, it is as if the self "were going both forward and backward, into the future and into the past. And there are times, often there are times, when these feelings are so strong that his life no longer seems to dwell in the present" (66). The death of the other becomes the centre from which all experience spins out; it is both a wound and a ground. As McGahern writes in reference to his mother's death, the knowledge of death shapes all perception:

> We grow into an understanding of the world gradually. Much of what we come to know is far from comforting, that each day brings us closer to the inevitable hour when all will be darkness again, but even that knowledge is power and all understanding is joy, even in the face of dread, and cannot be taken from us until everything is. We grow into a love of the world, a love that is all the more precious and poignant because the great glory of which we are but a particle is lost almost as soon as it is gathered. (36)

In both of these texts we see a true being-towards-death, for the singular death becomes universal in affect; it changes not only what comes after it, but also what comes before. The death of the other is what permits interpretation of the self, and what frees the self from the constraints of narrative causality. In all of these texts, the authors continually note the way in which, through the work of mourning, they are able to access elements of their own past that had previously been lost to them, or deemed unimportant. The story Didion finds in her husband's death is not a story she had known previously, but one that could only arise after that moment. It is in this way that the death of the other is, as Levinas has it, the "first death". The death of the other is both alien to everyday experience and at the same time the source of our understanding of it.

Doty's first memoir, *Heaven's Coast* (1996), specifically focuses on the way the death of a loved other alters one's perception of the self and the world by creating a new story. Like Didion's *The Year of Magical Thinking* (2005), *Heaven's Coast* was written in the immediate aftermath of a lover's death; as Doty introduces the volume, this death created a new perspective: "Loss brought with it a species of vision, an inwardness which was the gift of a terrible time – nearly unbearable, but bracingly real" (1996, ix). The memoir focuses both on the death of his lover and on a number of simultaneous friends' deaths as a way to locate individual experience. Self-consciousness, Doty discovers, is really "being aware of others" (124). In this awareness of others that crystallizes at the moment of the other's death, Doty argues that one becomes aware of one's own story: the narrative of his lover's death "offers me back to myself" (290): it offers a permanence that the writing self could not experience otherwise. Death yields a shaping narrative that had not previously been known, a narrative that can in turn be shared with others. As in McGahern's *Memoir* (2006), for Doty it is the very difficulty of the loss of a loved one that opens the world: "the thing that harms turns out, sometimes, to be the very thing that restores, the exact thing" (1999 191). It is only through this experience, and moreover through the writing of this experience, that the self comes to be the self, capable of recognizing its place in the world.

The creation or realization of the self in response to the death of the other can perhaps most clearly be seen in these accounts of grief and mourning. The death of the other is equally important however, both as a structural and thematic element, in the emergent genre of family histories; John Lanchester and Jeremy Harding's recent family chronicles, for instance, are both explicitly motivated by discoveries the authors made after their mothers' deaths. For Lanchester, the death of his mother reveals that: "The story of our lives is not the same as the story we tell about our lives" (2001 5). In tracing the untold history of his family, he develops a new self-conceptualisation: the story of his mother's life "is also the story of my father's life, and, to an extent far greater than I realised when I began this journey, the story of mine too" (5). Yet for Lanchester, this originary death raises not only problems of self-knowledge, but of self-interpretation. As he embarks on his own life story, he states that: "our motives aren't knowable, and our selves are not fixed [...] [T]he stability and continuity of the self is a comforting illusion" (259, 366). Like the autobiography, the family history, as an assessment of a fixed or constant self or group of selves, is an impossibility. For Lanchester, this problem can only be solved by locating the unfixed self in the death of the other: it is only when his mother has died, as he repeatedly states, that he can begin to write. Writing an autobiography, in the sense of attempting to present a totalized self, requires a deliberate falsification: for Lanchester, it is only in addressing this work to an absent other that the project is even possible.

In her own family chronicle, which includes a lengthy discussion of her mother's death, as well as throughout her nonfiction corpus, Didion (2006) also uses death as an organizing principle: *Slouching Towards Bethlehem*, *The White Album*, *Salvador*, *Miami*, *After Henry*, and *Where I Was From* all open with a discussion of a death. Sometimes, as in the first two volumes, it is a discussion of the death of an individual stranger. *Salvador* begins with a discussion of mass death, while the deaths discussed at the beginnings of *Miami* and *Where I Was From* are historically-based. Only *After Henry* opens with an account of the death of an individual known to Didion. Yet the death of the other is continually evoked as an explanatory principle. *Slouching Towards Bethlehem* identifies death and absence as significant cultural principles: once identified, they seem to explain everything else. She writes:

> The center was not holding. It was a country of bankruptcy notices and public-auction announcements and commonplace reports of casual killings and misplaced children and abandoned homes and vandals who misplaced even the four-letter words they scrawled. It was a country in which families routinely disappeared [...]. People were missing. Children were missing. Parents were missing. Those left behind filed desultory missing-persons reports, then moved on themselves. (2006 67)

For Didion, any understanding of the self, or of a larger culture, is predicated on the recognition of a necessary absence at the heart of experience. People know themselves only through whom they have lost, and are quickly lost themselves. To understand anyone, in this account, is to first understand how they are shaped by those they have lost. Andrew O'Hagan repeats this notion in *The Missing* (1996), a work that, like many of Didion's, attempts to bridge family and societal histories through an understanding of loss and death. He writes: "The world is full of missing persons, and their numbers increase all the time. The space they occupy lies somewhere between what we know about the ways of being alive and what we hear about the ways of being dead" (134). Like Lanchester, Didion and O'Hagan both represent knowledge of the self, and indeed of life itself, as something only available in the context of a dead or absent other. It is this confrontation with otherness that Geoffrey Hartman claims has led to the rise of autobiography itself. As he writes:

> The inflation of autobiographical writing, a relatively minor genre in literary history, previously limited to individuals caught up in exceptional happenings, is also related to the mounting number of refugees in the world and our awareness of their ordinary yet extraordinary situation. [...] Facing that strangeness in others, we become more aware of the other in ourselves: of what remains ambivalent, unintegrated, in between. (10)

The "strangeness in others" underlies all of Didion's non-fiction: it is as present in her account of her husband, a man she knew intimately for forty years, as it is in her accounts of displaced young people with whom she only spent a few days. In both cases, however, documenting this strangeness or alterity is not only a method of engaging with the other, but also of revealing the self. Autobiography can only arise in confrontation with, and relation to, absolute alterity.

Midway through *The White Album*, Didion introduces herself to the reader, in the process of contemplating divorce and watching for a tidal wave. She writes: "I want you to know, as you read me, precisely who I am and where I am and what is on my mind" (2006 277). Who and where and what she is is "radically separated": for the reader to approach the writer as an individual, they must see her both as part of the world – their own other – and also as something separate from it. This separation, as she repeatedly makes clear, is both particular to her and universal, for it is the separation that ensues from witnessing – and in her case recording – the death of the other. For Didion, the ability to say "I" is only achieved by this separation. In a memorial talk for Levinas, Derrida too focuses on the idea of "radical separation". Radical separation is both the "experience of the alterity of the other" and "relation to the other" (1999a 46). This separation is what permits the other to be known as other, the self to be known as self, and the two to be mutually defined. This notion of separation allows Didion's works to be read both as journalism and as autobiography: in delineating her own relation to the other, a relation typically predicated on the other's death, Didion opens the space of autobiography.

This autobiographical space allows for a discussion of much broader ideas, particularly illuminating the relation between consciousness and the body, and that between the writing self and the reader. In a brief passage at the beginning of his memoir, Auster notes that: "Death takes a man's body away from him. In life, a man and his body are synonymous; in death, there is the man and there is his body" (10). This distinction is at the centre of Douglas Hofstadter's recent book of reflections on the nature of the conscious self, *I am a Strange Loop* (2007). In setting forth an argument that the embodied self is ultimately illusory, and that consciousness should rather be understood as the "dance of symbols in the brain" (276), Hofstadter employs a wide range of arguments from philosophy, cognitive science, and especially mathematics. Hofstadter attempts to overturn both neuroscientific reductionism and high-level psychologism in order to develop a new theory of consciousness. At its most succinct, his argument runs: "The cells inside a brain are not the bearers of its consciousness; the bearers of consciousness are patterns" (257). Yet, quite remarkably, Hofstadter explicitly grounds his ideas in his own lived experience, specifically in relation to the death of his wife. In establishing a theory of entwined selves, he locates the development of this argument at the moment he realized that, although his wife "had died, that core piece of her had not died at all, but [...] lived on very determinedly in my brain" (228). He goes on to argue, in terms familiar from the authors discussed above, that after her death he has become his wife's "best representative in the world" and is "deeply responsible to her" (233). Even Hofstadter, approaching the idea of consciousness from a background in cognitive science, must refer to a personal experience with the other's death in order to develop a complete theory of the self.

In his preface, Hofstadter writes that: "this book is not about me, but about the concept of "I". It's thus about you, reader, every bit as much as it is about me" (2007 xv). Similarly, in his brief work on Dutch still lives, Mark Doty allows for a transition from the relation between the self and the other in death to the relationship between the text and the reader:

> Where there was a person, a voice, a range and welter of experience compressed into lines and images, now there are only lines and images. Where there was a life, now there is a form.
>
> And the form, spoken, breathes something of that life out into the world again. It restores a human presence; hidden in the lines, if they are good lines, is the writer's breath, are the turns of thought and of phrase, the habits of saying, which make those words unmistakable. And so the result is a permanent intimacy; we are brought into relation with the perceptual character, the speaking voice, of someone we probably never knew, someone no one can know now, except in this way. (2001 50)

The story that death provides, the structure that the death of the other allows, becomes itself an opening to a relationship, through the text, with an unknowable self. In all of the texts discussed above, whether they are categorized as autobiography, memoir, or family history, the central relationship between the self and the other becomes the catalyst for the relationship between the text and the reader: it is only in seeing this originary relationship between the self and the other, revealed in the other's death, that we can come to know our own selves.

Bibliography

Amis, Martin (2001), *Experience*. 2000. London: Vintage Books.

Antrim, Donald (2006), *The Afterlife*. New York: Farrar, Straus and Giroux.

Auster, Paul (2003), *Collected Prose*. London: Faber and Faber.

Cavell, Stanley (1994), *In Quest of the Ordinary: Lines of Skepticism and Romanticism*. Chicago and London: University of Chicago Press.

de Man, Paul (1984), *The Rhetoric of Romanticism*. New York: Columbia University Press.

Derrida, Jacques (1999a). *Adieu to Emmanuel Levinas*. Trans. by Pascale-Anne Brault and Michael Naas. Stanford: Stanford University Press.

—— (1993), *Aporias*. Trans. by Thomas Dutoit. Stanford: Stanford University Press.

—— (1999b), *Circumfession*. In *Jacques Derrida*. Trans. by Geoffrey Bennington. Chicago and London: University of Chicago Press.

—— (2007), *Psyche: Inventions of the Other*. Vol. 1. Ed. by Peggy Kamuf and Elizabeth Rottenberg. Stanford: Stanford University Press.

—— (1994), *Specters of Marx: The State of Debt, the Work of Mourning and the New International*. Trans. by Peggy Kamuf. New York and London: Routledge Classics.

—— (2003), *The Work of Mourning*. Ed. Pascale-Anne Brault and Michael Naas. Chicago and London: University of Chicago Press.

Didion, Joan (2006). *We Tell Ourselves Stories in Order to Live: Collected Nonfiction*. New York and London: Everyman's Library.

—— (2005), *The Year of Magical Thinking*. London: Fourth Estate.

Doty, Mark (2007). *Dog Years*. New York: HarperCollins.

—— (1999), *Firebird*. New York: HarperCollins.

—— (1996), *Heaven's Coast*. London: Jonathan Cape.

—— (2001), *Still Life with Oysters and Lemon*. Boston: Beacon Press.

—— (2000), *Turtle, Swan & Bethlehem in Broad Daylight: Two Volumes of Poetry*. Urbana and Chicago: University of Illinois Press.

Franzen, Jonathan (2007). *The Discomfort Zone: A Personal History*. 2006. London: Harper Perennial.

Freud, Sigmund (2006). "Mourning and Melancholia." *The Penguin Freud Reader*. Ed. by Adam Phillips. London: Penguin Books: 310–26.

Handke, Peter (2002). *A Sorrow Beyond Dreams*. Trans. by Ralph Mannheim. New York: New York Review Books.

Hartman, Geoffrey (2004). *Scars of the Spirit: The Struggle Against Inauthenticity*. New York and Basingstoke: Palgrave Macmillan.

Lacoue-Labarthe, Philippe (1998). *Typography: Mimesis, Philosophy, Politics*. Stanford: Stanford University Press.

Lanchester, John (2007). *Family Romance: A Memoir*. London: Faber and Faber.

Levinas, Emmanuel (1999). *Alterity and Transcendence*. Trans. Michael B. Smith. London: Athlone Press.

—— (2006), *Entre Nous*. Trans. by Michael B. Smith and Barbara Harshav. London and New York: Continuum.

—— (2000), *God, Death, and Time*. Trans. by Bettina Bergo. Stanford: Stanford University Press.

—— (1998), *Otherwise Than Being, or Beyond Essence*. Trans. by Alphonso Lingis. Pittsburgh: Duquesne University Press.

McCarthy, Mary (1989). *How I Grew*. 1987. London: Penguin Books.

McGahern, John (2006). *Memoir*. 2005. London: Faber and Faber.

Marcus, Laura (1998). *Auto/biographical Discourses: Theory, Criticism, Practice*. Manchester and New York: Manchester University Press.

Morrison, Blake (2006). *And When Did You Last See Your Father?* New edn. London: Granta Books.

Motion, Andrew (2007). *In the Blood: A Memoir of My Childhood*. 2006. London: Faber and Faber.

O'Hagan, Andrew (1996). *The Missing*. 1995. Basingstoke: Picador.

Ondaatje, Michael (1993). *Running in the Family*. 1982. New York: Vintage Books.

Peterson, Linda H (1986). *Victorian Autobiography: The Tradition of Self-Interpretation*. New Haven and London: Yale University Press.

Roth, Philip (1989). *The Facts: A Novelist's Autobiography*. 1988. New York: Penguin.

—— (1996), *Patrimony: A True Story*. 1991. New York: Vintage International.

Rousseau, Jean-Jacques (1953). *The Confessions*. Trans. by J.M. Cohen. London: Penguin Books.

Semprun, Jorge (1997). *Literature or Life*. Trans. by Linda Coverdale. New York: Viking.

Wieseltier, Leon (1998). *Kaddish*. New York: Alfred A. Knopf.

Wordsworth, William (1995). *The Prelude: The Four Texts (1798, 1799, 1805, 1850)*. Ed. by Jonathan Wordsworth. London: Penguin.

16

'The Contrived Innocence of the Surface': Representing Childhood Memory in Recent British Autobiography

Nicola King

In this chapter, I explore the ways in which some recent autobiographers attempt to recreate the experience of childhood in language. Paul John Eakin claims that 'the overwhelming majority of autobiographers continue to place their trust in the concept of an invariant memory that preserves the past intact, allowing the original experience to be repeated in present consciousness' (1999, 107). This trust in early memory is informed by Rousseau's belief in the language of the child as pure and direct, providing unmediated access to experience. As Jacqueline Rose explains, in Rousseau's *Emile* (1762), 'the child is being asked not only to retrieve a lost state of nature, but also to take language back to its pure and uncontaminated source in the objects of the immediate world' (1984, 47). One could cite many 'autobiographies' – by Georges Perec (1975) and Carolyn Steedman (1986), for example – which question the reliability of memory and foreground it in their texts, but Eakin's claim holds good for many more, and autobiographies are often praised for the immediacy and freshness of their reconstructions of the experience and point of view of the child. Of the texts I discuss here, Andrew Motion's *In the Blood* (2006) makes the most direct claim to this preservation of childhood memory: Hilary Mantel (*Giving up the Ghost*, 2003) and Richard Wollheim (*Germs*, 2004) both reconstruct childhood memory 'as it was', but also modulate and inflect it in the light of later understanding. Even Motion, however, acknowledges that the apparent 'innocence' of the text has to be, in some sense, 'contrived', and it is this 'contrivance' that I discuss here.[1]

Richard Wollheim provides a nicely clear example of one way in which the 'innocence of the surface' may, in fact, be the effect of 'contrivance'. His memoir, *Germs*, begins with an account of what seems to be his earliest memory:

> It is early. The hall is dark. Light rims the front door. The panes of violet glass sparkle. The front door has been left open. Now I am standing outside in the sun. I can smell the flowers and the warmed air. I hear the bees as

they sway above the lavender. The morning advances, a startled bird runs
fast across the dew ... (9)

This precise and sensuous account continues until the climax when the child
begins to walk forward, into the garden, when he trips and falls. The language
then imitates the expectation, and then the experience, of the fall: 'if I trip,
and when I trip, and now at long last, the waiting is over and I have tripped,
and I am, am I not? Falling, falling ...' (9). This account, with its short sentences, simple vocabulary and focus on the senses, creates the illusion that
this is a memory untouched by later experience, as fresh and immediate as
its original occurrence, although, as I shall explain in a moment, this impression soon modulates into a much more sophisticated account of this fall, of
later falls, and what they meant, and now mean, to the narrator. Nevertheless, it still comes as something of a surprise to read later in his text, that, in
writing the account of this early fall, he had set himself 'a task that lacked all
rationale, except that it blocked all progress':

> For I had decided ... that each sentence, beginning with the first sentence,
> which was three words long, would be one word longer than its predeces-
> sor, up to the moment when I trip, and then the words would stream out,
> one tumbling over the other, like a body in free fall. (124)

Wollheim does not explain any further the reasons why he gave himself this
task, nor why he found himself unable to abandon it. The long and breathless
sentence he refers to is a good example of the way in which early childhood memory, however 'fresh' and 'immediate' it seems to be, is inevitably
inflected by subsequent experience and by the re-tellings of that memory. In
this sentence Wollheim wonders whether, on the occasion of that first fall,
he did what he was to do on later occasions:

> and I stretched out my hands rigid in front of me so that my fingers formed
> a fan, not so much to break my fall ... but rather to pretend ... that things
> were not so bad as they seemed, or disaster so imminent, and that this was
> not a fall but a facile descent through the air, which would leave me in
> the same physical state, clean, ungrazed, uninjured, that I was in before I
> tripped ... (10)

Later experience of later falls influences the reconstruction of the memory
of this first fall: the garden setting, the repetition of 'fall' and the desire to
remain 'clean, uninjured' suggests also the fall from grace in Eden, Rousseau's
'lost state of nature'. Wollheim's explanation of how he came to write this
account also makes clear that it takes some 'contrivance' to 'take language
back to its pure and uncontaminated source in the objects of the immediate
world' (Rose, 47). Wollheim goes on to talk about the 'pattern' of emotions

that he 'loved to trace back to this isolated event', even before he began psychoanalysis: 'In doing so, I gave way to the most persistent of all these patterns: that the earliest identifiable self ... was the real thing, tap it and it rang true, so that any change I contemplated in myself would be a betrayal of myself by myself' (12–13). Here he acknowledges a belief in an 'original' self, founded in first or early memory, which is nevertheless a 'persistent ... pattern', one upon which ideas about identity within Western culture are, perhaps unconsciously, based.[2]

Andrew Motion grew up in an upper-middle class family in rural Hertfordshire and, later, Essex. Riding and hunting were important activities, especially for his mother, to whom he was clearly very close, and the title of his memoir *In the Blood* (2006), indicates the ways in which the child and adolescent he once was negotiated ideas of belonging and separation, similarity and difference. He begins his memoir with an account of the day which ended with his hearing the news of his mother's eventually fatal accident – she was thrown from her horse whilst hunting with her younger son, Kit, and went into a coma from which she never recovered, although she lived for several more years. Motion was away from home, staying at the house of a girlfriend, where he was given the news. He remembers and reconstructs the way he felt the next evening, once he was back home and had realised how serious her injuries were: 'A lumpy thought is stuck in my head', he writes, and disentangles it to realise that his childhood, unlike that of most people, had ended abruptly on that day.

> Then I'm thinking something else – no, not thinking. Wishing. I want to lock into my head everything that's happened in my life up to now, and make sure it never changes. If I can keep it safe, I'll be able to look back and feel safe myself. I don't want to explain it. I don't want to talk about it in the grown-up language I haven't learned yet. Maybe I don't even want to understand it. I just want everything as it was, when I saw the world for the first time'. (16)

Motion's book is an account of that childhood, reconstructed in full and immediate detail: the jacket blurb claims that this is executed 'without the benefit of adult hindsight', and Motion has said that his memory of his early years is 'uncannily good'. His desire to preserve and recreate the world as it was when he saw it 'for the first time' is close to Rousseau's desire for the pure and unmediated language of the child – and it is this kind of language which Motion largely deploys in his memoir. All memory, however, at least once narrated in language, must be reconstruction, and the amount of detail, particularly of conversations, in this memoir makes it clear that much of his account must be reconstruction, not the 'pure' and immediate access to memory which the 17-year-old Motion claims, or aspires to, in the extract quoted above. Motion has said that readers are 'prepared to accept that a certain amount of licence is sometimes taken: the essence of what was said being as or more important in most contexts than the exact words used':[3] although, of course, only the writer can know what is most important, what is the 'essence'. The language of the section of the memoir quoted above deserves closer examination, as does the notion that the experience of childhood can be recreated 'without hindsight'. There is an interesting use of tenses in the passage: Motion is narrating a moment from the past, when he was 17, but it is narrated in the present tense, as if it is happening now: the first chapter, leading up to his mother's accident and its immediate aftermath, is narrated in the present tense, as is the last, when he visits his mother in hospital. The story of his childhood and adolescence is narrated in the past tense, suggesting that it is the memory of the day of his mother's accident that is, still, the most 'present', and that his childhood, from that moment on, is now in the past. Commenting on previous attempts he made, in prose and in poetry, to write about his childhood and his mother's accident, Motion says: 'I only found a way into the whole thing when I realised I could do it as though it was in a sense still happening':[4] it is this sense of immediacy which memoirs of childhood judged to be effective, or successful, seem to recreate. Hilary Mantel (2005), similarly, says that 'I've never felt disconnected from my early childhood. I've always been able to summon it up, as a sensory experience, and so, I hope, get it onto the page as if it were happening now.'[5] I explore this effect in Mantel's memoir later on. 'Hence the teenage voice', continues Motion, but a large part of this text describes the experience and recreates the perspective of the child, whose 'voice' modulates into that of the teenager. Motion's reference to 'the grown-up language I haven't learned yet' suggests the attempt, in his and other accounts of childhood, to use only the language, and hence the understanding, of the child who is being remembered as experiencing the events of his or her childhood and adolescence. But the idea that as a child he 'saw the world for the first time', and the desire to preserve this vision, may also belong to the longing for childhood – and the time before his mother's accident – on the part of the 50 year old writer, as well as the 17 year old just leaving that childhood behind.

Motion returns to this moment at the end of his memoir, when he reconstructs once again the days immediately following his mother's accident. This time it is in a conversation with his brother Kit:

> "I'm going to keep everything that's happened", I say, remembering what I told myself yesterday ... "I'm going to keep *everything*. The whole of the past, locked up inside my head, just as it was." "You can't do that," Kit says ... "Whatever happens next will interfere with it. And anyway, you'll want to understand it. That'll change it all." "I know," I tell him. "I don't mean I won't think about it – I expect I'll think about it for ever. I just mean I'll keep it safe inside me as well. Separate." Kit nods, slowly. "And write it down eventually?" "Perhaps," I say ... '. (312–13)

In this exchange Motion reconstructs his memory of what he told himself 'yesterday', and through this conversation with his brother acknowledges the way in which 'memory' changes, as events from the past are remembered in different circumstances by a subject whose understanding and perspective inevitably changes over time. He reconstructs his 17-year-old self who believed that he could keep his memories of childhood 'separate' from his later understanding and 'thinking about it', disputing his brother's claim that 'whatever happens next will interfere with it' – although, of course, his memory of his recent, 'safe' childhood has already been 'interfered with' by his mother's accident and absence. Here a more sophisticated understanding of memory is ascribed to a 14-year-old, perhaps as a way of preserving the 'innocence' and faith in the accuracy of memory of the 17-year- old Motion. The conversation briefly capitulates recent and complex debates about the nature of memory – and also its relationship to writing. Motion has acknowledged the deliberate framing of his memoir: 'I was entirely aware of wanting the frame the book with an outline (at least) of thoughts about how even the most accurate re-callings of past experience inevitably involve some kind of distortion – either simply by remembering them "inaccurately", or by arranging them in such a way as to misrepresent their actuality'. The reader, of course, has no way of judging the accuracy of the writer's memory, and any narrative must involve some 'arranging': this, at least, is something the reader is in a position to observe and analyse. He has also admitted that 'below the contrived innocence of the surface, there's a lot of pretty furious padding going on'. Kit suggests that his brother – who by this stage we are aware of as an adolescent becoming aware of the power and possibilities of language – might one day write an account of his childhood. 'Not now', says Motion, but of course the reader does not know when the process of writing started, nor what finally prompted it, if, as seems to be the case, it began in middle-age. A sequence of poems published in 1978 in *The Pleasure Steamers* describe his visits to his mother in hospital on the anniversaries of her accident, and Motion has also said that he had tried to write about his childhood in shorter pieces of prose. What is evident from a close reading of these two passages is that Motion is aware of the debate over the functioning and accuracy of autobiographical memory, and frames his own reconstruction with a claim to accuracy prompted by the shock of his mother's accident. The memory of the trauma prompts a doubling of memory, in which the 50-year-old writer remembers his 17-year-old self, going home from a friend's house on the day after the accident, remembering his 10-year-old self: 'and suddenly I see myself leaning out of a carriage window at Euston. Where has that come from? I'm ten years old again, waving to mum as the train shovels me off to school. But it's not her I see on the platform, it's myself, shrinking in the steam' (7).

One way in which Motion both reconstructs childhood experience and, at the same time, provides the reader with a fully evoked landscape of the past, is to describe the way in which he and his brother explored the territory of Little Brewers, in Hertfordshire, the house where they lived as children. This seems to have been a way of making the house and garden his own, and of reclaiming it on his returns from boarding school. In the reconstruction of memories such as these, a generalised account gradually becomes a more specific one, of a particular – and perhaps typical – day with reconstructed thoughts and conversations. Like many autobiographers, Motion first provides a narrative of family history – obviously gleaned from parents and grandparents – in order to locate and orientate his own sense of self. His own earliest memories are those of Little Brewers and of his parents, especially his mother, and in Chapter 4 his reconstructed tour of the garden and house leads to the kitchen, where his mother is cooking lunch. In his account of his exploration of the garden with his brother, Motion recreates the sense that he was seeing the world as if 'for the first time', partly by means of questions: 'So we were off again, heaving our bikes up the weird earth mound that stood on the edge of the spinney. Was it part of the war, a shelter of some kind?' (45). On this occasion,

we still had the tunnel to explore, the one inside the laurel hedge ... We fell into single file, me leading and Kit crouching ... At the mouth, which was big enough for us to stand side by side again, we faced the house for the first time. We weren't ready for indoors yet – there was the rest of the garden first, the flowery bit. In fact, there was mum now, shoulder-deep in her border, wearing her straw hat'. (47)

In a later chapter Motion describes how, on the day before he had to go back to boarding school, he 'walked round the garden the wrong way, starting with the roses, to make sure I was seeing everything from a surprising angle and wouldn't forget it' (169): he describes a similar 'tour' around the grounds of his prep school, which takes him to the lake where he could feel 'secret' and 'closer to things' (116). There is a sense here, as in his tours of his garden, of the young Motion making these places his own, securing them 'in the blood', of locating his identity securely in a sense of place and close observation of the natural world, and also of the older writer using these landscapes as mnemonic devices, as *ways* of remembering – as well as reconstructing them for the reader. In his *Memoir* (2005), the Irish novelist John McGahern (whose mother also died young, of cancer, when McGahern was about 10) repeats at intervals this account of the walk to school with his mother:

With her each morning we went up the cinder footpath to the little iron gate, past Brady's house and pool and the house where the old Mahon brothers lived, past the deep, dark quarry and across the railway bridge and up the hill by Mahon's shop to the school ... (80)

The repetition re-enforces the memory – and, perhaps paradoxically, its freshness – and becomes the writer's token of remembrance of his mother: as in the case of Motion, the walk also becomes part of his mental landscape and his belief that 'the best of life is lived quietly, where nothing happens but the calm journey through the day, where change is imperceptible and the precious life is everything' (80).

The chapter in which Motion reconstructs his tour of house and garden ends with an interesting moment. The boys have come in early for lunch on this occasion and their mother tells them to go away for a while, and Motion uses this as an opportunity to reconstruct his memory of the house itself. When they hear the radio pips for the one o'clock news, they rush downstairs to the kitchen. The chapter ends, like several others, with a moment frozen in time, in which his mother is held in memory: 'She was standing at the head of the table with one hand on her hip, and the other holding a battered spoon. Like a fat cook in a picture, except she was so thin the light from the stable yard shone straight through her' (53). Chapter 12, which describes some embarrassing attempts to socialise with neighbouring children, ends with his mother comforting him whilst doing the washing-up: 'Her thin shoulders rolled again, as she whisked the mop round my plate. It made her look as though she'd once been a bird, and was remembering her wings' (166). These chapters end with memories of his mother which seemed to be informed by the knowledge of her imminent loss or disappearance. The ending of Chapter 5, in which Motion becomes aware of his mother's tenderness to animals as she handles some new-born puppies, but also of her own fragility, her frequent illnesses, is a more direct premonition of loss: he remembers himself lying in bed that night watching the lights of the cars on the ceiling: 'When I got out of bed and opened the curtains to look towards the Tree of Heaven, smashed bits of light were spreading across the lawn like a disaster' (67). He has already described the 'Tree of Heaven' in his garden: here it also becomes an embodiment of the 'paradise' of childhood which he will have to leave when he goes to boarding school, but which, some ten years later, he will lose more irrevocably with his mother's accident. The final moments of these chapters are memories reconstructed with the eye of the poet who Motion was later to become.

A similar moment, but one not involving his mother, ends Chapter 16, which describes his last term at Maidwell, his prep school, and which also reconstructs the memory of when he first heard the folk songs which gave form to his experience of the countryside and country people, and which partly created his desire to write poetry. Here a teacher nicknamed 'Rhubarb' is playing the piano and singing 'The Ashgrove': Motion calls it 'The Ashground' (229) which may be an error at this point in the text, but which makes concrete the way in which it is linked with the abandoned wood, predominantly ash, at the end of the garden of their new house, near Sisted in Essex, which he and his brother reclaim. Motion is halfway up the stairs, looking down on a group of boys gathered around the piano as the teacher sings:

> Down yonder green valley where streamlets meander,
> When twilight is fading, I pensively roam ...

'The words hung in the air as if they were fireflies in a wood, buzzing and gleaming, then scooting into a deep green silence when others took their place' (229). Other boys are listening too: nobody moves when the song is over, and the 11 year-old Motion knows that he will never see Rhubarb or his schoolmates again. 'The Ashgrove' is a song of parting and separation, but of lovers, an experience of which the boy knows nothing yet: the reconstruction of the moment is, however, informed by the narrator's memory of knowing and feeling the imminence of partings of other kinds.

Much later, when he is in the sixth form and beginning to learn about poetry, one of his teachers reads the class Thomas Hardy's 'I look into my glass': at first he is puzzled by this choice of poem, but then: 'I could hear a man singing to himself, in a shadowy room by a log fire', and sadness of the poem makes him push the book away as if it were a dangerous weapon.

> Nothing like this had ever happened to me before – but the poem reminded me of 'The Cumberland Farmer' and 'The Ashgrove' and every-day things I loved, such as peering into a bird's nest and seeing the eggs when I hadn't expected any. Come to think of it, the words made the whole of Sisted gush through my mind like floodwater. All I had to do was say them, close my eyes, and I saw the horses' field glittering with frost, ... and the Ashground In the distance ... (285)

The poems of Hardy and Philip Larkin 'gave me the same mysterious feeling of discovering things I didn't realise I already knew '(285). Later, describing his own attempts at writing poetry, Motion says that his first poems 'were just words, thrown like stones at whatever happened to be passing through my mind. They made my thoughts stop and turn round to look at me' (286). What Motion reconstructs here is the gradual awareness of the power of language to capture experience, to make the world one's own, and to articulate the thoughts one did not, until then, know that one had. In this sense, his memoir becomes the story of the beginning of his development as a writer – as are the memoirs of Mantel and Wollheim – as well as the reconstruction of the childhood which provided the experience and memory which were the foundation of the identity which his work articulates.

Hilary Mantel's memoir is framed by her account of selling her cottage in Norfolk and moving into yet another house. 'You come to this place, mid-life. You don't know how you got here, but suddenly you're staring fifty in the face. When you turn and look back down the years, you glimpse the ghosts of other lives you might have led. All your houses are haunted by the person you might have been' (2005 20). In a sense, Motion's memoir is haunted by the possibility of what 'might have been': his mother might so easily not have had her hunting accident, and have survived into old age, in which case Motion would not have had the acute incentive to preserve his childhood intact, and would not have written the memoir he did write. But Mantel, who was unable to have children due to the endometriosis that went undiagnosed for many years, is more specifically haunted by what might have been, by the 'side-shadows' evoked in Michael Andre Bernstein's analysis of narratorial point of view. According to Bernstein, as opposed to 'foreshadowing', which constructs a narrative from the perspective of the way in which it ends, sideshadowing pays attention to 'the unfulfilled or unrealised possibilities of the past' (1994, 3), acknowledging that '[e]very counterlife is composed of countless counter-moments' (7). Mantel's memoir is haunted by these counter-lives or counter-moments: 'The country of the unborn', she writes, is criss-crossed by the roads not taken, the paths we turned our back on. In a sly state of half-becoming, they lurk in the shadowlands of chances missed' (228–9). It is, of course, only from the perspective of the present – Mantel's present as she writes her memoir – that these sideshadows become apparent, particularly those that offered themselves in childhood, so that her memoir is inevitably informed by hindsight.

I focus here on the section of the text which recreates her childhood: she continues her narrative through her adulthood, focussing on her medical and psychiatric (mis-) treatment, her childlessness, the houses in which she has lived and her writing, often linked with the idea of her childhood self and her unborn children. *Real* children are also shadows of a kind, she suggests: as a child '[y]ou had to construct yourself and make yourself into a person, fitting somehow into the niche that in your family has always been vacant, or into a vacancy left by someone dead' (223). Children are always part of someone else's story: '[e]very event that happens to you is appropriated by others, who think they know better than you do what is going on in your head'. She is writing this book, therefore, in order to 'take charge of the story of my childhood and my childlessness; and in order to locate myself, if not within a body, then in the narrow space between one letter and the next, where the ghosts of meaning are' (222). These 'ghosts' allude to the things which were never explained to her as a child, such as the gradual disappearance of her father (who becomes a shadow and then a side-shadow) and his replacement by her step-father Jack; to the distortions of vision caused by her migraines, which accustomed her to seeing things which 'weren't there'; to things which might have happened –'the ghostly fading boy I still carry inside' after she failed to turn into the boy she longed to be; and her memories of the dead. The boundaries between these *unheimlich* categories are often blurred: *unheimlich* is a word she learned later to describe these experiences (65).

At the end of her first chapter, which centres upon her recent memories of her Norfolk cottage, Mantel reflects upon the process of memory and the possibility of reconstructing childhood experience in writing: structurally, this section occupies a similar space to Andrew Motion's reflections on memory discussed above. The death of her god-mother takes her back to her native village, and she walks again up the carriage drive that led to the church, a convent (her family was Catholic) and her school: the walk creates the same sense of fear and oppression which she experienced as a child, and which almost stops her before she embarks on the project of writing her memoir. But '[b]efore I went to school there was a time when I was happy', she writes, 'and I want to write about that time'.

> The story of my own childhood is a complicated sentence that I am always trying to finish and put behind me. It resists finishing, and partly this is because words are not enough; my early world was synaesthetic, and I am haunted by the ghosts of my own sense impressions, which re-emerge when I try to write, and shiver between the lines'. (23)

Memories of childhood are here equated with ghosts, and Mantel suggests that it is in the process of writing that they emerge more fully, although they can never be completely recreated, just 'shiver[ing] between the lines'. She reflects on the inaccuracy of memory, on how easily people believe that they remember things which never happened: but, '[t]hough my early memories are patchy, I think they are not, or not entirely, a confabulation, and I believe this because of their overwhelming sensory power ... As I say "I tasted", I taste, and as I say "I heard", I hear. I am not talking about a Proustian moment, but a Proustian cine-film' (23–4). She here lays claim to the immediacy and accuracy of memory which her memoir reconstructs. She also acknowledges that children have a strange sense of time, 'so although I feel sure of what happened, I am less sure of the sequence and the dateline'. A family habit of secrecy also leads to distortion – in her case, primarily the gradual replacement of her father by her step-father – 'so you cobble together a narrative as best you can' (24). Mantel rejects the by-now commonplace description of memory as geological excavation, with the most distant in time the hardest to reach: rather, she suggests, memory is 'like St Augustine's "spreading limitless room". Or a great plain, a steppe, where all the memories are laid side by side, at the same depth, like seeds under the soil' (25). This analogy suggests the timelessness and accessibility of early memory, whilst Mantel also acknowledges that, in committing them to the page, a narrative is 'cobble[d] together'.

A key – possibly *the* key – memory of Mantel's childhood is one that took place in the 'secret garden' of her second childhood home, when she was seven, and which 'wrapped a strangling hand around [her] life' (106). She prefaces her account with a hesitation: '[s]ometimes you come to a thing you can't write. You've written everything you can think of, to stop the story getting here. You know that technically, your prose isn't up to it' (105–6). A serious Catholic child, she believed that she had a space inside her filled with God: but, alone in the garden she sees, or senses something – 'a ripple, a disturbance of the air ... a spiral, a lazy buzzing swirl, like flies'. 'It is as high as a child of two', and 'its motion, its insolent shift, makes my stomach heave' (106). It is a formless shape which drains her sense of grace and fills her instead with 'some formless, borderless evil, that came to try to make me despair' (107). This moment, this apparition, is not explained any further: the child clearly could not understand it, and it is as if the writer herself has never been able to explain it, although the reader might be tempted to connect it with the 'auras' or her migraines, her visions of 'ghosts'. Much later, in the context of her self-diagnosis with endometriosis, she says of her associated migraine, which she has also been reading about in medical textbooks: '[I]t stirred the air in dull shifts and eddies, charged it with invisible presences ... it gave me morbid visions, like visitations, premonitions of dissolution' (193). But this account is not applied backwards, with hindsight, to 'explain' the moment in the garden: it is only explicitly mentioned once again, in comparison with her experience of akathasia, the appalling side-effect of an anti-psychotic drug which she was prescribed in her twenties, which feels, she says, 'exactly like madness' (181): her 'meeting in the secret garden', however, was worse. For this reader at least, the 'meeting' haunts the rest of the narrative and is, by the end, associated with her illness, the fibrous growths of endometriosis which made her infertile and filled her womb with emptiness instead of the 'grace' of children. This association is not at any time made explicit by the writer, although the comparison with the height of a 'child of two' suggests it.

Mantel ends her memoir with a description of the apartment she lives in at the time of writing, after the sale of Owl Cottage in Norfolk. It is part of a converted 'lunatic asylum' in Surrey, which was once surrounded by fields and market gardens. An elderly man has told her about his activities there as a boy, rabbiting and falling into ditches, and his stories now form part of her 'own terrain' (251). She often stands on her balcony, looking out over where the fields used to be, and sees, or thinks she sees, a figure 'picking a way among the treacherous rivulets and the concealed ditches'. At first apparently the elderly man, a boy again, the figure becomes the writer herself, wrapped in a cloak and carrying bulky objects which turn out to be books she still hopes to write. She thinks about 'other houses, which seem not so long ago', and her last paragraph takes her, and the reader, back to 20 Bosscroft in Hadfield, near Manchester, where she lived as a child, and where she now imagines the dead – those 'who have crossed into the land where only the living can provide their light' (252) – gathering and waiting.

> I will always look after you, I want to say, however long you have been gone. I will always feed you, and try to keep you entertained; and you must do the same for me. This is your daughter Ilary speaking, and this is her book. (252)

The mutuality – intimacy, even – of the living and the dead is here suggested, in a partly-humorous tone which Mantel develops in fictional form in her subsequent novel, *Beyond Black* (2005). The dead have given her life, and the material for her writing: in return as it were, she preserves them in memory by writing about them.

This, of course, is what Andrew Motion does in *In the Blood* (2006), preserving the memory of his mother as well as that of his childhood. In the last chapter, when he returns to the 'present' of the days following her accident, he describes his first visit to her in hospital. The account is informed by the knowledge of what happens afterwards, of her continuing coma, very partial recovery and eventual death. 'What do you think?' asks Motion's father, uncharacteristically.

> '... I don't answer him because just for a second I can see the future. Mum's going to die. Maybe not soon, she's too much of a fighter for that. Maybe not here. But eventually. She's never going to recognise us or speak to us – not for years. And even when she wakes up again, she's never coming home.' (324)

Motion's ability to 'see the future' here provides a means of telling the reader what was to happen to his mother. The last paragraph of the memoir is narrated in the future tense, as Motion describes their journey home after this, the first of many visits to the hospital, and all their other returns: '... the Ashground will be stirring as a breeze works up the valley behind us, ... The light will be shining above the front door because I remembered to turn it on before we left ... because mum used to do that if we were going to be late, so when she saw it through the branches ... she could always say "Here we are", and pause, then almost repeat herself as if she didn't believe what she was seeing: "Here we are at last" ' (326). As in the first passage from his memoir discussed earlier on, the use of tenses here is an indication of the disruption to the usual passage of time caused by traumatic experience, and an attempt in language to hold on to what is almost already lost. Motion evokes the succession of evenings when he, his father and brother return home after their hospital visits – as the series of poems published in 1978, 'Anniversaries', describe a series of visits to his mother in hospital in subsequent years – to her house from which they know their mother and wife is absent, but which remind them of her, acutely, over and over again. Like McGahern's repeated account of his walk to school with his mother, this last sentence is both a memory of presence and an evocation of absence, and also of the sense of home which the text has established so firmly as the ground of being.

Andrew Motion frames his memoir with an account of the day when he sensed that his childhood had ended: Richard Wollheim ends his with three ideas about how childhood ends. One is when the child or adolescent – like Motion at 17 – recognises that childhood *will* end; another is when time, having seemed so endless, contracts, and 'gilded mornings' lose their 'compendiousness' (308). The third way, Wollheim suggests, is when one realises how impossible it is to say what one really means, and compromises by saying the next best thing, the thing closest to it, hoping, by this means, to come closer and closer to the truth, 'to spill the beans', or to find himself, 'with one broad archaic gesture, scattering the germs' (309). Loss of childhood is here linked with the loss of the 'pure and uncontaminated' language of the child, but the hope is expressed that language may, once again, approach the 'truth'. Wollheim, Mantel and Motion all became writers who, having 'lost' the language of childhood, recuperate it in various ways in order to negotiate complex ideas, to tell stories, to affirm identity and to locate themselves in time, place and memory.

Notes

1. This phrase is taken from a personal communication from Andrew Motion to the author, 13 July 2007.
2. For a fuller discussion of these ideas about the representation of memory and of the 'autobiographies' of Perec and Steedman see King (2000).
3. Personal communication from Motion to the author.
4. Ibid.
5. 'Behind the Scenes', in the appendix to the Harper edition of *Giving Up the Ghost*, p.7.

Bibliography

Bernstein, M. A. (1994), *Foregone Conclusions: Against Apocalyptic History* (Berkeley: University of California Press).

Eakin, J. P. (1999), *Making Selves: How Our Lives Become Stories* (London: Routledge).

King, N. (2000), *Memory, Narrative, Identity: Remembering the Self* (Edinburgh: Edinburgh University Press.

Mantel, H. (2003), *Giving Up the Ghost* (London: Harper Perennial).

Mantel, H. (2005), *Beyond Black* (London: Fourth Estate).

McGahern, J. (2005), *Memoir* (London: (Faber and Faber).

Motion, A. (1978), *The Pleasure Steamers* (London: Carcanet Press).

Motion, A. (2006), *In the Blood: A Memoir of My Childhood* (London: Faber and Faber).

Perec, G. [1975] (1988), *W Or The Memory of Childhood*, trans. David Bellos (London: Harvill Press).

Rose, J. (1984), *Peter Pan Or The Impossibility of Children's Fiction* (London: Macmillan).

Steedman, C. (1986) *Landscape for a Good Woman* (London: Virago).

Wolheim, R. (2005) *Germs: A Memoir of My Childhood* (London: Black Swan).

17

The Relics of St David Wojnarowicz: The Autobiography of a Mythmaker*

Richard Maguire

David Wojnarowicz's writing from his first monologues collected in *The Waterfront Journals* (1996) to his posthumously published diaries all conspire to tell a story of loneliness and solitude lived out on the streets of New York or in the barren interior of America itself. It's a story of cruising and sex, of illness and death, and of desire thwarted and fulfilled, increasingly played out in the arena of the AIDS epidemic in North America in the late 1980s and early 1990s. It's an angry story but it's written with brutal poetry. Even if he is cruising, searching for company or looking for sex, it's still a solitary occupation and, after any sexual contact, Wojnarowicz quickly returns to his own company. His cruising grounds are sometimes swarming with men, but often the derelict warehouses located on the now vanished piers and docks of New York are empty:

Looked out the side windows into the squall, tiny motions of the wet city. Inside, for as far as the eye could see, there was darkness and waving walls of iron, rustling sounds painful and rampant, crashing sounds of glass from remaining windows, and no sign of people: I realized I was completely alone. The sense of it slightly unnerving in the cavernous space.

(Wojnarowicz 1992a: 19)

Wojnarowicz returns again and again to his solitary self in much of his work; not just in his autobiographical essays, but also in his paintings and photographs. In his memoirs he walks the city streets alone after dark or speeds through the expanses of America searching for company at rest stops. This lone figure also appears in his most famous artwork- the series of twenty-four photographs entitled *Arthur Rimbaud in New York* from 1978 to 1979. In these almost iconic shots a man wearing a paper mask representing the face of the French boy poet stands in front of graffiti proclaiming 'the Silence of Marcel Duchamp is Overrated' or loiters in a cut-off denim jacket in Times Square or more darkly, shoots up heroin or masturbates on a grimy bed. The photographs show the wandering artist simultaneously at odds and at home in the cityscape. It's a relationship that Wojnarowicz himself shares. The city's streets became a haven from the hardships of his life at home. Born in 1954, he is soon sent away from his estranged parents to live with distant relatives or in orphanages. He is 'kidnapped' by his father and David has a family life of sorts for awhile. But his father, a violent alcoholic kills the family pets and beats David who runs away to begin his life hustling on the streets:

> There were times in my teens when I was living on the streets and selling my body to anyone interested. I hung around a neighborhood that was so crowded with homeless people that I can't even remember what the architecture of the blocks looked like. Whereas I could at least spread my legs and gain a roof over my head, all those people down in those streets had reached the point where the commodity of their bodies and souls meant nothing more to anyone but themselves. (32)

Even when he lives with his mother he still prefers life on the streets. He returns again and again to the nocturnal desolate highways of New York and as Rebecca Solnit points out in her study of walking, the streets become a refrain in his writing (Solnit 2002:194). They are the site of his homelessness, the inspiration for his graffiti-styled art and the location for his constant cruising. Also the streets are the battleground for the queer activism of the period; the marches, the demonstrations where activists 'died' in the streets causing havoc in the financial quarter, the noisy whistle-blowing rallies, Wojnarowicz's funeral itself. With AIDS decimating the artistic community in New York from the mid-1980s all of Wojnarowicz's work after this period becomes more politicised.

One of David Wojnarowicz's most famous group shows was entitled 'Witnesses: Against Our Vanishing' held at the Artists Space in 1989. He wrote an essay for the catalogue which criticised public figures such as New York's Catholic bishop Cardinal John O'Connor for their refusal to condone safersex practices. This damning essay caused the National Endowment for the Arts (NEA) to retract their money which helped fund the exhibition. The exhibition contained work by many artists already dead. Artist and actress Cookie Mueller had already vanished by the time the show began; her husband, the artist, Vittorio Scarpati, too. Likewise photographers Peter Hujar and Mark Morrissoe. Their art remains even if they do not. This essay is about remains. As the curator Nan Goldin writes:

> I have sometimes experienced survivors in these times criticizing themselves or one another about appropriate or inappropriate ways of mourning. We are all clumsy in dealing with grief. I do not believe we need to develop a correct etiquette. Every one of our responses is valid, passivity and silence the gravest dangers. It is not the time to distract ourselves with divisiveness.

I have also witnessed this community take care of its own, nurse its sick, bury its dead, mourn its losses and continue to fight for each others' lives. We will not vanish.

(Goldin 1990:5)

Wojnarowicz's two most famous books *Close to the Knives – a Memoir of Disintegration* (1992a) and *Memories that Smell like Gasoline* (1992c) are responses to the AIDS epidemic and the American government's handling of the crisis but they also are versions of his life. However, John Carlin warns against reading Wojnarowicz's work – his paintings, films, books and performances – as autobiography and instead says, 'they are about the tattered edges of self awareness where the artist becomes an apparition in his own imagination' (Carlin 1990: 31–2). *Close to the Knives* is a collection of essays which loosely and chronologically tell his story from childhood to illness. Other essays are furious calls for justice and a cure for AIDS. They resist the equation drawn up by the activist group ACT-UP (the AIDS Coalition to Unleash Power) that 'Silence=Death'.

They are works of mourning for his friends and colleagues, the foremost among them his ex-lover and close friend Peter Hujar. Soon after Hujar's death in 1987, Wojnarowicz finally takes an HIV test and discovers that he is positive. His work now becomes a self-elegy as he mourns his own imminent demise. But as he loses one life, a life he loses to abuse from his father, and later from AIDS, he simultaneously constructs another life loosely based on these same hardships, but which instead gestures towards myth, and hence immortality. He died on 22 July 1992 but he will not vanish. It is this strategy of mythmaking and its effects that forms the rest of this essay.

Myth, fiction and fact

It is sometimes difficult to separate fiction from embellishment and the propaganda in Wojnarowicz's work, especially that written in the last years of his life. Yet, it is not the purpose of this essay to discover the facts from the fiction, but instead to concentrate on the way he elevates episodes from his life into myth. Myth is a more powerful tool than simple recollection in the fight for life. Wojnarowicz was always aware that myth was sometimes more valuable than straightforward biography. When he looks back to his past he remembers that even as a young boy he wove himself into stories:

I think of these trees and how they look like the winter forests of my childhood and how they were always places of refuge: endless hours spent among them creating small myths of myself alone ... I realized then how I always tend to mythologize the people, things, landscapes I love, always wanting them to somehow extend forever through time and motion. It's a similar sense I have for lovers, wanting somehow to have a degree of permanence in my contact with them but it never really goes that way.

(Wojnarowicz 1992a:79)

In his study of both classical and contemporary myths, Laurence Coupe (1997) says that mythopoeia, that is myth-making in literature, is often about creating order. Coupe turns to an article by T.S. Eliot on James Joyce's *Ulysses*, which is itself a refashioning of the *Odyssey*. Eliot says that Joyce's mythopoeia is 'simply a way of controlling, of ordering, of giving shape and a significance to the immense panorama of futility and anarchy which is contemporary history' (Eliot cited in Coupe 1997:35). In a way, the writings of Wojnarowicz also constitute a journey, or an odyssey, except that there is no real goal to Wojnarowicz's wanderings, unless it is death, a death that is always preinscribed in his writings of illness, of the expansive emptiness of rural America, of the bittersweet sex on decaying piers, and of the quick stench of desire as he finally succumbs to the virus. Nevertheless these seemingly random and nocturnal explorations do create some order in a community ravaged by AIDS and poverty. By 1989 art collective Gran Fury was producing posters with shocking statistics. One campaign proclaimed 'The U.S. Government considers the 47,524 dead from AIDS expendable. Aren't the "right" people dying?' (Hoyt L Sherman Gallery 1989:62). About a quarter of these people had lived in New York (4). Indeed Charles Kaiser estimates that half of the gay men living in Manhattan died from AIDS in the 1980s and 1990s (Kaiser 1997:283). Wojnarowicz uses myth in order to prolong his own life and the lives of his friends at the time. Myth becomes a prophylactic against disappearance.

Coupe believes that the makers of myth and, indeed, the readers of myth are attracted by three terms; 'paradigm, perfection and possibility' (Coupe 1997:9). The paradigm of a myth is its ordering pattern, often a cyclical pattern because of its basis in fertility rites. Myths can be reassuring as they signal a continuance of human existence, but myths can also seem imprisoning as they signal inescapable doom through repeated sacrifice and inherited family curses. This pattern, whether comforting or ensnaring, should be ideal though, in that it should be representative of the perfect harvest, the perfect conclusion, endlessly repeated. The myth 'perfects', but as Coupe suggests this is a 'curse because it ... allows us to conceive of the "perfect" victim or scapegoat, and so the "perfection" of sacrifice' (8). However, Coupe rejects the idea that all myths are closed circuits forever preventing change. He believes that some myths signal towards future possibility and that the cycle of myth can be overcome. He says, 'myth may imply a hierarchy, but it also implies a horizon ... it ... carries with it a promise of another mode of existence entirely, to be realised just beyond the present time and place. It is not only foundational ... but also liberating' (8–9).

Wojnarowicz's careful mythmaking holds up to Coupe's simple, but useful framework. The New York artist continually presents himself as the perfect 'victim' of abuse whether it comes from the hand of his father, violent men with whom he has sex for money, or the HIV virus which eventually kills him. Though, as he says many times throughout his journals and his performances, it's not just AIDS that kills him. The most powerful rendition of this famous line comes in his performance of ITSFOMO (In the Shadow of Forward Motion), a collaboration with musician Ben Neill first performed at the theatrical space Kitchen in New York in 1989. In his wonderfully deep and sexy voice, Wojnarowicz says over an urgent electronic music text 'When I was diagnosed with this virus it didn't take me long to realise that I had contracted a diseased society as well' (Wojnarowicz and Neill 1992). Wojnarowicz becomes the perfect sacrifice, and with this comes the possibility of redemption. By offering himself up for sacrifice, a paradigm which follows one of the most powerful and 'perfect' myths ever recorded, that of Jesus Christ, Wojnarowicz is hoping that society can be cleansed and redeemed. Although in an interview he explicitly denies that he is a living martyr asserting 'But I ain't no Jesus' (Wojnarowicz 1992b: 29), he's still part of a heritage of queer saints from Oscar Wilde to Jean Genet; the latter was declared a saint whilst he was still living by his biographer Jean-Paul Sartre.

Across the Atlantic, Derek Jarman could be seen as Wojnarowicz's British equivalent: they are both artists, filmmakers and ardent autobiographers. They both discover their HIV diagnosis in 1987 and both fuse their art with that of activism. Their lives, and their self-recording of their lives become a politics in itself: a writing of resistance and protest. They become martyrs for their cause. In 1991 the British activist group The Sisters of Perpetual Indulgence proclaimed Jarman 'St Derek of Dungeness', and his own autobiography *At Your Own Risk* (1993) is subtitled 'A Saint's Testament'. Two of his films *Carravagio* (1986), and *Edward II* (1991) chart the martyrdoms of two historical queer saints while *The Garden* (1990) is a queer reimagining of Christ's Passion. These hagiographical myths, like Wojnarowicz's autobiographical myths, act as paradigms and protests. They may be pessimistic, but they illustrate how same-sex desire and homophobia have existed throughout history. They also confirm the possibility of escape from this cycle of history. Indeed, in his adaptation of Marlowe's play, Jarman allows Edward II to escape from his executioner, a gesture at a happier ending, a gesture of escape from the horrors of AIDS and government sponsored homophobia in the late twentieth century.

Wojnarowicz has a similar strategy for his mythopoeia. The myths contained in his monologues of people on the street collected in *The Waterfront Journals* and in his journals, which, as Amy Scholder says were ultimately meant for publication, all contribute to the struggle against the conservative government of America at the end of the twentieth century (Wojnarowicz

1999: v). As Felix Guattari attests, in his notes in the catalogue to Wojnarowicz's art show 'In The Shadow of Forward Motion' held at the P.P.O.W. gallery in New York in 1989, 'Wojnarowicz is explicitly ideological: his aim is to affect the world at large; he attempts to create imaginary weapons to resist established powers' (Wojnarowicz 1989a: no page numbers). By writing myth, Wojnarowicz is writing about future possibility. He uses symbols and characters from his memories and fantasies in order to create new myths:

> I like playing with images that are loaded for me, emotionally or otherwise. It's like fucking with the images, putting them through some sort of change so that they mean something else, or pushing them in new directions so that they can express a variety of things.
>
> (Wojnarowicz 2006: 164)

These reworkings of established myths allow different people to identify with them and see them as allegory rather than straightforward autobiography. Also by writing of same-sex desire Wojnarowicz is able to create images and testimonies of an affirmative homosexuality that were unavailable to him as a boy:

> Everybody else who's not homosexual or doesn't have leanings that are that far outside the norm are totally supported by every image that they see in media, movies and books. They find comfort in all these normal lives because they find direction. I had no direction. I had to pretend I had it, but at the same time try and figure out where I was. (164)

Wojnarwicz's writings and pictures become maps – indeed some of his pictures *are* maps – where the queer boy and girl can locate themselves, and even if these maps became increasingly pessimistic in the AIDS era with the government doing little to ameliorate the situation at least it was better than no representation at all. It's a myth that now invites participation.

Of course, his mythmaking is a response to the hardships in his life and the intervention of his imagination in recalling episodes from his life – such as the rape which takes place in the back of a stranger's van and the virus which ravages him – is a common enough response to trauma. As he says it doesn't matter if the myth is fabricated because it is a way of understanding the world:

> Also just about any artist can endlessly invent rationalizations for what they have done. I don't think these inventions whether true or false are worthless: for all inventions whether truth or a lie are part of one's personal myth: how one sees oneself in relation to the world: what one thinks the world is. I am after some personal truth in my life and it reflects in my

work. Whether others like or don't like what I do is really outside the personal process of exploration. It's the freedom in that exploration that is important to me. It makes a kind of sense of my life and the things I grew up in.

(Wojnarowicz and Zwickler no year: 4)

The solitary self he advances in his own writings also, cynically, helped his career as an artist. In the recently published *David Wojnarowicz a Definitive History of Five or Six Years on the Lower East Side* (2006) we are confronted with a new version of the artist as testimonies from his fellow artists highlight his work ethic of collaboration. This new version is more gregarious, more companionable as friends and colleagues talk of the trips across America they took with him, or the bands they formed, or the work on which they collaborated. These associations do not correspond with the lonely awkward artist working (and walking) in solitude. As Steve Doughton, a fellow collaborator, says in his testimony:

David was an excellent promoter of work. He constructed this myth about himself. That was no accident. He knew the story of a nine-year-old runaway was a very romantic notion to critics, collectors, and people in general. And although these stories were basically true, he also knew their value. His work was easily marketed as the pure expression of this ex-street hustler who got his education suffering, fighting, and surviving on the mean streets of the big city and not at art school ... People ate it up ... David wasn't at all naïve; he was very sophisticated. His life has this mythic status, which he himself created. And others are very quick to perpetuate this myth.

(Wojnarowicz 2006: 52–3)

Wojnarowicz and those who edit his work seem only to record his lonely wanderings rather than his social life or his artistic projects. For instance, Amy Scholder, the editor of his posthumously collected diaries, acknowledges that her selection only comprises ten to fifteen per cent of his journals and that any other editor would inevitably come up with a different selection (Wojnarowicz 1999: v). A different selection would inevitably lead to a changed Wojnarowicz. The version of his life that we do have can be misleading as his political activism and his sense of humour which are more apparent in his unpublished work can sometimes be overshadowed by the sex and loneliness that is promulgated by his published work and those who write about him. Patrick Moore sustains this myth and, in his history of the period, has Wojnarowicz 'driving with a horny wonder across the harsh flatness of America's deserts or striding the ruined piers' (2004: 101). Moore continues, 'not only did he mark his path through the decaying landmarks of downtown through his writing, David blew smoke from his ever present cigarette out over the

Hudson, "spilled his seed" on the dirty floors of the piers' (101). This post-modern romanticism is what he is remembered for: these myths are his relics which we have come to honour.

In the 1994 biopic, *Postcards from America*, directed and written by Steve Mclean, this myth of Wojnarowicz is continued and the result is an almost familiar gay tale of childhood and unhappy adulthood punctuated by homophobic beatings and deaths from AIDS. As unpublished letters testify, initially the film was only going to be forty minutes long concentrating on the political and artistic activism of the time. Paintings by Wojnarowicz would be screened as artists spoke about the AIDS epidemic decimating the New York art scene. Also planned was footage of an ACT-UP demonstration with Wojnarowicz providing a commentary. However the final cut carries none of his art and there is no record of the activism which helped shape his art at this time. Indeed, apart from one short conversation with a john about a painting of a dog, and a quick shot of some paintbrushes in an overflowing sink that Wojnarowicz (played by James Lyons) leans over, running the tap to splash his face and cool his AIDS-fevered brow, the uninformed viewer would not know that Wojnarowicz was a visual artist. Cindy Carr agrees and as she watches the film being shot she says, 'it concentrates on what I like to think of as the "Genet material" in his [Wojnarowicz's] work – tragic boys, violent tricks, sexy outcasts, landscapes of danger and desire that can lead one to a singular self-definition. Or perhaps to a singular doom' (Carr 1993: 307). The film, despite its postmodern nonlinear narrative devices – the film tells the story of the boy, the teenager, and the adult Wojnarowicz simultaneously – still manages to create a teleology of his life, a teleology that is perhaps missing from the writings, published or not. In his journals it is sometimes difficult to separate actual events from imagined, dreamt or recalled scenarios. The film of his life is easier to follow and the blurb on the back of the video helps to sort out the three stories by saying that the film

> follows the life of David from a 60's [sic] dysfunctional family dominated by his abusive father.
>
> As a moody teenage hustler surviving the New York streets, he forms bizarre relationships with fellow rent boys and clients alike.
>
> Finally escaping a brutal world of debased sexual violence, David continues his search for anonymous sex by wandering into the vast landscape of the American desert.
>
> (Dangerous to Know Videos 1996)

Carr, a friend of Wojnarowicz, believes that he rejected the first documentary style script that Mclean prepared, and that he was happier with the final scripts that offered his life as a more conventional narrative. Carr writes that Mclean remembers Wojnarowicz telling him, ' "This isn't me, but I like it" ' (Carr 1993:306). However, unpublished letters written by McLean and his partner Jimmy Somerville to Wojnarowicz suggest that it was the film's financial backers who required the changes to the script; the politics and the activism had to be compromised if the film was ever to be made. By the time that filming begins, Wojnarowicz is dead.

There is little AIDS activism in this version of Wojnarowicz's history. Instead his life survives as the familiar myth of a queer boy growing up in a small town, with a violent/absent father and absent/weak mother. In the writings of Wojnarowicz there is a more direct political angle especially in the material he produces after Hujar's death. Though even in *Close to the Knives* and the later *Memories that Smell like Gasoline* Wojnarowicz returns to his childhood of hustling and abuse. This retelling and constant backward turn towards his adolescence strengthens the myth he wants to create by turning his stories into cycles, into Coupe's paradigms. The lack of dates and the lack of place-names also help his myth to grow as this invented self seems to cruise endlessly and rootlessly throughout his work. By resisting dates and explicit locations Wojnarowicz no longer is telling his autobiography but a biography of a community which shares a common history and has the same problems. In his short study of the recent Downtown New York scene, Marvin J. Taylor says that Wojnarowicz was among the artists who 'mounted a full-scale assault on the structures of society that led to grinding poverty, homelessness, the Vietnam war, nuclear power, misogyny, racism, homophobia, and a host of other problems' (Taylor 2002: 386). In his work Wojnarowicz is telling all these stories; not just the story of AIDS. The objects and the landscape around him can be used by other viewers and readers in order that they recognise their own story in allegorical form.

Wojnarowicz is more interested in imparting his essence than merely recounting dreary lists of dates and places. The titles of his essays signal this move from particularity to formlessness; 'Self-portrait in Twenty-Three Rounds', 'Losing the Form in Darkness' and 'Being Queer in America – A Journal of Disintegration'. For Wojnarowicz, the self is hidden by facts and figures and is seen better in snapshots and shadows. He catches the self, naked, in the way it appears rather than the way it is:

It is the appearance of a portrait, not the immediate vision I love so much ... the image of Jean Genet cut loose from the fine lines of fiction, uprooted from age and time and continent, and hung up slowly behind my back against a tin wall. It's the simple sense of turning slowly, feeling the breath of another body in a quiet room, the stillness shattered by the scraping of a fingernail against a collar line. Turning is the motion that disrupts the vision of fine red and blue lines weaving through the western skies. It is the motion that sets into trembling the subtle water movements of shadows, like lines following the disappearance of a man beneath the surface of an abandoned lake.

(Wojnarowicz 1992a: 9–10)

I'm conscious that 'essence' is a loaded word, and for Wojnarowicz it's not just that kernel of belief in a Romantic self, a self that is individual and different, coherent and whole. For him it's also a belief in a self that stretches back to his queer literary fathers whose images are also tacked up on the imaginary wall behind him: Genet and Rimbaud, of course, but also John Rechy, Jack Kerouac, William Burroughs, Frank O'Hara, Tennessee Williams and Walt Whitman. Living in the poststructuralist era, Wojnarowicz was well aware of the discourse that ideology, hegemony and capitalism all banded to construct the self. This self he believed was, in his words, 'pre-invented' or 'robotic'. This self is almost powerless, almost resistant to agency. He sees himself as 'the robotic kid with caucasian kid programming trying to short-circuit the sensory disks'; he's the 'robotic kid looking through digital eyes past the windshield into the pre-invented world' (1992a: 63). Despite these claims in the unmodifiable self, this does not prevent Wojnarowicz from stubbornly trusting that there is a core of self within him, and that to see it for himself he has to travel, cross boundaries, literally live on the edge, *close to the knives*, on the streets, in the wilderness, or the dilapidated piers as far as possible from the panoptical gaze of government and authority. In these blind spots he is able to connect with history and an older, more authentic self. Here 'all civilization is turning like one huge gear in my forehead' and where he finally knows 'the exertion it takes to move these programmed limbs' (63). It's the mythical struggle of one man against the omnipotent gods.

This mythmaking strategy is employed by many autobiographers. Edmund White communicates his essence not only by repeating episodes from his life but also by couching it within the confines of fiction. White wrote the first modern coming-out narrative based on his own life with *A Boy's Own Story* in 1983 which concentrates on his childhood and his realisation that he is gay. Further books chart his battle with repressive psychotherapy to cure him of his homosexuality and his struggles in a world that is torn apart by AIDS. These books are nominally fictional but in his autobiography *My Lives* (2005) he retells his life all over again. It's a story, give or take a few changes, that has also been reproduced in his biography written by Stephen Barber in 1999. His story's very repetition with its combination of real and fictional events elevates his life-story into myth. On a practical level White would have been more likely to sell many copies of his first autofiction in 1982 if the tale was a fictional childhood rather than an autobiography of a very minor (at that time) author.

Of course, this strategy is a method of survival especially in the time of the AIDS epidemic. Making one's life into a myth is a stab at immortality. Wojnarowicz admits that he isn't just writing in order that others will not feel alienated in their childhood, 'but I also wanted to leave a record. Because once the body drops I'd like some of my experience to live on. It was a total relief to have to put words to what I put words to, an enormous relief' (1992b: 29).

Jean-Jacques Rousseau, the second great autobiographer after Augustine, also wrote his story many times. He tried many times to get it right, but always felt that he failed to communicate the truth about himself. As he says in his *Confessions* (finished in 1770, but not published until the 1780s), he thought that the point of an autobiography was to tell the truth. He declares that his 'purpose is to display to my kind a portrait in every way true to nature, and the man I shall portray will be myself' (Rousseau 1953: 17). Seeking complete transparency, the record of his life, while very clear as he remembers his childhood and younger years, degenerates into meandering confusion as he recalls his more mature years. And while perhaps this is the way that memory works, in that it privileges episodes from one's childhood while more recent events remain indistinct, it doesn't always make for good reading. Or indeed for easy listening because Rousseau is disappointed at the response of the audience to which he has been reading his *Confessions* out loud:

> Thus I concluded my reading, and everyone was silent. Mme d'Egmont was the only one who seemed moved. She trembled visibly but quickly controlled herself, and remained quiet, as did the rest of the company. Such was the advantage I derived from my reading and my declaration. (606)

Rousseau believes that he has failed in his attempt at self-representation and so, undeterred, tries again. His next autobiographical project *Dialogues* (completed in 1776, published in 1782) is an homage to the Platonic structure where he splits himself into characters such as 'J.J.' and 'Rousseau'. James Olney believes this too is a failure and says that 'Rousseau is trapped in his writing, in his text, in the written performance ... and all he can do...is fall silent again' (Olney 1998:191). The reasons for his failure are many: the trappings of memory, his love for aesthetics. His love of language will always eclipse the subject matter. Rhetoric will always override truth.

Jean Genet, the subject of a mammoth biography by White, and an influence on Wojnarowicz also blurs autobiography and fiction in the same volume aware that a love of aesthetics will prevail over a fascination with facts. Responding to the question of why he had never written a book dealing with gay liberation, Genet replies 'I wrote my books for a completely different reason: for the taste of words, even for the taste of the commas of punctuation, for the taste of the sentence' (Genet 1993: 314).

Indeed, aesthetics get the better of Rousseau in his final attempt to display himself in *Les Rêveries du Promeneur Solitaire* (uncompleted but published in 1782) where he turns away from conventional narrative and reminisces in chapters which are 'promenades', literally walks, which shows that walking and the self have a long relationship. It is in the description of these walks that Rousseau, and later Wojnarowicz in the description of his cruising, come close to self-definition. These descriptions impart essence rather than facts: it's the walking, the journey not the goal, that is vital. Wojnarowicz never wants to arrive:

> Transition is always a relief. Destination means death to me. If I could figure out a way to remain forever in transition, in the disconnected and unfamiliar, I could remain in a state of perpetual freedom. It's the preferable sensation of arriving at a movie fifteen minutes late and departing twenty minutes later and retrieving an echo of *real life* as opposed to a tar pit sensation.
>
> (Wojnarowicz 1992a: 62)

The self which is unburdened by facts, figures, dates, locations, times and destinations has the best opportunity in revealing itself, as well as repeating itself. As Olney says of Rousseau's final attempt:

> In the *Rêveries* there is a steady movement away from singularities and contingencies through repetition to essence, a movement from the particularities of history to the universals of myth ... and from events taking place in time to a state transcending time. But is this not the natural effect of all repeated acts of memory and narrative? The more times an event is recalled and the more times its story is retold, the more often it occurs – it occurs again with every retelling – and the larger the significance that accrues to it. (197)

For Olney, Rousseau's ultimate success in the self's display lies in his repeated determination, and for me, Wojnarowicz comes close too in his repeated and fictionalised attempts at his life. By the time that Wojnarowicz is writing poststructuralism has destroyed any hope of telling the truth about oneself and he resorts to myth. He's 'afraid about ... getting trapped in language' and does not want to be frozen by words especially as he becomes sick with AIDS; 'the more I think about death, the less I want to find my feet in the cement of one thought or another'(Wojnarowicz 2006: 179). And yet as his illness progresses and as he withdraws from society his manifestations at self continue: 'The only thing that remains constant, the only thing that ever made sense or given me proof that I was here – because I felt so completely alien – was trying to find some form of expression to people' (179–80).

Wojnarowicz repeats his life story, knowing that it will be repeated. And it is repeated in Carr's short biography of him in her book on performance art, in Amy Scholder's introduction to his edited diaries, in the film charting his life, in his obituaries, and here, even as I throw doubt on its reliability. Though I don't want to give the impression that his whole life is made up;

I'm sure that most of what he says happened, happened. Steve Doughton agrees and says

> I don't think he did a huge amount of fabrication, but he certainly held back information that ran contrary to this myth. He was no fool about his career. David came to really understand the power of myth. And once he had achieved some notoriety due to the perpetuation of the myth of David Wojnarowicz, he used this notoriety to say some very crucial things. Myths contain important lessons. Without the myth, we're left with dry, dull, important information, but who wants to learn that? The myths enable the lessons to be spread around.
>
> (Wojnarowicz 2006: 53)

These lessons that Doughton mentions are the ways in which Wojnarowicz positions his self, a threatened but nevertheless enduring self in the America of the 1980s and 1990s. His myth, Doughton implies, is pedagogical. An untitled print of 1990 contains a photograph of Wojnarowicz as a child and the text behind begins with the words 'One day this kid will get larger' and Wojnarowicz records every possible hardship the boy will encounter once his homosexuality is discovered. 'The myth of David Wojnarowicz' would go some way to ensure that future queer kids would not be punished.

In his essay, 'Autobiography as De-facement', Paul de Man warns against seeing any autobiography as a truthful enterprise and says,

> We assume that life *produces* the autobiography as an act produces its consequences, but can we not suggest, with equal justice, that the auto-biographical project may itself produce and determine the life and that whatever the writer *does* is in fact governed by the technical demands of self-portraiture and thus determined, in all its aspects, by the resources of his medium?
>
> (de Man 1979: 920)

By being selective Wojnarowicz will have the life he wants. He produces a self with which he wants to be remembered, a self that with each retelling he eventually becomes. As he says in his 1989 journal as he flies to Dallas, 'I want to open a window on who and what I am. I want to create a myth that I can one day become' (1989b: no page number). This is especially important to him when he begins to die because he wants to control how he will be remembered. His myth will be his self-written epitaph.

As de Man continues, a large part of autobiographical discourse is a 'discourse of self-restoration' in the face of death (925). Wojnarowicz chooses the details which will go towards his self-restoration; but unlike other auto-biographers who search for the truth Wojnarowicz is acutely aware that he is creating a mask, that he is caught up in the in the in the process of prosopopoeia.

De Man demonstrates that when authors are writing autobiography they unavoidably erase their selves in the very process of displaying them because language and its tropes will always say more than the author wants, and inevitably say something else other than the author's wishes (Anderson 2001: 13). As de Man says, 'by making the dead speak, the symmetrical structure of the trope implies, that the living are struck dumb, frozen in their own death' (928). Linda Anderson succinctly explains: 'autobiographies ... produce fictions or figures in the place of the self-knowledge they seek' (13). Wojnarowicz attempts to control this fiction by creating his own myth, rather than yielding to the fiction that would result in him trying to tell his past truthfully.

It is clear that Wojnarowicz is complicit in the retelling of his childhood, but as he gets older, and after Peter Hujar dies in 1987, he is more reticent on the subject. Carr says that 'he regrets all the mythmaking that came of it a few years ago, that "ex-hustler makes art" stuff' (293). In his journal of 1988 he travels to Spain and a gallery owner asks how much of the story of his childhood is true, and how much has been exaggerated. He records that he is 'angry' and 'I told her I no longer talk about my childhood – that as a kid I would have benefited had I read an interview with a writer who had experiences similar to mine – that it would have let me feel change was possible' (Wojnarowicz 1988: no page number). The truth may not be important for Wojnarowicz as he is not just telling the story for his own gains but he writes myth for a generation, his generation and the generation to come.

Myth and elegy

Wojnarowicz's autobiographical work is also his elegy, an elegy to himself and to his friends. It is a way of keeping himself and his friends, colleagues and lovers, alive as they struggle with AIDS and depression. Elizabeth Young comments on one of his essays about the suicide of his friend Dakota:

> As Wojnarowicz evinces an extraordinary empathy with his dead friend, as he magically animates his friend's lost life, Wojnarowicz loses the consciousness of his 'own' self that naturally propels a memoir. In achieving identification with his lost friend he achieves fiction and therefore achieves in art not only that part of it that must always signify corporeal death, but that part that has always signified permanence and immortality.
> (Young 1993: 222)

In his book *The English Elegy* (1985) Peter Sacks shows how the grieving poem is an artistic representation of Freud's process of mourning and melancholia. Sacks reveals how the elegy charts the mourning process of the grieving poet following the Freudian paradigm. The poet will slowly detach his affection from the lost love object and redirect it to a new love object. In the elegy this new love object appears at the end of the poem, and usually symbolises the rebirth of the dead and importantly the rebirth of the poet into language and society after his period of mourning. Sacks calls this symbol the elegiac substitution as it acts as a replacement for the dead, becoming the new object of affection. For instance, in 'Lycidas', Milton's elegy for his friend Edward King, the dead man is reborn as the sun sets. Although the sun is setting, it is certain to rise again and so King is reborn into an endlessly cyclical nature, giving him immortality. The poem ends with the lines

> And now the sun had stretched out all the hills,
> And now was dropped into the western bay;
> At last he rose and twitched his mantle blue:
> Tomorrow to fresh woods, and pastures new.

> (Milton 1955:170)

A similar elegiac substitution can be seen in 'Adonais', Shelley's elegy for Keats. After much grieving the dead poet is finally turned into a star, is 'made one with Nature', thus securing him a measure of immortality. The star and indeed the poem itself become elegiac replacements for the lost love object. They are the new love objects for the grieving Shelley. Other common substitutions are memorial monuments and epitaphs as seen in, perhaps, the most famous of all English elegies, Gray's 'Elegy Written in a Country Churchyard'. Like nature, these substitutions can be seen as permanent, opposed to the fleetingness of life.

Although writing primarily in prose, Wojnarowicz follows the tradition of the elegiac form by locating his mourning away from society. Shelley, Keats and Gray set their poems in the pastoral, but this Arcadian landscape of shepherds and fauns is unavailable to Wojnarowicz in the postmodern era. He has to find his own version, and he discovers it in the cruising grounds in New York; the cheap movie theatres in Times Square and the derelict piers jutting out into the Hudson River. The piers and warehouses had a special attraction for Wojnarowicz; they were 'as far way from civilization as I could walk' and 'they were good for solitude and being able to hear myself think' (Wojnarowicz 1990: 54). This is Wojnarowicz's pastoral and he alludes to them as his 'industrial meadows' (54). Once he even tried to grow grass in some of the rooms in the warehouses attempting to make them interior fields. He found sex there too, yes, but this should not be considered unusual. Since Virgil's *Eclogues* there's often homoeroticism in these meadows, a tradition that the original hagiographist of Edward II, Christopher Marlowe, continued in his poems. Though it's not only sex and desire that Wojnarowicz searches for in his meadows, but also some truth in the 'slow disintegration of these architectural structures' (54). These piers return him to some more ancient time, and when he walks their deserted passageways he stops and thinks

> of the eternal sleep of statues, of marble eyes and lips and the stone wind-blown hair of the rider's horse, of illuminated arms corded with soft unbreathing veins, of the wounding curve of ancient backs stooped for frozen battles, of the ocean and the eyes in fading light, of the white stone warthog in the forest of crowfoot trees, and of the face beneath the sands of the desert still breathing.
>
> (Wojnarowicz 1992a: 23)

It's his elegy for permancy and a less complicated time. Wojnarowicz's elegiac substitution is the myth that he weaves into his work. This is how he copes with his impending death, by creating a self that will endure, a self that will live on after his death.

Perhaps it is better in the case of autobiography to rename the elegiac substitution as the 'elegiac supplement' after Derrida's important essay '... That Dangerous Supplement ... ' in *Of Grammatology* (Derrida 1977). In looking at Rousseau's *Confessions*, Derrida shows how Rousseau privileges speech over writing, but still sees writing as inevitably necessary as sometimes speech exposes the absences that it is meant to cover. Speech is natural, while writing is something added on to represent presence when the speaker is gone. Remember that Rousseau wrote his *Confessions*, and then read them out loud in order to give his words greater immediacy, but he still was not entirely satisfied. Derrida explains Rousseau's ambiguous relationship with words saying that he 'valorises and disqualifies writing at the same time' (141–2). Rousseau 'condemns writing as destruction of presence and as disease of speech. He rehabilitates it to the extent that it promises the reappropriation of that of which speech allowed itself to be dispossessed' (142). For Derrida, Rousseau's attitude to writing is similar to his attitude to masturbation. Both activities are not 'natural', but something added on to nature and simultaneously something that acts as a replacement. Rousseau calls masturbation 'that dangerous supplement' and he often records in his autobiographies the shame he felt when he engaged in onanism. However, he sometimes still thinks it is a better activity than sexual intercourse with a woman because he is only hurting himself rather than entering into affairs with women he would only be using for sex. Masturbation, he thought, would prevent women from becoming emotionally hurt. Masturbation replaces sex, but while it can be seen how the act stands in for sexual intercourse it still is something else entirely. The word 'supplement' has two meanings, like its French equivalent – it means to add something on, and also to substitute. Derrida says 'the supplement adds itself, it is a surplus, a plenitude enriching another plenitude' (144) but also 'the supplement supplements. It adds only to replace. It intervenes or insinuates itself *in-the-place-of*; if it fills, it as if one fills a void' (145). Derrida believes that writing acts like a supplement too. It is a replacement for speech, but simultaneously it adds something surplus. Words, especially written words as they will be able to be read and reread, will always yield meanings and angles not originally intended. This is how the elegiac substitution works too; it replaces the dead but, at the same time, it is something more than the dead.

The myth that Wojnarowicz leaves us with is much more than his life, as well as a replacement for it. His myth will endure more than the flesh and bones of his body. It is more than flesh and bones. It is a search for authenticity which somehow lies in the very myth that Wojnarowicz makes, in the uber-marginal life he creates for himself. Jonathan Dollimore has explored this territory in his study of John Rechy, another author of melancholic cruising:

> It is tempting to see Rechy as trapped in romantic/tragic self-glorification inseparable from naïve fantasies of revolutionary omnipotence. And there may indeed be a sense in which *The Sexual Outlaw* signals at once the apotheosis and the demise of the romantic quest for authenticity, the last stage of its restless search ever further outward in search of new marginal extremes of being. As the quest exhausts itself in one domain, it moves to another temporarily more invigorating because more marginal, yet destined also to become exhausted. Eventually the search must expire altogether at some point so distant from its origins that regeneration becomes impossible.
>
> (Dollimore 1991: 214)

Likewise it's tempting to see Wojnarowicz moving from margin to margin to discover authenticity, an authenticity that he nevertheless doubts exists in the postmodern, from the piers on the very edge of Manhattan, to a life sleeping on the street. He mixes with some dangerous people on the streets who engage in violence and bloodletting. Wojnarowicz says that this violence 'contained some unarguable truth' (Wojnarowicz 1992a: 172–3). For Wojnarowicz a chance meet through cruising is charged with both sexual and political satisfaction; he becomes that outlaw self. Wojnarowicz's cruising is a search for the self; he's cruising for the self. It is a search for the truth on the margins. Any truth found in the centre of society (or as far as to the centre a gay man could ever get) would lead to a social death, what Wojnarowicz calls 'a death more terrifying than physical death: an emotional and intellectual strangulation' (170). In the heteronormative centre Wojnarowicz would have to surrender his sexuality and his artistic expression. And while it is perhaps impossible to stay on these margins all the time, Wojnarowicz's myth goes someway to letting this happen. In real life Wojnarowicz has friends, family and for the last few years of his life a faithful lover in

Tom Rauffenbart, though Tom is hardly mentioned in the published autobiographical projects. Tom has only a slightly clearer presence in his unpublished journals.

Death becomes the last margin for Wojnarowicz, and it is here perhaps that he imagines a more fructifying authentic authenticity, but this too will always be sullied with fiction. He struggles with the idea that there is no self, and although the descriptions of the self he finds as he dies are grounded in postmodern denial, something of his self still persists.

Despite his regret at his mythmaking, his last book, *Memories that Smell like Gasoline* still manages to follow the same trajectory of a man living on the edge of society. This time he tells his story in an almost Romantic style, just concentrating on a few episodes from his life. They become like Wordsworth's 'spots of time': tableaux overexposed to the sublime. Yet there are no mountains or dark rocks in Wojnarowicz's sublime. His sublime is a violent and vertiginous space of sex and rape and death. Though in the last section of the book he now surrenders his myth to nothingness. As he slowly dies he feels that he is moving further away from society and is disappearing, becoming transparent. He says:

> Sometimes I come to hate people because they can't see where I am. I've gone empty, completely empty and all they see is the visual form: my arms and legs, my face, my height and posture, the sounds that come from my throat. But I'm fucking empty. The person I was just one year ago no longer exists; drifts spinning slowly into the ether somewhere way back there. I'm a Xerox of my former self ... I am glass, clear empty glass ... I am no longer animal vegetable or mineral. I am no longer made of circuits or disks. I am no longer coded and deciphered. I am all emptiness and futility. I am an empty stranger, a carbon copy of my form.
>
> (Wojnarowicz 1992c: 60)

He succumbs to the postmodern idea that there is no subjectivity outside of language, and begins to doubt that there is an essence of self within him. He continues 'I can no longer find what I'm looking for outside of myself. It doesn't exist out there. Maybe it's only in here, inside my head. But my head is glass ... I am a glass human. I am a glass human disappearing in rain' (60–1). He does not resist making an elegiac substitution, but rather creates a substitution out of nothingness. This is what he becomes. But following Derrida's theory on supplement this nothingness, or vacuum, becomes more than a simple denial of self. This nothingness, this disappearing act is given outlines and contours. It's not that there is no essence, but that the essence *is* of nothingness. Instead of vanishing he becomes a trace, an essence of ghostliness always on the point of disappearing. He's forever *losing his form in the darkness*, but this is where the self can be imagined, if not grasped. This is how he endures whether he wants to or not.

As Derrida says there is always a supplement; there is never an origin. It is similar to his concept of *différance* where signifiers always give way to signifiers with the signified always out of reach. He writes

> The supplement comes in the place of a lapse, a nonsignified or a nonrepresented, a nonpresence. There is no present before it, it is not preceding by anything but itself, that is to say by another supplement. The supplement is always the supplement of a supplement. One wishes to go back *from the supplement to the source*: one must recognise that there is *a supplement at the source*.
>
> (Derrida 1977: 304–5)

The self, like the signified, is forever out of reach. Wojnarowicz can never entirely lose himself in order to find himself. But like Rousseau, perhaps some lines of the self are breached in the arduous task of telling it mythically, fictionally or even repetitively.

For David Wojnarowicz even as he dies in pain, even as struggles against flimsy transparency, he is still leaving something of himself behind. It may not be his actual self, but a supplement of his self. The last words in *Memories that Smell like Gasoline* are 'I am disappearing. I am disappearing but not fast enough' (61). There is always something that remains, or replaces that which is lost. Wojnarowicz's elegiac substitution is his myth and his ghost forever walking the streets of New York, or driving through the deserts of America. This is what remains. It may eclipse his sense of humour, his collaborative spirit and his AIDS activism, but this is what remains.

Note

* Thanks to the Fales Library and to Tom Kauffenbait.

Bibliography

Anderson, L. (2001), *Autobiography* (London: Routledge).

Carlin, J. (1990), 'David Wojnarowicz: As the World Turns' in D. Wojnarowicz and B. Blinderman (eds), *Tongues of Flame* (Normal: Illinois State University) 21–33.

Carr, C. (1993), *On Edge – Performance at the End of the Twentieth Century* (Hanover, New England: Wesleyan University Press).

Coupe, L. (1997), *Myth* (London: Routledge).

Dangerous to Know Videos (1996), *Postcards from America* (Video) (London: Dangerous to Know Videos) Directed by S. Mclean.

de Man, Paul (1979), 'Autobiography as De-Facement' in *MLN* (*Modern Language Notes*) Vol. 94, 919–30.

Derrida, J. (1977), *Of Grammatology* (London: Johns Hopkins University Press).

Dollimore, J. (1991), *Sexual Dissidence – Augustine to Wilde, Freud to Foucault* (Oxford: Oxford University Press).

Genet, J. (1993), 'An Interview with Jean Genet', Interview with Edward de Grazia in *Cardozo Studies in Law and Literature*, Autumn, Vol.5, No.2, 307–24.

Goldin, N. (1989), *Witnesses: Against Our Vanishing*, Catalogue for group show at Artist's Space, New York, 16 Nov.-6 Jan. 1990.

Hoyt L. Sherman Gallery (1989), *AIDS: The Artists' Response* (Ohio; Ohio State University) Curator – Jan Zita Grover, 24 Feb.–16 Apr. 1989.

Jarman, D. (1992), *At Your Own Risk: A Saint's Testament* (London: Hutchinson).

—— (1993), *At Your Own Risk, A Saint's Testament* (London: Vintage).

Kaiser, C. (1997), *The Gay Metropolis – The Landmark History of Gay Life in America Since World War II* (San Diego: Harvest, Harcourt Brace).

Milton, J. (1955), in H. Darbishire (ed.), *The Poetical Works of John Milton Vol. II* (Oxford: Clarendon Press).

Moore, P. (2004), *Beyond Shame – Reclaiming the Abandoned History of Radical Gay Sexuality* (Boston: Beacon Press).

Olney, J. (1998), *Memory and Narrative – The Weave of Life Writing* (London: University of Chicago Press).

Rousseau, J. (1953), *The Confessions* (Harmondsworth: Penguin).

—— (1989), *The Collected Writings of Jean-Jacques Rousseau* (Hanover: University of New England Press).

—— (2004), *Reveries of the Solitary Walker* (London: Penguin Classics).

Sacks, P. (1985), *The English Elegy, Studies in the Genre from Spenser to Yeats* (London: Johns Hopkins University Press).

Shelley, P. (1971), in T. Hutchinson (ed.), *Poetical Works* (Oxford: Oxford University Press).

Solnit, R. (2002), *Wanderlust A History of Walking* (London: Verso).

Taylor, M.J. (2002), ' "I'll Be Your Mirror, Reflect What You Are": Postmodern Documentation and the Downtown New York Scene from 1975 to the Present' in J.G. Hendin (ed.), *A Concise Companion to Postwar American Literature and Culture* (Oxford: Blackwell Publishing) 383–99.

Wojnarowicz, D. (1988), *Journal Spain/Paris/U.S.*, Series 1, Box 1, Folder 20, David Wojnarowicz Papers, Fales Library, New York University.

—— (1989a), *In the Shadow of Forward Motion*, exhibition catalogue, (New York: P.P.O.W. Gallery).

—— (1989b), *Journal 1989 Dreams-Drawing-Notes*, Series 1 Box 1, Folder 21, David Wojnarowicz Papers, Fales Library, New York University.

—— (1990), B. Blinderman (ed.) *Tongues of Flame* (Normal: Illinois State University).

—— (1992a), *Close To the Knives – A Memoir of Disintegration* (1st edn 1991) (London: Serpent's Tail).

—— (1992b), Interview with Nan Goldin in *QW*, No. 42, 23 Aug. 1992 (New York gay magazine).

—— (1992c), *Memories That Smell Like Gasoline* (San Francisco: Artspace Books).

—— (1996), *The Waterfront Journals* (New York: Grove Press).

—— (1999), in A. Scholder (ed.) *In the Shadow of the American Dream – Diaries of David Wojnarowicz* (New York: Grove Press).

—— (2006), *David Wojnarowicz A Definitive History of Five or Six Years on the Lower East Side* (New York: Semiotexte).

——, Letters at the Fales Library, Mclean correspondence in Series 2, Box 3, Folder 29 and 31, David Wojnarowicz Papers, Fales Library, New York University.

—— and B. Neill (1992), *ITSFOMO* (audio CD) (New Town Recordings, Rob Droli).

Wojnarowicz and Zwickler (no year), Image Script for Video *Fear of Disclosure Part 2 (self)*, Series 3 Sub Series F, Box 6, File 266, David Wojnarowicz Papers, Fales Library, New York University.

White, E. (1983), *A Boy's Own Story* (1st edn 1982) (London: Picador).

—— (2005), *My Lives* (London: Bloomsbury).

Young, E. (1993), in E. Young and G. Caveny (eds), *'Shopping in Space' American Fiction from the Blank Generation* (New York: Atlantic Monthly Press with Serpent's Tail).

Part III
Writers

18

Reflections on Life and Writing

Alan Sillitoe

A novelist milks life, not as in the cowshed with hands on a more hygienic machine, but in silent reflection as he does his work – even in a book lined room, if he can, or can afford one. From the beginning he milks the life – in a search for art and reality – of his own background and family, until there is nothing left, after which his imagination strays elsewhere for what is so crudely called 'material'. As for the family, no members of it can hide from his ruthless eye.

Writing novel after novel is little more than a serial attempt to bring to life a character he will recognise immediately as himself – somewhere along the line. Luckily, this never happens, because if it did the writer would surely cease to write, the only reason for being alive cut from under his feet. So no members of the family can hide from him, nor indeed he from them, a triumph of symbiosis.

All members of the family are vividly fixed in his memory from too early on for him to forget their influence. For mysterious reasons they appear in larger measure than himself. A novelist, the least trustworthy person, thus sucks his family dry, then vamps on people passing in the street, or old friends until, having run out of reality, he has to rely more and more on the imagination – not quite entirely, but that is the only way I can explain it.

For donkey's years I vowed never – never – to write an autobiography. But we all know what happens when you say never, the word being a sure indication that sooner or later you are going to do whatever it was that you said never about. It has always been so with me.

One day, trawling through my notebook between one novel and the next, I thought how interesting it might be, to me at any rate, if I told the story as to how someone from my background turned into a writer. A novelist, who is nothing if not self obsessed, tries to hide the fact of how he did so by writing novels which he claims to be about others.

In my family there were no books until I started bringing them into the house. Perhaps having a father who was mostly unemployed during the nineteen-thirties, a labourer who could neither read nor write, was the perfect condition for such as me who was to become a storyteller.

As if in opposition to him, I learned all that was possible in school, and read devotedly whatever book I could find. Many excellent novels existed in those days for young people, by such writers as Rider Haggard, Conan Doyle, G. A. Henty, Richmal Crompton, etc. as well as works by Victor Hugo and Alexandre Dumas.

One of the first books, given to me by a schoolmaster, was called *History Day by Day*. I have no idea who the compiler was for that instructive volume, but it was my mainstay for a long time. It was a kind of almanack, of seven hundred and fifty pages or so, which meant a double-page entry for every day of the year. Open it anywhere, and I would find a biographical sketch on the left hand page of a celebrated statesman, soldier, artist or writer born on that day, and on the facing page something more specific about a certain period of his life. If an author, there would be an extract from one of his or her novels.

It was as engrossing and almost inexhaustible book for a boy of ten, and I'm forever grateful to the man who gave it to me. When I was eleven my grandmother who, incidentally, came from County Mayo, encouraged me to sit for the scholarship examination which, if I passed, would enable me to go on to a grammar school. Among other things I would be taught French there, a language I already knew something of.

Perhaps due to lack of coaching, or the kind of conundrums I was expected to solve, I didn't get through. It could be that I was rather close to doing so – or that's what I like to think! – because I was allowed to take it again the following year. Disappointed yet not downhearted, I didn't triumph that time either, so at least I could tell myself later that I was not just the only English novelist to fail his Eleven-plus (as it came to be known) but had done so twice.

This lack of luck or intelligence (or whatever it was) meant that I would go to work in a factory as soon as I was fourteen. This was no hardship, rather an adventure in fact, and in any case there were many more lads in the same circumstances. My life would make some kind of story, or pattern, a sort of novel even, a rags to (comparative) riches tale with a beginning and an end – almost the shape of a novel. I decided that a satisfactory cut-off point for the memoir would be at thirty three years of age, when I was writing the filmscripts of my first publications, *Saturday Night and Sunday Morning* and *The Loneliness of the Long Distance Runner*.

Neither of those first two books was in any way autobiographical, though I did use details of the background from which I came. Such work marked a success after struggles of earlier years. The device of ending the autobiography at that point left open the possibility of my writing volume two at some point in the future – should I need to relax from writing novels (on the premise that a change could be as good as a rest) – or it might be a rather backhanded way of earning some money!

But I couldn't think that the continuation of my autobiography could be anywhere as interesting at the first volume, since it would be a boring account of how I wrote one novel after another (more than twenty when last counted!) the stepping stones of what now might seem as unremitting work, too linear to draw a reader's attention, of no real interest to anyone except possibly other writers – not even to them.

The book was published in 1995 by Harper Collins, and is still in print from JR Books. At the beginning I quoted from the Jewish Scriptures in the King James' Version, with which I've always been familiar. I quite often pick up the Book at the end of the day and read a page or so in order to know what real English is like. The quotation is from 1 Samuel 31-9: "And they cut off his head, and stripped off his armour, and sent into the land of the Philistines round about, to publish it in the house of their idols, and among the peoples" which sounded apposite at the time.

I wondered, while writing *Life Without Armour* – such was its title – what plasma of memory autobiography was formed by. What makes one choose certain memories and not others, from many that must be left out, which seem so important afterwards that they should have to be put in. I hadn't written the book in a hurry, either. Searching for recollections in a half charted ocean of the past (through what I was only half-convinced was my past) I was like a hydrographical surveyor on an ocean trip, pinning the detail of distant coastlines and islands finally and firmly down. The occasional lighthouse illuminates a particular scene from some far gone era that was once the present, each journey vivid with reminiscence, pictures like maps spread out for my delectation. A lighthouse could also have warned me of areas from my past which have to be 'given a wide berth'.

Marcel Proust clarifies the process in notes and letters that go towards forming his great novel *A la Recherche du Temps Perdu*. He shows how memory must become the overriding factor in such a purpose. Incidents thought to have been forgotten, never to return into consciousness, suddenly come back into the light, and become part of the machinery and shape of a novel – or autobiography.

One might say that the novelist writes biographies all the time, creating people and doing what he wants with them, using methods which are hardly definable but more often than not drawn out of his imagination, or by recollection, or kidnapped from other peoples' memories without intending to do so. Even someone walking along the street – or especially someone walking down the street – whom you don't know and will never in reality meet, enters the mixing process to produce what you think and hope will turn out to be an original and realistic person whom readers will relate to or even recognise as someone they once knew, possibly even better than the author in his book.

You think of those you make up as people rather than characters, a distinction which surely gives them more dignity. This technique, closer to that necessary for writing an autobiography is, or should be, a different art when it comes to writing biography, which deals with someone's whole life and not only a part. The difference is that the biographer has solid and incontrovertible facts which leads the subject from stage to stage, from birth indeed to death.

I recently read George D. Painter's biography of Proust, which seemed necessary before tackling (the right word, believe me!) the twelve volumes for the second time, first come across in my youth. Much was forgotten, after so long. In fact almost all was forgotten. But I wanted, as a reader, to be entranced again. It was a different novel from the one I'd found before, nothing unusual.

Painter's biography of Proust was published by Penguin Books in 1983, and had lain on my shelf for over ten years. It was a volume of nearly eight hundred pages, of fairly close print, the longest introduction to the seemingly endless novel itself. All the fascinating details of Proust's life are gone but Painter brings them both back to life; most importantly intuiting when Proust first knew he would become a writer.

Painter points out what induced Proust to think about all who would inhabit his novel, in his biography seeming to know his subject as well as, or conceivably better than, he knew himself, as if he had taken as long to write the book as Proust his novel.

A literary biography (and an autobiography of merit) can be a work of literature, and I not only read Painter's to see how someone with a similar obsession to my own managed to live and survive but also, above all, how he managed to go on writing, and the techniques that were used. I witnessed his life as a story of the common struggle, an account as firmly fixed to the truth as it is possible to get, as true to the subject which provides, for another writer, not only information but also inspiration.

Aiming for truth in the writing of such work is not a scientific activity, since there is no way of measuring the accuracy of verisimilitude. Facts are collected, and the imagination is sympathetically deployed in choosing some from many, though who can claim that the work is even then close enough to the truth? This applies to novelists as much as to biographers.

Such problems as these faced me when writing *Life Without Armour*. If there is any such thing as the truth, and there must be more of it available to the biographer than to the novelist, who can take more risks, truth can only be harnessed on the one hand by imagination, and on the other by patient detective work. Imagination is a tool for sorting the relevant from the dross, and increases the enlightenment in getting near the truth.

It is more difficult for a biographer to achieve the truth than a novelist, truth that the novelist can hardly dream about in his desire to make up people out of nothing. He, the biographer, has to be somewhat more devious, and take greater risks. All this may be hypothesis on my part, and I'd have to write the biography of a biographer to clarify my ideas.

A novelist is expected to make up the truth, to fabricate endlessly out of his imagination, go to great lengths in making people seemingly real, while the biographer is yoked to verifiable facts. He can, the novelist, make the *golem* live for him, and even create people to live for the golem, not exactly like a holy man or like God Almighty, but certainly like the Devil himself. Writers of fiction can be endlessly inventive in using the imagination (plus lies) to get as close to the truth as possible, a concept to be discarded as soon as they have achieved their purpose.

The biographer, with sharper tools and perhaps more skill (though of a different sort) may feel greater responsibility for what he writes, having noted in the process how much more difficult the task must be for him or her. There is some advantage on discovering that his subject is already dead, or even nearly so, an advantage novelists aren't always able to enjoy. Even so, he still needs the essential ability of the novelist who – like Proust while dunking his fluted small cake into a cup of herbal tea unexpectedly offered him by his aunt – suddenly sees revelations of his coming into place which are personal and unique to him alone.

As a novelist one reads literary biographies with interest. Luckily, so do many others who are not writers, and one of the reasons they are drawn to them with such enthusiasm must be that even before starting to read they know how the book is going to end. The following is a record of how I felt soon after *Saturday Night and Sunday Morning* was published in 1958. It is I suppose an example of how work and life can overlap unpredictably.

There was something which did not allow me to enjoy my so-called fame to the extent I should have been capable of doing. Perhaps it was just as well. I persuaded myself that such an afflicted state was necessary in order to go on writing. The wheels of fame and artistic success did not lock into each other, and I distrusted any feeling which came from a whiff of either.

Lack of enjoyment could have been caused by something in me, or factors exterior, or a mixture of both. The only success which meant anything was that of doing good work, and my increasingly hypercritical faculties never allowed me to acknowledge that sort of achievement. I learned to regard good reviews with the same objective appraisal as bad ones, realizing that success which eluded me in one book could always be aimed for in the next.

An eternal refugee from such ambiguous feelings, I immersed myself in work that came out of the coal mines of my subconscious, and never allowed sufficient time to elapse between novels in which I could be intimidated by what the 'normal' world looked on as 'success'. Nor was it possible for me to work *and* live, and though that decision was to be a mistake as far as my life was concerned, it was necessary because there was not enough energy in me to do both.

Facing such truth reinforces my inherited conviction that, having chosen what to do in life, you must go on with it to the utmost. Choices have to be paid for, and those half hidden ones that you allow to be made for you, or which Fate makes, cost even more.

Many aspects of life were too difficult for me to endure. They always had been. Why this was is hard to say, but I suppose a possible answer might be that dissatisfaction supplies the power for the mill of the imagination, out of which one endeavours to create works which leave the reader (and therefore the author) in favour of life by the end of the book rather than in a state of despair at all the vile things that go on in the world.

(15 April 1993)

(*Some questions raised by this talk are addressed in the second half of Chapter 19.*)

19
A Writer's Work and Life

Ruth Fainlight

Richard Bradford (RB)

I'd like to introduce Ruth Fainlight and then we'll carry things off to questions, both to Ruth and Alan. As you can see from the flier, Ruth Fainlight is primarily a poet but she has also written fiction, translated an enormous amount of verse and written three libretti. Today she will be talking about (I hope she will anyway) the autobiographical aspects of her verse and I must confess that having asked her if she'd be willing to do this I began to have second thoughts and I'll tell you why. Ruth's poetry, and particularly when she reads it aloud, has the power to fixate the listener; we are drawn to those points where moments of crisis, loss, feeling, inspiration, suddenly intersect with words, so that in a way her poems are vividly autobiographical in their own right. They are not just beautifully crafted artefacts, they are that as well, but also gripping introductions to the person behind them, Ruth might well disagree, I'm not sure, but anyway you will enjoy what is to come.

Ruth Fainlight (RF)

What I am going to do is just give a poetry reading with rather more talking about the poems. I've chosen poems that are 'quote' autobiographical 'end of quote', because as Richard so correctly says and as I believe, everything one writes as a poet cannot help but be autobiographical. I've written various sequences of poems like the 'Sibyls' and 'Sheba and Solomon' – I suppose they have autobiographical aspects, but they are not as overtly autobiographical as the poems I'm going to read you now. I'm going to read you about ten poems and talk a little bit about them. The first is called 'Passenger'. The circumstances of writing it were that I was sitting on a train which had stopped in a railway station in a large city and of course when you are on a train you are raised quite high above the level of the people on the platform. I saw on the platform an adolescent girl and she was looking up at the train and our eyes met and suddenly she reminded me of myself at that age when I would have been the girl on the platform and I would have been looking at the woman in the carriage and fantasising, 'when I'm grown up I'm going to get on that train, leave here, leave everything and go into the great world', etc. etc. So that was the inspiration of this poem.

'Passenger'

Not watching trains pass and dreaming of when
I would become that traveller, glimpsed
inside the carriage flashing past a watching
dreaming child, but being the passenger

staring out at tall apartment blocks
whose stark forms cut against the setting sun
and bars of livid cloud: balconies crowded
with ladders, boxes, washing, dead pot plants,

into lighted steamy windows where women
are cooking and men just home from work, shoes
kicked off and sleeves rolled up are smoking, stretched
exhausted in their sagging half bought chairs,

under viaducts where children busy
with private games and errands wheel and call
like birds at dusk: all that urban glamour
of anonymity which makes me suffer

such nostalgia for a life rejected
and denied, makes me want to leave the train,
walk down the street back to my neighbourhood
of launderettes, newsagents, grocery shops,

become again that watching dreaming girl
and this time live it out – one moment only
was enough before a yawning tunnel-
mouth obscured us both, left her behind.

Now I'm going to read a few poems connected to my parents. During the war, the Second World War, I was in the United States with my mother and my brother, and my father was in the air force and so my parents didn't see each other for six years and there was a great deal of correspondence between them. That's what this is about, and of course, the effect it had on me. It's called 'Handbag'.

'Handbag'

> My mother's old leather handbag,
> crowded with letters she carried
> all through the war. The smell
> of my mother's handbag: mints
> and lipstick and Coty powder.
> The look of those letters, softened
> and worn at the edges, opened,
> read, and refolded so often.
> Letters from my father. Odour
> of leather and powder, which ever
> since then has meant womanliness,
> and love, and anguish, and war.

The next poem is called 'Early Rivers' – which is a variety of plum. I make jam most summers, and this is about jam made from Early Rivers.

'Early Rivers'

> This jar of rosy purple jam is labelled
> Early Rivers August '84 - *

Interrupts – I'm stopping. I'm going to start again because I've forgotten to give you a vital piece of information – otherwise something that comes up will seem mysterious. I talk about a cotton sock. When you make plum jam, you cut the plums and take the pips out, but you have to use the pips because the pectin comes from them. Years ago I started putting all the pips into an odd white cotton sock, not a muslin bag, knotting the top and putting it into the boiling fruit, so that's the explanation for the sock .

> the date I made it, the name the farmer gave
> those plums, smooth as onyx eggs, but warmer.
>
> The dimpled groove, bloom-dusted, down each fruit
> pouted at the touch of my knife, yielding
> a stone I put inside a cotton sock
> (relict of a worn-out pair – every
> boiling dyed it darker crimson – from one
> plum-season to the next I saved it) then pushed
> the lumpy tied-up bag into the centre of
> the pulpy amber halves and melting sugar
> in the preserving kettle, and let the mixture
> ooze its pectin, odours, juices, flavours,

until the chemistry of time and fire
produced this sharpness, sweetness, that I'm eating
now, straight from the jar, smearing my mouth,
digging the spoon in deeper, seeking a taste
undiluted even by nostalgia.

I didn't start writing poems about my parents until they were both dead. This is one about my father, it's called 'Learning about Him'.

'Learning about Him'

A sheep bleated, and sounded
exactly like someone imitating a sheep,
which made me think about my father –

the sort of thing he'd do,
suddenly start to clown and act crazy, or like
a warning cough of static

from the jelly mould
Art-Deco shape of the big valve radio,
its glowing amber dial

marked with places he'd been to.
I'd twiddle the knobs and move the needle through
London, Bombay, Rio.

'Look after my Feigele',
(the Yiddish name meant 'little bird)' her dying
mother said to the lodger,

my father, so they got married.
I heard the story after his funeral
and finally understood

why I was born in New York.
I'd recognised another melancholic
early on, but not

the autodidact's hunger
for self-improvement; he'd dissembled (as though
it would be shameful if

any of us knew) until
clearing his room, choosing which books to keep,
I found old favourites.

I hate to read books marked
with comments in the margins, underlinings,
but these were different.

I was learning about him.
For instance, how he'd saved what seemed every
postcard I'd mailed home –

grudgingly dutiful –
and pasted them in scrapbooks, marking my routes
red and his bright blue.

We'd almost meshed the globe.
I wonder if his restlessness was soothed
by mine, or irritated?

Dear father, now your crazy
daughter's weeping sounds like bleating or
a faulty radio.

And this is a memorial poem for my mother. It's called 'The Crescent'

'The Crescent'

My stick of lipsalve is worn away
into the same curved crescent
that was the first thing I noticed
about my mother's lipstick.

It marked the pressure of her existence
upon the world of matter.

Imagine the grim fixity
of my stare, watching her smear
the vivid grease across her lips
from a tube shiny as a bullet.
The way she smoothed it
with the tip of a little finger
(the tinge it left, even after
washing her hands, explained
the name 'pinky') and her pointed tongue
licking out like a kitten's,
fascinated, irritated.
It was part of the mystery of
brassières and compacts and handbags

that meant being grown-up. I thought
my own heels would have to grow
a sort of spur to squeeze right down
the narrow hollow inside high-heels.

Now I am calmer, and no longer
paint my lips except with this,
pale as a koshered carcass
drained of blood in salty water
or a memorial candle,
wax congealed down one side,
as though it stood in the wind
that blows from the past, flame
reflected like a crescent
moon against a cloud
in the pool of molten light.

I carry the sign of the moon
and my mother, a talisman
in a small plastic tube
in my handbag, a holy relic
melted by believers'
kisses, and every time
I smooth my lips with the unguent
I feel them pout and widen
in the eternal smile
of her survival through me,
feel her mouth on mine.

Now I'll read a poem about myself in Spain when I was a young woman in
my twenties and it's called Agua de Colonia, which is Eau de Cologne in
Spanish

'Agua de Colonia'

The sharp smell of cheap eau-de-cologne,
agua de colonia , will call it back:
every aspect of the lonely summer
in that other era, when I was young.

Watered pavements of narrow streets between
old buildings. Dim high-ceilinged cafes blue
with smoke from yellow-papered cigarettes.
The almost neutral taste of almond *horchata*

in a tall glass beaded with moisture. I pressed
my wrists against its sides to cool my blood.

Molten sunlight through the shutter slats
corrodes the floor-tiles' lozenges and arabesques.
Insomnia under a mosquito net.
My scent. My languor. My formal clothing.

I should have told you – again I'm not giving you enough information – I said I would be talking about the poems but I'm not. I must explain: 'the almost neutral taste of horchata'. Horchata is a thick syrup made by boiling almonds. At that time, decades ago, I don't know if it still exists, it would be in bars and you could get a tall glass with some horchata syrup poured into it, then add some water to dilute it – it was a very pleasant drink and the nearest equivalent I can think of in England is barley water. If you think of the word 'horchata' and the medieval word orgeat, which is syrup made from barley, I'm sure they're directly related. So I'll read the middle stanza again:

Watered pavements of narrow streets between
old buildings. Dim high-ceilinged cafes blue
with smoke from yellow-papered cigarettes.
The almost neutral taste of almond *horchata*
in a tall glass beaded with moisture. I pressed
my wrists against its sides to cool my blood.

So that is what horchata is, and the yellow-papered cigarettes were like those French *Gitanes*, those terribly rough, black tobacco, cheapest work men's cigarettes which I used to smoke when I smoked.

Now I'll read you some poems from my latest book. The first six that I read were from my *Selected Poems*, from earlier books. My last book, *Moon Wheels*, which was published last year, is divided into three sections, one section of new poems, one of translations and one section which is poems from a book that was published in 1994 called 'This Time of Year'. It not only went out of print but there just don't seem to be any copies available, it seemed to have vanished. I didn't want those poems to be totally lost so I put some of them at the back of this book and that's the final third. I'll read two poems from that collection, then I'll read you a new one, and then one more.

This poem is about my aunt. I lived in America for the first five years of my life, in England for the second five years, America for the third five years and I've lived in England since I was fifteen – or in Europe anyway. Not in America. I've only been back to America for work really. My mother's elder sister, who was only about eighteen months or two years older, didn't have any children. She was a much stronger personality than my mother, completely dominated her, and she more or less adopted me when I was an infant, she decided that my mother could have my brother and she could have me. She was a terrifically important influence in my life. There are many references to her throughout my work. When I was between the ages of twelve and fifteen we lived with her in Arlington, Virginia. As I said, she didn't have any children – so there was this rather comfortable middle aged, middle class childless couple, and suddenly the wife's younger sister with her two children turned up and lived with them for three years. It was a complete disruption to their lives. My uncle Roscoe came from a mid west farming family, from a Scottish Presbyterian background, completely exotic to us. He just put up with us. Every weekend he would just sit on the porch and drink and sing little songs to himself. He was an engineer, a very intelligent successful man and I mention his guns in the poem because he had a few, and used to make bullets for them. I was quite a good pistol shot at this time with my uncle Roscoe's guns. My aunt was crazy about opera and she introduced me to it. Every Saturday afternoon we used to listen to the opera broadcast from the Met (the Metropolitan Opera House in New York) which now one can hear in England, and I often listen to it now. I used to go to art classes in the morning at the Corcoran Art Gallery in Washington, and I'd come back and have lunch, and then my aunt and I would sit in the sitting room listening to the opera, it was almost like a religious occasion, and in this room was the cabinet in which my uncle... Anyway it is all in the poem.

'Tosca'

> Above the walnut cabinet where
> Uncle Roscoe kept pistols and bullets,
> moulds and targets and tins of pellets,
> dust motes drifted through a shaft of sunlight
> while my Aunt Ann and I listened
> to *Tosca* broadcast from the Met.
>
> I know it was summer, because a layer
> of dust below the glittering swirl
> dulled the linoleum's pattern, and that meant
> the carpets had been stored until winter.
>
> But which pattern was it, which room –
> before or after our move –
> am I remembering, where we sat
> between the radio and the cabinet,
> which sunny Saturday afternoon,
> during the war, assembles
> around me as I listen to *Tosca*
> now, in a half-dismantled apartment
> the day before a new departure.

I have heard Tosca so often,
I think I know each motif
by heart. The grand themes of my life
must have been already waiting
in the wings, incarnated as
the jealous woman artist,
Scarpia's potent menace. Those two
make the couple. Cavaradossi's
revolutionary fervour can
never deflect their trajectory
of mutual destruction.

Uncle Roscoe's guns and bullets
somehow stay connected to the story,
but he was gentle, indifferent
to the passions of the music –
and the wife he had chosen:
that thwarted fantasist of every
métier and alternative.

So much talent misdirected
into trimming hats and bottling fruit.
She taught me to listen to opera,
to believe I was an artist,
to read Baudelaire and to iron a shirt
as well as a Parisian laundress.

Tosca is telling the whole world
how she has lived only for art, and I
an in another place and apartment,
writing my notes, watching dust motes drift
in the sunlight, about to move on.

Aunt Ann's floral-patterned linoleum
on one or other living room floor
crumbled decades ago. Each house
was gone when I tried to find it,
the gardens asphalted over.
I never learned what happened to her
walnut cabinet, or Uncle Roscoe's
collection of guns, after they died.

And here's another poem about my mother. My mother and her family
went to America at the beginning of the twentieth century from what was

then part of the Austrian and Hungarian Empire. Now it is in the Ukraine, and between the First and Second World War it was Poland and Romania – it was in that area of shifting borderland of eastern Europe. So that's 'the old country'.

'Lineage'

When my eyes were sore or tired or itched,
clenching her hands in a loose fist,
my mother would rub her wedding ring,
carefully, along the closed lids,
sure the touch of gold was curative.

She also believed in hot water
with lemon, first thing in the morning
and, at any time of day, drank awful-
tasting infusions and pot-liquors
to purify her blood. She warmed
a spoonful of sweet almond oil to pour
into my aching ear, wrapped torn
old woollen vests around my throat,
and blistered my chest with a poultice
if I came down with a cold.

Remedies and simples from the old
country, still useful in the city,
were passed from mother to daughter
and not yet scorned. We rarely saw
a doctor. When I was little
it seemed normal to be sickly
for half of the year. I never told her
that I was proud she was a witch.

And this is a much more recent poem from *Moon Wheels*. When I was a child in London, between the two stays in America, I had two blue woollen Whitney blankets on my bed. I vaguely remembered them but when I cleared my parents' house after their deaths I found these same two blankets, terribly threadbare and worn but they were there. I took them and I still use them now. I make a reference in the poem to the way they say that the black death was introduced into Europe by the Mongols catapulting the body of someone who had died of the plague over the walls of a besieged city – and I conflate that with the fact that when Europeans went to the United States, in order to obtain the land of the Indians, they gave them infected blankets to kill them off – you know, *ethnic cleansing*.

'Blankets'

The stuffy ground-floor bedroom
at the back of our flat. The bed,
covered with blue Witney blankets
bound with paler blue velvet.

Measles, scarlet fever,
influenza, whooping cough.
The night I tripped over the oilstove
Mother lit to warm the bathroom.

From hip to heel, burning
paraffin splashed. Weeks in bed
under a sort of cradle made
to hold the weight of the blankets off.

Bunches of flowers, orange and red,
climbed the faded papered walls
up to the ceiling. My eyes rolled back
in their sockets, counting the nosegays.

Nightmares under the blankets.
Like sodden tufts of moss
bulging virulently green,
mounting the window ledge

and oozing through the open gap,
sooty spores clogging my
nostrils and mouth, the touch
of velvet would make me scream.

I still sleep under those blankets
(their velvet binding rubbed bare)
the self-same ones I pulled around
my shoulders and hid beneath:

now potent and dangerous
as plague-infected blankets thrown
over the walls of a city besieged,
or exchanged for the sacred land

of people with no more immunity
to the pathogens they carried, than I

> to the fevers of memory in the folds
> and the weave of these old blue blankets.

And then I thought I would close with a poem, an older poem, whose subject is autobiography, which seemed very appropriate.

'Author! Author!'

> What I am working at and want to perfect —
> My project – is the story of myself: to have it
> Clear in my head, events consecutive,
> To understand what happened and why it happened.
>
> I wander through department stores and parks,
> beyond the local streets, seem to be doing nothing;
> then an overheard phrase or the way light slants
> from the clouds, unravels the hardest puzzle.
>
> It takes all my time, uses so much energy.
> How can I live, here and now, when the past
> is being unwound from its great spindle, and tangles
> forgotten motives around the present? Rather
>
> than set the record straight, further knowledge
> complicates. I cannot stop the action
> to make a judgement, or hope for better.
> Every gesture casts a longer shadow
>
> into the future, each word shifts the balance.
> I see myself as one more character
> in this extravagant scenario,
> the story not yet finished. And who's the author?

Thank you.

This question and answer session occurred after the papers delivered by Ruth Fainlight and Alan Sillitoe, and involves questions to and replies from both; the latter's paper is reprinted as Chapter 18 of this volume.

RB

Thank you. Are there any questions that anyone would like to address to either or both of them, or a general question which each of them might like to leap at.

From the audience (unidentified)

I have a question for Ruth Fainlight. It seems in your poems sometimes a Jewish feel comes out so could you explain a little more about it

RF

I'm Jewish so that's why!

Response

There are a lot of Jewish writers and poets and they express it in different ways so I was wondering what it meant for you?

RF

Well, I'm not an observant Jew at all but it's just a fact about me, I don't know how I can answer your question. I could write a long considered piece about what it means for me to be Jewish but otherwise I just can't give you a quick answer I'm afraid. Maybe we could talk about it later.

Response:

Would you like to like to elaborate on the image of the lipstick as a washed out kosher carcass?

RF

Well it's just a fact that when an animal is slaughtered, according to Jewish laws, every drop of blood must be washed out of the carcass because blood is absolutely not allowed. Blood carries life so you can't eat the blood, not a drop of animal blood... so I'm just referring to the regulations concerning the slaughter of an animal that makes it kosher for Jewish people to eat.

Response

So in that case, religion itself sometimes...

RF

Yes, it's just a fact, a non Jewish person could say that as well, that a carcass of animal that has been prepared by a Jewish slaughterer will have all the blood washed out - that's all it means. In that poem I also have candle imagery: 'melted by believers' kisses', something like that, and memorial candles because I lived in Spain for some years in my twenties so actually I'm quite knowledgeable about Catholicism but again that is completely objective, factual knowledge because I was there and I picked it up but it hasn't impinged on me, I've never had a crisis of Catholicism.

Tim Hancock

Can I just ask Ruth a question? When you are writing poems which draw on your own memories and autobiography do you find that the writing process is trying to distil the essence of this memory or do you find that it sort of transforms that memory and turns it into something different or how do you generalise?

RF

That's an interesting question...I don't know how I should answer it. Everyone writes either in poetry or prose. In either case language transforms memory. How exactly it does so or whether it distorts the truth; this we can never know. We can't recover the past without language.

TH

Are you conscious of manipulating the memory or whether it's language that is doing it itself:

RF

No, I don't consciously try to manipulate the memory. I try to remain faithful to it.

RB

Since poetry has played such a part in your life, so continuously and for such a long time, do you think you remember poetically? I mean what I'm doing is adjusting Tim's question. Apart from the conscious act of using memory as the foundations of a poem, aside from when you do that, when you sit down deliberately and decide to draw upon your memories and make use of them in a poem do you think more casually, instinctively? Do you believe that the way in which you recall facts or even think is in some way affected by your familiarity with your, I was going to say, your state of mind as a poet..

RF

Well, I imagine it must be but it's so integral and central that it's very hard to remark on. It isn't thinking about a memory and then thinking 'how can I write a poem about it' that starts a poem. A poem always starts with words, with the language, the crystallisation of something I'm thinking about, but I can't make it happen, alas.

RB

No, I wasn't suggesting that you can and obviously a lot of work and effort goes into those poems, self-evidently, but I was just wondering if being a poet makes you think differently from us.

RF

You mere mortals!?
(Laughter)

Deirdre O'Byrne

Richard can I intervene on this because it's very interesting? I just want to take it back to the poem about the leather handbag and the Coty lipstick and the way that poem ends, particularly the thrill administered in the last line which ends on the word 'war'. This of course is the manipulation of language by the poet to create rhetorical and emotional effect which is why we get an affective association between with the lipstick and the handbag. And it reminds me of the piece that Alan read at the end of the autobiography where he's talking about hope being alive in the writing process in spite of the violence that goes on in the world and the curious thing is that you seem to get a sense of excitement from the word 'war', which is curiously hopeful, because what you seem to be saying is that the writer is retreating to language as a last resort, that poetry is a medium in which horror can be faced and overcome.

RF

Yes but it's a most interesting comment which I shall certainly have to think about. Poetry is not a refuge, at least I don't treat it as such, when I'm composing it. But later, then my relationship with the poem is more complicated.

RB

Alan, I remember reading something, I ought to be able to remember where, when you said, and I'm paraphrasing very badly, that you feel responsible for the characters in your novel in a way similar to the type of responsibility that we would normally associate with our affection or attachment to real human beings.

Alan Sillitoe (AS)

Well, if you make a person in this way, and so suddenly, you don't know quite how to deal with this man or women. They've come down from somewhere, and you've never known them before. You did not anticipate that some-one like them could exist, and suddenly they are part of your novel, they are directing other people and making them have reactions towards them as well. It's very difficult to understand. That has no connection at all to biography or autobiography, that's another game as it were. Sometimes real people resurface, or I should say are redistributed, in fiction, in my fiction. But just as often characters come from elsewhere, like strangers. And then after a while these people control your novel. Okay that's fine, and you know a novel is very easy to stock, it's like filling and piloting a big commercial aeroplane, you take off fine, you simply pull back the stick and increase the howls of the engine and then the plane, with all your people travels at 3000 feet with all the action going on and then of course you have to end it, so you have to be very careful in landing the plane, ending the novel, and then they are out of your mind, you are onto another novel and you've forgotten about them and you wonder at the responsibility of having left them in that situation. And you have a sort of nightmare scenario sometimes where on a bleak morning one of your past inhabitants, with a knife between his teeth, gets through your bedroom window and says 'Why did you leave me in that situation? You used me so unnecessarily brutally in all your novels. Why?' and you think 'Did I know that person in real life or was that person actually invented'. So I have to correct myself, slightly. It is not intended to be biographical or autobiographical but because you spend so long with these people, people you have created, you begin to feel the borders between the emotional and moral responsibilities of the real world and those of the novel begin to break down.

RB

So there is a connection between your writing and autobiography?

AS

To an extent, yes. But it is not that simple. As I said in my talk, Writing *Life Without Armour* was both like and unlike writing fiction.

Paul Perry (PP)

Question for Alan. You started your talk by referring to a writer using their family as source material, I wonder did you ever experience or fear a sense of estrangement from your family that you used for your writing?

AS

My family reacted particularly humanely, in fact, they didn't kill me and they didn't drive me away. My father couldn't read what I wrote, my mother read some of it to him and, sadly, he died soon after I'd found my feet as a writer. My brothers and sisters were very happy about the fact that that I'd become a writer and didn't mind, and I don't think I maligned them particularly because when you use people, at least when I use people, I do try to disguise them as much as I possibly can so they can't say this is me 100 per cent by any means. Writing realism and making it successful as a kind of work of art needs imagination and hard work. Recording facts transparently, naturalistically, is commendable I suppose but the book will be very boring. You have to tell the truth but at the same time you have a responsibility to the reader, to give them something they want to *read* rather than just witness. It's a process which you get used to. Myself, I don't even realise what I'm doing, I've never been particularly interested in analysing how I write, it's of no interest to me because I simply do it. On the other hand, I do sometimes I wonder how the process works but not sufficiently to write about it with any deadly seriousness.

Andy James

This is a question for both Ruth and Alan. I wonder have either of you (I'm sure you have been but I hope you can give me a good answer) been irritated or angered by something that a critic or reviewer wrote about your work, where you said that this guy has got it all wrong; that this is bollocks?

RF

In a word, yes. (laughter)

AS

It doesn't much matter what critics say because you know if they say anything at least you are getting some attention. If they don't say anything or don't notice your work you keep on with the blinkers down doing what you want to do, of course.

AJ

So it really doesn't have much effect on you what critics say then?

RF

You know, it doesn't matter what the review says, just how big it is, how many words. No one remembers what a review says, they just say 'Oh, I saw that big review of your book' and it might be the most vile review and they really don't remember. That often happens.

Kevin De Ornellas

This is going back to question of memory if you don't mind, and clearly your poetry draws on particular memories, often around objects, quite sensual images. I'm interested in the relationship between narrative and memory and I'm just wondering whether as a poet [Ruth Fainlight], and a writer of novels who has also written poems and autobiography [Alan Sillitoe], if either of you have any thoughts on the question between truth and memory. This relates to what Tim was saying. You might feel yourself to have captured the truth of the memory in writing but of course the reader will never know. You've both written short stories too and it seems to me that memory is often very fleeting and coheres around images. Therefore short fiction seems like a good medium for the representation of memory. Martin Amis said in his interview that he thought a life is not like a story, it was more like a short story. I am fascinated by the relationship between memory and narrative and memory and imagery as a medium for dealing with or using memory.

AS

Well, it's impossible for the memory not to be transmuted by my imagination to a greater or lesser degree, and then when it comes out, and becomes language, and when the narrative process takes over. So many stages of refashioning and reprocessing occur that what might once have been a pure image or experience must eventually become something else. I mean almost nothing you write is transparent, true to its origin. By the time it has been processed by your brain, by language – which we all share – and by my particular massaging of language, it seems not the truth at all. Only a picture, something you recognise, perhaps recognise as you, but which isn't you. It is a representation, the result of many stages of transposition.

RF

I've written prose, I've written short stories, some autobiographical, some not at all. Prose that has been autobiographical has always been very short, intense, going towards the prose poem but that's just how my mind works. I couldn't write a long narrative memoir I don't think. I could only do it in sections, either in poems or short prose fragments, so it's quite similar to poetry, using prose in that way, yes, it is objects and images around which the words cohere. Certainly not the other way around – by which I mean the poet plays tricks with words, creates beguiling effects, irrespective of what inspired the poem *for them*. I suppose the so-called Martian poets did that.

RB

There might be another question or two.

Nicola King (NK)

This is a question for Ruth. You say that words come first when you go to write a poem but I thought it might be feeling that came first and then the craft came after it? When you speak of the little girl in the poem, it seems to be that you felt first and then the words came after that?

RF

Yes, in that case. But it was she who reminded me of my own feelings, seeing her reminded me of my feelings of being in her situation but that's not enough. If words had not come I couldn't have written a poem, I might have written a little account of it of 'watching trains pass and dreaming'. I mean it was the actual rhythm of words coming to me that initiated the poem but yes, the process was first of all the experience, then thinking about it or brooding more than thinking. It's more musing or brooding and then a phrase comes out of it, but if it doesn't get to a stage where language enters then it's just something that you think about. I mean I might think about something for years and years before words will come. I wrote a long poem about a trip I made to Russia in 1965 and I didn't write a poem about it until 1992 and I'd been thinking about it the whole time knowing that there was something niggling at me that had to turn into a poem and finally it did turn into a poem. That's the longest gap I think, from 1965 to 1992.

PP

That was the poem about your travels with Beryl Graves, and I just have a question about the significance of your meeting with Robert and Beryl Graves, how significant was this meeting?

RF

Very, very significant. Because he was the first major literary figure I met. I didn't go to university so that was the only situation in which I've been in what might be called a student/tutor relationship, and when we visited him sometimes he would show me the poems he was working on and I looked at these corrected pages of manuscript. It was all written by hand, he didn't type... I mean this wasn't a frequent thing but it happened regularly over the course of those years and he would explain what he was doing, you know 'Look, I've done this because...' It was thrilling, and also incredibly valuable, he was a sort of mentor at that time.

Jan Jedzrejewski (JJ)

Just a quick question. What I was struck by in both the reading and the commentary that you gave this evening was the dependency of the truth on the facts, factual explanations. You said a couple of times 'I haven't given you enough information on this' so background is very important to you. I was just wondering then would I be over-interpreting things if I said that your poetry is about looking for truth with a capital 'T', but an emotional kind, truth about mysterious, even magical underpinnings of the mundane? Would that search for the truth be central to your work as poet?

RF

Well, it sounds so pretentious to say so but I suppose so yes. I think that must be so for every poet, don't you think so?

JJ

I don't know. I mean poetry is supposed to be about creating imaginative worlds, postmodern worlds. Playing with conventions. I find it immensely refreshing that the concept of the search for truth is there, that sense of contact with a reality of some kind which is surprising...

RF

Well, I mean there are enjoyable games that one can play as a writer. I can't disagree; I can't say 'no you got it wrong completely.' But bringing oneself, and other people, into the poem is I think more important than showing off with conceits and devices.

NK

If I can add to that. I was at a conference in Wales, just a couple of weeks ago. The Poet Laureate was there, who is also of course an academic, a critic, and he read out four poems and asked us which one he had really experienced, suggested that only one was 'authentic'. He disclosed finally none of them had been his experience, and the game he was playing was actually a sense of the autobiographical approach to other people's lives, setting himself a task of describing something so well that we assumed he had experienced it when he'd invented, or at least borrowed it.

RF

Like Browning?

NK

I like your approach much better.

RF

I mention Browning because there is a very respectable tradition, the completely imagined biographical poem which is full of very wonderful made-up characters in poetry, like Shakespeare. But then how can you tell which is real and which invented? Larkin's personae are just as vivid as Browning's but each was a version of himself, very autobiographical. At least in Richard's [Bradford's] opinion.

Paul Davies

Do you have any thoughts about the essential art of poetry, Alan, as you've written quite a lot of poetry?

AS

I've always understood that poetry comes from a far more instinctive level than a novel. A novel might come out of the air but a poem has to come from deep within the heart and in a sense dictates how you are to write it, complete it or try to get the truth of it, which is more necessary in a poem and which takes a lot more time. A novel might go through six or seven drafts but sometimes a poem twenty, twenty-five. You can go on writing it, while trying to keep alight the flame of inspiration which set it off in the first place, but still you do seem to write draft after draft to get what is necessary.

RF

So when you say a more instinctive level, you mean deeper?

AS

I certainly do, as deep and fearful as a the coal mines.

Stanley Black

Did I detect a hint of possible regret in the final two pages of your autobiography, about the workaholic approach to your writing or is that just the vocational demands of the chosen career?

AS

It might have been something like that, yes, the fact that I'd been lumbered with this obsession which is what being a writer is. When Robert Graves published a series of essays, he thought 'what shall I call the book?' He called it 'Occupation: Writer', because a writer is an occupation. Mine is a little bit more obsessive, in that I would love to have £100,000 or £200,000 a year and just be able to travel around and do what I want with no strings attached but I can't because I've got to write. That's the way it is. Slight regret in that sense...

RB

Without seeming to speak on your behalf with regard to that question, there is one piece of fiction in particular that springs to mind, it's called *The Story-teller*, came out in 1979 and the title I suppose explains the novel, it's about the storyteller who is addicted to telling stories, can't stop telling stories continuously...

AS

But he doesn't write them though, he tells them in pubs, clubs, parties and he gets paid for it and he makes a living out of it, he's an imaginative person of course.

RB

Of course you wouldn't think that this person might be in some way generically related to a novelist?

AS

No. No. It was an experiment. But on the other hand...
 (Laughter)

RB

Let's move to the particular. Both of you [Alan Sillitoe and Ruth Fainlight] knew Ted Hughes and Sylvia Plath very well indeed, were close friends in fact. There can hardly have been two writers in recent decades who have drawn so much attention, and wrath, as those two – by which I mean that their lives have become entangled with their work. Knowing them as you did how do you feel about this?

AS

It was terrible. Ted was scapegoated. None of us is perfect but he was certainly not responsible for what happened to Sylvia, who was mentally ill. Their lives were appropriated by others, who had their own agenda.

RF

Yes, I agree, and using their work as a prism for speculation on a very complicated relationship which only they and those closest to them understood, was malign, unfair. I knew Ted and Sylvia very well. I think their work has been tainted by supposition.

RB

Thank you.

20

Richard Bradford Interviews Martin Amis

First of all I'd like to thank you for agreeing to do this interview. I don't think I need to introduce you to the people here because if they read books and if they don't know anything about the work of Martin Amis then they've probably been in a coma for about the past thirty years. I'll be asking a few questions, particularly regarding the background, personal and circumstantial, to your work and I'll start logically and rather innocuously enough with your first novel, *The Rachel Papers* which was published in 1973 when you were twenty-four.

Its hero and narrator is Charles Highway and the thread of the story involves Charles's pursuit of the elusive Rachel. Now, Charles Highway reminds me of a chap called Jim Dixon created thirty years earlier by one Kingsley Amis in his first novel *Lucky Jim*. Both are precocious, acerbically witty characters and each serves their creator well as a channel for cynical observations on the mores of contemporary Britain. Were you aware when you were writing it of the potential similarities between Highway and Jim Dixon or was this merely coincidental?

Martin Amis (MA)

Well, one unsympathetic reviewer said that you'd expect the son of a writer to go in the opposite direction, but then he said rather obliquely that a really obnoxious writer would purge the influence by imitation and there's something in that. It's a much nastier novel than *Lucky Jim* and if he's like Jim then it is Lucky Jim thirty years on and much less innocent; Jim is rather innocent about many things. There is actually a bit where I do paraphrase *Lucky Jim*; there is a passage in *Lucky Jim* where Dixon is comparing nice, pretty women to their exhausting intellectual counterparts and he says that he was always sure of his view that nice things were nicer than nasty things. In the *Rachel Papers* at some point I say that nice things are dull and nasty things are interesting so there's a kind of consciousness of *Lucky Jim* – not quite imitating and not quite going against – but certainly aware of the other book. Kingsley was deliberately dividing his readership, in that in those days some would inevitably loathe Jim and others love him. I don't think I wanted anyone to sympathise with Highway.

Richard Bradford (RB)

Thanks; and did your father know before it came out that you were working on the book? Did you make it clear to him or was he interested in your literary ambitions before this first novel was published?

MA

I think he knew that I was writing something. I wasn't secretive about attempting what would be my first novel and he didn't pry. When it came out he was slightly enthusiastic and nice about it but not fulsome in any way and seemed slightly vexed with it. He was of the nature to want all the oxygen for himself and I remember seeing him on a TV programme several years later being asked about me and quite honestly in my eyes he was having to suppress a great deal of irritation. But later in his life he loosened up about it and he told me he'd laughed when he read it. He met a women at a party and she asked him what it was like to have a son who's much more famous than you and he said 'he's not more famous than I am' and she said 'he's much more famous than you' and by then he did find the whole situation genuinely funny. Back to the books themselves, he didn't like my second novel and liked the third one a little bit. He couldn't get on with my use of time travel in *Time's Arrow* I think because of his interest in science fiction; he thought it an ostentatious borrowing from the genre. He enjoyed reading my criticism, perhaps because in that respect we did have some things in common. The first novel, my first novel, was a shock to him, maybe a little painful, but by the third he'd got used to things. He said so anyway.

RB

Are you sure he meant it though?

MA

Meant what?

RB

When he said things like that to you, or was he being playfully provocative?

MA

Well what he thought was that I was the best of a bad lot, my generation in other words; he quite liked William Boyd, especially his short stories, and that was about it but don't forget that his take on prose was very low-middle-brow, you know; what he enjoyed was Dick Francis and he liked genre-fiction to read for pleasure. The only contemporary writer he read with unfeigned enjoyment was Anthony Powell, and he didn't like Nabokov and he certainly didn't like Joyce. His taste in poetry was the reverse and that was his real passion. He admired poetry that combined elegance with meticulous craftsmanship, and of course Philip [Larkin] was his favourite. Fiction he thought should be entertaining and not much else, well that at any rate was the line he was giving.

RB

We might return to this but if you don't mind I'd like to talk about your second novel *Dead Babies*. It could remind one of *Vile Bodies* updated to include an appropriate excess of sex, drugs and alcoholic abuse, it being late twentieth century. The obvious difference, of course though, is that each of these hedonists is systematically slaughtered by their host, the enigmac Villiers. So were these individuals modelled on the people you met at Oxford and later in London and did they deserve to die?

MA

Well, I may sound like a case study here but how it works with me is that you write the first novel and all you know about at that point, at that age, is your own consciousness and then in your second novel you write about feelings and states of mind beyond your own, then your third you write about cities, in the fourth you compare two cities with each other and then later on these boundaries become more porous, you are aware of the world expanding, becoming far more complex and recondite than you previously conceived it to be. *Dead Babies* is my exotic period novel and it was very loosely based on the characters that I shared a house with in Oxford. It was pretty druggy and it did often get out of control; nothing like what I put in the novel but there was that feeling of the dark side of permissiveness. This was around the time of Charles Manson where it – the hedonistic indulgent state of the late 60s and 70s – was all showing its dark side, so it was of that time, of my time.

RB

Very intriguing, but it's just that Villiers, although he is not the narrator, seems in a way to be in control of the novel. Of course he operates only within the text but I wonder if he is to an extent an extension of his author.

MA

Yes, he's not the narrator but he's the *deus ex machina*; we don't know until the conclusion what he has been up to but yes, behind the scenes he is in control.

RB

So I'm thinking there is something of you in him, given that you've said that it is a novel of 'your time'. Perhaps his acts reflect your feelings about that time?

MA

Not much, not really. I mean one of the things it is, is an update of the country house mystery murder, you know, who did it and it plays with that. But, well, looking back there was a kind of incurious narcissism abroad, waiting for someone like Villiers to dismantle it.

RB

Ok, moving on a bit further chronologically, to probably my favourite, *Money*, starring the outstanding John Self, a narrator like none before, who combines I suppose the tragic dignity of Charles Ryder on speed with the presence of the late lamented Bernard Manning. He is probably the most loathsome and repulsive individual to have ever appeared in fiction but he's also one of the most brilliant storytellers. He is the energy of the novel and when compared with him one other character in it, that is Martin Amis, comes across as rather feckless, cryptic, less interesting. So what are you doing?

MA

Well, I was being postmodern and it has a comic side. I mean it's not what you set out to do but you realise at a certain point that this is indeed what you are doing, so you form a relationship with this narrator, who is more or less as you describe him, although I think you neglect to say how very endearing he turns out to be ...

RB

Oh yes, I like him immensely ...

MA:

As for this rather uptight, studious, ridiculously idealistic and dedicated figure that I turned myself into...as you can imagine I did that to myself so that no one would confuse me with John Self. The way the process works is that you take what might be three or four percent of your character – and I certainly have at least that much of John Self in me – and you imagine that there is nothing else there and that's how you end up with someone like John. Then you can contend with all your worst qualities.

RB

One more attempt to track you down in one of your novels then we'll leave it and turn to something else. *The Information* is a novel I like very much and just to bring people up to date and remind them of what happens here, it involves two central figures, Richard Tull and Gwyn Barry, who are both novelists. Tull has published two serious avant garde novels, of the first we are informed that nobody understood it or even finished it but equally no one felt able to say that it was self indulgent tripe. Richard flourished briefly, in that he was feted as a challenging radical new presence until common sense in the market took over and he found that he couldn't publish anything else, and he ends up as a reader, ghost-writer and editor for a vanity publisher. And it sounds to me as if a new circle of hell has been created for ambitious radical young novelists who want to keep the flames of modernism alight (I love this personally). Alongside him we have Barry who writes novels that people read, becomes exorbitantly rich with a beautiful wife and has a wonderful life. And I'm wondering: are you explaining, apologising or what? In short, you're as popular as Barry and as intellectually respectable as Tull: having your cake and eating it?

MA

No. You wouldn't write a novel to do that. The thing about Gwyn Barry is that he's completely up the arse of generational ideology, which we know about initially as PC, also known as relativism or multi-culturalism and he incorporates them in his writings, soothing tracts that control/console everyone hungry for similar delusions, whereas Richard Tull writes novels so that the reader gets a nosebleed by about page six. I think I wanted to deal with the subject of literary envy which is one like no other because it's to do with the novelist's ego, a great curse, and it's something that you have to fight all the time. What you must deal with is the temptation to treat as trivial everything except your own literary universe and many writers oscillate continuously between raging egotism and anxiety, it's just part of the job. I wasn't even fully aware of just how debilitating that can be, at least until I created Tull and Barry. I don't really suffer from it as much as some people because being the son of a writer – you have already witnessed it firsthand, and I don't just mean Kingsley; as I grew up his friends, and competitors, were always around. Whereas it must strike most writers as a complete miracle that

that's what they've been able to do with their lives, sometimes coming from an unlikely background, a non literary background, they must be pinching themselves, whereas I never did pinch myself because nothing in a way is more banal than what your father does for a living so I could come at it with a bit of detachment and have fun with it.

RB

We've only an hour and we'll have to move onto another topic, but before that, to think about what your father did was 'banal' or routine, you make him sound like a road sweeper.

MA

That's what he was like every day: he went into his study after breakfast and managed to create time in the evening and it just looked like an ordinary way of **making** a living ...

RB

If you wouldn't mind, some questions regarding your opinions on some general issues, one of which is particularly relevant to this conference, that is literary biography. I have a quotation here from the *War Against Cliché*, it's from a review that you did quite a while ago of a literary biography of Coleridge. And you begin by saying:

> The critical biography has several claims to being a dead genre. The main aim of criticism nowadays is to provide intellectual stimulation. The main aim of biography, or so it seems to this reviewer, is to amuse the over-sixties. The knowledge of a writer's life may give the odd insight into his work but you don't have to be a structuralist to see the dangers in studying them in tandem.

Later on you say that

> no biographer meant to me to put on a fresh suit of clothes for the poetry so perhaps it ought to be left alone and we should simply be told where the genuine criticism is to be found.

Now I'm praying that you've changed your mind or at least had cause to adjust your opinions.

MA

No, I think I was right on the money there; I think I was twenty-three when I wrote that piece and I do think it's a flaw or a trap – the critical biography. To take an example, Andrew Motion's biography of Philip Larkin where he said again and again *ad nauseum* that how interesting it is to take the life and, separately, explain the work, but they can't help doing the opposite or implying a causal relationship (how else can they get by?). That's the dilemma that they can't ignore, nor is it true that there is no relationship whatever, so that inevitably is what they're sniffing out even if, like Motion, they're too fastidious to admit to it. You don't have to be a genius to see that the life is one thing and the work is another but at the same time only an idiot would pretend that they are not to an extent interdependent. I honestly believe that literary writing is a lonely isolated activity, but you cannot completely ostracise your personal life from it.

RB

I see your point but my view is that it depends on what sort of literary biographer you are, and I don't think there's a general formula that you can apply, in the sense that some writers lives have very little relevance to their works – one won't enlighten the other – but there are ways that one can find channels between the lives and the works that don't involve simply grubbing away for nasty detail. I think a thoughtful presentation of the life can be a means of offering a perspective on the work which in many ways does no harm to its intrinsic qualities. I'm apologising for something I'm doing myself I suppose.

MA

Well, the reason I liked your biography of my father is that it didn't mess around or generalise, your insights elucidate the life as well as the fiction itself, and there's certainly a sense in which a novel, more than a poem or more than any other art form, a novel does take your whole being, and your whole personality and your psychology and even your sexuality, and it's all there on the page. A novel tells you everything there is to know about someone's mind or make-up, which is why J.G. Ballard kept his novel hidden from his children when they were growing up, so much so that they were hardly aware that he was a novelist. It is possible to achieve this with a certain level of decorum – balance your life against your inventions I mean – but sometimes the mask can slip. There's one great difficulty with literary biography and that is the kind of hatred that the biographer begins to feel for the writer after he spends several years on end on it and this can get completely out of control. It can become impossible to go back to the time when he felt something like the admiration or even the envy that first inspired the project and a kind of vindictiveness takes over. He's spent so long gathering evidence and the rewards diminish correspondingly. There are many strains on your sympathies when you fasten your mind to someone else's, it's not a fictional process where you're responsible only to yourself, and while an ideal exists, it is very seldom achieved. I thought you did very well with Larkin.

RB

Thanks, I think. One brief last question and then if we have time a few from the floor and I'll let you go. Your next novel, to be called it is alleged, *The Pregnant Widow*, is going to be autobiographical, blatantly, involving quite a few of the figures closest to you, most obviously your father, Philip Larkin, quite possibly Christopher Hitchens and a whole group of people from the seventies onwards. Would you like to say anything about it or not?

MA

Sure, it is blindingly autobiographical but it is fiction and there are several provisos for keeping it at one remove from reality. It is tremendously difficult to make a collection of lives look like a novel, because what they may resemble is a book of short stories written by various hands, some of them sardonic, emphasising their twists and surprise endings, some of them carving their lives in their dirty realism, some self evidently literary and a few of them incredibly brutal, so that that novel turns out to resemble a file of case studies, each fighting for prominence and demanding stylistic autonomy. It is immensely difficult to find a style of writing that suits a real person, you are framing them and your technique determines the way that they appear in the novel. This is fine if they are a tapestry of borrowings and inventions, but if you've decided to base them on people you have known then their presence even as a memory is unsettling. If you get it right and the mood, perspective seems faithful and authentic, then fine, but you do run the risk of appropriating their personality. Of course most readers wouldn't know how well, or otherwise, you've done the job, but nonetheless you feel privately an obligation. I would never write about their sex lives and that sort of thing. You see when I wrote *Experience* I didn't do love life in any way; it is always disgusting when someone writes about their love lives, there is no way of doing that.

RB

You mean your own or the love lives of people you know?

MA

That too but you certainly can't do your own in fiction or non-fiction; it has to become displaced otherwise it becomes pitiable, you lose the universal. That was actually Kingsley's objection to writing about sex. There are no explicit descriptions except the failures and histrionics in his fiction and not very much in mine after a while; I sort of got over it. And when you write about sex you inevitably start to talk about your own iniquities and your fetishes, the minute you do that you're stirring prurient interest and it ceases to be literature. There are two or three things that fiction cannot do; one is dream. Henry James said that 'dreams are real'. Kafka tried to do this and he couldn't finish those novels and neither can we, his short stories are immortal but in his dream-like novels nothing worked. And fiction can't do sex. Some writers try much harder than others, like John Updike for instance, who gave it a real good go but you either revert to orotund symbolism, coy metaphor, or swing toward lurid detail; both are for different reasons toe-curlingly embarrassing. That's what you remember about John Updike, long, consistently embarrassing sex scenes. Is it possible to have a universalist public sex life? No. Putting it into words that others will read is the equivalent of doing it on a bench, in a crowded park, at noon.

RB

I agree with you there, there's nothing really that prose … on that dreadful thought, are there any questions from the floor?

Paul Davies

I have a question about the kind of fiction writing which is the host of auto-biography, and I wanted to ask you about Hanif Kareishi and his recent short story writing from *Intimacy and Around that Time*. Do you feel that it worked, because he has talked a lot about this problem of writing from one's personal reality and whether such writing can also involve universality?

MA

Well, I haven't read that book and I know only a little of it so I can't really answer that question, except I agree with what he wrote about divorce. Now, that is one thing that I do not go near in *Experience,* where I wrote about my life and I'm not going to go near it in my fiction either, mainly because of the children from my first marriage, my sons, so I couldn't do it. But then we all know how difficult it is to say nothing and how Saul Bellow is the great example of going right in there – his wife calls it mugging the muse – but he is I think unique and I don't think anyone else has ever gone as far with the materials of what actually happened. So I can't judge Hanif's book but it's subject no doubt to the usual pitfalls and terrors and eggshells of making fiction from what you know.

RB

Andrew James, who is actually working on a thesis on Kingsley's novels.

Andrew James

Here's my question. In a sense I think that your father never got over his marriage to Elizabeth Jane Howard. In *The King's English*, he uses an example sentence: 'he served in the royal ice staff from 1965 to 1980'. Then in *The Biographer's Moustache* he has the writer Jimmy Fain writing his 6th and final novel in 1965 and as you know your father wrote *The Egyptologists*, his sixth novel in 1965, the same year he married Elizabeth Jane Howard. So my question is, do you think that after Kingsley was re-installed in the 1980's with Hilary looking after him that he regretted leaving your mother to marry Elizabeth Howard for creative reasons, that when he looked back did he think that he could have written better fiction had he stayed with Hilary?

MA

Yes, the marriage he didn't get over was the one to my mother and as he would tell it later on he left her by accident really. He thought he could have his cake and eat it and have affairs and write and my mother would always be there, but it didn't work out that way. Actually, just looking back at all that James Bond stuff my father did – and *The Egyptologists* was in that period too – I think he must have been tremendously unmanned artistically after the break up because he wrote three books about James Bond and the essentially frivolous *Egyptologists* in collaboration – that he had never done before – and I think during that period his energies were weak, but then he wrote *The Anti-Death League* which was a new departure and pretty impressive. Then he hit a good vein and was producing one very interesting novel a year through the late 60s and early 70s, many of them dystopian or escapist and which might indicate his feelings about life. When he was reinstated with my mother it was a completely new arrangement where she was there for him and he got out of that misogynistic phase and wrote *The Old Devils* and I think that was very much due to forgiving women, the act of forgiving women, which my mother's reappearance in his life enabled him to do. *Stanley and the Women* was his first major novel after splitting up with Jane Howard. The feminists hated it of course but Stanley only seems unpleasant if we ignore, or rather indulge, the undeviating nastiness of all the women he knows. Stanley doesn't hate women, he simply accepts, without bitterness, that most of them seem determined to make him miserable. That, I suppose, was Kingsley's view of things – with the very notable exception of my mother. I think you suggest as much in your biography, Richard [Bradford].

RB

I do, yes. You got on well with Jane Howard though, did you not?

MA

Oh certainly, and I still do.

RB

Well, I'd like to thank you for providing such intriguing responses to these questions. And I think the bar is open.

Index